P9-CJD-291

LARSON, Bruce L. Lindbergh of Minnesota; a political biography.
Harcourt Brace Jovanovich, 1973. 363p il bibl 73-6596. 14.50.
ISBN 0-15-152400-9.   C.I.P.
The elder Charles Lindbergh has long deserved a full-scale biography, and Larson's essentially political one, though somewhat plodding and too uncritical, is a competent and informative first. As a case study of a Republican insurgent during the Progressive Era, it supplements biographies of LaFollette, Borah, and others of similar persuasion, and, in addition, sheds interesting light on the vigorous and socially productive politics of Minnesota. It deserves a place in larger college libraries. Family photographs; bibliography; index.

Lindbergh of Minnesota

Photo by Charles Schmid

Bruce L. Larson

a native Minnesotan, is a graduate of Concordia College and the universities of North Dakota and Kansas. He is a member of the History Department of Mankato State College, Mankato, Minnesota.

Lindbergh of Minnesota
A Political Biography

BRUCE L. LARSON

Foreword by Charles A. Lindbergh, Jr.

New York
Harcourt Brace Jovanovich, Inc.

LIBRARY

JAN 1 7 1974

274947

Copyright © 1971, 1973 by Bruce L. Larson

All rights reserved. No part of this publication may
be reproduced or transmitted in any form or by any means,
electronic or mechanical, including photocopy, recording,
or any information storage and retrieval system,
without permission in writing from the publisher.

Printed in the United States of America

The author wishes to thank Princeton University Press for permission
to quote material from *A Monetary History of the United States,
1867–1960* by Milton Friedman and Anna Jacobson Schwartz, copyright © 1963 by National Bureau of Economic Research, and *Wilson:
The New Freedom* by Arthur S. Link, copyright © 1956 by Princeton University Press; and Vanguard Press, Inc., for permission to
quote material from *The Lindberghs* by Lynn and Dora Haines.

An excerpt of this book previously appeared in *Minnesota History*.

Library of Congress Cataloging in Publication Data

Larson, Bruce L
Lindbergh of Minnesota.

Based on the author's thesis, University of Kansas.
Bibliography: p.
1. Lindbergh, Charles August, 1859–1924.
2. United States—Politics and government—1901–1953.
3. Minnesota—Politics and government. I. Title.
E748.L74L37   328.73′092′4 [B]   73–6596
ISBN 0-15-152400-9

First edition
B C D E

To
the late Professor George L. Anderson,
University of Kansas
and to
Eva and Charles,
in memory of their father

"We must get away from the idea that money is created to serve any other purpose than that of an exchange agent."
—*Banking and Currency and the Money Trust,* 1913

"Mankind is now subject to the prey of monopoly, as primitive man was subject to the prey of fierce animals."
—*The Economic Pinch,* 1923

"The war hysteria has so unbalanced the world that it is even considered traitorous to suggest terms of peace, or to plan for conditions upon which to propose peace."
—*Why Is Your Country at War,* 1917

Contents

Contents

Illustrations

Between pages 172 and 173

xi

Foreword

Through childhood and youth, as the son of an immigrant fron-
tier-homesteader, my father's life rooted in the wilderness and
in the soil. He never severed himself from these roots, for they
seemed to him universal. A study of his political career can best
be approached with this background in mind.

My earliest memories hold stories about my father's Minnesota
frontier days, stories of fishing in the lakes and rivers, of hunting
in the forests, of breakplowing virgin land. They formed the
warp through which an increasingly complicated culture wove—
a schoolhouse, a sawmill, a railroad slashing across the territory.
His father, August Lindbergh, welcomed that railroad, my father
told me, for it moved civilization closer and eased the heavy
burdens of frontier life. Its trains brought in money to buy farm
produce, and money could be exchanged for such essentials as
tools, clothing, and books.

But along with its benefits, the railroad created problems that
occupied much of my father's attention up to the time of his
death, and these problems were closely related to the money it
brought in. A large part of my father's political career was devoted to the study of money and its misuses.

Investment interests accompanied the rails to Minnesota, resulting in the exploitation that investment for a money profit
usually brings. Land values went up, and taxes with them. Farm
income was low while bank loans were expensive. "A man can't
pay off a mortgage at twelve per cent no matter how hard he

works," my father said. "Taxes ought not to be raised because of farm improvements."

He believed that national prosperity is founded on the farmer, that government policy should be based on the welfare of the farmer and the land, and that the farmer should have a fair share in a prosperity that results from his labor. The intensity of my father's belief caused him to run for Congress and, after his election, to champion the causes of men who live by labor, especially of those who live by labor with the earth. These causes, he felt, required major changes in the financial policies of government, banks, and business. As a congressman, he soon achieved a leading position in the attempt to bring such changes about.

My father approached life philosophically and seriously, but with a quiet, underlying sense of humor. He had complete control over his facial muscles, and he enjoyed the impression he could create by exercising this control. When he was most amused, he would often appear to be not amused at all. He laughed inwardly rather than outwardly, but his laughter was deep and frequent. He liked being with simple people: dinner with a threshing crew or with log drivers, nights in farmhouses or dollar hotels. He placed great confidence in his children, supported their developing interests, and always treated them as older than they were. "You and I can take hard knocks," he said before I was halfway through grade school. "We'll get along no matter what happens."

My father was fascinated by thoughts of the future, but he was at the same time apprehensive. "Great changes are coming," he would tell me. "I won't live to see them, but you will." I remember him discussing overpopulation problems when I was less than ten years old. He was not a pacifist, but he spoke to me on occasion about the danger and effects of war. "The trouble with war is that it kills off the best men a country has," he once said.

Living in the city of Washington, D.C., separated my father from the fields and forests he loved, and he missed them keenly. On walks with me through the Capitol grounds, he would talk about returning to Minnesota as soon as the current session of

Congress was over. Then he would tramp through the woods and visit the farmers. But back in his Sixth District, he became so absorbed with farm and labor reforms, and so angered at abuses by "money interests and big business," that he returned term after term to Washington for a total of a decade, and thereafter entered unsuccessful senatorial and gubernatorial campaigns.

Near the end of his life, my father again achieved close contact with the land and open skies he loved, working with real estate in Minnesota and Florida. He carried a tent in the back of his car and delighted in telling about how he slept out in the open under the stars. But he continued his interest in political and financial reform. Only illness and death removed him from another gubernatorial contest.

In this biography, Professor Larson, after years of scholarly research, accurately and perceptively treats my father's life as it related to his political career. The scope of the biography is national as well as local, for similar farm, labor, and financial problems existed in every state in the union; and congressional reform, of course, spread nation-wide. The account is of universal interest because it describes the impact of a civilization on early frontier life—on the human rooting that my father realized is of such great importance.

CHARLES A. LINDBERGH, JR.

July 18, 1972

Preface

Charles A. Lindbergh, Sr., a progressive Republican congress-man from Minnesota during the early twentieth century, con-tributed both to the national development of reform thought and action, and to the tradition of American protest politics. Since the historic transatlantic flight by Lindbergh's son in 1927, a number of journalists, most notably Lynn and Dora Haines, have studied the political career of the father. However, no historian to date has examined in depth the public life of the elder Lindbergh, and, as Professor Richard Leopold wrote in the *Mississippi Valley Historical Review* in 1951, Lindbergh remains one of the "rich biographical opportunities" not yet pre-empted by historians. The purpose of this study is, in part, to fulfill that need.

Among the many persons interviewed during the course of the research I am most indebted to Charles A. Lindbergh, Jr., and Eva Lindbergh Christie Spaeth, both of whom gave generously of their time and made available specific Lindbergh materials. Their cooperation, including helpful comments on the manu-script, has been invaluable in examining the public life of their father. My association with them has been a most pleasant and rewarding experience.

The research has also involved the time and effort of many librarians and archivists at several depositories. Among those who aided the author were the staffs at Sterling Library, Yale Univer-sity; Alderman Library, University of Virginia; Chester Fritz Library, University of North Dakota; Memorial Library, Mankato

State College; and the Michigan Historical Collections, University of Michigan. Equally helpful were the staffs at the Wisconsin State Historical Society; the University of Michigan Law School; the Manuscript Division in the Library of Congress; the Minnesota State Archives; and the National Archives.

The knowledgeable and thorough assistance by the entire personnel of the Manuscript, Newspaper, Reference Library, and Photo departments in the Minnesota Historical Society was indispensable. To all of them, especially Lucile M. Kane, Catherine Rafter, Faustino J. Avaloz, John A. Dougherty, Dorothy Gimmestad, and Eugene D. Becker, my sincere thanks.

To Russell W. Fridley, the Society's director, I owe a special obligation, not only for reading the manuscript, but for counsel, encouragement, and time spent in extended chats about Lindbergh data and Minnesota history.

For valuable criticism in the preparation of an earlier version of this study as a dissertation at the University of Kansas, I particularly wish to thank my major advisers, the late Professor George L. Anderson, who guided its initial development, and Professor Donald R. McCoy, who expertly saw it to completion. For help and inspiration, I am also indebted to Vice-Chancellor Ambrose Saricks, and Professors James C. Malin and W. Stitt Robinson.

For professional reading and editorial counsel I wish to thank William Jovanovich and William B. Goodman of Harcourt Brace Jovanovich, Professor Carl H. Chrislock of Augsburg College, and Professors Donald G. Sofchalk and David G. Taylor of Mankato State College. I am further indebted to Professor Sofchalk for advice and encouragement over a long period of time.

Many friends and professional colleagues, especially Bradford D. Garniss, Jr., David L. Nass, Gary M. Fink, Hiram M. Drache, Darryl B. Podoll, John W. Hevener, Jon and Ruth Wefald, Donald H. Strasser, and Burton J. Williams, offered suggestions and simple encouragement along the way. I will long remember the congenial associations with neighbors on Sylvan Shores, the winter retreat near Brainerd, Minnesota, where the initial draft of the manuscript was written.

Preface

To Helen Sofchalk, expert typist and helpful critic, I give my most appreciative thanks.

For financial assistance partially covering travel costs, and for adjustments in teaching schedules allowing blocs of time for research and writing, the author wishes to thank the Minnesota Historical Society, the University of Kansas, and both the Department of History and the Faculty Research Council at Mankato State College.

The author especially acknowledges a grant from the Elmer L. and Eleanor J. Andersen Foundation that enabled him to complete the final manuscript for publication. Governor Andersen's keen interest in the project was most gratifying.

To Audrey and Gordon, Eric, Mark, and Sara; and to Virginia, Athar, and Miriam, I extend thanks for time which might otherwise have been spent with them.

To Ida, who encouraged academic learning as a way of life and demonstrated an appreciation for the human mind and spirit, I owe a debt I cannot repay.

Finally, the author alone is responsible for all statements of fact and interpretation made in this book.

BRUCE L. LARSON

October 25, 1972

Lindbergh of Minnesota

Chapter I

Swedish Immigrants on
the Minnesota Frontier

No state in the American union has had a more vigorous or a more socially productive politics than Minnesota. Both the Republican and Democratic parties have enjoyed periods of control. A strong tradition of reformist protest, moreover, lies deep in the state. The Grange, the Populists, the Nonpartisan League, and the Farmer-Labor party have been major factors in the mix of its politics. From Minnesota have come such varied and nationally known public figures as Ignatius Donnelly, Oliver H. Kelley, John Lind, John A. Johnson, Arthur C. Townley, Frank B. Kellogg, Floyd B. Olson, Harold E. Stassen, and, in more recent years, Hubert H. Humphrey, Eugene J. McCarthy, and Walter F. Mondale. Less well known is the political career of a Little Falls lawyer, Charles A. Lindbergh, Sr., an early-twentieth-century Minnesota congressman. Overshadowed by the fame of his flier son, the elder Lindbergh played a significant role in the development of Minnesota and American reform politics. Rooted in the Western agrarian tradition of political protest, Lindbergh's position on issues cut across party lines, and his public career encompassed without principled contradiction the progressive wing of the Republican party, the Nonpartisan League, and the Farmer-Labor party. He is best remembered for his attack on the Money Trust, his support of the insurgent revolt in Congress, his opposition to American entry into World War I, and his deep commitment to the needs of the Midwestern farmer.

3

Lindbergh's concern for the farmer grew naturally out of his immediate family background, for his parents, August and Louisa Lindbergh, were pioneer farmers on the Minnesota frontier. These first Lindberghs were Swedish immigrants and therefore a part of the classic pattern of population growth in nineteenth-century Minnesota. Significantly, such pioneer and Scandinavian origins were typical characteristics of successful Minnesota politicians at the turn of the century.

In other respects, however, the Lindbergh family history was not typical. Unique was the fact that August Lindbergh, known in Sweden as Ola Månsson, had enjoyed a public career in his native land prior to his emigration. From 1847 to 1858 Månsson represented a district in Skåne, Kristianstad län, in the southern part of Sweden, as a member of the Riksdag, the Swedish parliament. Also unusual was the fact that when he chose to leave for the United States in 1859, Månsson was fifty years old.[1] These circumstances suggest that, unlike the great number of Swedes who left for America because of economic hardships and famine during the period, Månsson had other reasons for leaving Sweden.[2] Indeed, it was his political activity and related business difficulties that were basic considerations in his decision.

The main thrust of Ola Månsson's politics was reform. Representing the agricultural estate in the Riksdag, Månsson gained a reputation for his liberal views. Among the issues he championed during his career was the abolition of the whipping post as a means of punishment. Although Månsson was successful in this quest, and in certain other political matters, his thinking was often in opposition to the political climate of the times. Politically, Sweden, like the rest of Europe, was still experiencing the post-Napoleonic era, and the movements of liberalism and nationalism had not yet come into their own.[3] Ultimately it was the action of political enemies who brought charges of embezzlement against Månsson, a director in the Bank of Sweden at Malmö, together with the apparent need to turn over his resources to cover notes, that forced Månsson to leave his native land. On the basis of

1. Notes are on pages 295–342.

4

available evidence, Grace Lee Nute has concluded that "from the vantage point of today we can judge that Ola Månsson's enemies—and he had many, largely because of his liberal ideas—'framed' him, and that he was guilty only in a technical sense."[4]

When Ola Månsson sailed for the United States in 1859, he began a new life. He had remarried, and with him came his second wife, Louisa, thirty years his junior, and their new son, Charles August,[5] born on January 20, 1859. The son was named Charles in honor of Crown Prince Charles, a personal friend of Månsson, who in September, 1859, became King Charles XV. Left behind were his homeland and his Swedish name. There was nothing extraordinary about changing one's name in Sweden, and Månsson simply took the Lindbergh name that the two eldest sons of his first family, Måns and Jöns, had chosen to avoid confusion in the mails and elsewhere with their widely used surname, Olsson (according to Swedish custom, any "son of Ola" was named Olsson). The selection of the name Lindbergh had no special significance, but Månsson's choice for a new first name, August, was likely inspired by its frequent use by the royal family of Sweden. Thus Ola Månsson became August Lindbergh.[6]

Like many Swedes, August and Louisa Lindbergh selected Minnesota, the "Glorious New Scandinavia," as their American destination. The emigrant journey was typical. The voyage from Sweden to New York took six weeks; there followed travel by railroad from New York to Dubuque, by Mississippi River boat from Dubuque to Minneapolis-St. Paul, and by oxen and prairie schooner from there to Stearns County, Minnesota. Although the original plan had been to settle near Litchfield, where a number of Swedish immigrants lived, August Lindbergh stopped on the south bank of the Sauk River near Melrose. German settlers were far more numerous than Swedish settlers in this area, but there was also more timber, wildlife, and water than existed on the prairie perimeter thirty miles to the south. August apparently felt that it would be easier to provide food and shelter for his family during the first immigrant years in this setting.[7]

The initial years in Minnesota were not easy for the Lindberghs. Since August had been forced to liquidate virtually all his material possessions when he left Sweden, little cash was available to help him get started in the New World. Louisa exchanged her gold watch for a cow, and August sold a gold medal given to him in Sweden in order to purchase a plow. Prior to using the plow, however, portions of his acreage had to be cleared of timber. Although the plentiful wood supply was welcome for constructing a cabin and providing fuel, hard physical labor was required to make use of it. But hardships and hard work were an inevitable part of frontier life, and the Lindberghs responded to the challenge. Their original cabin and its furniture were homemade and crude; the cabin floor was earthen. Yet this shelter was their new home, and in it August and Louisa ordered their new life in America, treasuring the few dishes and books that added a civilizing touch from the old country.[8]

For Minnesota pioneers, other common hardships included transportation difficulties and the lack of available medical help. A team (of oxen or horses) and wagon, horseback, or walking were the only means of transportation. For the Lindberghs, despite their nearness to the small settlement at Melrose, the closest stores, services, and medical aid were thirty miles to the east, at St. Cloud.

These frontier facts caused a near tragedy during their second year in America. In 1861 August decided to improve life by building a frame house. To accomplish this he had to take his logs to a sawmill for cutting, which meant traveling ten miles west, to Sauk Centre, the nearest mill. While there, on August 2, according to the *St. Cloud Democrat,* "Mr. Lindbergh . . . fell and was caught by the saw, horribly mangling his left arm and side." Mill hands at the scene claimed they could see his heart beating through the opening in his side. August was laid on a cushion of hay in a wagon and taken over rough roads to his home. A doctor was summoned from St. Cloud, thirty miles away. According to the Reverend C. S. Harrison, who was with the family and aided in dressing and cleaning the wounds, twenty-four hours passed before help arrived. Louisa, Harrison, and other friends gathered at the home expected August to die. But despite the loss of blood and the danger of infection, he lived. When the doctor finally came, he successfully amputated the arm near the shoulder and sewed up the body wound. After the operation, August worried that he could not pay the fee. At this point Harrison came to the rescue, for he wrote shortly afterward: "Next day, I headed a paper with a dollar and raised the whole amount, of $25, much to the joy of the old man."[9]

Because of the accident, certain adjustments were made in the Lindbergh household. A long period of recovery prevented August from doing any farmwork for two years. In view of this crisis Louisa wrote the children of the first family in Sweden. Two sons, Måns and Per, or Perry, responded by sailing for the United States in the spring of 1862. At Chicago they were met by their father and young Charles. Only Perry accompanied August and Charles to Minncsota, however, for Måns remained to enlist in the Eighty-second Illinois Volunteer Infantry. His decision to join the Union Army was not unique to his experience, for Måns, in some ways a soldier of fortune, had served with a British regiment in the Crimean War and had spent five years as a member of the Royal South Scanian Infantry Regiment in Sweden. He rejoined his Swedish unit in 1866 after the Civil War, but not before seeing Minnesota and planning to lead a colony to the new state.

Måns Olsson Lindbergh's intention was to bring a group of about a thousand people to form a homogeneous Swedish colony. His efforts to promote the venture in 1868 were hampered, however, when the conservative press in Skåne led a vigorous campaign against the "son of Ola Månsson." The hostile Swedish papers, according to Lars Ljungmark, charged that "one of the reasons for the project was Månsson's efforts to make money with his son through illegitimate business transactions involving land and necessities for the emigrants in America." Although liberal papers came to Måns's defense, the sharp attack, plus the intervening activity of Minnesota immigration promoter Hans

Mattson, in connection with Governor William Marshall and the railroads, changed the final outcome of the plan. Ultimately, Måns led a group of about two hundred Swedish immigrants to Minnesota in 1869, most of whom settled in Sherburne County. The group was too small for the proposed colony, and Måns returned to Lund, Sweden. There, in 1870, he died of tuberculosis at age thirty-five. Significantly, the emotional response of the Swedish press to the colonization project tends to validate the political nature of Ola Månsson's sudden departure from Sweden in 1859.[10]

A routine expectation of frontier life in Minnesota during the 1860's was the threat of marauding Indians. Although the Chippewa tribes in the area were friendlier than the Sioux, there had been a long history of fighting between the two. In addition, white settlement aroused, with some justification, a hostile Indian reaction. In 1862 the situation in Minnesota worsened with the Sioux Uprising, which erupted in the Minnesota River valley. It was caused by failure of the federal government to make annuity payments, lack of food, poor crops, inadequate reservation lands for hunting and living, and incompetent Indian agents. Blood was shed on both sides, and in the end the Sioux were forced out of the state. In the words of Theodore C. Blegen, "The Sioux Uprising was a frontier and national calamity, a blood-spattered commentary on the failure of American Indian policy, a terrible ordeal for the people of Minnesota, a tragic final act in the drama of the Minnesota Sioux."[11]

For the Lindberghs, the unpredictable Indian activity meant living in constant uneasiness, and on more than one occasion they fled to the safety of St. Cloud. At other times there was no opportunity to flee, and the Indians had to be faced directly. One such incident was a confrontation between Louisa and a group of braves. When the Indians, fortified with whisky after trading skins, demanded food at the Lindbergh farmhouse, Louisa, alone with the children, refused. The Indians left, but as they walked away one of the braves grabbed August's ax from the woodpile. Of Louisa's reaction to this theft, her grandson later wrote: "My grandmother took time to change her clothes before she ran after those Indians." Louisa's reason for putting on a silk dress

8

was that she felt a dignified appearance necessary in dealing with Indians. Without apparent fear, she pursued the small group down the road some distance, and, after arguing and threatening them, succeeded in retrieving the ax. Her action was motivated primarily by the costliness of the ax, which they could ill afford to replace, and by the fact that it was designed especially for August. Weighted and shaped for single-handed use, it enabled him to do regular work after his accident.[12]

It seemed inevitable that August Lindbergh would emerge as a local leader. Because of his natural abilities and his considerable experience in Sweden, he was exceptionally well equipped to handle responsibility. Simple proof of his contributions to Melrose may be found in a listing of the official positions he held. They included town clerk for eighteen years, village recorder in 1888 and 1889, clerk of School Districts 41 and 49 for twenty-one years, justice of the peace for sixteen years, and postmaster from 1863 to 1865 and again from 1879 to 1887.[13] August and his family were assimilated as quickly or perhaps more quickly than most immigrants; he became a citizen of the United States in 1870. It is noteworthy that the Lindberghs stressed the use of English immediately after their arrival in America. Evidence of August's written mastery of his adopted language is revealed in his fine English handwriting.[14]

The Minnesota frontier made its mark on the character of young Charles Lindbergh. Pioneer life demanded self-reliance and independence. Each member of the family was expected to contribute to the homestead; for Charles, this duty involved hunting to keep the family table supplied with fresh meat. No one in the family could later remember when Charles did not know how to handle a gun. His older half-brother Perry carried on the major part of the farmwork, and his younger brother Frank handled the chores during the early years; younger sisters Linda and Juno helped their mother with the household tasks. Three other children of August and Louisa Lindbergh—Louisa, Victor, and Lillian—died during childhood in the 1860's and 1870's, yet another reminder of the hardships of frontier existence.[15]

Hunting was one job that Charles did not mind, for it allowed great freedom in roaming the woods. Both game and fish were abundant along the Sauk River during these years. Charles later recalled for his own son the plentiful game: "There were thousands of duck . . . so many that the sky was blackened."[16] He used either a muzzle-loading rifle or a shotgun, depending on the quarry. Ammunition was so expensive that when he missed a bird he tried to get two birds with the next shot. Shells were counted against birds when he returned home, although there were no questions asked when he brought in a deer. It is likely that Charles came upon Red River oxcart caravans during his hunting forays, because the trails passed within a quarter-mile of the Lindbergh house. Until the mid-1870's the loud and creaky oxcarts were used to bring furs from Pembina, on the Red River near the Canadian border, to St. Paul and to haul supplies back to that distant settlement. The hours Charles spent alone in the woods certainly added to the feeling of independence that was so much a part of his character. Biographers Lynn and Dora Haines suggest that "in the solitude he learned to think." Lindbergh himself later wrote of his days on the farm as those "when I was happiest."[17]

Formal educational opportunity was limited on the frontier. What Charles absorbed as a youngster was a combination of grammar-school training and strong home influence. His father, a self-educated man, had been instrumental in organizing the first school district in Melrose Township in 1861 and later donated a granary on the farm to be used as a schoolhouse. This was Charles's first school. He did not accept confinement in a classroom without opposition, however, and often escaped to the freedom of the surrounding woods and water. He also dreaded the occasions on which his father, in broken English, spoke at the school. Understandably, the teachers worried about Charles, for "his A.W.O.L. record was easily the outstanding feature of those early educational years."[18] Nonconformity nonetheless was to be a Lindbergh characteristic that grew as the boy became a man.

The Lindbergh home was an important source for learning. Both August and Louisa Lindbergh read a good deal; the most frequently used volumes were a lengthy *History of the World* (1878) by James D. McCabe and the Bible. August read the history book several times through and delighted in discussing other lands and other peoples. Lindbergh family discussions were serious and intellectual rather than petty and personal. Then, too, the many travelers and neighbors who frequented the Lindbergh house were an added source of information and stimulation for Charles. The warm hospitality of August and Louisa was widely known, and immigrants regularly stopped at the Melrose homestead, literally on the edge of the frontier during the 1860's, on their journeys north and west into Minnesota and the Dakotas. In fact, Charles himself remarked years afterward: "I have seldom stayed with anybody up north who did not stop over night with my father and mother in the 60's and 70's."[19]

At about the age of twenty Charles improved his formal training when he attended Grove Lake Academy, a nearby preparatory school. The school had begun in 1876 in the open country near Prairie Lake, but in 1883 it moved to Sauk Centre and became known as the Sauk Centre Academy and Business College. Founded by Father Daniel J. Cogan, a Catholic priest, the academy was based on individual instruction. There was no religious discrimination in accepting students, and the emphasis on individual progress was particularly well suited for farmers' children who could attend only for short periods, usually in the winter. The academy's catalogue boasted of the lack of embarrassment or distraction to students under its specialized program, and noted that "a student can accomplish more here with greater thoroughness in three months than he can accomplish in schools that use the class system in six." According to N. K. Strande, a student at the academy in the winter of 1882–1883, the work was demanding. For the sixty-five male students—there were no girls—school lasted from nine in the morning until nine at night. Each student recited his lessons alone, lived in a dormitory during the week, and was usually called by number rather than name. Tuition was six dollars per week. No official records of Grove Lake Academy exist, but it is safe to estimate that Lind-

bergh's attendance at the school included the winters of 1879–
1880 and 1880–1881; one report stated that he attended for five
years (terms). The needs and temperament of this young man,
still engaged in hunting and trapping, seemed naturally fitted to
the individual approach of the academy.[20]

Just how the political and economic views of the future re-
form-minded congressman were shaped during his formative
years in Minnesota can only be guessed. During the 1860's,
American agriculture began an important transition from sub-
sistence to intensive farming. Industrial expansion and widespread railroad development made this transformation possible,
but in the process certain inequities rankled Midwestern farmers.
Most pronounced among their grievances were discriminatory
railroad freight rates and high interest charges for credit. Consequently there developed a wave of political discontent during the
1870's, primarily aimed at the railroads, the machine companies,
and big business in general. In Minnesota the Grange and the
Anti-Monopolist party of Ignatius Donnelly were the most prominent voices of protest during the decade. At the same time, the
Republican party controlled state administrative offices and the
legislature. Discussions in the Lindbergh home could not have
failed to embrace these issues.[21]

Without question, the seed of belief in political reform passed
from father to son. The Swedish career of August Lindbergh
clearly indicates his deep concern for democratic change in the
interests of humanity. In America, he joined the Republican
party. In this he may have been influenced by the Republican-
oriented Swedish-American press. After a new constitution and
other reforms became law in Sweden during the 1860's, August
voiced his apprehension about the effectiveness of these reforms
and his deep distrust of the rich. In a letter dated April 28, 1866,
he declared: "The constitution is changed after the English, all
most in the favor of the wealthy." He felt strongly that it would
not do much good for the Swedes, asserting in particular that the
position of the Lords in the Riksdag had not been overthrown.
The former Riksdag member further predicted that the Swedish

people would discover the real meaning of the document and leave for America, noting that "it is the same mistake in the new Constitution as in the old one, not half of the people are represented, only the rich, and pretty rich, too." In the years ahead the attacks on Wall Street and the Money Trust by his son Charles would reveal a striking similarity to these earlier views of the father.[22]

Young Lindbergh had his first contact with the worlds of business and labor while still on the Minnesota frontier. His business venture involved shooting and marketing small game birds, probably some type of grouse.[23] In the beginning he had been shooting fowl and muskrats on his father's farm and selling them in the village for 12½¢ per bird or animal. One day a man stopped him on the road and suggested that he send his birds to Chicago for a better price. Accordingly, he sent a barrel of game to the address given him, and to his delight received payment at 50¢ per bird. What followed was good business on a small scale. In the succeeding months Charles hunted only game fowl, paid other young men in the neighborhood the regular rate of 12½¢ for their birds, borrowed $200 on a note from the bank to pay his hired hunters, and sold the birds to the Chicago source (a restaurant) at the higher price. Within a few months the lucrative business ended, when the Minnesota legislature passed a bill prohibiting killing birds for shipment out of state. Significantly, the profits earned in this activity became the financial base for the next step in Charles Lindbergh's life; namely, the decision to study law. As he himself remembered the episode during a campaign for governor, "In six months from the time I started I had paid back the loan, paid my hunters and . . . had $850 to spare. . . . With the money I thus earned I went to college at Ann Arbor and financed my law course."[24] But he added to that amount enough cash for clothes and transportation by working on a gravel train the summer before entering law school. His brief participation in railroad activity provided a new dimension to his understanding of transportation and labor, issues to which he later addressed himself as a politician.[25]

In the fall of 1881 Charles entered law school at the University of Michigan. His decision to attend Michigan was probably based on its good reputation, its reasonable fees, and the fact that its established program, going back to 1859, was the largest in the Midwest. Moreover, there was no option in Minnesota, for the fledgling University of Minnesota did not yet have a law school. Admission requirements at Michigan stated that a student be eighteen years of age, of good moral character, and possess a college or normal-school diploma or pass an examination. Charles apparently met the last requirement by examination and entered a degree program that involved two six-month sessions at the school. As it turned out, Lindbergh's 1883 class was the last allowed to pursue that particular program, for in the following years the sessions were lengthened to nine months.

Later writers have described the early 1880's at Michigan as the end of the first of four periods in the history of the law school. During this initial period, the "lecture" method was the major form of instruction. Accordingly, "Students attended Moot Courts, were 'examined' on their lectures, were advised to purchase and refer to specified textbooks and cases, and were required to prepare a thesis as a graduation requirement. . . . and toward the close of this first period, there was formal instruction in 'leading cases' and recitations on text assignments were held."[26] Department records reveal that 216 members of the junior class in 1881–1882 and 158 members of the senior class in 1882–1883 were engaged in law studies, and that the daily routine included at least two lectures a day, five days a week. Since out-of-state students numbered 260 out of a total enrollment of 395 in 1881–1882, and 236 out of 333 in 1882–1883, Michigan could fairly be termed a "national" law school at the time.[27]

The Michigan faculty under whom Lindbergh studied was composed of men with distinguished careers outside their association with the law school. Among its members from 1881 to 1883 were James V. Campbell and Thomas M. Cooley, both judges on the Supreme Court of Michigan; and Alpheus Felch, former governor, U.S. senator, and university regent. Cooley was unofficial dean of the loosely organized department. All six faculty members who served during the two terms were practicing lawyers and taught on a part-time basis. Weaknesses were inherent in this system, and when five of the six faculty members retired between 1883 and 1887, many changes were made.[28] Lindbergh and the class of 1883 thus were trained by men nearing the end of their teaching careers, averaging about sixty years in age, in a "school designed to teach the man what the law was and how to practice it." To what degree the politics of these young law students may have been influenced by the Michigan faculty seems a logical question, particularly since a high percentage of Michigan law graduates went on to be elected to Congress at the turn of the century. The reader may wonder whether Charles Lindbergh acquired reformist ideas while at Michigan. In general, the evidence does not support such a conclusion. For one thing, the many class members who became congressmen over the years were divided rather evenly between the Republican and Democratic parties. More explicit is the record on faculty views. Elizabeth Gaspar Brown declared emphatically that the Michigan law faculty of the 1880's was "absolutely not" progressive, adding that "I doubt if a liberal or unorthodox idea was around on the faculty."[29]

There was one significant exception to Brown's thesis—the liberalism of Judge Cooley. Although Cooley's views were by no means thoroughly liberal, many of his writings and legal decisions had reformist and democratic substance. For example, as early as the 1840's and 1850's, Cooley defended free trade and free public schools and attacked war, slavery, banking monopolies, unfair railroad practices, and special incorporation laws. In his *Treatise on the Constitutional Limitations Which Rest upon the Legislative Power of the States of the American Union* (1868), Cooley discussed the need for constitutional limitations to prevent unequal legislation, "as well as the identification of legislation with privileged and powerful capitalists." Further, he stressed the "pervading nature" of state police power rather than its limitations, and gave special attention to issues of human liberty and individual rights. There was, in fact, a Jacksonian tincture to some of Cooley's writings, an interest in the common man. In certain of his views, from monopoly to war to individual rights, then, there would appear to be a conspicuous legacy to later reform positions taken by Lindbergh as a congressman.[30]

At the same time, Cooley's democratic bent was tempered by a deep respect for common law tradition and English history. According to Alan Jones, Cooley's total position was an "ambivalent mixture" of conflicting principles. In short, he was both a conservative and a reformer. As Jones puts it, Cooley

regretted national political centralization but understood its necessity; he resisted the politics of plunder and special privilege but feared a retaliatory radicalism based on demagogic resentment; he deplored the pace of change and the self-satisfied pride that flowed from a national sentiment to become immediately rich and great yet believed that change was inevitable and that it developed from popular needs and sentiments which the law must heed.[31]

Further insight into life at Michigan during Lindbergh's stay is provided in a brief volume by the class historian, Charles I. York. His account, *History of Law Class of 1883 of Michigan University,* is one of the few extended class histories there are for the nineteenth century. York suggests that the "Laws" gained a campus and town reputation for colorful activity, noting that his class was involved in "rushes," "military parades," "championships," and "indignation meetings." Boasting that the law students "in mental contests, as well as physical . . . had no equal in the University," York recounts their success at Field Day. He also relates a "Law" victory over a challenge from the "Lits" and "Medics" during the junior year. According to York, the class of 1883 was largely responsible for a well-publicized incident involving the attempted ouster "without cause" of a Medic from the Opera House by a local policeman. During the affair the class held a meeting for all departments, demanded and got an apology from the *Ann Arbor News,* and ultimately led a march of twelve hundred persons through the city. A more typical procession took place the same year when university president James B. Angell returned after two years as envoy to China. Historian York sums up the first year of law school by commenting on heated elections for class officers and the organization of six moot courts; namely, "Ohio," "New York," "Indiana," "Pennsylvania," "Michigan," and "Trans-Mississippi." Since the courts were designed to fit the locality of intended practice, lawyer-to-be Lindbergh undoubtedly participated in the "Trans-Mississippi" court.[32]

The two terms at Michigan were mainly study and work for Lindbergh. He may have been involved in some extracurricular activities, but his personality and purpose were such that he probably was not an active participant. Always independent and a "loner" by temperament, as well as a closely scheduled student because he worked part-time as a waiter, the chances are that he had little time or taste for recreation. In fact, Lindbergh told his second wife that he "kept away from girls" at Michigan and at one point moved out of a house "where a girl roomed in whom he found himself taking too great [an] interest." He did become friends with roommate Orville C. Trace, a medical student, who later practiced in the Minnesota town where Lindbergh settled. Whether Lindbergh was among the law students who "held in question the extravagance [the class history] might impose" is not known, but he was one of fifteen class members whose biographies do not appear in the volume.[33] His earnings while at Ann Arbor, plus what savings he had brought from home, probably no more than covered the total minimum cost of his legal education.[34] On March 28, 1883, Charles August Lindbergh, product of the Minnesota frontier, received his Bachelor of Law degree in a graduating class of 155 members.[35]

Chapter II

Little Falls Lawyer

As a young lawyer, Lindbergh faced the crucial issue of finding a suitable place to start his practice. Shortly after graduation he investigated the possibilities of the South Dakota frontier. He decided against it, and instead selected his home state as the base for his career. Lindbergh joined the firm of Searle, Searle, and Lohman in St. Cloud as a student and junior member, practicing law there for about a year. On June 22, 1883, he was admitted to the Minnesota bar. The following spring he set up permanent practice in a neighboring community to the north, Little Falls.[1]

Little Falls, a village of less than two thousand persons, offered promise to newcomers during the 1880's. It was situated on a slight rapids, or falls, on the Mississippi River where river transportation and water power were readily available. From the first real settlement during the 1850's the fur trade, farming, and lumbering were the chief elements of the local economy. By far the most important of these in the growth of Little Falls was the lumber business. Surrounded by good pine forests, Little Falls emerged as a major mill site for the Weyerhaeuser lumbering interests during the later part of the nineteenth century.[2] Morrison County, of which Little Falls is the county seat, experienced substantial population growth in the years just prior to Lindbergh's arrival in 1884. It had a population of 618 in 1860; 796 in 1865; 1,681 in 1870; 2,722 in 1875; 5,875 in 1880; and 9,406 in 1885.[3]

With attorney L. W. Bills, Lindbergh opened his first law office at Little Falls. The association lasted only a few months—

Bills ultimately relocated at Park Rapids, and Lindbergh moved to "Marotte's Brick Block" in downtown Little Falls and established his own private practice in the fall of 1885. In November the *Little Falls Transcript* announced that Perry Lindbergh had arrived from Melrose and "is assisting his brother, C. A. Lindbergh, in his law office."[4] Later in the decade the younger brother, Frank, joined C. A., as he was often called, in the firm as a fellow lawyer. Frank, a graduate of Melrose High School, attended the normal school in Valparaiso, Indiana, for a year before coming to Little Falls in 1889. He was admitted to the bar by examination at Elk River in 1891, completed his law degree at the University of Michigan in 1892, and became a full partner in the practice now renamed Lindbergh and Lindbergh.[5]

From the very beginning C. A. Lindbergh specialized in real estate and land sales. As country lawyers C. A. and Frank no doubt engaged in a wide variety of legal matters, including trial work, but C. A.'s particular interest and competence always involved real estate. It was an important asset to his success as a lawyer and businessman. Years later, Frank recalled of C. A.: "Well, he was a good office lawyer, but I don't think he was a good trial lawyer. . . . In fact, he didn't do much trial work . . . mostly office work."[6]

During the 1880's regular law matters kept Lindbergh busy. Morrison County records reveal that he handled civil actions for a large number of clients, several of whom apparently retained him on a permanent basis. Most frequently represented by Lindbergh during the early years at Little Falls were the McCormick Harvester Machine Company; the Little Falls Lumber Company; Fuller and Johnson; Rosenberger Brothers; Singer Manufacturing Company; C. Aultmann and Company; Wander, Bushnell, and Glessner; and the W. A. Butler Company. By 1890 Lindbergh had gained a reputation as an honest lawyer—he had turned down his first client because he was guilty—was known for his special knowledge on real estate and land matters, and had been admitted (in 1886) as a practicing attorney in the Circuit Court of the United States for the District of Minnesota.[7]

When Lindbergh first came to Little Falls, he lived at the home of Moses and Harriet Bridget Finnegan La Fond. La Fond, a French Canadian, and his wife, a native of Ireland, were among the original settlers of the community during the 1850's. He was active in several businesses and had been a member of the state legislature. There Lindbergh met and courted the youngest La Fond daughter, Mary ("May"), and in April, 1887, they were married. The years that immediately followed were happy ones for the Lindberghs. Mary was known to be "naturally artistic" and to possess "a quiet, competent genius for homemaking." She was well liked in the community and an active member of the Congregational church. Three children were born to the Lindberghs—Lillian in 1888, Edith, who died at ten months, in 1891, and Eva in 1892. The family circle grew larger as Lindbergh's parents moved from Melrose to Little Falls in 1889, and his sisters, Juno and Linda, also settled in Little Falls. For a time Juno worked as a stenographer in Lindbergh's office. Lindbergh loved young people and was close to his children while they were growing up. Two nieces, Mrs. P. W. Huntemer and Mrs. G. V. Butler, recalled his fondness for children, and noted that "Uncle Charlie" liked to roughhouse and play with the youngsters. And the children loved it. These years were shadowed first by the death of Edith in 1891, and, two years later, by that of August Lindbergh. Thereafter "Grandma" Louisa lived in her own house in Little Falls, warmly surrounded by her children and grandchildren.[8]

During the 1890's Lindbergh's interests in the community and business deepened. He was officially associated with both banks in town, the First National and the German-American National. Lindbergh was an original shareholder in the First National Bank and served as a member of the board of directors at the time of its organization under President Andrew R. Davidson in 1889. He owned ten shares valued at one thousand dollars in the bank, which was capitalized at fifty thousand dollars. Lindbergh's association with the German-American Bank, whose board in 1892 included lumbermen Charles A. Weyerhaeuser, W. H. Laird, and Clarence B. Buckman, came during the 1890's. His name also appeared in the original articles of incorporation of the Transcript Publishing Company in 1892. Although Little Falls already had three newspapers, the new firm was set up to publish a daily paper and to engage in other aspects of the printing business. Lindbergh was selected to serve as a member of the board of directors and as vice-president with fellow officers John Berkey, president, and W. M. Fuller, secretary and treasurer. It seems clear, judging from the positions of the men who started these corporations and from entries in the *Little Falls City Directory for 1892*, that Lindbergh was emerging as a leader in the economic development of the community. The Lindberghs, the La Fonds (ten were listed in the *Directory*), the Davidsons, the Butlers, the Weyerhaeusers, and the Mussers were among the founding families of Little Falls.[9]

Lindbergh's business activities began to take more of his time during this period. Thomas Pederson, who first knew Lindbergh in 1893, later commented that "one of his early real estate deals, and one which I always believed help put him on his feet financially, was the purchase of a long, low gravel ridge alongside the roadbed of the Northern Pacific Railroad 'cut-off' between Little Falls and Staples." According to Pederson, he resold the valuable land to the railroad company, "which hauled hundreds of trainloads of gravel along the ridge every summer for more than twenty years." C. A. continued to buy more land and real estate during these years, although his brother Frank qualified Lindbergh's success a bit when he observed: "I know he owned considerable farm land, but I don't know how much attention he paid to it." This comment is perhaps offset by the fact that Lindbergh's business interests were now aided by an important new associate, Carl Bolander. Bolander, a native of Wrigstad, in the province of Småland, Sweden, began working with him in 1893, and his activities revolved about land matters and the construction of houses and buildings. Martin Engstrom, a friend of the Lindbergh family, described Bolander as a man who knew land well, a "kind of architect" on building projects, who acted as C. A.'s "right-hand man." Engstrom noted that Bolander's suggestions often became realities with Lindbergh's money, and emphasized that "C. A. and Bolander worked well together."[10]

When, in a 1937 interview, Bolander recalled his association with Lindbergh, he discussed certain incidents that reveal Lindbergh's compassion for human suffering. One story, which he recounted in great detail, involved Lindbergh and a needy farm family in about 1895 or 1896. According to Bolander, Louie, a local farmer, had come to Lindbergh's office to pay overdue interest on a loan. Louie, like many farmers during the agricultural recession of 1890's, was in danger of losing his farm. When it became clear that the payment left the farmer nearly broke, Lindbergh scrawled something on a piece of paper and gave it to Louie, saying, "Take that to the mill, get a hundred bushels of seed wheat, twelve sacks of flour, . . . and pay me when you can." Two weeks later Louie made another payment on the interest coupon, and Bolander marked it paid although the cash amount was lacking thirty-five cents. To Bolander's surprise, Lindbergh expressed displeasure over the incident, asserting that "it isn't good business."[11]

Bolander went on to recount a subsequent meeting between Lindbergh and the farmer. In the fall, Lindbergh and Bolander were invited to hunt ducks on Louie's land. With obvious enjoyment, Bolander recounted the hunting party's astonishment when C. A. abruptly stripped to the waist and retrieved their bag of mallards, which had floated out of reach in the icy water. Then, only partially dressed, he hopped about on the bank shooting at a flock of ducks that had come up suddenly. Bolander was puzzled by Lindbergh's silence on the way home, much in contrast to his good humor on the trip out and during the hunting episode. It was not long, however, before C. A. explained his changed feelings to his friend. According to Bolander, Lindbergh declared: "Carl, did you go into Louie's house? . . . Why, Carl, you can see daylight between the cracks in those walls and floors! There's ten little youngsters, and most of 'em barefoot and nearly naked! There's next to nothing on their beds, and probably the same is true of their cupboard. . . . We've got to do something,

Carl. We've surely got to do something about it." What occurred the next morning was a simple act of direct humanity. Lindbergh and Bolander canvassed the town, rounding up coats, dresses, shoes, bedding, and groceries, and saw that the supplies were loaded onto Louie's wagon. Bolander said of Lindbergh: "There you have the man—worried over a missing thirty-five cents in a business deal—but giving time, money, labor, thought, to a needy man who had no other claim than his need."[12]

The Lindbergh law firm went through a number of changes during the decade. Apparently, after Frank joined the firm in 1889, there was a two-year period during which he was intermittently absent while attending law school at Michigan. E. P. Adams worked with Lindbergh from late 1889 through late 1891, and for a short time the firm was known as Lindbergh, Adams, and Lindbergh. When Frank returned permanently to Little Falls after receiving his law degree in 1892, the firm became Lindbergh and Lindbergh. At this time the offices were maintained in the "Butler block," property owned by W. A. Butler, businessman and banker husband of C. A.'s sister Juno. In 1894 Arthur P. Blanchard joined the two brothers, and the firm became Lindbergh, Blanchard, and Lindbergh. This partnership remained intact until Frank withdrew in 1899; thereafter the letterhead read Lindbergh and Blanchard.[13]

Frank's withdrawal from the firm was probably due to his growing involvement in local politics. He had been a candidate for mayor in the spring of 1898, and he also ran for county attorney in the general election that same year. On both occasions he was defeated. In the opinion of the *Little Falls Weekly Transcript,* Frank's defeat was due to the "Buckocrats," a "combine" of Republican Clarence B. Buckman and a number of local Democrats. The group, the paper noted, had successfully backed the candidacy of Charles Vasaly, editor of the *Little Falls Herald,* for mayor. Frank, the *Transcript*'s choice for county attorney, was a staunch Republican but without Buckocrat support. In view of this political alignment it is interesting to note that Frank had married Buckman's daughter, Mamie, in 1897. Frank's vote-

getting ability changed in November, 1900, when he was elected
county attorney. He served three successive terms to January,
1907.[14]

Actually, C. A. had held public office prior to Frank's campaigns—he had served one term as county attorney in 1891–1892.
In the general election of 1890, running as a Republican (although, as customary, ballots for county office did not specify
party label), he defeated attorney F. W. Lyon by a 1,379 to 1,143
vote. While in office, Lindbergh, according to a sampling of
correspondence, was mainly involved in such legal issues as incorporation rules for a savings and loan association, the handling
of homicide cases and coroners' inquests, the manner in which a
county board of commissioners should apportion funds, the publishing rights of newspapers, and the procedure for using separate ballots for women in the election of a superintendent of
schools.[15] He also initiated court action growing out of a misunderstanding between himself and the Morrison County Board of
Commissioners. Lindbergh's chief complaint was that the county
attorney's annual salary of nine hundred dollars was inadequate
in view of the time and work that the job required. The commissioners argued that there had been ample opportunity for
Lindbergh to appear before board meetings and voice his criticism at the time he took office. Ultimately Lindbergh conceded,
and Judge D. B. Searle dismissed the appeal without costs. But
in his final statement Lindbergh maintained that his action was
"based on facts that justified the appeal," and emphasized that
the commissioners were mistaken in their affidavits about his alleged poor attendance record at board meetings. He indicated
that his appeal had not been intended as an "expression of disap-
probation" against the commissioners, and explained that "I am
however able to contribute to the county more than it is willing
to pay for since it is asked that I do so." Undoubtedly the affair
influenced Lindbergh's decision not to run for reelection in 1892.
That same fall he stated publicly that he was not a candidate
for the district judgeship. Lindbergh certainly could not be
termed a politically ambitious lawyer at this point in his career.

His daughter Eva later said simply of his activities during these years: "Father had no idea of politics at that time."[16]

Meanwhile, the Lindbergh law practice continued to be very active. When Lindbergh was doing trial work or traveling to a nearby town on business he would often take his daughters Lillian and Eva with him. It pleased him to have his girls along, and nothing would hold them back when their father gave them the chance to go. Noticeable among additions to the Lindbergh firm's already substantial list of clients at this time were the Pine Tree Lumber Company, the Little Falls Improvement and Navigation Company, Howard P. Bell, the First National Bank, the German-American National Bank, and the Transcript Publishing Company. In view of Lindbergh's official connection with the two banks and the Transcript Publishing Company, those new accounts are easily understood. Most important for Lindbergh, though, would be his association with the Pine Tree Lumber Company and Howard P. Bell.[17]

The Pine Tree Lumber Company of Little Falls was a combined effort of several influential lumber families—the Weyerhaeusers of St. Paul; the Mussers of Muscatine, Iowa; and the Lairds and the Nortons of Winona. In 1891 the Pine Tree firm purchased the Little Falls Lumber Company mill on the east side of the Mississippi and during 1891 and 1892 constructed a new mill on the west bank of the river. This large new mill was one of several Weyerhaeuser mills in Minnesota (the others were at Cloquet, Virginia, and Minneapolis). At Little Falls, Charles A. Weyerhaeuser, one of the four sons of Frederick Weyerhaeuser, emerged as a major figure in mill operations until its collapse about 1919 or 1920, when the supply of available pine ran out. Agnes Larson describes the Weyerhaeuser mills as well equipped, well organized, and efficient. The Little Falls plant, she writes, "had two McDonough band saws that could cut 300,000 feet in a double shift day." During these years the general lumber activity precipitated a boom for Little Falls. While the population of the community had been 2,354 in 1890, just prior to the opening of the Pine Tree plant, the first city directory placed its population at 4,699 in 1892. Officially, Little Falls had, in fact, more than doubled in size between 1890 and 1895, when the state census recorded a population of 5,116. A leveling period of relative stabilization followed, with the population reaching 5,856 in 1905.[18] One commentator relates that the Pine Tree Company "employed about 450 men when running day and night and 150 men on the river and their payroll was about $60,000 per month when ordinary workmen got $1.50 per day." A former employee of the firm, however, stated that employment figures ran as high as eight hundred men. For Lindbergh, the Pine Tree account was obviously an important asset. John C. Patience, longtime wholesale accountant and office manager for the Pine Tree Company and the later Pine Tree Manufacturing Company, stated that Lindbergh acted as legal representative for several corporations of the Weyerhaeuser-Musser interests. He also indicated that Lindbergh was involved in buying timber land, cutting the timber, and then selling the land. Patience, who characterized him as a "pretty shrewd businessman," emphasized that Lindbergh's land deals were his own, without any ownership by the Mussers or Weyerhaeusers.[19]

The contact with Howard P. Bell proved to be both a productive business relationship and a close personal friendship for Lindbergh. Initially Bell came to Little Falls seeking financial investments, and after meeting Lindbergh was so impressed that he arranged for him to handle many of his property and loan dealings. Eva remembered Bell as a multimillionaire "character" who thought a great deal of her father and tried to persuade him to move to the East Coast. From the first meeting between Bell and Lindbergh, probably in the late 1890's, until Bell's death in 1908, the two men wrote each other frequently and periodically met in Minnesota or in the East. Most of their correspondence concerned specific land or real estate transactions and the larger issues of general economic conditions and the nature and influence of Wall Street.[20]

In January, 1903, Bell predicted in a letter to Lindbergh that the long "boom" period of business from 1898 to 1903 would break. In his opinion it had not taken a particularly wise person to make money during these years, but the situation, he felt, would be reversed during the coming years. Bell asserted that Wall Street had a definite advantage during a decline and could make just as much money then as in a boom economy. Perhaps because of this economic fluctuation, he was anxious about the success of his Minnesota investments with Lindbergh, revealing that "I don't like the extra risks that come with grasping the last profits." At the same time he told Lindbergh that he believed the chance of loss was small, and commented that "I still feel I would like to see you actually clean up a good thing." The following March, Bell expressed worry because a large number of Minnesota farms purchased on speculation were still unsold. He wrote Lindbergh: "Out of $75,000 paid for farms we have left $52,000," and he estimated that the actual cost of unsold lands in their joint account was about $40,000. Stressing the existence of a tight money period in business and inaccurately predicting a long decline from 1904 through 1907, Bell advised Lindbergh to "SELL, SELL, SELL."[21]

In 1906, Lindbergh and Bell discussed the advantages and disadvantages of owning country bank stock. Apparently they were considering an investment in the German-American Bank in Little Falls at the time, and Lindbergh informed Bell that the bank management would pay about 40 per cent on its stock, "at least as long as the Pine Tree people are here." Bell's main objection to country bank stock was that it had very limited demand and thus might have to be sold at a concession price, but he assured Lindbergh that he would go along with the deal if they could be certain of at least a 25 per cent gain over several years. He wrote Lindbergh that "the $24,000 cost of the bank block is not material," provided that it was used for a bank, and advised him that "book value plus good established business beats any depreciation on building." Bell also suggested to Lindbergh that "in taking stock I think it might be better (appear better to the Pine Tree boys) for you to take it in your own name." Lindbergh's association with wealthy capitalist Bell was undoubtedly financially profitable for him, and this friendship reveals the early stages of his absorbing interest in the field of money and banking.[22]

Certain changes occurred in Lindbergh's personal affairs during the Little Falls years. Throughout the 1890's his private life revolved largely around the close-knit Lindbergh families. The "Charlie" Lindberghs, the Frank Lindberghs, the Butlers, the Seals (Linda Lindbergh married Joseph Seal), and Grandmother Louisa all lived on the same block on Broadway East during these years. Daughters of these families developed a closeness that was more like that of sisters than of cousins. But the decade was not without its sadness for Lindbergh. In the spring of 1898 his wife Mary, just a few days before her thirty-first birthday, died of complications following surgery for the removal of an abdominal tumor. According to reports Lindbergh's shock was heightened by the fact that he had been assured of his wife's full recovery after the operation. Lindbergh continued to live at 608 Broadway East for about two years, employing a kindergarten teacher, Helen Gilbert, to live with the children. Grandmother Louisa also moved in with the family. Eva recalled one crisis during that period in the old yellow brick house. During the night a burglar had gained entrance to the home; Eva and Lillian were awakened when a gun fired in the upstairs hallway, but they were told it was just thunder. The stories of what actually happened vary. Eva remembered that her father later claimed that although he had always said he would shoot anyone who broke into his house, when confronted with the situation he could not fire at the man. According to Eva, Lindbergh actually "had grasped the man in the upper hallway and held his arm and made him discharge his revolver into the wall—then the man eluded him—he was in his stocking feet, and as he slipped down stairs—Father shot over his head." Charles, Jr., however, recently wrote: "The story I was told was that my father shot the burglar with his Smith and Wesson revolver as the man was escaping through a window, and that blood was found on the window sill."[23]

About 1900 Lindbergh met Evangeline Lodge Land, a young woman from Michigan who had come to Little Falls to teach science in the high school. She was attractive, intelligent, and well educated. Her father was Dr. Charles Henry Land, a Detroit dentist who was best known for his invention of the porcelain jacket crown. The Land family ancestry was English and Scotch (Lands fought for King George III in the American Revolution), and the Lodge family was of English and Irish background. Evangeline Land had been educated at Miss Ligget's School for Girls in Detroit and the University of Michigan, from which she graduated in 1899 with a major in chemistry. While at Ann Arbor she developed a romantic notion about teaching in a frontier mining town. After securing several leads through a teachers' agency, Evangeline settled on Little Falls, a decision influenced by reading Willard Glazier's *Down the Great River* (1881). Her job at Little Falls ended within four months, following a confrontation with the school principal. Refused permission to move a class from a laboratory she considered too cold ("usually about 54°"), she "simply set the apparatus on the floor" and left the school building. "Father," Evangeline later wrote Charles, Jr., "did not like the situation and advised me to resign."[24]

Lindbergh and Evangeline both lived at the Antlers Hotel (with room windows facing each other for "easily arranged" signals, said Evangeline), and their relationship began naturally with walks along the same route to school and office. They soon became engaged, and they were married on March 27, 1901, in Detroit. They had one son, Charles Augustus Lindbergh, Jr., born in Detroit on February 4, 1902. In 1898 Lindbergh had purchased some land about two miles south of Little Falls, just north of where Pike Creek flows into the Mississippi River. For a short time he and Evangeline lived in a quickly constructed cabin on the low river bank while a large frame house was being built on the high bank. The house, built by Carl Bolander and completed in 1901, was impressive. It was, according to Bolander, a handsome three-story structure, "richly furnished and planned with taste and care." Red oak paneling, big fireplaces, furnishings from Grand Rapids, Michigan, and a third-floor billiard room were among the features of the new house. Bolander called the dining room "one of the loveliest rooms I've ever known."[25] Although Howard Bell had written Lindbergh that, with cheap lumber and Bolander's skill, he could build a house for $2,000 to $2,500, the finished product undoubtedly was more expensive. Bolander admitted that it cost "much more" than the original estimate, but divulged no actual figures. According to Bolander, Lindbergh had made him promise not to. "Carl, keep it under your hat," he had said. "We're going to have it *right,* but we won't ever tell what it costs." Social life at the new house consisted mainly of visits, and return entertaining, with such families as the Weyerhaeusers, the Tanners, the Williamses, and the Mussers. Typical entertainment included card playing and acting. Lindbergh played billiards and occasionally joined in a pinochle game.[26]

The physical focus of Lindbergh home life ended abruptly when, on August 6, 1905, the three-story house burned to the ground. The report in the *Little Falls Daily Transcript* indicated that the spectacular fire started on the third floor shortly after the family's Sunday dinner and quickly went out of control. Efforts to save the house were hampered by the fact that there was not sufficient water pressure from the gravity tank in the barn hayloft to reach the third floor; nor would hoses reach that height. Everything on that floor, including part of Lindbergh's library, as well as the contents of the basement and kitchen were lost, but much of the furniture and other belongings from the first and second floors were saved. Charles, Jr., despite the fact that he was only three years old at the time, still remembers the event and recalls that he was caught up by a nurse and taken to a safe distance around the corner of the barn. The cause of the fire was never clearly established, but one theory was that a maid had started it by turning over a lamp while curling her hair. Another theory blamed a pile of oily rags in the attic. In any event, Lindbergh immediately announced that the house

was covered by a fair amount of insurance and that he would re-
build on the same foundation. For a time the Lindberghs resided
at the Buckman Hotel in Little Falls (later Evangeline and
Charles, Jr. took an apartment in Minneapolis), until a second,
somewhat smaller, gray and white house was constructed on
the same property in 1906–1907.[27]

About the time of the house changes C. A. and Evangeline
became estranged. According to Charles, Jr., they were never
divorced, but "they lived apart most of the time after the first
several years of their marriage." In the years afterward Charles,
Jr. lived with his mother in Detroit, in Washington, and in Little
Falls. But Lindbergh visited his wife and son frequently, and
Charles often joined his father on the farm, on campaign trips,
and in Washington. "Their relationship was a tragic situation,"
Charles, Jr. has said of his parents, and he emphasized that they
continued to care for one another. Eva stated that her father and
stepmother "were attuned mentally, but not emotionally." Apparently Evangeline was a woman of rapidly changing moods.
Her emotions were highly charged and often unpredictable,
giving her a temperament not well suited to that of her husband.
Lindbergh was the sort of man who did not show emotion at all.
Perhaps a contributory, albeit minor, factor in their relationship
was their quite different senses of humor. C. A.'s humor was
"deep, subtle, straight-faced," whereas Evangeline's wit was
"rippled, light, quick, and laughing." Evangeline herself later
recalled two incidents symptomatic of this difference. In one
instance a farmer visited C. A.'s office shortly after his marriage
to Evangeline and remarked that Mrs. Lindbergh was surely
much younger than he (she was seventeen years younger than
C. A.). "No," Lindbergh replied with a straight face, "she is as a
matter of fact five years older." It was a long time before
Evangeline forgave him for that remark. On another occasion
Evangeline slipped on the grass along the Mississippi and
plunged "up to my arm pits in the cold water." C. A. "stood on
the bank and laughed." Evangeline was furious.[28]

There apparently always existed a basic misunderstanding between husband and wife. Charles, Jr. suggested later that his mother's protected family life and education were "not good background for a Minnesota one-generation-beyond-the-frontier life." Nevertheless, as correspondence between C. A. and Evangeline clearly substantiates, a strong bond of affection endured between them for years after their separation. The marital situation was not uncommon, but it no doubt deepened Lindbergh's aloneness and sensitivity. Eva described her father as a "lonely but basically not unhappy man." His essential nature was reflective and tolerant, which probably made him better equipped to handle loneliness and disappointment than most men.[29]

Lindbergh's demeanor was reserved and modest, and most people regarded him as a serious, even scholarly, man. Former Minnesota governor Elmer Benson described him as "austere" and difficult to know. To Admiral "Jerry" Land he was "a rather severe individual, hard to approach, and eccentric." Mrs. A. M. Opsahl of Brainerd stressed Lindbergh's straightforward speech and honesty as the basis for an enduring friendship between him and her husband. Fred Larson, longtime Little Falls county official, "never heard him crack a joke" and expressed the opinion that Lindbergh was not a natural "mixer" nor given to the usual small-town coffee breaks. Charles, Jr. recently wrote: "My father mixed easily with individuals and groups—when he wished to." In a 1900 letter, presumably to Lindbergh, Grace Van Sickle told him: "You businessmen take life *too* seriously; it would be good for you to indulge in some of the frivolities of life. Now I suspicion that Mr. Lindbergh *thinks* too much, *reads* too much, even outside business matters." Eva, who probably knew her father's political and economic views better than anyone else, called her father "mainly an intellectual man" and felt that he had a "judicial mind." Friend Thomas Pederson referred to Lindbergh simply as a "deep thinker."[30]

The serious bent of Lindbergh's character coincided well with an interest in ideas and books. An examination of the remaining books in his personal library reveals several fields of interest. Most numerous are the volumes dealing with history, evolution, economics, psychology, philosophy, politics, sociology, and select literary classics. Significantly, the largest single segment in the Lindbergh library is made up of books on evolution and the related debate between science and religion. There are several volumes of Herbert Spencer and Charles Darwin, as well as a number of analytical works by such authors as John Draper, John Fiske, Oscar Schmidt, Henry Drummond, and Ernest Haeckel. In addition, although the works are no longer in the collection, Lindbergh was influenced by the writings of T. H. Huxley.[31]

Historical books in the library range from Prescott's *History of the Conquest of Peru* and *History of the Conquest of Mexico*, Macaulay's multivolume *The History of England*, and Von Holst's *The Constitutional and Political History of the United States*, to studies on ancient history and the Protestant Reformation. Among the classics are the novels of Victor Hugo and the works of Washington Irving, while political material includes the *Addresses of Abraham Lincoln*, Lynn Haines's *Your Congress*, and H. P. Hall's *Observations* on Minnesota politics. Other representative volumes deal with such areas as linguistics, mental health, and geological surveys. Lindbergh may have been further influenced by the ideas in periodicals, and in the Lindbergh home were *Harper's, The Atlantic*, and, a bit later, *La Follette's Magazine*. In view of Lindbergh's interest in agriculture and money, it is not surprising that he read Sidney Owen's Populist-oriented magazine, *Farm, Stock, and Home*, and W. H. Harvey's *Coin's Financial School*.[32]

According to Eva and Bolander, Lindbergh's reading interests included poetry. They both recalled his keen liking for American writer Elbert Hubbard, and Eva also noted that her father enjoyed Tennyson. Bolander later told of spending a cold evening with Lindbergh and a volume of Hubbard's poems in the living room of the first house by the river. "The weather turned cold, it started to snow," Bolander said, "but we were cozy by the fire, and there we sat for hours—talking, reading aloud by turns, and eating crackers and cheese."[33]

Lindbergh was not inclined to follow the regular patterns of organized religion, but he did believe in God. Eva stated that in later years he became a Unitarian and was particularly influenced by the lectures of John Dietrich of the Unitarian Church in Minneapolis. Charles, Jr. remembers being taken to church by his mother one Sunday shortly before his father's election to Congress. For the young boy in a new suit and tight stockings, hemmed in by the hot building, it was a frustrating experience. After all, any sensible boy would prefer the river breezes and open space of the pine woods on the farm to close confinement in church. Years afterward, Charles, Jr. wrote that he was sure Lindbergh was aware it was "a good move politically" to have his son seen in church, and he thought that his parents had probably discussed the matter in advance. "But on the whole," he stated, "his actions were natural rather than political." Carl Bolander discussed Lindbergh's expression of a belief in God in a different way. In his 1937 interview Bolander recalled driving with Lindbergh into the lake country north of Little Falls and stopping on a hill overlooking a lake and a yellow road winding through the pines. After viewing the scene for a time, Lindbergh broke the silence "with an outburst of such eloquence and impassioned feeling that I'd never heard from him before." According to Bolander, Lindbergh declared: "Some men tell us there is no God!—or that God is a puny creature shut up in churches and creeds." Looking over the horizon, he exclaimed: "I need no scientific analysis or theological arguments to show me the reality or the bigness of *my* God when I look at this!"[34]

Understandably, Lindbergh was known for his financial and business success. His law practice was well established. His land holdings were considerable. By the early 1900's, he and Bolander had built thirty-five houses and three commercial brick buildings on the west side of the river in Little Falls. Lindbergh later claimed he had built "six blocks" of his own in town. A hotel, a cold storage plant, and a general store building were planned for the three commercial structures. Apparently Lindbergh's investment in the buildings did not pay off, however, for Frank

Dewey stated that his father, T. H. Dewey, and Martin Engstrom, who opened a hardware store, eventually bought the buildings for less than the cost of construction. One reason for the limited success of the Lindbergh-Bolander commercial venture was the fact that the west side of Little Falls did not develop into a major business district, as some had anticipated. As a lawyer, Lindbergh probably lost some money on accounts he endorsed on behalf of clients, much as his father had done in Sweden. Nonetheless, even though many of his assets were not liquid, Lindbergh was reasonably well-to-do at this point in his life.[35]

Perhaps the clearest statement of his financial worth is contained in a letter to Evangeline in December, 1905. He stated simply that his assets were valued at over $200,000 in property against $36,710 in debts. But his main point was that he was "exceedingly poor in cash" and that "we will have to be governed by our condition and not by our needs." He complained of being a slave to the taxes on his properties and noted that he could probably send Evangeline only money for necessities. Lindbergh further revealed that unless there was a dramatic change in his financial situation, he could not send his daughter Lillian to the university the next fall. "I can send her the next year but certainly not 1906, unless it's on the scale I had to go on." With a touch of frontier philosophy and rugged individualism, Lindbergh instructed: "They both, our little daughters, have got to work and it will be better for them," adding that "there wasn't as much spent on me from the time I was 3 years till I was 20 as is spent on L. and E. each 6 mos."[36]

Intermittently during the Little Falls years Lindbergh made public statements on the questions that mattered to him. In 1887, for example, he delivered a Memorial Day address expressing gratitude to the veterans of the Civil War and praising the economic prosperity and lack of governmental restraint in the United States since that divided time. An industrial edition of the *Little Falls Transcript* on January 1, 1894, carried a statement on the economics of Morrison County. In it Lindbergh strongly emphasized the diversity of soil and landscape in the county. Not only were water and timber readily available, but the variety of farming activities—from wheat, corn, oats, and potatoes to cattle, sheep, and fowl—gave the Morrison County farmer a definite advantage over the Dakota wheat farmer. Lindbergh stated that there were area farmers who had sold out, gone to the Dakota prairies, and returned to Morrison County as virtual paupers. But Morrison County was not immune to the hard times of the 1890's. A number of mortgage foreclosures occurred there during the decade, and the Lindbergh law firm necessarily handled many of these legal actions.[37]

When, in the fall of 1900, Lindbergh's failure to accept local Republican speaking engagements was interpreted as indifferent Republicanism, he felt obliged to answer. In a letter to the editor of the *Little Falls Transcript,* after noting that he did not wish "to become prominent in print," Lindbergh made it abundantly clear that he was indeed still a Republican. Although he demanded that people respect the sincere beliefs of any citizen whether he be Republican, Democrat, or Populist, Lindbergh stressed that "most practical and reasoning people" were Republicans. Moreover, since the Republican party had been in power roughly forty years, it was the "executive" party and the one most likely to accomplish its purposes, while the Democratic party was the "critic" party. In Lindbergh's opinion, the Republican was the party best equipped to meet the pressing current need for laws to curb the abuses of the great national trusts—a particularly relevant statement in view of his later reform thought. Finally, he offered his evaluation of the presidential campaign by describing Democrat William Jennings Bryan's arguments as inconsistent and advising support of the full Republican ticket.[38]

The race problem in America was the subject of several newspaper statements by Lindbergh in early 1903. After taking a trip to the South, he recorded his firsthand observations. Lindbergh believed that the Negro was destined to a subordinate role in American social and political life. His reasons were threefold:

(1) "By nature he is inferior to the white race"; (2) "he is natural to a climate that tends to sluggishness"; (3) "there is not sufficient inducement for him to become progressive." Lindbergh further viewed the Negro as the "happiest of all races," noting that this was a sustaining characteristic in that it helped to offset the "cloud of race prejudice that holds them down." Politically, he stated that the Negro, despite his legal rights, was "nevertheless forever barred from hopes of being stamped with the glories accorded to complete American citizenship." Lindbergh pointed out that many Americans might criticize the South for its treatment of the Negro, but "we cannot condemn, for we in the north would, if we had an equal colored population, render the same treatment." In his opinion it had been a mistake to extend the franchise, and the only hope of this condition actually working might be the establishment of a separate state for the Negro population, where they might "exercise national character" and "rapidly improve to a higher morality." But the race matter was practically settled, Lindbergh contended, for the Negro "will be kept down." The only long-range hope he saw was miscegenation. "It may not elevate the white race," he said, "but it will eventually lift the black."[39]

Lindbergh's views on the racial issue were formed largely as a result of his absorbing interest in Darwinian thought, but his interest in the problem may also have been prompted by Theodore Roosevelt's attention to the question about the same time. The president was disturbed with lynchings in the South and felt that total disenfranchisement was wrong, an opinion that was probably formed in part as a result of political and public pressure. According to scholars, it is also clear that Roosevelt accepted the basic notion of biological inferiority of the Negro. He did, however, believe that a better environment would improve the race, and he recognized the accomplishments of individual Negroes. Lindbergh, an admirer of Roosevelt, apparently endorsed the same type of physical-environmental analysis of the Negro. Considering this aspect of his thinking on race, he was not among the extreme racists of the period, and Eva stated that her father later repudiated even these views. The seeming contradiction between Lindbergh's reformist beliefs and his racial views is, in fact, not unusual, for most progressives formed similar judgments. Progressives in the South sought to "purify" politics by disenfranchising the Negro. In general, as C. Vann Woodward states, progressives "reflected [their times] awfully well: They were thoroughgoing spokesmen of contemporary attitudes."[40] There is, in fact, some evidence that individual progressives, among them Senators Robert M. La Follette of Wisconsin and Albert Cummins of Iowa, defended the rights of the Negro. Although Lindbergh may indeed have changed his views on race, and his reform thought was often parallel to that of La Follette and Cummins, he made no recorded public statements on the subject while in Congress.[41]

The most dramatic of Lindbergh's public efforts during the Little Falls period was his involvement in founding an experimental farmers' cooperative and in publishing a related reform-oriented magazine. On February 28, 1905, the Industrial Adjustment Company was organized, with C. A. Lindbergh (treasurer), Frank Lindbergh (secretary), Carl Bolander (vice-president), Arthur P. Blanchard, and Charles H. Land (president) named as its incorporators. The incorporation papers outlined four broad areas of proposed company activity: (1) General dealings in lands, tenements, and hereditaments; (2) the wholesale mercantile business; (3) acting as "an adjustment agency between creditors and debtors"; and (4) operating a storage facility for goods and produce and advancing money and credit to depositors on this same merchandise.[42]

More specifically, according to Carl Bolander, the company "was principally intended for the purpose of buying and storing and selling farm produce." To this end "310 acres of land one mile west of Little Falls was purchased and a large barn was built upon it. The intention was to buy up stock and hogs and keep and finish them on the land, and to erect a butchering plant and butcher the stock so bought and kept." A substantial cold storage plant was also a part of the company plan, and subsequently a two-story brick building with full basement was constructed on the west side of the Mississippi near the railroad tracks in Little Falls (one of the three commercial buildings Lindbergh and Bolander built and promoted). The overall plan called for insulating the building and installing an ammonia cold storage unit so that it could efficiently store and cool meat, potatoes, and other produce. In essence, the primary purpose of the cooperative company was to benefit local farmers by eliminating unnecessary costs.[43]

Closely related to the proposed Industrial Adjustment Company was the publication of Lindbergh's magazine, *The Law of Rights: Realized and Unrealized, Individual and Public.* It was designed as a quarterly bulletin to be sold at thirty-five cents annually or ten cents per copy. Essentially *The Law of Rights* was the organ of the company, and its purpose, in part, was to focus attention on the farmer's economic problems and the cooperative's answers to them. The magazine also provided a place for Lindbergh to express his emerging views on economic, political, and social reform. Just prior to publication Lindbergh announced in the *Little Falls Herald* that "the aim is to get the people interested in their own behalf, and to act on matters in promotion of their interests." To that end, he went on, "I have formulated a system of studies and work in connection with the development of our county and other counties that I will introduce through the bulletin." Three thousand copies of the initial March, 1905, issue were printed.[44]

In the first issue, after explaining that the publication itself was not a "financial scheme," Lindbergh argued that the small manufacturing plant could operate successfully for a home market. "The main thing in all these considerations is to prevent the waste of energy in the individual as well as in the community." Obviously the Industrial Adjustment Company was an example of such a plant. Lindbergh, really writing as a crusader for reform, called for the organization of farmers, adjustment between producers and consumers, reasonable rates of interest, cheaper transportation costs, and an end to "uneconomic competition."

His comments on Little Falls as a community with undesirable business competition must have appeared a bit radical to many local citizens. Noting that the city of 6,000 persons was located in a county with a population of 27,000, Lindbergh asserted that Little Falls, with three banks and sixteen grocery stores, had more such establishments than it really needed. If instead the community had only one bank and three groceries, which, in Lindbergh's opinion, would be sufficient to handle the needs of the population, he estimated a total yearly savings to the people of $8,400 for the banks and $17,400 for the grocery businesses. He also revealed his growing concern about the centralization of capital and the trusts. In his judgment, the "advancing education of the people" and the "irresistible energy of the people" would act as a partial remedy to these evils.[45]

Except for the brief existence of *The Law of Rights,* the Little Falls project failed to materialize. Three issues of the magazine were published, but its unattractive format and the vague, complicated sentence structure of Lindbergh's writing probably hampered its success. In the case of the Industrial Adjustment Company, $26,000 out of an anticipated $75,000 investment was actually spent on land and buildings. When it became clear that neither Bolander nor Lindbergh would have enough time to devote to the project in the months before the proposed opening of operations in 1907, "the cold-storage building was rented out to other parties and afterwards sold, and the land was sold in small tracts, and that was the end of it." The building was rented and eventually sold to T. H. Dewey, who operated Dewey's Produce Company. Walter E. Quigley, a later associate during Lindbergh's political career, wrote that Lindbergh lost about $20,000 on the Little Falls affair. Lindbergh's failure to watch the project more closely was due to the fact that, in 1906, he became actively involved in politics.[46]

Chapter III

Sixth District Congressman

On June 20, 1906, Charles A. Lindbergh, Sr., of Little Falls announced his candidacy for the Republican nomination from the Sixth Congressional District of Minnesota, stressing that, in his opinion, "the determination of all questions of governmental policy rests with the people." In a statement in the *Little Falls Daily Transcript*, Lindbergh told the voters:

There is now a pressure for legislative action on more intricate questions of national policy than there has been in any previous period and the wishes of the people must be shaped into legislation through their servants in office, and as a candidate I wish to study with the people the questions that interest them and solicit their consideration with me.[1]

With Lindbergh's declaration the stage was set for a vigorous and fiercely competitive Republican primary race, which, in turn, was followed by a less provocative general election campaign.

Lindbergh's entrance into political life was sudden. It was a surprise to nearly everyone close to him, for as his friend Thomas Pederson put it, "He had never meddled in politics, nor expressed any desire to hold office." Lynn and Dora Haines suggest that his decision to run for Congress came after a late-night chat with an old friend on the Mississippi River bridge in Little Falls in the early summer of 1906, but they do not identify the friend. Frank Lindbergh agreed that "I think there were some people who urged him," but he, too, was unable to name those who convinced C. A., explaining, "I don't know just who." This

41

view was later supported by a report in the *Minneapolis Evening Star* that a "delegation" of Lindbergh's friends were determined to put up his name for Congress, and, under the circumstances, he entered the race. In a 1964 interview, Frank emphasized the abruptness of his brother's congressional activity by pointing out that "there was an idea that I was going to run for the legislature." When C. A. declared his candidacy, said Frank, "I didn't pay any attention to that." In reply to a question on the seriousness of his running for the legislature, he stated: "Oh, I probably would have . . . if he [C. A.] hadn't gone and become a candidate for Congress," further clarifying that "no, I never had any great ambition to get into politics."[2]

The first indication that Lindbergh was interested in pursuing a political career is shown in a March 5 letter to him from Howard P. Bell. Bell, writing from Sea Breeze, Florida, and apparently answering an earlier letter from Lindbergh, could not see any advantage in running for public office. Bell discussed Lindbergh's political possibilities in terms of running for a legislative seat, and concluded that "the legislature can't look especially attractive to you and only a sense of duty can draft you. . . . But I think your duty is to yourself—not to the 'dear public.'" Either Lindbergh had actually considered running for the state legislature, or, more likely, Bell was confused about his interest in Congress. Interestingly, Bell made a few critical comments about Lindbergh's office staff, warning that he must have better help. "I don't notice anything that you can *safely* leave to your office force," wrote Bell. "You have so little aptitude to figures and accounts and can use your rare executive ability to so much better purpose that it seems too bad to suffer year in and year out these annoyances." For Bell, of course, Lindbergh's entrance into politics would bring into question the future of their active working arrangement on land and real estate dealings in Minnesota.[3]

Lindbergh reached his decision to seek the Republican nomination about the middle of April. Weighing heavily the judgment of Bell, Lindbergh wrote to him about the congressional race on April 11. In reply, Bell wrote Lindbergh a brief note on April 14, advising him "to let the thing run a bit through your silence and throw a scare into Buckman." Clarence B. Buckman, to whom Bell referred, was the two-term Republican incumbent in the district and would be Lindbergh's major obstacle in a bid for Congress. Bell answered Lindbergh more fully on April 16 and April 17. He still voiced strong doubts about the desirability of becoming a candidate, commenting that "congressmen don't amount to much in Washington" and noting that a congressman "has to mix in with the little squabbles all over his District and get a good round cussing from the crowd he decides against." In Bell's opinion the lost time, money, and opportunities at home, together with the necessary associations with "low down politicians" were too high a price to pay. One advantage Bell did foresee was that Lindbergh would become better known in his state. If an actual campaign materialized, Bell felt that Lindbergh's Swedish name and his reputation as a man of intelligence and conviction would have strong voter appeal. His most urgent point in the letter was that Lindbergh not spend any of his own money or "hustle" to get the nomination.[4]

Lindbergh expected to win if he entered the race for Congress. Writing to his wife on April 17, and referring to his attendance at a meeting in St. Paul that evening (in all likelihood a meeting with Republican leaders who supported his candidacy), he stated: "If it looks tonight as if I will have an easy victory I may go in." He pointed out that he would not shrink from a "big fight," but he preferred to avoid that kind of a race. "If I go in I will expect to win," he boldly wrote Evangeline. The same day he received another letter from Bell. Explaining that the pacemaker in a race has the most difficult role, Bell warned Lindbergh to "go slow" in his political bid, noting that it would be dangerous to "kill off" Buckman too soon; if Lindbergh instead "let C. B. kill off the others, you could still *do* him." Even though Bell was now giving Lindbergh explicit campaign advice, he still voiced strong reservations on the whole matter and concluded: "I am unalterably opposed to your candidacy unless the nomination attracts you—thereby minimizing the features that would be most disagreeable to you."[5]

To Lindbergh the attractions of candidacy outweighed the disagreeable features. One week later a communication from Bell indicated that C. A. was "in by invitation." Bell was unsure whether Lindbergh should publicize his candidacy before nomination and cautioned that once he did start addressing the public he should avoid coming on too strong, sticking only to a policy of genuine inquiry about the conditions in the district. In a letter to his wife during the first week of May, Lindbergh exhibited some enthusiasm for the coming campaign. Calling his candidacy "a battle against ignorance," he declared: "I think the people will win—I do not feel anxious about it and am really enjoying it." He assured Evangeline that he was "in trim for one of the most interesting campaigns the 6th District has ever seen." Charles, Jr. stated in an interview that his father was physically "trim all his life," with his weight at 175 and his height at 5 feet 11 inches.[6]

The Sixth Congressional District of Minnesota was located in the geographic center of the state. In 1905 the twelve-county district had a total population of 227,827, of which 75,293 was urban and 151,027 was rural. Major communities included St. Cloud (population 9,422), Brainerd (8,133), Little Falls (5,856), Alexandria (3,051), Sauk Centre (2,463), Litchfield (2,415), Staples (2,163), and Melrose (2,151). A substantial proportion—22.4 per cent—of the Sixth District's population was made up of foreign-born citizens. The most numerous immigrant groups in the district were the Germans and Swedes, followed by the Norwegians and Canadians, and then lesser numbers of Finns, Danes, Irish, Poles, and English. The total number of German foreign-born (17,255) and Swedish foreign-born (14,076) in the Sixth District represented approximately 14 per cent and 11 per cent of the state's German and Swedish population, respectively.[7]

From the time of Sixth District's creation in 1893, its congressional representation had, with one exception, been Republican. The exception was the single term of its first representative, Democrat M. R. Baldwin, who served from 1893 to 1895. He

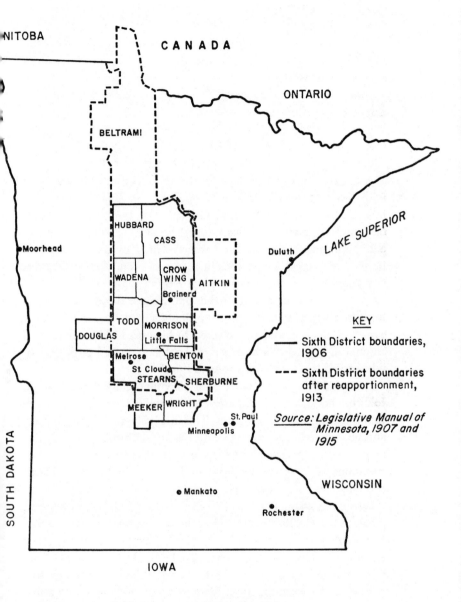

Sixth Congressional District of Minnesota

was followed, in turn, by Republicans Charles A. Towne (1895–1897), Page Morris (1897–1903), and Clarence B. Buckman, a two-term incumbent in 1906.[8] During the same period, from the 1890's to 1906, the Republican party held control of the Minnesota state legislature, but the party's control of the office of governor had been broken. With the agrarian revolt of the 1890's came support for candidates representing the Farmers Alliance and the Populist party. For example, Editor Sidney M. Owens of *Farm, Stock, and Home* made strong showings as an Alliance and Populist candidate in the gubernatorial races of 1890 and 1894. But the first real break in Republicanism came with the election of Democrat-Populist John Lind as governor in 1898. Swedish-born Lind served only one term, however, and had limited success with his reforms because of opposition from a Republican legislature. Lind was defeated by narrow margins in his campaigns for governor in 1896 and 1900. The Republican governors during these years were Norwegian-born Knute Nelson, who opted for a seat in the U.S. Senate during his second term in 1895; David Clough, the lieutenant governor who took over from Nelson and was elected in his own right in 1896; and Samuel R. Van Sant, a former river boat captain and businessman who served two terms from 1901 to 1905.[9]

In 1904 Minnesotans voted into office another Swede, John A. Johnson, editor of the *St. Peter Herald* and a Democrat. By 1906 Johnson had established himself as a highly popular governor, and he enjoyed some success with the legislature because he was able to win bipartisan support. In national elections Minnesota continued to cast the majority of its votes in the Republican column, as it had in every election since its first presidential vote, favoring Abraham Lincoln, in 1860. In 1904, in the most recent presidential election prior to Lindbergh's entrance into politics, Minnesota went overwhelmingly (by a four to one margin) for Republican Theodore Roosevelt. To Lindbergh, the Republican party seemed to offer the best opportunities to a prospective politician. Although many of his views were akin to the Populist ideology, he was a practical politician in that he knew the value of belonging to the party in power. Lindbergh felt quite simply that it would be the party most likely to run the country as well as the party most likely to be able to bring about needed change.[10]

During the 1906 primary most newspapers of the Sixth District supported incumbent Congressman Buckman. Buckman had a record of accomplishment in his adopted state. A native of Pennsylvania, he came to Minnesota and founded the town of Buckman in 1872, moved to Little Falls in 1880, and established himself in the lumber business and the manufacture of railroad ties there. He served in the state house of representatives from 1881 to 1883 and in the state senate from 1887 to 1891 and from 1899 to 1903, and by 1906 he was nearing the end of his second term in Congress. Many Republican papers, which outnumbered Democratic newspapers in the district by five to one, emphasized Buckman's political experience as a sound basis for his reelection.[11] In contrast, the *Litchfield Saturday Review* pointed out, Lindbergh "has no legislative record at all." The *Long Prairie Leader* put it simply: "Buckman has given us action and results" and "Lindbergh promises us theory and talk." In Little Falls, the home community of both candidates, the Republican *Little Falls Daily Transcript* strongly endorsed Buckman. The *Transcript* praised Buckman as "a congressman who gets everything possible for his district" and carried prepared advertisements that singled out such Buckman accomplishments as the installation of 194 free-delivery mail routes, winning an appropriation for a public building in Brainerd, securing pensions for veterans, and obtaining a U.S. land office site at Cass Lake rather than Bemidji.[12]

Among the pro-Lindbergh publications during the primary were the *Buffalo Journal,* the *Todd County Argus,* and the *Hubbard County Enterprise.* In supporting Lindbergh they stressed his willingness to speak to the people during the campaign ("His opponent is seeing the ward workers"), his ability and integrity as a lawyer, and his progressive views on political economy. He would devote more attention to national questions than Buckman, they said, but at the same time would not neglect the local district. The Buffalo weekly was impressed that Jacob F. ("Jake") Jacobson, a well-known Republican state leader, was stumping the district for Lindbergh, while the *Argus*, a Long Prairie publication, attacked Buckman for voting with the railroad interests in the state senate. Of some interest was another paper, the Democratic *Little Falls Herald*, which ran guest editorials sympathetic to Republican Lindbergh. Typical were statements from Sixth District papers that strongly identified Buckman with the "political machine" of the party, and, in turn, viewed Lindbergh as a progressive Republican, anticorporation, and challenger to the party machine.[13]

A key factor in the Lindbergh-Buckman primary race was the split in the Republican party. The Republican difficulties dated back to the gubernatorial race of 1904, when Robert Dunn won the nomination from Minnesota associate justice L. W. Collins. In the general election, Dunn, who had been editor of the *Princeton Union* and whose background included experience as both state legislator and state auditor, faced opposition in his own party. Despite the support of popular senior senator Knute Nelson of Alexandria, charges against Dunn's political ability and personal character hurt him in the campaign. The result, in a year when eight of the nine congressmen Minnesota elected were Republicans and Theodore Roosevelt received a 163,000-vote margin in the state, was victory for Democrat John A. Johnson. By 1906 the old wounds in the party had not yet healed, and they were aggravated by a sharp contest between two candidates for the gubernatorial nomination during the state convention in Duluth. The leading candidates were Jacobson, a west central Minnesota businessman from Madison and a former state legislator and member of the State Board of Control; and Albert L. Cole, a merchant from Walker (in the Sixth District) and a member of the state legislature. Although Jacobson led on the first two ballots and appeared to have the support of the majority of the delegates, Cole was nominated on the third ballot. Dunn, still smarting from 1904, vigorously opposed Jacobson's candidacy. Alva Eastman, one of Jacobson's campaign managers, angrily charged that "Mr. Jacobson's defeat was accomplished by the efforts of the railroad and lumber interests."[14]

During the primary campaign Lindbergh was correctly identified with the pro-Jacobson forces, but he also acquired the label of belonging to the anti-Nelson faction of the party. Clearly Jacobson had been involved in promoting Lindbergh's candidacy. Furthermore, according to the *St. Cloud Daily Times*, James A. Martin, another Republican leader and a Jacobson backer, managed Lindbergh's campaign. Martin, a former executive clerk to the governor, chairman of the State Board of Control, and recently resigned St. Cloud postmaster, had a reputation as a "political boss." As the *Times*, the *Brainerd Dispatch*, and the *Little Falls Daily Transcript* saw it, the Lindbergh candidacy was an attempt by Jacobson and Martin to repay Buckman and his backers for leading the shift of delegate support at the state convention to their own Sixth District candidate, A. L. Cole, and thus "disobey[ing] Jim Martin's orders."[15] Moreover, to the pro-Buckman press the political figures surrounding Lindbergh represented an affront to Senator Nelson. Although Nelson did not spend much time in the district during the primary, he did endorse Buckman, and, in a confidential letter to Chris Heen of Osakis, found the congressman "as effective, energetic, and efficient as a new member can be expected to be." In the opinion of the *Long Prairie Leader* the Lindbergh candidacy was a "sorehead campaign," while the *Pine Tree Blaze* of Pine River editorialized: "It isn't the 'better' element that opposes Buckman. It is the 'bitter' element."[16]

In making his appeal to the voters of the Sixth District, Lindbergh stressed his broad views on political economy and reform. In a speech at Sauk Centre on July 4, he argued that to have a representative government everyone "must work to the end that all people and all places may possess all the general social opportunities that any possess." To bring this about, "there must be positive laws to prevent discrimination against individual persons or places." Reform for Lindbergh meant taking away from "special interests" the advantage they had over the public. More specifically, Lindbergh felt that there was "an unreasonable discrepancy between the price received by the producer and that paid by the consumer for many farm products." But he cautioned that "it is not contended that middlemen should be eliminated, for they are, in this age of specialties, necessary."[17] A Lindbergh pamphlet distributed during the campaign described his concern over railway favoritism in transportation rates, the building of cities in places to suit private rather than public interests, and the problems of labor. In Lindbergh's opinion, "The government must not be too far behind the people's needs, lest the loyalty of its citizens be shaken," and he cited Russia as an example of what could happen in such a case. Lindbergh strongly advised that individual patronage be taken away from officials and be determined by "general law." He discounted the praise given Buckman for bringing local benefits to the district and consistently maintained that Buckman deserved no special credit for the free-delivery mail routes, the Brainerd public building, or the Cass Lake land office.[18]

Lindbergh was a forceful and straightforward campaigner, but his attraction did not lie in his ability as a public speaker. He was no William Jennings Bryan. During the campaign the pro-Buckman *Alexandria Citizen* harshly declared that "his talk closely resembles the first oratorical efforts of the average school boy—filled to the brim with high-sounding phrases and wholly devoid of all practical common sense logic." Later in the campaign, however, the *Little Falls Daily Transcript* lauded Lindbergh as "one of the most effective talkers in the campaign for the entire Republican ticket."[19] More reliable in assessing Lindbergh's ability on the political stump are the comments of friends and relatives close to him. Eva stressed that her father was a competitive person, particularly in the field of ideas, but noted that he liked people and was a good listener. She revealed that he did not use notes when he spoke, and that, in her opinion, he "really orated" as a public speaker. In a letter, Eva again drew attention to her father's competitive nature, noting that he often told her that he enjoyed "a scrap" if it was an objective one. Charles, Jr.

recognized many of the same characteristics in his father's political campaign style. He, too, emphasized that C. A. spoke extemporaneously ("I don't remember ever seeing him read a speech") and was a good listener, "but I think not always ready to consider carefully the other side of issues." During later campaigns Charles, Jr. traveled with his father, and it was obvious to him that C. A. "enjoyed campaigning."[20]

Curiously, Frank Lindbergh never heard his brother speak publicly. When asked about C. A.'s speaking ability, Frank remarked: "Well, I never heard him myself, but I don't imagine it was too good—I don't think he was a very good speaker—and he was quite emotional, if I can put it that way—get pretty loud when he was talking about some things." Even though Frank stated that he was active in C. A.'s 1906 congressional campaign, there seemed to be some political remoteness between the two brothers, probably because Frank, as a "standpat" Republican, was opposed to many of C. A.'s reform ideas. Lucile Butler remembered her uncle as a forceful but uncharismatic speaker who had "a trace of dry humor." Other observers commented that although Lindbergh never became a fluent public speaker and was not a spellbinder, he always knew what he was talking about. John M. Baer, colorful North Dakota congressman and political cartoonist for the Nonpartisan League, recalled that Lindbergh's speeches were "as dry as poker chips." Baer, thinking primarily of Lindbergh's 1918 campaign, felt that he was too serious, never "told stories," and "went over the farmers' heads" too often. According to Baer, Lindbergh occasionally practiced his speeches at farmers' dinner tables, and he confided that he [Baer] enjoyed those talks more than the formal addresses. Baer's memory may have improved on reality a bit, however, since Charles, Jr. does not remember his father rehearsing speeches in this fashion. He did reveal, though, that Lindbergh would sometimes rehearse portions of a speech "in full voice" either outdoors or pacing up and down the living room. What stood out, then, about Lindbergh's speaking ability and campaigning style, were his forcefulness, sincerity, and obvious knowledge of the issues. Although he knew Swedish and would occasionally use it in casual conversation, he did not use it in his campaigns or in his home.[21]

During the last days of the Lindbergh-Buckman primary campaign strong attacks were directed against both candidates. In fact, the degree to which the campaign "heated up" amounted to mudslinging. Buckman faced charges that his dealings in the lumber business had been dishonest. According to some reports, Buckman as a "cruiser" had "wrongfully and unlawfully entered upon lands of the state and cut and removed large quantities of timber." When Buckman was questioned about these charges, he made a somewhat disingenuous reply. "I admit," he stated in a press release,

> I have a row on in my district. But I am not worrying much. I never let such things bother me. I have always had them, the four times I was elected to the legislature and two times I have made the run for Congress. . . . I have had some opponents go at me pretty roughly, but I have never made an attack on any man working against me. I stand on my merits. The weakness of an opponent is not my strength.[22]

Lindbergh was accused of being associated with corporate interests and of profiting from foreclosure activity from 1894 to 1896. The formal charge, credited to the *Royalton Banner* and reprinted in the *Little Falls Daily Transcript* on September 10, condemned Lindbergh for having "a record of riches amassed out of the sorrows and suffering of the poor and the weak. Its pages are the darkest blots on the County's history." According to the *Banner* editorial, Lindbergh had shown a profit of $7,287.41 on 184 foreclosures during the period. An article in the *Wadena Pioneer-Journal* singled out his connection with New York financier Howard P. Bell as illustrative of corporate orientation and warned readers that Bell had taken "personal charge" of Lindbergh campaign headquarters at Little Falls. The *Pioneer-Journal* was disturbed, too, about the cold storage plant development at Little Falls, which it felt would force local retail merchants to go out of business. Certainly Lindbergh's association with Bell and his foreclosure record were matters of fact, but to what extent these activities were opposed to the "interests of the people" is a matter of opinion. In examining Book 12 of Deeds in Morrison County records, this writer counted 99 foreclosures that were not credited to the Lindbergh law firm out of a listing of 279 cases from June, 1895, to August, 1899. A number of entries were only partially completed, and thus fewer than the remaining cases may actually have been Lindbergh's. Frank Lindbergh signed virtually all of the entries. In any case, the general statement about 184 cases is probably fairly accurate, but no records exist to show the profit earnings. Fred Larson, longtime register of deeds for the county, did not think Lindbergh should be blamed for the foreclosure activity. In his opinion it was merely part of Lindbergh's job as a lawyer with the largest firm in town. Frank pointed out that the foreclosures took place during a depression and noted simply of his brother: "Oh, yes—of course, he got attorney fees out of it."[23]

On the day of the primary election, September 18, Lindbergh served notice on W. M. Fuller, editor of the *Little Falls Daily Transcript*, "demanding a retraction of certain statements printed in the *Daily Transcript* of September 10, regarding Mr. Lindbergh and some mortgage foreclosures." There followed an editorial entitled "A Retraction" on September 22. In it the *Transcript* asserted that promiscuous loans had been made on cutover lands and farm lands in Morrison and Crow Wing counties during the 1880's and 1890's, but that in reassessing it had ascertained that the firm of Lindbergh, Blanchard, and Lindbergh had, whenever possible, "assisted in securing time on any loan where there was any prospect of payment." Thus the *Transcript* admitted that the earlier article on Lindbergh had given "an impression different from the real truth." Although there is some question as to the true origin of the charges, general press consensus in 1906 viewed them as the work of the Lindbergh opposition.[24] But Edward M. La Fond of Little Falls leaves room for reasonable doubt on the issue. In a letter to Dora Haines in 1930, La Fond wrote that "the charges were absolutely untrue and I am of the opinion that they originated in the brain of one of his [Lindbergh's] advisers at the time, knowing full well that they would react to his benefit, which was what happened." He further revealed that "the retraction was written before the charges were published and the retraction had the O.K. of Lindbergh a day before the charges were published." Perhaps the mortgage charge issue was the episode to which Thomas Pederson referred in his reminiscences about Lindbergh. According to Pederson, Lindbergh had hired a "trained campaigner" well into the campaign when it appeared he might lose the election. Afterward, Pederson wrote, "Never in his later political campaigns did he employ professional politicians," adding that Lindbergh "evidently did not like their methods."[25]

On September 18, Sixth District voters made their decision. The returns showed Charles A. Lindbergh, Sr., the new Republican nominee for Congress. Carrying nine of the twelve counties in the district, Lindbergh received a 1,253-vote margin over Buckman. Buckman won in Cass and Sherburne counties, and had an 8-vote edge over Lindbergh in the home county of both candidates, Morrison. The total vote in the 1906 Republican primary was: Lindbergh—9,962; Buckman—8,709. Nina Hollister Sullivan, a business college student and campaign worker for Lindbergh in 1906, remembered him calling her on election night, saying, "Come on, get up, we won and we're going to celebrate." Mrs. Sullivan also recalled that the local campaign headquarters were in Lindbergh's office above the bank, and that George La Fond was campaign manager. Meanwhile, Democratic voters endorsed Merrill C. Tifft, a Long Prairie lawyer and banker and a former probate judge, as their congressional candidate. The Democratic turnout was comparatively light, with only 5,623 votes cast.[26]

The most noticeable response in the press during the seven-week general election campaign between Lindbergh and Tifft was the unity with which the Republican papers now supported Lindbergh. For example, the *Cass Lake Voice* revealed that Buckman followers were not "sulking," but were "right in line for Mr. Lindbergh," while the *Hubbard County Enterprise* pointed out, quite accurately, that "every county in this district, with the exception of Stearns, is Republican on state and national issues by a large majority." A persistent Lindbergh advocate after the primary was the *Little Falls Daily Transcript,* which formerly had been one of his sharpest critics. Its editorial column now called Lindbergh "one of the coming leaders of his party in Minnesota." And the *Litchfield Saturday Review* accurately predicted that Lindbergh "will look good enough to the voters to remain in Congress five or six terms."[27]

One of the goals of the Lindbergh camp was to promote a strong identification between Lindbergh and the policies of President Theodore Roosevelt. Illustrative of the approach was an advertisement for candidate Lindbergh that stated: "He stands distinctly for the interests of the masses as against the interests of the classes; favors revision of the tariff, and is in accord with President Roosevelt on all the great issues that are before the American people today." Most other press comment for Lindbergh made a direct appeal to Republican party loyalty.[28] Meanwhile, the Democratic campaign concentrated on lauding Tifft's personal and public record and attacking Lindbergh as a representative of corporate interests. Early in the campaign the Democratic *Little Falls Herald* could not resist joshing that "Lindbergh and the Long Prairie man are going to have a Tifft." Another Democratic paper, the *St. Cloud Daily Times,* located in traditionally Democratic Stearns County and a major party organ in the district, charged that Lindbergh was "an apologist and advocate of the catalog [mail order] houses." Tifft, it pointed out, opposed this kind of corporate influence and would look after local "farmers, workingmen, and merchants." Tifft also received strong support from *Der Nordstern,* one of three German-language papers in St. Cloud and the most widely circulated (7,320) newspaper in the entire congressional district.[29]

On November 6 the voters of the Sixth District registered a second decision. Once again Lindbergh was victorious, this time winning by 3,637 votes, roughly the same margin as that given to Buckman in 1902 and 1904.[30] He won all but two of the twelve counties in the district. As had been expected, Stearns County went Democratic, as did Benton County. Lindbergh received the highest percentages in Hubbard, Sherburne, Douglas, Cass, and Crow Wing counties, most of which had a solid base of Scandinavian-American population. The total district vote in the 1906 general election was: Lindbergh—16,752; Tifft—13,115. The same district returns showed an 8,203 majority for popular Democratic Governor Johnson. Clearly the primary campaign had been the real contest of the 1906 congressional election, and in future years it would prove to have been the most controversial and challenging of Lindbergh's congressional campaigns.[31]

Shortly before the election Lindbergh had written Carl Bolander about a business matter related to his probable election to public office. On October 15, 1906, he wrote: "As I expect now to be mixed up in congressional work, I want to cut out all my personal interests in real estate in Little Falls, so no one can claim that I am influenced by my own personal holdings." He referred specifically to unloading his major commercial buildings on the west side of Little Falls, and he gave Bolander several leads in terms of parties to contact on the sale of the hotel, the creamery, and the storage building. Lindbergh suggested various prices on individual buildings, noted he would extend any time period payable at 6 per cent interest annually, and observed that buyers could probably get monthly rents of $185 and $145 on the hotel and the creamery. Another option he saw was to sell the entire property for $33,000 to Swedbeck Nelson & Dewey and Nelson & Peterson, and handle the transaction through the Internal Adjustment Company. Apparently the latter course was taken, for Swedbeck did purchase the property and later sold it to Dewey. In any case, some time elapsed before Lindbergh was free of these real estate holdings. When the Sixtieth Congress opened in December, 1907, a Bradstreet report summarized Lindbergh's financial status. The report, issued in March, 1908, but based on data from the preceding December, cited one authority as stating that Lindbergh owned ten thousand acres of land worth $75,000, with no more

than $10,000 owed on the lands. Another authority, said Brad-
street, estimated Lindbergh's worth at $100,000 plus his home,
valued at $10,000.[32]

Lindbergh spent most of 1907 in Washington, getting used to
his new job and to Capitol Hill in general, attending to the routine political matters of his constituency, and anticipating the
formal session of Congress that would open in December.[33]
Anxious to be placed on a committee of some relevance to his
training and constituency, Lindbergh contacted the Speaker of
the House, Joseph G. Cannon of Illinois, requesting a position on
the Indian Affairs committee. He also wrote Knute Nelson, U.S.
Senator from Minnesota since 1895, politely requesting to talk
with Cannon about his appointment. Nelson replied to Lindbergh on June 28, noting that it was "uphill work" and "difficult
for a new member to get a place on the Judiciary Committee."
Instead, he suggested that Lindbergh try for a spot on one of the
good committees such as Public Lands, Indian Affairs, or Post
Office. A handwritten note by Lindbergh at the bottom of Nelson's letter explained that he had, in fact, requested support for
an Indian Affairs committee appointment, not the Judiciary
Committee. "Guess my writing was bad in the letter I wrote," he
apologized.[34]

On December 2, 1907, the First Session of the Sixtieth Congress began. Five-year-old Charles, Jr. was present on the floor of
the House of Representatives during the opening-day ceremonies,
and he would often spend time there with his father during the
years ahead. It was yet another sign of Lindbergh's desire to be
near his children, but for young Charles the political talk was
both mysterious and boring, and the large, stuffy chamber reminded him of church. Of the nine Minnesota congressmen during Lindbergh's initial term, only Winfield S. Hammond of St.
James was a Democrat. As a Republican Lindbergh thus be-
longed to the ruling party in his own Minnesota delegation and
in the House itself.[35] On the immediate questions of the organization of the House, Lindbergh voted for the retention of Joseph
Cannon as Speaker and for the adoption of the rules from the

Fifty-ninth Congress. Both resolutions passed despite approximately 160 opposition votes in each case. In essence their passage meant continued powerful control by Speaker Cannon. Lindbergh later regretted having voted as he did in 1907, explaining to his friends Lynn and Dora Haines: "I had come to Washington to do something, so I voted with the herd, but I am going to wipe out that stigma if I can." Within a couple of weeks appointments to House committees were made, and Lindbergh was named to serve on the Committee on Indian Affairs, as he had hoped, and on the Committee on Claims.[36]

Lindbergh felt it necessary to attend to the local needs of his constituency during his first term. On several occasions he wrote Senator Nelson seeking his opinion on postmaster appointments at Garfield, Carlos, and Pine River, and asking the Senator to do him the favor of writing a letter of introduction to the Minister of Norway for his friend A. M. Opsahl of Brainerd. In Lindbergh's opinion, patronage was a curse that came with the job. In another instance, he wrote M. M. Williams of Little Falls asking if he might "take a hand in getting any dissensions in harmony in Brainerd" over his recommendation of Opsahl to the postmaster spot there. In early 1908 Lindbergh assured M. N. Koll of Cass Lake that despite rumors the General Land Office would not be removed from that community, and the next fall he recommended that Lester Bartlett be named office register. On September 24 Senator Nelson wrote Lindbergh, indicating that he was surprised at him for not remembering Franklin Eddy and "Captain" Wood by the action. "I think you owe more to both Mr. Eddy and Capt. Wood for your nomination than to anyone else," Nelson stated. On the following day Eddy, a former Republican congressman from 1895 to 1903, wrote Nelson that he thought Bartlett would make a good land officer, and clarified: "As for myself I am asking no favors at Mr. Lindbergh's hands, nor would I, *under any consideration,* accept any." These minor crises in the district were exactly the kind about which Howard Bell had forewarned Lindbergh in 1906, and during the first term Bell reminded him of his prediction.[37] Further evidence of

Lindbergh's political responsiveness to his home district were his unsuccessful complaint to the War Department about the removal of artillery units from Fort Snelling and cavalry units from Forts Assiniboine and Keogh, and the introduction of a bill (H.R. 12401) "to legalize a bridge across the Mississippi River at Rice, Minnesota."[38]

Lindbergh's first serious exposure to his colleagues and the nation came on March 4, 1908, when he delivered a lengthy speech on the floor of the House on financial conditions in the United States. The subject was a familiar reform one. In January, 1907, President Roosevelt had asked Nelson Aldrich of Rhode Island, one of the kings of the Senate, whether "something can be done about the currency this session." That session, however, had passed without remedial legislation. The panic of 1907 followed and intensified public sentiment for reform. The currency crisis therefore was one of the chief issues during the next congressional session. According to financial historians Milton Friedman and Anna Jacobson Schwartz, "Contemporary criticism centered on the alleged 'inelasticity' of the stock of money" in the country. In order to correct the situation by bringing about "effective interconvertibility between currency and deposits," the Congress had three main lines of legislative action open to it: (1) "The establishment of some central reserve of currency which would be made available to meet the demand for currency whenever it arose but would be held idle in ordinary times"; (2) "the provision of some method of issuing currency on a fractional basis to meet emergency needs"; or (3) "a guarantee of bank deposits to make it less likely that a few failures would start a chain reaction involving a widespread attempt by the public to convert from deposits to currency." All three possibilities received considerable discussion in Congress, but by the end of the first 1908 session attention was largely focused on the proposed Aldrich-Vreeland bill, which emphasized the second approach as a temporary solution.[39]

When Lindbergh addressed the House on March 4 he prefaced his main remarks with several criticisms of certain operative features of the House, and with statements emphasizing the principal problems facing his constituents. For one thing, he said, the immense number of private bills before the House impeded "the efficiency of main work" and in most cases led to favoritism. A general law, Lindbergh argued, could better regulate such matters as the construction of bridges and buildings. Although he accepted that a certain amount of "spectacular political talk" was necessary to voice legitimate opinion in the House, he pointed out that so much was said on general questions that House records were "overcumbersome." Problems most important to his district, Lindbergh said, were those dealing with finance, downward revision of the tariff, and reasonable regulation of transportation. "There is some impatience," he added, "with the dilatory practice in the passing of such laws as will respond to the common needs."[40]

Lindbergh then proceeded with the topic of his expertise, finance. According to his own analysis, the recent financial panic had no relation to any political party. Moreover, he observed, President Roosevelt's actions against the "evil practices" of a number of corporations "have saved the country from a far greater panic than would have taken place if these concerns had been permitted to go on uninterrupted in laying their foundations to sap the substance and appropriate the energy of the well-meaning and law-abiding people." Despite his sympathy for those investors who lost money, Lindbergh noted that they were few in number compared with the general public and "must be subordinate to the general good." At this point two representatives attempted to gain the floor from Lindbergh. He refused them both, explaining that "it is the only time I may speak this year," and the Chair continued to recognize him.[41] Lindbergh went on to say that he believed that "panics are more likely to occur in the most highly developed systems of credit. The danger of money panics increases in the direct ratio to our opportunities and our enterprise." He expressed amazement at the strength of the general banking system in the country, particularly since "our banking laws are quite imperfect." In his view, the greatest need was "to root out bad banking, not only promoters, but those who do not protect their depositors by moderating their loans prudently." And he expressed serious doubt about the much-discussed idea of guaranteeing bank deposits:

I have grave fears as to the ultimate success of a guaranty of bank deposits. In the first place, unless there should be some provision prohibiting certain kinds of speculation, or unless human nature should change, even the guaranty of bank deposits will not prevent panics, but would simply defer the day by postponing the hour of fear; for, by the very nature of things, when a bull market starts, the momentum continues until it reaches a point when economically a breakdown is inevitable.[42]

Lindbergh strongly condemned "speculative parasites" for oversubscribing credit and forcing out legitimate industry during the 1907 panic. He warned that the common people must be aware of the threat posed by speculators on both rising and falling markets. Those gambling on the bull market relied on a sense of public confidence in money, while the bear gamblers took advantage of the element of distrust. In addition, Lindbergh felt that guaranteeing bank deposits would not work because the current manner of examining banks was too "loose" and left the door open for trickery. He cited a hypothetical case in which, under the present system, ten men might start a national bank with only 50 per cent of the capital required by law, and then borrow enough money from deposits secured to recoup their 50 per cent and pay up their stock "so as to leave no capital in the bank except their promissory notes." The only concession Lindbergh made in his strong opposition to deposit guarantees was to state that if public sentiment demanded the change, he would vote for it despite his lack of confidence, but he would urge that not more than one thousand dollars be guaranteed to any individual in any one bank.[43]

In other sections of his address Lindbergh discussed money as a means of exchange, as a commodity, and as a reserve. He was sharply critical of the reserve system because he felt it was "not properly handled." In his opinion, Grover Cleveland had been the first president to correctly make "conspicuous practical use of the gold reserve." He also outlined in some detail a plan for structuring a bond-secured emergency currency, citing statistics and interest rates that might be employed. Lindbergh stressed that the currency was to be payable in gold, at an interest rate high enough "to insure its retirement" when the emergency was over. He expressed fear of creating a monopoly in large cities during such a crisis and vigorously urged protection for "remote farming districts." Obviously his own Sixth District of Minnesota was such a rural district. Lindbergh then presented a broad assessment of his fear of overspeculation and his general theory of money:

The United States requires a system that will make the capital of the country available to develop its natural physical conditions. Everybody desires to encourage enterprise. But in enterprise there is a tendency to bull everything, and as the country is honeycombed with speculators of a gambling instinct, these speculators are constantly interfering with the equilibrium; constantly the mark is being overshot. Setbacks are the economic penalty.

There is no fixed science about money and credit, except so far as we can evolve it out of experience. Human nature cuts a great swath on this subject, and as human nature is not steady, neither is money and credit, for the value of both are more or less seated in the human brain.[44]

Lindbergh's speech must have been an eye-opener for many of his colleagues and administration leaders. He had clearly demonstrated that he was a serious student of finance and that he was not afraid to say what he thought. Lindbergh had released earlier statements to his home district about his money views, but his reform thinking on money and credit may have been a surprise even to many people there, and some may have questioned the apparent inconsistency between Lindbergh the Little Falls attorney who represented various lumber companies and corporations and was interested in banks, and Lindbergh the crusading congressman. Yet belief in reform was a fundamental part of Lindbergh's character all along. He had indicated as much in *The Law of Rights,* but it was only after 1906 that he could express his beliefs in a more national and thus more effective forum.

The congressional debate on currency continued, and on May 14 Lindbergh made a much briefer presentation to the House explaining his vote against the Vreeland currency bill. He had taken a position different from that of most other Republicans, he said, because he believed that every member of the House must represent his own district, "free from any outside domination." In his opinion the Vreeland bill was simply unsound. Lindbergh used the same hypothetical case of ten men investing in banks that he had presented in his March address, but he expanded his example to show that if just $250,000 were reinvested ten times, and an additional $250,000 were borrowed from deposits in each case, the Vreeland bill's requirement that a bank have $5,000,000 in commercial paper in order to be incorporated as a clearinghouse could legally be met. Lindbergh also stated that he felt it grossly unfair to ask a congressman to vote on a bill with a change made known only three hours before the roll call. When the major Aldrich-Vreeland bill came up at the end of May, Lindbergh voted against the measure. The bill passed, however, providing as a temporary measure the issuance of emergency currency, based on assets, by groups of banks, and outlining penalty provisions to ensure retirement of the currency after the crisis. The Aldrich-Vreeland Act also called for the formation of a National Monetary Commission, to be headed by Aldrich and Vreeland and consisting of nine senators and nine representatives. Lindbergh's opposition vote, along with the negative votes of several other Western Republicans, was indicative of a growing split in the Republican party. In the words of historian George Mowry, "An ominous open break had . . . appeared in Congress."[45]

In 1930 W. Jett Lauck wrote perceptively about Lindbergh's views and about his involvement in the Aldrich-Vreeland controversy. Lauck, a private economic consultant and a former academic and government economist, argued with justification in his unpublished manuscript that Lindbergh's economic views were based on his belief in democratic and humanitarian values. Lauck wrote: "What Lindbergh was primarily interested in were the fundamental principles involved or the relation of banking and credit to democratic institutions, and to the economic and social welfare of all classes of people in our self-governing republic." Furthermore, according to Lauck, Lindbergh "specifically disclaimed any knowledge or interest in the technical aspects of problems of money and banking." Lauck stressed that Lindbergh's views were, in part, a reaction to the chaotic state of American finance in the post–Civil War era. In his opinion, then, Lindbergh's theories on money, banking, and credit "grew out of western conditions of overdevelopment, low prices and suffering, currency and silver inflation, and later (after 1900 especially) of trust movement." Lauck praised Lindbergh for his "innate soundness of judgment" and "adherence to practical and safe methods of procedure" in opposing government guarantee of bank deposits and voting against the Aldrich-Vreeland bill. He also singled out Lindbergh's speech after the 1907 panic as a good example of his knowledge of both the practical aspects of banking procedure and the general causes of financial overexpansion and inflation. In the speech, Lauck asserted, Lindbergh showed "unusual powers of analysis and discrimination." Lauck saw Lindbergh as opposed to the banking system, not to individual bankers; his intent was simply to educate people about the facts of the situation so that specific reforms could be made. His position was not unlike that of the Populists, who, in the opinion of some writers, were not as opposed to individual exploitation as to the institutions that fostered exploitation.[46]

"Lindbergh gave himself completely to his work in Congress," wrote Lynn and Dora Haines. He gained an immediate reputation among his colleagues as a hard worker given to long hours and regular work habits. He had been an early riser ever since his days on the farm, and his routine in Washington reflected that training. Lindbergh usually got up at about 4 A.M., took a walk, had a couple of apples, and was in his office about 5 A.M. He found that this schedule gave him precious uninterrupted time for study and writing. Although always courteous and

friendly with the many people who visited his office, Lindbergh
found this necessary diversion from more serious matters frustrating. "People on my back all the time," he wrote Evangeline,
and Charles, Jr. remembered that during some of the years in
Congress his father often worked "at a small desk amid the book
shelves in a storage area of the Congressional Library." Charles,
Jr. often visited his father in this quiet "office" away from the
office, largely because he "delighted" in running the self-service
cable elevator one had to take to get there. Lindbergh often
simplified his schedule by having only a sandwich for lunch in
his office; according to Charles, Jr., there was almost always a
bottle of milk and some bread on hand there. At times he even
slept in the office. The social whirl of Washington held little
appeal for Lindbergh and his family, and Lindbergh did not
smoke or drink. Even when Evangeline, Lillian, Eva, and Charles,
Jr. were with him in Washington, there was no regular formal
entertaining as there had been in Little Falls. Although Lindbergh appreciated the beauty of the city of Washington, he in-
tensely disliked its climate. "This is the hottest hole I ever got
in—sweating all the time—terrible climate," he remarked in a
note to Carl Bolander.[47]

With the conclusion of the first session of the Sixtieth Congress in May, 1908, Lindbergh's attention turned to re-election.
One worry was whether he would face opposition from former
congressman Buckman again. As early as February, Lindbergh
had confided to M. N. Koll that Buckman had told him that he
had no intention of running, and "I think he means it." In the
spring he wrote M. M. Williams that although he still considered
himself an "amateur in politics," he was now choosing his friends
with an eye to their future helpfulness, mixing "in nothing that
does not concern our people," and preparing for "long range
shots." In another letter Lindbergh told Koll that he would not
have committees working in his behalf during the election, but
rather would feel free to consult with "any and all of the people."
Thus the endorsement of a congressman would rest solely "where
it should, with the individual voters . . . at the primaries." In

writing to Bolander, Lindbergh revealed that he still retained land properties in the Little Falls area, and he complained that taxes were too high. "A man is a *damn* fool for getting real estate when taxes are so high," he declared in a note written on white scratch paper, and another time he claimed that $135 taxes on two hundred acres of land were enough to make a man "put up a fight." He then gave Bolander instructions as to which taxes to pay and which he would not pay. In a letter to Williams, Lindbergh declared he was certain he was losing money because he had chosen to serve in public office, but he added that "I really love the work better than anything I ever did." He must have been pleased with political developments in the summer of 1908, for no one filed to oppose him in the Republican primary. On September 15, 1908, in what amounted to a mere formality, Sixth District voters endorsed Lindbergh as the Republican nominee for Congress, and Dr. A. J. Gilkinson of Osakis as the Democratic nominee.[48]

The general election campaign of 1908 was low-keyed and posed no real threat to Lindbergh. Gilkinson, experienced only in local politics, conducted an active campaign, but his appeal was limited to the district's Democratic minority. There was no real invective or personal attack during the campaign. Perhaps the strongest argument advanced against Lindbergh was the statement that to elect a Republican congressman was to endorse "Cannonism." A Democratic advertisement in the *Long Prairie Leader* played down Lindbergh's vote against the Aldrich-Vreeland bill, explaining that the measure was so "obviously corrupt" that for Lindbergh to claim credit for his negative vote was "like asking for remuneration for repeating his own prayer." Despite this sort of criticism, an editorial in the *Brainerd Dispatch* was probably correct when it commented that Gilkinson was "no real opposition" and that the Democrats were merely trying to strengthen the ticket for Governor Johnson rather than expecting to defeat Lindbergh.[49]

The Republican campaign based its appeal on Lindbergh's qualities as an independent-thinking and forceful representative, and on his solid identification with the Republican party and the policies of Theodore Roosevelt and presidential candidate William Howard Taft, Roosevelt's chosen successor. W. M. Fuller of the *Little Falls Daily Transcript* labeled Lindbergh "progressive" and pointed out that "with him there is no juggling of issues or straddling of fences for votes." Other press comment emphasized that Lindbergh had been far more influential than was normally the case for first-term congressmen.[50]

Lindbergh directed his campaign statements toward both the broad issues of national policy and matters of local politics. In an early statement he reminded voters that he held the same position he had taken two years ago: "The people first, the party second, and the individual third, with full respect to all parties and all persons." Though campaigning as a progressive Republican, he was in fact making a Populistic appeal to the voters. In the same statement Lindbergh came down harshly on what he called the "demagogic leadership" of Charles Vasaly in Morrison County Democratic politics. At a Brainerd rally on October 30, Lindbergh spoke more fully on broad issues and on his record as a congressman. His main topic that evening was finance. He explained to the audience that while the Democratic panic of 1893 had been both "industrial and financial," the recent panic of 1907 had been only "financial." To prove that industry had not suffered greatly in 1907, he pointed out that the prices of products of labor (both farm and manufactured goods) had not fallen as they had in 1893. Lindbergh also discussed the general unrest in the country over the growth of business combinations in the post–Civil War period. In his judgment this growth had been allowed to continue not because the Republican party favored these trusts, but rather because the American people had insisted on a policy of no governmental interference in private business. He assured the Brainerd crowd that the Republican party "had proceeded in this respect as fast as the people would support them." Lindbergh also informed his listeners that he supported a revision of the Dingley tariff, and he urged strong backing for Minnesota's Republican gubernatorial candidate, Jacob F. Jacobson. The Brainerd engagement was a busy political day for Lindbergh, what with an informal noon reception with local businessmen at the Ransford Hotel, a Republican meeting in nearby Deerwood in the afternoon, and the evening address complete with the arrival of a "Lindbergh Special" train, which brought more than two hundred people from Little Falls to hear the congressman.[51]

On November 3, 1908, Sixth District voters returned C. A. Lindbergh to Congress for a second term. Lindbergh received a majority of 63.1 per cent of the vote, carrying all counties in the district except Stearns. The final count was: Lindbergh—22,574; Gilkinson—13,174. Minnesotans also returned Governor John A. Johnson for a third term in a reasonably close race with his Republican challenger, Jacobson, and selected William Howard Taft (by approximately a two to one margin) over Democrat William Jennings Bryan as their choice for president. For Lindbergh, reelection meant a new sense of political security, and he attributed his strong showing at the polls to the fact that he had been "actively at work in the duties of his office" and had a record that "satisfied the people."[52]

insurgent revolt represented a move against one type of political tyranny—the abuse of the congressional system.[3]

The agrarian roots of Lindbergh and the other insurgents were evident in the causes they espoused as congressmen. Western frontier adjustments to a changing agricultural structure, the new industrialism, and the problems of credit and finance in the post–Civil War era had their impact on these men. The insurgent movement was not unlike the Populist revolt of the 1890's, for both movements were concerned with the same reform issues. As political historian Kenneth Hechler writes: "Both groups clamored for railroad regulation, conservation, more equitable taxation, postal savings banks, more direct democracy, and the rights of the individual against the depredations of the plutoc-racy."[4] In the broad sense the insurgents were to the Republican party what the "Pops" had been to the Democratic party. The insurgents, however, viewed the most desirable change as coming within their own political party, the Republican, and during the revolt they emerged as the progressive wing of the party.

In addition to the attack on Cannon, the Republican House insurgents during the late Roosevelt and early Taft administrations split with regular Republicans on such matters as the Payne-Aldrich tariff bill of 1909, the Mann-Elkins rate bill of 1910, and the Ballinger-Pinchot conservation controversy. Insurgents like Lindbergh continued to voice their opposition to the trusts, and urged a more equitable distribution of wealth in the country. Furthermore, with the exception of the Cannon fight, which was an internal House matter, insurgent counterparts in the Senate vigorously supported similar positions on the tariff question, the railroad rate debate, and, in 1911, debated the question of Canadian reciprocity. Leaders of the insurgent Senate group during the Taft period of 1909 and 1910 were Robert M. La Follette of Wisconsin, Albert Cummins of Iowa, William Borah of Idaho, Joseph L. Bristow of Kansas, Moses Clapp of Minnesota, Coe I. Crawford of South Dakota, Albert Beveridge of Indiana, and Jonathan P. Dolliver of Iowa. Although La Follette was not a direct House participant, John Nelson credits the Wisconsin senator with being "the moving force behind this great fight to reform the rules of the House of Representatives"—that is, behind the attack on Cannon.[5]

During the lame duck session of the Sixtieth Congress from December, 1908, to March, 1909, House insurgents laid the groundwork for their challenge to Cannon's power. Their primary aim was to restrict the Speaker's prerogative to appoint committee personnel, his arbitrary power over granting recognition to members on the floor of the House, and his domination of the Committee on Rules. On December 11, 1908, twenty-five insurgents, including Lindbergh, met in the office of Representative Peter Hepburn of Iowa. Of particular concern at the session was recent action taken by Cannon against three insurgent Republicans. Because they had dared to oppose legislation backed by regular Republicans, Henry Allen Cooper of Wisconsin, Fowler of New Jersey, and Murdock of Kansas had been removed from, or demoted on, certain House committees. In response the group issued a report after the meeting, calling for the following changes in rules to be demanded when the special session of Congress convened in March, 1909: "First—to abolish the arbitrary power of recognition by the speaker and restore the rule in force prior to 1879;[6] Second—a representative committee of seven or more on rules *to be elected by the House;* and Third —the compulsory calling of the committees on two or three days of each week, specified."[7]

Understandably, House insurgents tried to win open support from President Roosevelt and President-elect Taft in early 1909. Both Roosevelt and Taft were sympathetic to the revolt against Cannon, but they never fully endorsed the insurgency. A special House insurgent committee, made up of John Nelson of Wisconsin (who served as the group's secretary), Madison of Kansas, and Augustus Gardner of Massachusetts, approached Roosevelt directly on rules reform. According to Nelson, Roosevelt greeted the small committee "with his choicest toothy grin," asking "What can we anarchists do now?" The outcome of the interview resulted only in a promise by Roosevelt to write a letter, not for publication, indicating his position on the issue. Thus Roosevelt's assurance to Nelson, Madison, and Gardner that "I'm with you" was of minimal value, especially since he withdrew even the promise of a letter toward the end of the lame duck session. Taft's clear desire to unseat Cannon at first seemed more promising, but within a few weeks, cautioned by Roosevelt, he too gave in to political expediency. Both men simply were persuaded that the revolt would not succeed. As Taft instructed Nelson during a personal chat: "I'd like to help you, but such a fight will disrupt the party." Nelson's reaction, like that of the other insurgents, was to consider Taft an enemy of their cause. However, the insurgents still thought of their several issues as being aligned with Roosevelt's policies, and he remained an inspiration to them.[8]

More successful in early 1909, however, were insurgent moves to gain support from the Democratic minority in the House, to promote exposure of their movement through the publications of certain journalists, and to solidify unity within their own ranks. The Democrats were essential to insurgent success, for the overthrow of Cannonism relied on a total combined vote of Democrats and insurgent Republicans. During the lame duck session, an agreement was made between insurgent leaders Nelson and Gardner and Democratic Minority Leader Champ Clark. Clark promised total Democratic support in exchange for thirty-two insurgent votes. Among the journalists who helped to publicize the aims of the congressional insurgent faction were Mark Sullivan of *Collier's Magazine,* Ray Stannard Baker of *The American Magazine,* Judson C. Welliver of the *Washington Times,* and William Allen White of the *Emporia Gazette.* Other sympathetic publications included *McClure's Magazine, Everybody's Magazine,* and *The Outlook.* Also crucial to insurgent victory was a stable number of voters within their own group. To guarantee such stability, Nelson utilized such techniques as recording all activities at insurgent meetings and appointing certain members to committee chairmanships to maintain the interests of the selected chairmen as well as the group. These devices, he believed, helped to keep the group "tied together." The first concrete evidence of insurgent solidarity came in February, 1909, when twenty-nine insurgents signed a Norris resolution calling for the abolition of the Speaker's power to appoint committees; the existence of a new, elected Rules Committee; and the establishment of "Calendar Tuesday," on which all committees would be allowed to present legislation. In an attempt to isolate the radical insurgents, the regular Republicans countered with a compromise "Calendar Wednesday" bill. The compromise measure passed by a narrow 168 to 163 roll call vote, but the insurgents were encouraged by their show of strength.[9]

Among the insurgent Republicans "Charles Lindbergh of Minnesota was perhaps the most radical and independent of the group." This statement by Nelson simply reinforces the fact that Lindbergh was a man of deep conviction and not prone to compromise. In keeping with these traits, he was not particularly active in planning insurgent policies or in the leadership of the effort, but he was behind the movement "heart and soul." For Lindbergh the fight against Cannon was clearly a struggle against the opponents of progressive legislation. In his opinion the rules of the House were organized "to the advantage of a certain few." In a statement to the press early in 1909 he explained that "it is in the interests of trusts and monopolies to keep politicians so organized as to make it possible to create a dominant central power and build up a mutuality of interests with it; for, to achieve their ends and prevent legislation for the people, all that is necessary is to reach those in control." That comfortable condition was a virtual conspiracy against the public interest. It demanded change, and, although Lindbergh normally believed in the party structure, he did not hesitate to desert the Republican caucus on a matter of this magnitude. Like other insurgents, he viewed the caucus as little more than a rubber stamp presented with legislation by party leaders that was automatically approved as a matter of party discipline.[10] In any event, Lindbergh's dedication to the House revolt was complete, and the insurgents knew that they could depend on the Minnesota congressman when insurgent votes were being lined up. As

John Nelson put it, "When Lindbergh was with you, he was with you until Hell froze over."[11]

Certain members of the insurgent group developed close associations with Lindbergh during his years in Washington. In an interview, Grace Nelson recalled that her father, John M. Nelson, and Lindbergh were "very close." The friendship apparently extended beyond politics and Capitol Hill, for Lindbergh helped Nelson build a tennis court in a ravine behind the Nelson home. In another interview, Fola La Follette related that there likewise existed a close feeling between her father, Robert M. La Follette, and Lindbergh. "Father admired C. A. very much," she said. Unfortunately it is difficult to document the extent of these relationships or of the ideas exchanged in detail, for, as is often true in the case of individuals working together, almost no correspondence exists. Former U.S. senator Gerald P. Nye of North Dakota told the author, for example, that although the Lindbergh-La Follette association must have been close, he was not surprised at the difficulty in finding correspondence, because the relationship was "personal." He likened the Lindbergh-La Follette relationship to his own close association with Hiram Johnson, George Norris, and William Borah, in which most communication took place "in the office, at the lunch table, or on the floor of Congress." One of the Kansas insurgents, Victor Murdock, was also a friend of Lindbergh. During a trip to the Panama Canal as a member of a congressional investigating committee, Murdock later related, he came to know something of the personal side of Lindbergh. According to Murdock, the two congressmen spent time on the deck together during rough weather on the Caribbean Sea, and there Lindbergh recited original poetry while viewing the moon and an angry sea. In a 1930 letter, Murdock claimed that Lindbergh had confided to him that it had been his desire to make poetry his life's work, but fate had put him on the farm and at the law. Murdock described his friend Lindbergh as "absolutely independent, one of those marvelous souls who lived out of his time and in the midst of an environment absolutely independent of him." His one-word summary of the Minnesota congressman was "unowned." Eva verified that Murdock was indeed a friend of her father, but she called the story about the poetry and the Panama boat trip "far-fetched." In the opinion of Charles, Jr., Lindbergh's statement about making poetry his life's work "was probably one of his straight-faced jokes."[12]

The Panama journey to which Murdock referred took place in late December, 1908. The purpose of the trip was to investigate conditions and progress on the construction of the Panama Canal. Members of what was apparently a special committee included Representatives Murdock, Lindbergh, Gilbert N. Haugen and Charles A. Kennedy of Iowa, and Asle J. Gronna of North Dakota. The group, arriving aboard the steamship *Advance,* preceded another official investigation by members of the House Committee on Interstate and Foreign Commerce. As Lindbergh wrote Evangeline on December 17, "We go in ahead of the main squad"; and, in view of the House situation, he also informed her that "Cannon is not in my party." Completion of the canal, of course, had been one of Theodore Roosevelt's pet projects from the beginning of his presidency in 1901. But because of the unfriendly relations between the United States and Colombia, the Panama Revolution of 1903, the question of international economics, the cost of the project, construction problems, and the danger of disease to workmen, Roosevelt and the canal project came under substantial criticism. The report by Lindbergh and the special committee, however, strongly backed the project and expressed satisfaction with the rate of progress. One statement by Murdock indicated that the committee favored proceeding with a lock canal rather than a sea-level canal, which had been another issue of some controversy.[13]

Lindbergh's own evaluation of the Canal Zone project is evident in a statement of commendation released after the trip:

In general terms I would say the completion of the canal is summed up in health of the workmen, time and money. The health question has been solved and dangerous diseases are within control. There is good food for workmen and at present plenty of labor. Money is being expended in profusion. I believe the management honest and that it fully understands the work and is doing the work right and with great speed. . . .

Our people have really started a great job—a job that when completed will in no small degree change the transportation and commercial relations of the world. . . .

The burden is on us and the benefit, commercially, is to all the world equal to us. The government will charge the same toll to all, designed ultimately to cover interest charge and cost of maintenance. In a military sense we will secure an advantage.[14]

Moreover, Lindbergh, an admirer of Roosevelt, accepted speaking invitations in order to defend the purpose and administration of the project. His efforts did not go unnoticed by the president. In a brief note to Lindbergh on January 16, 1909, Roosevelt wrote: "I am as pleased as I can be with what you say about the Panama Canal. I hope you will lecture as often as possible on the subject."[15]

Lindbergh also directed his attention during the lame duck session toward bills affecting his home constituency; he spoke in the House on the issues of natural resources and ship subsidies; and he became involved in a unique plan to select a new postmaster for Little Falls. In January and February of 1909, for example, he authored bills calling for the payment of $18,671 to Chippewa Indians in his district to cover the difference in the value of coinage from the time of the original treaties in 1863 and 1864; authorizing the sale of public lands in his district; and granting an extension of the time needed to construct a federal dam across the Mississippi in Stearns and Sherburne counties.[16] On March 1, 1909, Lindbergh addressed the House briefly on the conservation of natural resources. He was a staunch advocate of conservation, explaining that "no one can be more enthusiastic for the preservation of our natural resources than I," but he was worried about pending legislation that would result in absolute government control over national forests. In Lindbergh's opinion, "The policy should be materially changed, so as to look forward to a broad policy of general supervision of all forests, public and private, by a regulation of the cutting of the

timber and the prevention of destruction by fires, something
along the lines established in the Scandinavian, German, and in
some of the other progressive countries." He also expressed the
view that, although he approved of the maintenance of areas of
great natural beauty, such as Yellowstone Park, he did not feel
justified in taxing the public to conserve forests in ordinary
places for park purposes. This expenditure, he felt, would serve
simply "to cater to the enjoyment of a comparative few who can
afford to make long trips to visit these reserves." A day later
Lindbergh told the House that he believed the ship subsidy bill
then under consideration was inadvisable. He agreed that an
effective navy was necessary, but, he argued, the projected bill
outlined monies only for merchant marine vessels. Instead, Lindbergh advised, there should be an attempt to construct marine
vessels that could be converted for naval use during a time of
need. This would, of course, entail a lesser expense to the American people.[17]

When W. M. Fuller of Little Falls died in 1908, Lindbergh
faced a problem familiar to many congressmen—that of appointing a new postmaster. On this occasion, Lindbergh, perhaps
spurred by the insurgency spirit, decided to fulfill the obligation
by the unprecedented method of election. Naturally, many Republicans opposed the move on the grounds that it would not
reward the party faithful. Lindbergh, on the other hand, felt that
patronage was one aspect of party politics that was often abused.
Accordingly, in March, 1909, an election was held. Of the
fifteen candidates who ran, Ethan S. Brown, the assistant postmaster, emerged the winner, receiving 224 of the 881 votes cast.
The *Little Falls Daily Transcript* seemed pleased with the results, pointing out that in its judgment Brown's vote had been
largely Republican. Praising Lindbergh, the paper noted that
"it is not often that party welfare and the principle of civil service reform get recognition at the same time." Lindbergh was
no political novice, however, and he realized that his experimental referendum at Little Falls would have little effect unless
a general law on appointments were passed. Such a law was

never passed. The Brown appointment was pigeonholed in the House, and Mrs. Clara Fuller, whom Lindbergh had appointed as interim postmistress, continued in that position for a period of five years until a Democrat was named by President Woodrow Wilson. According to Edward M. La Fond, the congressional response to the Brown appointment "amused Lindbergh," and he had no objection to the extended service of Clara Fuller.[18]

Prior to the opening of the special session of the Sixty-first Congress the Republican insurgents launched another attack on Speaker Cannon. They were heartened by the fact that the new House included an increased number of insurgents. Nine first-term Republican congressmen immediately came out in opposition to the regular party organization. The new insurgents plus two converted Wisconsin regular Republicans outnumbered any losses due to election; they gave the group a reliable total of about thirty members. Since Republicans in the House numbered 219, only 24 insurgents, together with the 172 Democrats, would be needed to form a majority for revision of the rules. But the Cannon machine was not unaware of these congressional changes, and its political force was put into full operation. In the end, apparently, a deal was made between the Cannon organization and a group of Tammany Hall Democrats led by John J. Fitzgerald of New York. In exchange for certain tariff favors, some twenty-odd Democrats promised to support Cannon on the old House rules. Shortly before Congress actually convened on March 15, 1909, President Taft made a last effort to work out a compromise by proposing that the House fight be postponed until the regular session of Congress opened in December. The suggestion was rejected. Since the primary purpose of the special session was to bring about tariff revision at Taft's request, the president no doubt was hopeful that this legislation might take precedence over the Republican House rules battle. The president, however, had weakened his position with the insurgents by succumbing to pressure from the Cannon people, who had threatened blockage of tariff revision should he aid the insurgent cause.[19]

When the direct challenge to Cannon took place in the House

balloting on March 15, Lindbergh remained true to radical insurgency. As expected, Cannon was reelected to the post of Speaker by a 204 to 166 margin over Democrat Champ Clark of Missouri. Lindbergh, however, along with eleven other extreme insurgents, had not voted for Clark. Eight of this radical core voted for Cooper of Wisconsin, two for Norris of Nebraska, one for John Esch of Wisconsin, and Lindbergh cast his ballot for Hepburn of Iowa. The vote for Cannon was no surprise, for most of the insurgents were concerned with overthrowing the Cannon machine by changing House rules rather than with waging a personal vendetta against the Speaker himself. The real showdown came, then, on the crucial roll calls on House rules. The insurgents lost. Even though thirty-one insurgents voted with the minority party, twenty-three Democrats bolted their party to vote with the regular Republicans, insuring defeat for the insurgent attempt. Most members of Congress, with Lindbergh being no exception, were convinced that a Cannon–Tammany Hall deal had, in fact, been made.[20] After the House confrontation, *La Follette's Weekly Magazine*, like other progressive publications, praised the insurgents for their courageous stand against Cannonism, which it viewed as a "menace to our free institutions" and the "bulwark of Special Privilege." The *Little Falls Daily Transcript* also supported the insurgent revolt, editorializing that Lindbergh had acted "entirely for the people" in opposing "Czar Cannon."[21]

Once the House rules vote was over, the special session immediately began concentrating its attention on the tariff problem, and within a matter of days, on April 2, 1909, Lindbergh presented his views on the tariff in a House speech. He began by pointing out that the Payne bill under consideration was one that "proposes to tax most of the things that we eat and wear, the materials of which our homes are constructed and a part of their furnishings, and the tools and implements with which we work." Since everyone had to be fed, clothed, and housed, he believed it was wrong to impose a tariff on these commodities. Although the tariff debate was mainly an economic question, Lindbergh urged that it also be examined "from the view point of the common interests of the American people." In his opinion the Payne bill had two principal objectives—to raise revenue, and to protect American producers. He admitted that the bill might be somewhat effective in these areas, but he felt it was unsatisfactory; unless it was "materially amended," he would vote against it. Again objecting to the plan of levying a tariff on "things of common necessity," Lindbergh argued that the House should "rather frame a tariff that equalizes the advantages of producing at home those commodities which are natural of production in our country so as to meet foreign competition, thereby keeping prices fair and also securing more revenue."[22]

Lindbergh went on to cite specific examples of industries with tariffs on goods of common need. One was the sugar industry. In 1908, he noted, the United States imported $181,125,523 worth of sugar, figuring at wholesale rates and including the duty. In the same year a similar amount of sugar at wholesale price in free trade England was worth $100,611,158. "Thus," asserted Lindbergh, "our tariff enabled the sugar trust to charge us $80,514,365 more than was charged in England for the same amount." Despite the fact that the federal government received $52,232,041 in revenue, "the people, besides having that amount added to the price of sugar, paid the trust $28,282,324 in addition because of a prohibitive tariff." Lindbergh, opposed to this approach, believed that goods such as coffee, tea, and possibly sugar, should be admitted to the country duty-free.[23]

Other illustrations used by Lindbergh were the Standard Oil Company and the Backus-Brooks Company. In his opinion Standard Oil had been protected to such an extent that it now had "an iron grip on the people's earnings, and we now require protection against it rather than for it." Lindbergh charged that the oil company had representatives in Washington exerting influence on tariff legislation. Although he gave Standard Oil credit for reducing prices somewhat, Lindbergh asserted that Americans nonetheless overpaid the Rockefeller-owned company for oil. Again he utilized a comparison with foreign sales. The United

States annually purchased 1,500,000,000 gallons of oil from the Standard Oil Company. Standard Oil, however, sold the same amount of oil in England, France, and Germany for approximately 2 cents less per gallon. The difference amounted to an additional tax of more than $30,000,000 on the American people. Lindbergh further pointed out that Rockefeller and other owners of the company had achieved enormous wealth with very little capital, and he disclosed that Standard Oil had paid an average annual dividend of more than 42 per cent during the last nine years. The Backus-Brooks Company, to which Lindbergh also referred, was a lumber firm with extensive holdings of Norway pine in Minnesota and Ontario. Lindbergh was disturbed that the firm, established in 1884 with virtually no capital, had by 1909 acquired assets conservatively estimated at five million dollars. "Do you think it needs protection now?" he asked House members. "Or do you think the farmer who wants to build a barn, or a granary, or repair a building, or the humble citizen who wants to build a home, needs some protection against the climbing prices of lumber?"[24]

It is clear from Lindbergh's April address that he, like most of the insurgent Republicans, did not oppose the basic concept of a protective tariff. What did disturb him were what he called prohibitive tariffs, which he viewed as abuses of the system. Lindbergh was also troubled by the fact that, as far as he could tell, the House Ways and Means Committee was not investigating such factors as the differences between American physical conditions and those of other countries, and the corresponding differences in labor costs—factors he felt were essential in deciding whether a protective tariff was necessary. To illustrate this point, Lindbergh cited the case of the Washington coal industry, where inferior coal and difficult mining conditions as compared with Canada dictated a policy of no additional tariff on Canadian coal.[25]

Lindbergh's insurgent and progressive Republican orientation came through strongly in yet another portion of his speech. He made the accusation that the tariff bill would be structured and

put through by the House organization, not the House membership or the Republican party. This degree of centralization, he
insisted, prevented elected representatives from responding to
the people in their home constituencies and enhanced the dominant influence of trusts and monopolies. Political parties shared
the blame, too, Lindbergh stressed, declaring that "no political
party as such has authority to make itself master of the House"
or the right to oppose the "will of the majority" of the membership. Lindbergh also attacked the procedure of having state
legislatures elect U.S. senators. In his mind, this process constituted "the hub of political organization."[26]

At the conclusion of his speech, Lindbergh stated: "I have
voted for this bill as now amended simply because in some respects it is better than when first introduced and better than the
present law." He approved, for example, of provisions in the bill
for revising some schedules downward, such as those on iron and
steel, removing the tariff on petroleum, and placing coffee and
tea on the free list. But he still found objectionable features in
the bill, and he hoped that these features would be altered in
the Senate before the bill was returned to the House. Certain
provisions, like the tariff on hosiery, gloves, and shoes, Lindbergh considered "outrageous." A tariff on these clothing items
reminded Lindbergh of the following poem, which he read before the House:

> Fence our European rivals out,
> Keep the duty steep,
> Save our honest workingman
> From foreign labor cheap.
>
> Build a tall old tariff wall,
> Thus produce a dearth,
> And make the honest workman pay
> Twice what things are worth.
>
> When his cheek is thin with want
> And thinner is his calf,
> Fill his place with an immigrant,
> Who'll do his work for half.[27]

Lindbergh and the other insurgents voted with regular Republicans, and the Payne bill was passed on April 9. Although, as indicated by Lindbergh's speech, they were not pleased with many parts of the bill, the insurgents, after Democrat Champ Clark's resolution for recommittal of the bill, had no other option. When the greatly amended tariff bill was introduced in the Senate by Nelson Aldrich on April 12, there began an extensive and heated debate that lasted throughout the spring and early summer. Insurgent Republicans in the Senate joined Democrats in fighting a high protective tariff and in challenging the power of Aldrich. Among the most vocal critics were Senators Beveridge, Dolliver, and La Follette. On July 8, when the Senate debate finally reached its climax, the Payne-Aldrich tariff bill passed by a 45 to 34 vote. Among the Midwestern insurgents who voted against the bill were both Minnesota senators—Moses Clapp, who was consistently sympathetic to Republican insurgency, and Knute Nelson, whose record vacillated between insurgent and stand-pat Republicanism. Nelson's position was best explained by political responsiveness to strong insurgent sentiment in his home district, but he may also have been irked by a threat by Aldrich to oust from the Republican party any insurgents who voted against the bill. Addressing the Senate, Nelson's reply to this threat had been: "I simply wish to say on this occasion that it takes more than the state of Rhode Island to read the state of Minnesota out of the Republican Party."[28]

The day after the Senate vote, on July 9, 1909, Lindbergh voiced his criticism of the modified tariff bill. Obviously displeased with the bill's contents, he termed congressional inability to implement a downward revision of the tariff "an insult to the American people." He interpreted the compromise corporation tax included in the new bill as a sop to postpone income tax legislation, and he accused Aldrich of using the tax to counter a provision introduced by Senator Joseph W. Bailey of Texas calling for a general tax of 2 per cent on incomes over five thousand dollars. Although he was not opposed to "corporations as such," he warned, and by now this was a consistent

Lindbergh theme, of the dangers of "corporations that exist by the plunder of the people," and he stated his belief that the Supreme Court would not again rule unconstitutional a "carefully-drafted income tax act." Overall, he viewed Congress' failure to sufficiently revise the tariff bill as a dark blot on the system of representative government. The interests of the common welfare had been ignored because the "favored interests" had dominated the legislative process. "The fault," declared Lindbergh on the House floor, "is not so much due to a lack of honesty and good intentions on the part of the members as it is to a determination to follow blindly a leadership which brings to naught all the original efforts which the people have put forth in the selection of their Members." During the weeks between the July 8 vote and the end of the special session in early August the Payne-Aldrich bill went through conference committees in both houses of Congress. Lindbergh's objection to this procedure—he would have preferred to send the bill back to the House Ways and Means Committee—had been to no avail, and the tariff bill, surviving the conference reports, became law.[29]

The tariff debate and the attack on Speaker Cannon caused an irreparable split in the Republican party and darkened the political future for President William Howard Taft. The insurgents' antagonism toward Taft was understandable, for he seemingly had misled and then deserted them on both issues. Lindbergh, however, expressed a flicker of hope for Taft as late as June, 1909, when he wrote Evangeline: "Taft so far has been a failure but he may show up yet—He was for the people till he had to make a sacrifice—then he wasn't—As usual no one wants to sacrifice but they all will in less than 10 years." But Taft's signature on the Payne-Aldrich bill and his vigorous espousal of its provisions during a fall tour of the nation sealed his fate with Lindbergh and the other insurgents. It was in Winona, Minnesota, in fact, that Taft described the Payne-Aldrich tariff as "the best tariff bill the Republican party ever passed." He chose Winona because it was located in the home district of Congressman James A. Tawney, who had been a supporter of the bill all along.

The president's Winona speech angered insurgents and, apparently, many Minnesotans; a day afterward, the *Minnesota Tribune* called the Payne-Aldrich tariff a "bunco law." Insurgent sentiment was strong in the state, and by the opening of the regular session of Congress Lindbergh told a Little Falls associate that even Eastern feeling was being directed against Taft and that "there is a united public in favor of Roosevelt."[30]

During the second session of the Sixty-first Congress, House insurgents rallied once again to overthrow "Uncle Joe" Cannon. This time they were successful. The first test came in January, 1910, on a vote involving the House investigating committee on the Ballinger-Pinchot controversy, another issue that divided the Republican party during the Taft administration. The controversy began with a report by Louis R. Glavis, a young investigator in the Interior Department, that Secretary of the Interior Richard A. Ballinger was conniving to turn over valuable coal lands in Alaska to the Morgan-Guggenheim syndicate. Gifford Pinchot, chief of the Forestry Department and a strong conservationist, publicly supported Glavis and urged a congressional investigation of Ballinger and the Interior Department. President Taft, however, exonerated Ballinger and called for the dismissal of Glavis for insubordination. Under mounting pressure, the president ultimately relieved Pinchot of his post. Thus the struggle pitted Pinchot and Roosevelt progressives against Ballinger and Taft Republicans. The Norris amendment before the House on January 7 gave the House membership, instead of the Speaker, the power to elect the Ballinger investigating committee, and the insurgent-Democratic coalition won by a 149 to 146 vote. Lindbergh was one of the twenty-six insurgents who voted with the Democrats. Although the House committee, dominated by old-line Republicans, found in favor of Ballinger, the insurgents were encouraged by their victory among the total House membership, and they prepared for the final attack on Cannon. By now the insurgent group was reasonably well disciplined, and Lindbergh was in attendance at a number of special meetings during the crisis period of 1910. At one gathering, at

From *The Literary Digest*, February 5, 1910. Minnesota Historical Society.

"Tottering." Bowers in the *Jersey City Journal*.

the apartments of Congressman Elbert H. Hubbard of Iowa, Lindbergh urged the group to remain out of the Republican caucus because the Republican party was not identified with the Cannon-controlled House organization. "We ought to act in accordance with the general sentiment of the people," he stressed.[31]

The showdown with Cannon came on March 17, when Norris, by a parliamentary maneuver, introduced a resolution to amend the House rules. There followed a continuous debate on the floor of the House throughout the night and next day, while both sides rounded up congressmen. The roll call took place on March 19, and the Norris amendment was adopted by a 191 to 156 margin. Once again Lindbergh joined forty-one other Republicans, primarily insurgents, and the Democrats on the vote. Thus the power of the Speaker was thwarted. During the confusion and emotion-packed moments after the historic vote, Democrat Albert Burleson of Texas presented a resolution calling for Cannon to vacate the chair of Speaker. Most of the insurgent Republicans were unwilling to deliver this personal blow to Cannon, and the Burleson resolution was defeated 192 to 155. But, significantly, Lindbergh and fellow Minnesotan Charles R. Davis of St. Peter were two of nine radical insurgents who joined the Democrats in voting for Cannon's deposition. Although Lindbergh's vote on Cannon may have been politically unrealistic, it was consistent with his belief in thorough reform.[32]

In the end the only major restriction imposed on Cannon was to remove him from the Committee on Rules, which he had once dominated. Although that change was indeed important, Cannon still retained appointive power and could work effectively with Republican leaders. As John Nelson commented years afterward:

> The 1910 fight for reform of the rules didn't basically improve the system, but merely diffused power among a few leading individuals and moved a few chairs around so that instead of having the power centered in the Speaker alone it was necessary for the Speaker to lean over and whisper with the Majority Leader and the chairmen of the important committees. But the machine control was still there as strongly as ever.

Furthermore, strangely enough, the insurgents allowed old-line Republicans to be elected to the new Rules Committee. They may have taken this seemingly weakened position in order to make it clear that as Republicans they had no permanent alliance with the Democratic party; another factor may have been an unwillingness on the part of Republican regulars to compromise with their own party rebels. A further result of the insurgent revolt was its identification with the American progressive movement. Actually, a substantial portion of progressive reform activity was at the state and local levels, but the success of insurgency in Washington in 1910 became a symbolic victory for everyone fighting against reactionary forces in America at the time.[33]

Throughout the insurgent battle against Cannonism, Lindbergh gave unwavering support to the effort. He took a radical stance within the insurgent group primarily because of the connection between the Republican machine and trusts and monopolies, but even so, he was considered almost independent within the group. As Russel B. Nye wrote of his participation in the movement: "Charles Lindbergh of Minnesota was a direct political descendant of Donnelly and Populism, a lone wolf in politics, the most leftish of the group, and a bitter hater of trusts and privilege." The revolt brought Lindbergh and other insurgents a degree of national notoriety. In February, 1910, for example, the *Washington Herald* and *Current Literature* carried stories on the insurgents including cartoons and photos of Lindbergh. On another occasion, Lindbergh summarized his reasons for participating in the insurgent revolt in a nationwide statement given to the *Chicago Tribune* and the *New York Post*. In the statement, later carried by the progressive *Record-Review* of Madison, Wisconsin, Lindbergh said:

I beg to state that I am an insurgent Republican because I have been designed such by reason of the fact that I have not accepted Cannon, Aldrich, and other bosses as my guides in political action. I consider that, as a representative of a sovereign people, I must act for and be responsible to my constituency, and do what seems to me for the common welfare.[34]

Another issue that drew comment from Lindbergh and other insurgents during the regular session of the Sixty-first Congress was the debate on railroad legislation. Congressional discussion in the spring and early summer of 1910 centered on the Mann-Elkins bill, which included provisions for certain changes in railroad rates and regulation. President Taft, who, along with the railroad interests, had a strong involvement with the bill, briefly courted insurgent support in an effort to gain solid Republican backing for the bill. His overtures were rebuffed, however, and the insurgent group, particularly in the Senate, gave the bill a hostile reception. House insurgents responded by opposing portions of the bill that legalized certain procedures on railroad mergers not allowed under the Sherman Antitrust Act, and by introducing amendments to the bill calling for such measures as the inclusion of long-and-short-haul regulation and the definition of telephone and telegraph companies as common carriers. The railroad debate, in short, crystallized the dissension between the conservative and progressive wings of the Republican party, and President Taft's commitment to the conservative faction was now irreversible.[35]

At the height of the Mann-Elkins debate Lindbergh declared his views on the railroad issue in a House speech. On April 21 he informed his colleagues that this "immensely important" bill must be amended to insure its "general advantage" to the public. Although he outlined several objections to the bill, Lindbergh emphasized that it was not his intention to cripple railways. He felt that they should be allowed to set rates that would give them a fair return, permitting them to properly compensate employees and at the same time show a reasonable profit on invested capital. In his opinion, the profits gained from discriminatory railroad freight rates did not constitute a fair return. He suggested that the Interstate Commerce Commission should determine the "proper value" of transportation systems and establish a uniform classification that would result in "impartial freight rates."[36]

Lindbergh went on to cite a specific example of unfair rate schedules used by railroads: the freight charges on goods traveling from the East and Midwest to the cities of Seattle and Spokane in Washington. According to the railway system, Seattle was a terminal point but Spokane was not; consequently, the railroad's lower long-haul rates applied only to the shipment of goods into Seattle, whereas high short-haul rates were charged on freight going to Spokane. For example, on one class of goods the charge via the Northern Pacific Railway from New York to Spokane was $1.25 per hundredweight, while the charge to Seattle was 95 cents. Moreover, the freight rate from Seattle to

Spokane was 26 cents, so that it was cheaper to ship goods on long-haul rates to Seattle and back to Spokane on short-haul rates than it was to ship directly to Spokane. Spokane consignees, however, were forced to pay warehousing costs and handling charges to Seattle middlemen before receiving their goods. In addition to criticizing the "absurdity" of the rates, Lindbergh pointed out that the railroads were wasting both manpower and the natural resource of coal by carrying freight an unnecessary extra distance of eight hundr 1 miles on the Seattle–Spokane run.[37]

Lindbergh then brought the discriminatory rate problem home to the Sixth District by giving an illustration involving the granite industry. He read a letter he had received from the Northwestern Granite Manufacturers' Association of St. Cloud comparing freight charges for granite quarried at St. Cloud with those for granite quarried at Barre, Vermont. According to the association, the railroad charge from Barre to Chicago, a distance of 1,220 miles, was 26 cents per hundredweight in carloads or 31 cents in less than carloads, while the freight rate from St. Cloud to Chicago, a distance of 507 miles, was 24 cents per hundredweight in carloads or 30 cents in less than carloads. The granite manufacturers told Lindbergh that they had taken up the matter with the railroads but were given little or no satisfaction on their complaints. The granite industry was not the only unhappy railroad customer in his district, said Lindbergh; in recent weeks he had received about seventy letters describing similar complaints.[38]

In another portion of his speech, Lindbergh attacked railroad tycoon James J. Hill. Although he had great respect for Hill's abilities and judgment, Lindbergh apparently felt that he was misusing his position. If Hill would handle his administrative functions without prejudice, he said, equitable rates no doubt could be achieved. But, Lindbergh charged, "Mr. Hill is not specifically interested in fixing freight rates for the people" or in securing a fair return for farmers or businessmen in small towns; rather, "what he is specifically interested in is to see that the volume of business is enough to give the railways all they can do." In other words, Hill was concerned only with high dividends to the stockholders.[39]

Lindbergh also expressed opposition to the Commerce Court proposed in the Mann-Elkins bill. It was his belief that a special court "in time would become narrow in its construction." As a lawyer, Lindbergh felt that judges in courts of general jurisdiction would be preferable because they acquired a "broadness of view" by practicing general jurisprudence; furthermore, he pointed out, the Commerce Court structure would be an unnecessary expense. Equally significant was the fact that the railroads vigorously supported the special court concept.[40]

Before concluding his speech, Lindbergh spoke of the need for a back-to-the-country movement in the United States, blaming the railroads for promoting unnatural growth in the cities of New York, Philadelphia, and Chicago. Discriminatory rates had helped to create a situation wherein New York City, for example, with an area of only about 300 square miles, had a population more than twice that of Minnesota, whose area was 83,000 square miles. Lindbergh noted that even though there was approximately thirty times more total wealth in New York than in Minnesota, "the average individual prosperity of Minnesota people is greater than in New York City." It was his belief that the overdevelopment of cities was an extravagance, draining the energies of people who, for the most part, came from the country, and thereby depriving rural areas of their "natural advantage." He warned that this trend could not continue indefinitely, for it was removing the manpower needed to produce "the necessary food, clothes, and other essentials of plain life." With a clear Jeffersonian tinge, Lindbergh boldly asserted: "Back to the farms and the villages is the remedy for most of the serious commercial and industrial evils so much complained of."[41]

For Lindbergh, then, restrictive amendments to the Mann-Elkins bill were necessary to correct the natural inequities that the railroads had inexcusably fostered. Paramount in his speech to the House was his plea that Congress deal with the matter of regulation in terms of economics rather than political science.

In Lindbergh's opinion government regulation of competition would be a costly and intricate administrative problem. He reiterated his belief that the Interstate Commerce Commission should deal directly with the basic economic factors—the proper value of transportation systems and the uniform classification of freight and freight rates. "To fix on that basis," he explained,

is immensely less difficult and less expensive, in the long run, than to attempt fixing and adjusting rules for competitive regulation, and the net result to legitimate investment of capital would be better preserved, stock gambling would cease, watered stock be unknown in this class of business, and the complicated procedure of courts would be simplified and their requirements reduced.[42]

One last aspect of Lindbergh's April speech was his discussion of President Taft's support of the railroad bill. In essence, he rationalized that Taft had probably backed the special court only because his advisers had recommended that he do so. Lindbergh seemed sincere in expressing respect for Taft as a progressive-minded lawyer, explaining that burdens of his office did not generally allow the president time to delve into the details of congressional legislation. Nonetheless, this somewhat apologetic statement for Taft did not stop Lindbergh from opposing his policies or from advising other House members to do the same.[43]

By the time the House debate on the Mann version of the railroad bill subsided, in early May, the representatives were presented with a substantially amended bill. The insurgents had succeeded in passing a number of important progressive-oriented amendments, but, stymied by a 140 to 140 tie vote, they were unable to counter the inclusion of the Commerce Court in the bill. On May 10, Lindbergh was one of twelve radical insurgents who voted with the Democrats to recommit the bill. The motion was defeated, 176 to 157. Lindbergh and the other radicals apparently were pleased with the overall impact of the legislation, however, for they solidly joined regular Republicans in passing the bill on a vote of 201 to 126. Meanwhile, the Senate fought its battle on the Elkins version of the bill, with Moses Clapp of

Minnesota one of the more outspoken insurgents. Finally the bills were sent to conference committee and, subsequently, conference reports were issued.[44]

During the final stages of debate on these reports, on June 16, 1910, Lindbergh made a second appearance on the House floor. Once again he made use of examples of discriminatory railroad rates and introduced broad philosophic concepts relating to natural conditions in economics and society. Lindbergh noted that, in terms of raw materials, conditions had changed since his boyhood days in Minnesota, when he could claim land, furs, meat, fish, and fruits with an "undisputed right." No longer could this be allowed. He accused the "special interests" of usurping the country's natural resources in direct contradiction to the general feeling in favor of conservation. "Unless we correct our present system," he declared, "disaster ultimately awaits the nation."[45]

In the June speech, in addition to repeating his earlier comments on James J. Hill and on freight charges on goods going to the state of Washington, Lindbergh provided another example of the economic inequities inherent in rail transport. Referring to his old boyhood home at Melrose, Lindbergh compared freighting costs from Melrose to St. Paul by wagon during his childhood with corresponding rail costs in 1910. In the 1860's, he revealed, "it would have taken 10 wagons, 40 oxen, and 5 men six days to haul 40,000 pounds of freight" the 145 miles between Melrose and St. Paul. By rail, the same freight load could be placed in one car, attached to a one-engine, sixty-car train, and shipped the 108 miles from Melrose to St. Paul in one day with a five-man crew. Thus modern methods and machinery enabled one man to perform 360 times as much transportation work per day by rail as could be done by wagon.[46]

But, Lindbergh queried, who profits by this the saving of energy? Certainly the people of Melrose were not given freight rates 360 times cheaper than the cost of the old ox system. Admittedly, everyone enjoyed a degree of convenience and luxury with the new system, but, Lindbergh charged, most of the surplus energy was absorbed by a few capitalists and their expenses, interest, and dividends. In fact, he stated, "80 per cent of the wealth in America is owned and controlled by 3,000 estates, corporations, and individuals." In Lindbergh's opinion this concentration of wealth was not in the best interests of the common welfare and, if continued, he felt, "our social system will crush under its own weight." The railway rate schedule, he concluded, was responsible for the sacrifice of the country to the cities; he blasted the Republican leadership for being tied to the special interests and unresponsive to the wishes of the majority. On the day after Lindbergh's June 16 speech, final approval of the reports on the railroad legislation was voted, and the Mann-Elkins bill became law. As a result of the congressional fight on railroads, the insurgent rebels had considerable success in changing provisions to their liking. The regular Republicans were willing to compromise on these provisions primarily because they were anxious to pass a bill in any form.[47]

In addition to participating in the Mann-Elkins debate, Lindbergh was involved with a number of issues relating directly to his home district. His activities during the regular session included the introduction of a bill to construct a post office building at Little Falls, and discussion of a problem regarding liquor prohibition as outlined in an 1855 land cession treaty between the U.S. government and the Chippewa Indians. As the ceded area became more densely settled, authorities found enforcement of the prohibition clause increasingly difficult, and in 1910 there was a movement to have the legislation revoked. One constituent who wrote Lindbergh about the matter was M. N. Koll of Cass Lake, an officer in the Northern Minnesota Development Association and an increasingly regular correspondent. He urged Lindbergh to do something to relieve the enforcement crisis despite his own predisposition favoring prohibition. Although Koll emphasized that he had no "sympathies" with the saloonkeepers, he felt that it was wrong for the government "at this late day" to try to enforce an 1855 treaty, especially since by now over 300,000 whites and only 6,000 Indians lived in the area.[48]

In a statement to Koll, Lindbergh agreed that the territory affected by the treaty had indeed changed, but he reserved judgment on enforcement of provisions of the treaty. He noted that there had been disregard for both state and federal laws on the liquor question. He did admit that there had been bad faith and perhaps criminal conduct on the part of federal agents, but he argued that this was a matter of administration rather than law. Unsatisfactory agents could be discharged. Lindbergh assured Koll that if legitimate complaints were forwarded to him he would ask for a congressional investigation, but he did not indicate whether he favored repealing the law. As it turned out, the attempt to revoke the liquor prohibition clause in the 1855 treaty failed.[49]

Also among Lindbergh's correspondence for the Sixty-first congressional period are a few items relating to business and personal affairs. Apparently Carl Bolander continued to handle the bulk of Lindbergh's business dealings in the Little Falls area. At his Washington office, Lindbergh appointed Magnus Martinson as his secretary early in 1909, replacing William Wood, who had entered law school. And, according to Lindbergh's letters to Evangeline, the tariff debate was not the only thing that was hot in Washington during the summer of 1909: the weather was almost unbearable. "The only place I have found that I could sleep is on my office floor with the electric fan turned on me," wrote Lindbergh. Three weeks later he still complained that "it's hot as the duce [sic] and I will be glad again to get a breath of Minnesota air." In other comments to his wife Lindbergh complained of debts on his properties, discussed the possibility of renting a cottage in the Forest Glenn area of Washington near good schools for Eva and Charles, Jr., and warned her not to let seven-year-old Charles "fool with loaded gun however careful it's not safe till I post him." In November, 1909, Lindbergh wrote Evangeline that his work, as usual, was "terribly crowded" and he might not reach Detroit on time. Perhaps a bit exasperated, he revealed: "Politics are awfully tiresome and at times bore me to the limit."[50]

The story of Lindbergh's campaign for reelection to Congress after the regular session of 1909 and 1910 is brief, for he faced only token opposition in the Republican primary and was unopposed in the general election. His challenger in the primary was P. H. McGarry of Walker, a businessman and state legislator. According to news reports, McGarry's candidacy was largely the work of the "interests" in Washington—another example of the influence of Cannon and Aldrich in attempting to counter insurgent forces. In fact, in the opinion of the *Minneapolis Tribune,* "the issues of Cannon and Cannonism were uppermost" in all Minnesota congressional primary contests in 1910.[51]

In the 1910 campaign Lindbergh aggressively publicized his identity as a progressive Republican candidate. When he filed for reelection at the secretary of state's office on September 1, a bit late, some Minneapolis-St. Paul newspapers interpreted his lateness as the result of "fixing up" his organization in the Sixth District. "I have no organization and don't intend to have any," Lindbergh retorted. His stand against political organization and special interests was by now well established, and it was one of the main points in his campaign literature.[52]

Included among the 1910 literature was a pocket-sized but fairly lengthy pamphlet that clearly labeled Lindbergh a progressive Republican and explained his views. On the first page of this brochure Lindbergh declared: "I am opposed to bosses and professional politicians administering the government." Government and political parties should be responsible to the people, he maintained, and errors in the system could be corrected through the influence of public opinion, with the daily press— "not always individually correct, but in the main reliable"— acting as a check. He emphasized his antiorganization and insurgent attitude by revealing that the "bosses" were waging "a back-room, dark-alley, secret fight" against him. He referred to the spread of slanders and lies against him, citing false stories printed about him during his 1906 campaign, and he revealed that political pressure had been exerted against him in an effort to interfere with his right of congressional patronage. Lindbergh then informed his constituents that his three years in Congress compared favorably with the four-year record of his predecessor, C. B. Buckman, noting that he had secured eighteen pensions for Civil War veterans and fifty thousand dollars for public buildings, whereas Buckman had obtained only twelve pensions and ten thousand dollars in funds during his tenure.[53]

Much of the material in the rest of the campaign pamphlet was taken from his speeches in Congress on Cannonism, the tariff, and railroads. Other portions dealt with his deep interest in the preservation of natural resources, his desire to insure that the energies of labor were justly rewarded, and his belief that future economic prosperity was threatened by "the present basis of economic trespass." He also called for the direct election of U.S. senators. In his discussion of discriminatory freight rates he used the Melrose-to-St. Paul example, although new research indicated that railroads were now 640 times more efficient than ox-and-wagon transport. In one section of the pamphlet, Lindbergh dramatized the insurgent attack on Cannon. According to Lindbergh, Speaker Cannon was the guest of special interests at a Waldorf-Astoria banquet in New York City on May 18, 1909. Allegedly, several members of the group, when asked what was to be done with the insurgents, replied, "Shoot them." To which, said Lindbergh, Cannon thundered, "Shoot them? That would be too honorable. Hang them." At the conclusion of the pamphlet Lindbergh stressed to his constituents that "the insurgents are not insurging against the party, but against boss rule." The insurgents, he summarized, "look to the substance of the people's rights; the Stand-patters look to the machine and special interests."[54]

The Sixth District responded warmly to the appeal to insurgent Republicanism, for Lindbergh received just over 73 per cent of the votes cast in the September 20 primary. Specifically, the results were: Lindbergh—13,415; McGarry—4,923. The general election was a formality, with Lindbergh, who ran unopposed, receiving all 25,272 ballots cast. Progressive Republicanism did well in other parts of Minnesota too: insurgents were returned to the House, while Payne-Aldrich supporter James Tawney was defeated in the First District. Minnesotans also elected Republican Adolph Olson Eberhart of Mankato to continue as governor (the former lieutenant governor had become governor upon the sudden death of John A. Johnson in 1909) and returned insurgent Moses E. Clapp to the Senate for another term. Elsewhere in the Midwest and West insurgent Republican candidates did equally well, but an even more serious blow to conservative Republicans were the many Democratic victories throughout the nation.[55]

For Lindbergh, the overwhelming majority with which he was elected to a third term clearly indicated a solid political base and may have encouraged him to think of seeking higher public office. Shortly after the election M. N. Koll advised him that "the best move for you to make would probably be governor first and then get the election of United States Senators closer to the people by law." Newspapers of the district agreed that any supposed threat to Lindbergh in 1910 had been a false alarm and that the insurgent movement was here to stay. In the opinion of the Republican *Duluth News-Tribune*, Lindbergh was "not a politician, as the term is usually applied; he is a student of economics and sociology, regarding politics as a means to an end."[56]

Chapter V

Canadian Reciprocity and the Money Trust

"It was a Swede from Minnesota who first raised in Congress the hue-and-cry of the MONEY TRUST HUNT—'a Swede who dreams,' a fellow member describes him—Charles A. Lindbergh," wrote Ida M. Tarbell in *The American Magazine*.[1] Indeed Lindbergh, who had voiced his concern about trusts and financial conditions in the United States as early as 1907 and 1908, was the first congressman to demand a congressional investigation of the Money Trust during the Sixty-second Congress of 1911 and 1912, and he continued to devote his considerable energies to an examination of the issue for several years. His views on the Money Trust were tenacious, and they became a central theme in his political career, often influencing his positions on other political and economic issues.

One such issue, taken up during the short session of the Sixty-first Congress, was the reciprocal trade agreement with Canada. The campaign for a reciprocal trade agreement was the natural outgrowth of political leadership and public opinion in both countries. President Taft urged acceptance of the measure in the United States; he saw its passage as a way to meet Western demands for tariff reduction after the Payne-Aldrich bill, to alleviate Eastern concern about the high cost of living, and to fulfill industry's desire for new markets for its exportable surplus of manufactured goods. In Canada, where there had been pro–free trade sentiment for some time, Sir Wilfrid Laurier, Liberal prime minister, advocated reciprocity because it seemed to offer a logical way of making use of the country's surplus of raw materials. Physical conditions also favored a trade agreement: an unfortified boundary of three thousand miles lay between the two countries; most Americans and Canadians spoke the same language; customs were similar; and the cost of living was roughly the same in both countries. Negotiations between the United States and Canada began in March, 1910, but a final agreement was not reached until January, 1911.[2]

The proposed treaty placed on the free list of both nations all primary foodstuffs, such as grain, livestock, and fish, as well as certain minerals, iron, steel plate, lumber, and paper pulp. Also outlined in the treaty provisions were sizable reductions in Canadian rates on such American manufactured goods as prepared meats, canned vegetables, farm implements, and a long list of nonagricultural products. Reaction to the reciprocity measure was perhaps predictable. American manufacturing and newspaper interests, looking forward to increased demands for their goods and to receiving Canadian newsprint duty-free, strongly supported the treaty, while farmers, seeing only open competition from Canada, bitterly opposed the agreement. On January 29, President Taft, recognizing that the treaty would face attack by insurgent delegations from Minnesota, Iowa, and Wisconsin when it was presented to Congress, wrote Nelson Aldrich:

> I don't know what they are going to do but probably they will oppose the agreement really because they cannot find it in their hearts to support any measure coming from me and ostensibly because they will contend, this is a manufacturer's agreement ignoring the interest of the farmer and seeking to put the whole burden of the change on him.[3]

The president's prediction was correct. Indeed, virtually all progressive Republicans in the House and Senate, together with a substantial number of regular Republicans, joined in forming an antireciprocity bloc during the debate on the treaty. Particularly outspoken in their opposition to reciprocity were congressmen from states along the Canadian border in the mid-continent, including Lindbergh; his Minnesota colleagues Andrew Volstead,

Sydney Anderson, Winfield S. Hammond, Charles R. Davis, and Halvor Steenerson; and North Dakota Representatives Henry T. Helgeson and Louis B. Hanna. Their position, a clear indication of their commitment to the farmers of the upper Midwest, was based on the fear that reciprocity would permit Canadian grain to flood the American market and lower prices, and that it would stimulate the migration of farmers from Minnesota and the Dakotas into Canada.[4]

The antireciprocity posture taken by Lindbergh and the other Minnesota and North Dakota congressmen was given substantial support back home. In Minneapolis, for example, P. V. Collins, editor of *Northwestern Agriculturist,* pointed out to Senator Knute Nelson that "the strongest opposition to Canadian reciprocity comes from the farmers of Minnesota, North and South Dakota, because they are the farmers most injured." In another letter to Nelson, Collins stressed that "35,000 signatures of actual farmers" were present on a petition against reciprocity given to the Senate Finance Committee by a Minnesota delegation, and termed the president's denial of any real opposition among farmers a "mendacious statement." To Collins and other farmers it was a "campaign of misrepresentation."[5] Antireciprocity sentiment was strengthened by the belief that James J. Hill and the Steel Trust were behind the agreement, since they would benefit from increased trade activity between the United States and Canada. In the rich northern wheat-growing region of the Red River valley, farmers gave further evidence of their feelings by gathering at protest meetings. Over fifteen hundred farmers denounced reciprocity at a Grand Forks, North Dakota, meeting, and similar rallies were held throughout the valley. Meanwhile, James J. Hill wrote President Taft that he was surprised that the opponents of reciprocity were not aware of the wide support for the preservation of Canada as a colonial market for England; this would, Hill admitted, cause American farmers to lose money. But Hill cheered Taft by noting that the Minnesota legislature had failed to pass a resolution opposing the reciprocity treaty.[6]

Lindbergh participated in the congressional debate on Canadian reciprocity during its early stages in 1911. In a February 14 natural conditions, a feat that would require willingness to accept change and to learn from experience. At this point Lindbergh added a somewhat critical note on human nature:

If we would enter into these business changes with the enthusiasm, patriotism, and willingness to sacrifice temporarily for the ultimate common good [and] in the same spirit that we would enter an international contest to be settled by force of arms, we should not be long in getting better conditions, and if all humanity labored with that idea in view, the foolish parade of war would disappear.

Overall, Lindbergh felt, the tariff laws of the United States could not be justified by the principles of philosophy or common sense, and the system amounted to little more than favoring the "privileged" few while taxing the "rest of us." Canadian reciprocity would not alter that arrangement. The only possible motive in voting for the agreement, suggested Lindbergh, might be the dim hope that trust-protected commodities would eventually be put on the free list, thereby destroying the trust.[9]

Continuing his speech, Lindbergh noted that many Americans, desperate for relief from the present tariff laws, mistakenly believed that the proposed treaty would mean low tariff or no tariff on all goods, "and reciprocity sounds good." In reality, he explained, "reciprocity" was a general term that could also be applied to high tariffs, as his reference to manufactured items demonstrated. Part of the reason many people failed to understand this was simply that they had not read the proposed agreement. Lindbergh substantiated this assertion by revealing that he had written to fifty constituents who had corresponded with him about reciprocity, asking them whether or not they had studied the bill. Replies came from fourteen constituents who had originally urged opposition to the bill and twelve who had favored passage. In all cases, he asserted, the constituents had neither studied the bill nor seen the provisions of the treaty. Lindbergh sympathized with his constituents, for he disclosed that although he regularly read approximately a hundred different newspapers in order to keep abreast of public sentiment in his district, "I failed to find one in which the bill was discussed in its provisions." In short, the American people had no opportunity to study the bill, and, as a result, they "think this bill is what it is not."[10]

President Taft, Lindbergh asserted, was earnestly seeking a satisfactory measure for the people, but he was likely over-anxious because of recent political disappointments. "It is pathetic to see how innocent the President is in his discussion of the bill." What particularly bothered Lindbergh was the apparent inconsistency of Taft's position. He referred to a speech made by Taft at Columbus, Ohio, on February 10, in which the president had stated: "The principle of protection takes away the justification for any tariff whatever by way of protection on articles imported from a country where the conditions as to labor and other circumstances are the same as in our own and this makes the cost of production substantially the same." Lindbergh agreed with the logic of Taft's statement, but he charged that it was glaringly inconsistent with the actual provisions of the proposed reciprocal treaty. What about the 131 items on his list of farm products and finished manufactured products? Even the president had recognized that conditions affecting the cost of production "are practically the same in the United States and Canada." In Lindbergh's opinion, the fault lay with the president's inability "to do all the work pertaining to his great office," and with cabinet officers who "have been educated in the schools of the special interests."[11] Concluding his address, Lindbergh said: "I unhesitatingly and unqualifiedly state that the terms of the proposed agreement, in practically one-half of the items enumerated, is in direct violation of the principles stated by the President and that if the President understood the agreement he could not ask us to support it on the principles named by himself."[12]

There was sufficient antireciprocity sentiment to block passage of the treaty during the third session of the Sixty-first Congress. As promised by President Taft, however, a special session of the new Sixty-second Congress was called in April, 1911, to settle the matter. Once again Congress debated the treaty. When it became apparent that the reciprocity plan would pass the House, Lindbergh offered an amendment that would postpone initiation of the agreement until January 1, 1912. Lindbergh told the House that his reason for introducing the amendment was simply that the bill affected crops that farmers had grown without prior knowledge of legislation that would materially affect prices. In other words, his amendment would at least protect the 1911 crop. The Lindbergh amendment failed, however, and the House approved reciprocity by a 268 to 89 vote on April 21. North Dakota Congressman Henry Helgeson's claim that reciprocity was "a plain case of the cities against the farmer" seemed valid, at least in the case of the Minnesota voting pattern, for Frank Nye of Minneapolis, Clarence Miller of Duluth, and Fredric Stevens of St. Paul voted for the measure, while Lindbergh and the remaining five congressmen, all rural-oriented, opposed the bill.[13]

Heated debate in the Senate followed, with Moses Clapp and Knute Nelson of Minnesota and Porter J. McCumber and Asle J. Gronna of North Dakota leading the antireciprocity group. In July the Senate finally approved the treaty by a 53 to 27 vote. In both houses it was the Democratic party that enabled the measure to pass, primarily because the Democrats were concerned about corn, tobacco, and cotton prices in the South. A large number of regular Republicans joined the insurgents in opposing Taft on reciprocity, but it was too late for a genuine rapprochement within the party. Ironically, it was the Canadian people who ultimately defeated the reciprocal trade agreement. In September, 1911, Canadians, influenced by nationalism, loyalty to the British empire, and manufacturing interests, voted down the reciprocity treaty with the United States. At the same time, they voted Prime Minister Laurier out of office. For President Taft, Canadian reciprocity had proved to be yet another political blunder in his growing difficulties as a public figure, and it cast an ominous shadow on his chances in the 1912 presidential election. As George E. Mowry wrote of Taft and the reciprocity issue: "At the cost of alienating the American farmer, irritating the friends of high protection, and the further fragmentation of his party, Taft had achieved nothing save an additional loss of prestige and public confidence."[14]

Although jokes and storytelling were rare with Lindbergh, he was occasionally prompted to relate a story explaining the meaning of the term "reciprocity." According to Lindbergh's story, a man was traveling in winter when his car broke down, and he was forced to walk to the nearest farmhouse for shelter. When he asked if he could stay until morning, the farmer replied that he was welcome but that he would have to sleep in the same room with the youngest child, since the only extra bed was there. The man turned in for the night and all went well until early morning, when the visitor, feeling an urgent need to relieve himself, awoke. Uncomfortable about having to go through the bedroom of the farmer and his wife in order to get to the outhouse, reluctant to face the bitterly cold weather, and feeling unwell, the man resorted to desperate action. Moving the child to his bed, the man urinated in the child's bed. When he moved the child back, however, the man discovered that the child had taken the opportunity to defecate in the bed assigned to the visitor. The exchange, of course, was an example of reciprocity.[15]

Congressional consideration of the so-called Aldrich plan on banking and currency reform gave Lindbergh his first real opportunity for constructive criticism on to the Money Trust issue. Although he had attacked the Money Trust before, he now had specific legislation to zero in on. The Aldrich plan grew out of the elaborate studies of the National Monetary Commission, a lengthy, multivolume set that dealt with subjects ranging from banking and currency systems in Europe and Canada to an examination of U.S. national banking structure, the independent treasury system, state banks and trust companies, and clearinghouses. In all some twenty-three monographs were published, plus the commission's final report in 1912. One newspaper reporter who covered Washington during Lindbergh's ten-year congressional career later observed that the Minnesota congressman was "the only man I have ever known who had read the

entire twenty [sic] volumes of the Aldrich Monetary Commission."[16]

The main feature of the Aldrich plan was the establishment of one large central bank, a National Reserve Association, with branches in each of fifteen districts to be set up throughout the country. These branches were to be controlled by member banks. The plan, drafted largely by Paul M. Warburg of the investment firm of Kuhn, Loeb, and Company, also suggested that the reserve association be capitalized at approximately $300,000,000 and that its charter run for fifty years. Other provisions were that "the National Reserve Association would carry a portion of member banks' reserves, determine discount rates, buy and sell on the open market, receive the deposits of the federal government, and, most important, issue currency based upon gold and commercial paper, currency that would be the liability of the Reserve Association and not of the government." Lastly, the Aldrich plan provided that the reserve association be managed by a governing board consisting of government officials and private members, and controlled by a forty-five-man board of directors made up primarily of bankers and businessmen. Since leaders in the banking and business communities favored private control of banking and currency, they were strong advocates of the Aldrich plan. They started the National Citizens' League for the Promotion of a Sound Banking System as part of an intensive propaganda campaign to sell the Aldrich plan to the American people.[17]

To Lindbergh, the Aldrich plan represented a final step in what he saw as a deliberate attempt by the Money Trust to take over the banking and currency system of the country. In his opinion the Money Trust had taken four major steps to insure the takeover. First, between 1896 and 1907, there was the manufacture, "through stock gambling, speculation and other devious methods and devices, of tens of billions of watered stocks, bonds, and securities." Second, there was the panic of 1907, "by which those not favorable to the Money Trust could be squeezed out of business and the people frightened into demanding changes in the banking and currency laws which the Money Trust would frame."

Third, there was the passage of the Aldrich-Vreeland emergency currency bill in 1908, "by which the Money Trust interests should have the privilege of securing from the Government currency on their watered bonds and securities." Lindbergh called attention to the fact that prior to passage of the bill, bank notes read: "This note is secured by bonds of the United States"; afterward, the wording was: "This note is secured by bonds of the United States or other securities." The additional comment, he said, was for the benefit of the "special interests." Another provision of the Aldrich-Vreeland bill that aided the Money Trust, Lindbergh asserted, was the creation of the National Monetary Commission, a body he described as banker-oriented.[18] The fourth and final step, explained Lindbergh, was the proposed Aldrich plan, which, he charged, would place the American people under "the complete control" of the "moneyed interests." "History records nothing so dramatic in design," Lindbergh wrote, "nor so skillfully manipulated, as this attempt to create the National Reserve Association—otherwise called the Aldrich Plan —and no fact nor occurrence contemplated for the gaining of selfish ends is recorded in the world's records which equals the beguiling methods of this colossal undertaking."[19]

In his book *Banking and Currency and the Money Trust*, published in 1913, Lindbergh notes that his interest in the operation of larger banks was prompted by the panic of 1903. At that time he observed that although there had been no attempt to form combinations to centralize deposits, banking associations worked closely together to promote their mutual interests, "even to the extent of maintaining efficient influence over legislation." In examining financial activities since that time, however, he determined that "there is a man-made god that controls the social and industrial system that governs us"—in short, a Money Trust. According to Lindbergh, no contract was necessary to establish a Money Trust. Instead, the large trusts such as J. P. Morgan and Company used such unfair practices as refusing financial loans to insure subservience to the trust firm. Neither the honesty of the applicants nor the value of their securities mattered to the trust,

Lindbergh said—"They had to be known to be subservient to that firm." In his opinion the Money Trust was the "father" of all other trusts, and he was displeased that the government took action against other trusts but, it seemed, blithely allowed the Money Trust to exist.[20]

Lindbergh made his initial contribution to the congressional debate on the Aldrich plan and the related Money Trust issue during the first session of the now Democratically controlled Sixty-second Congress. In a one-hour-and-thirty-minute House speech on June 13, 1911, he voiced his opposition to the Aldrich plan and the trusts, his proposals for a better solution to the problem, and his displeasure with the caucus system in Congress. He called attention to the fact that politicians were using the tariff to divert attention from the real issue affecting the cost of living, the industrial and speculative trusts. Lindbergh went on to relate certain actions by railroads that, he argued, were concrete examples of exploitation of the people by the trusts. He cited the construction of a $100,000,000 Pennsylvania Railway terminal in New York City as one instance. Lindbergh vigorously disagreed with a *New York Times* report that called the railroad a "public service corporation" and praised the new structure. On the contrary, he said, the people "are being daily charged on the food they eat, the clothes they wear, and the luxuries, if any, they enjoy, their quota for the construction, maintenance, and interest on invested capital for this 'purely voluntary addition' to the world's great terminals." Lindbergh further asserted that the Morgans, Rockefellers, Cassatts, and other large banking interests, aided by recent court decisions, would amass so much capital that these "special rights" would "make us and our posterity the abject serfs of the capitalists." He referred to the Minnesota rate case, a contemporary decision that gave railroad companies claim to 7 per cent as a reasonable return on their capital investment, as extravagant and unfair. In twenty-four years, he noted, the amount compounded at 7 per cent interest would be eight times the original investment, to the benefit of the railroads; he added that "already 80 per cent of the capital is

From *The Literary Digest,* March 15, 1913. Minnesota Historical Society.

"His Alibi." Macauley in the *New York World.*

owned by about 3,000 individuals and concerns" in the United
States.[21]

Basic to the financial problem of the country, Lindbergh told
his colleagues, was the "fictitious" nature of money in present
use. "Just as long as we treat money as our god and treat useful
property as of less value than money, fictitious money, just that
long most of us will be poor," he declared. To Lindbergh, property, not money, was the true servant of the people. In his opinion
a "commercial money backed by intrinsic value" would be
sounder than the money in current use. In essence, he viewed

the financial structure as out of step with natural conditions, a prostitution of property by money. In part, he blamed the arbitrary gold system, which he felt did not respond to natural commerce, and he concluded that silver or greenback monetization would be no better. According to Lindbergh, trusts began to grow and profit in 1893 and continued to do so into the twentieth century, while the nation as a whole also experienced prosperous times. But in the panic of 1907 many smaller institutions were eliminated, and the trusts gained greater control. The result, said Lindbergh, was simply this: "Money controls property, and since the money changers are by law given special privilege to regulate credit they control property." The only solution, he asserted, was "to make property, that which our everyday energy produces, the control of finances."[22]

Lindbergh interpreted the proposed Aldrich plan as a continuation of the old financial system. In his opinion the Reserve Association would increase the financial grip of Wall Street on the country. (When Lindbergh used the term "Wall Street" he did not mean only New York City interests. As he stated: "The Wall Street system is maintained in all of the large cities, and I include within the term Wall Streeters all those supporting the Wall Street system, wherever they may be."[23]) At the same time he labeled the management system proposed by the Aldrich plan a "masterpiece," and, "if controlled by the people," much of it could be copied in a system suited to the interests of the common people. His main attack on the Aldrich plan was directed against those provisions that gave bankers control of the system and centralized that control in one national institution. But even control of the nation's finances was not sufficient to satisfy the financial oligarchy, he contended, for they planned to control the world. As Lindbergh described the whole system:

Wall Street, backed by Morgan, Rockefeller, and others, would control the Reserve Association, and those again, backed by all the deposits and disbursements of the United States, and also backed by the deposits of the national banks holding the private funds of the people, which is provided in the Aldrich plan, would be the most wonderful financial machinery that finite beings could invent to take control of the world.

At other points in his statement he singled out the right of national banks to transact foreign business with government backing, the postal-savings bank issue, and the Canadian reciprocity agreement as further evidence of this "colossal scheme" to take over the world.[24]

In order to solve the financial crisis and establish a balanced relationship between property, money, and labor, Lindbergh offered an alternative plan. This tentative plan, he pointed out, was not yet complete or without fault, but it did suggest general principles applied to the common interest. Briefly, Lindbergh's plan, like the Aldrich plan, called for the creation of a reserve association for the United States. However, unlike the association provided for in the Aldrich plan, whose members would all be bankers, Lindbergh's association would charter all producers and property owners in the United States. The length of the charter would be the decision of the people, and the association's head office would be located in Washington, D.C. The Lindbergh plan also provided for one financial district in each state, "with the Treasury Department of the United States as the head and supervising office of all, to constitute a complete system for the issue of notes as currency, which should be exempt from State and local taxation, and that the amount of the issue should be limited as the charter would provide." In short, Lindbergh argued, his system would give producers and property owners the same privileges that the Aldrich plan granted to the "money changers."[25]

In the Lindbergh "people's plan," as he termed it, actual property would be hypothecated as a security rather than credit. Receipts would be given to owners, and on these—with a certain safe percentage of the value of the property—notes could be issued. These notes, in turn, would correspond in principle with bank notes. Under the "people's plan," each state association would be subdivided into local associations as necessary, with each local association serving an area with at least 300,000 population and having diversified business interests. These local associations would then "have charge of all hypothecated property and be subject to proper rules to safeguard securities." They would also guarantee these notes to the next division of jurisdiction so that ultimately the government would be responsible to the bearer.[26]

In regard to currency, Lindbergh's "people's plan" would operate for a time as a dual system. It would be a combination of the property notes just described and the gold system. The notes would be made legal tender, and would be able to be used "in payment of all taxes, excises, and other dues to the United States contracted after the enactment of the plan into law, and for all salaries and other debts, and demands owing by the United States to individuals, corporations, or associations, except obligations of the Government, which are by their terms specifically payable in gold." Anyone wishing to could pay debts with gold, but, Lindbergh advised, it would soon be discovered that gold would be less stable, except in its foreign utility, than staple commodities and the new system. "It would displace gold soon after it was established," he predicted, primarily because it was not a forced system but one left to "natural selection." Establishment of the new money system would help to reconstruct the true relationship between property and the means of production, labor. For example, he foresaw under the system a halt to the population exodus from the country to the city, for the country was the site of production. Lindbergh concluded his comments on his "people's plan" by claiming that the new system would make the farmer, laborer, and general producer "absolutely independent of the trusts." In answer to a countering statement that the trusts controlled factories and the means of production, he simply recommended that producers and labor—without which, he noted, the trusts could not function—set up independent production facilities.[27]

After some comments from the floor, Lindbergh ended his House discussion with an attack on the caucus system. It was not the first time he had voiced his displeasure with the caucus, for as an insurgent Republican his position was abundantly clear. His words were strong. Maintaining that no House member had any influence once the caucus had made a decision, Lindbergh bluntly charged that "any Member who surrenders his action to the control of a caucus, whether it be of one party or of the other, violates his oath, is a traitor to his constituency, and commits treason against his country." He directed his verbal onslaught specifically against the majority Democrats in the Sixty-second Congress. Emphasizing his own support of the initiative, referendum, and recall, because, unlike the caucus, this procedure brought legislation closer to the people, Lindbergh chided the Democrats for their false position in supposedly favoring these methods when in reality they accepted the totally opposite political philosophy of the caucus. He also accused the Democrats of using the caucus to decide the Canadian reciprocity issue and then allowing useless debate in Congress, deliberately distorting the function of that body. Lindbergh stated his recurrent charge that the caucus was closely tied to the "special interests," and pointed out that the system enabled a minority to control the legislative process. In a figurative sense, he said, "the tail wags the dog."[28]

Lindbergh made one further attack on the caucus system by assailing the manner in which congressional committee selections were handled. Busy congressmen, he said, were routinely appointed to special committees while many able representatives who had more time were limited to inactive committees. To Lindbergh, the practice was "a part of the general scheme to keep control in a very limited membership and to reduce the importance of membership as a whole," and he cited appointments on the Ballinger committees of the House and Senate to substantiate his claim. Perhaps this criticism was provoked by the fact that his new committee assignment in the Sixty-second Congress removed him from the Committee on Levees and Improvements of the Mississippi River, on which he had served during the Sixty-first Congress, to the relatively unimportant Committee on Coinage, Weights and Measures. He did, however, retain his membership on the Committee on Claims.[29]

Certainly the new assignment must have irked Lindbergh, and

it seems obvious that he, as a progressive Republican, received the unattractive appointment as a form of retribution. This idea is reinforced by the progressive journalist Lynn Haines, who noted in his study *Law Making in America: The Story of the 1911–1912 Session of the Sixty-second Congress* that Lindbergh was not alone in being placed on secondary committees. Among other progressives suffering a similar fate were Sydney Anderson, Henry A. Cooper, John M. Nelson, E. A. Morse, Stanton Warburton, William Kent, Charles R. Davis, and Henry T. Helgeson. They were placed on such "dead" committees as Elections, Pensions, Insular Affairs, War Claims, Expenditures in the War Department, Reform in the Civil Service, and Industrial Arts and Expositions. Furthermore, said Haines, only a single progressive Republican was appointed to any of the three most powerful House committees (Ways and Means, Rules, and Appropriations)—Wisconsin's Irvine Lenroot was given a seat on the Rules Committee. In analyzing House committee selection in 1911, Haines concluded that there were deliberate moves to place the most stalwart progressives "in positions where relatively unimportant matters would take practically all their time."[30]

Lindbergh's motive in attacking the Money Trust at this time was to arouse anti-Aldrich plan sentiment among the public, and he continued this quest with the opening of the regular session of the Sixty-second Congress in December. On the first day of the session, December 4, he introduced House Resolution 314, which would authorize a congressional investigation of the Money Trust in the United States:

Whereas the money, exchange, deposit, reserve, and credit systems are essential to the business relations of the people with each other, requiring that they should be administered on a commercial and not a speculative basis, in order to facilitate the dealing in, distributing and exchanging of products, services, and articles of commerce; and

Whereas it appears that our present system of money, exchange, and credit entail on the people enormous losses, due presumably to speculation, gambling, and manipulation, which are not necessarily incident to a natural commerce; and

Whereas it appears that these practices are directed through well-defined centers, the greatest of which it is believed does now actually have the power of controlling credit, exchanges, and deposits to the extent of being able to actually bring on business depression and even business disaster; and

Whereas there appears to be a constantly increasing power in certain individuals and corporate concerns to concentrate and control, for selfish purposes, the moneys, finances, and credits of the people; Now, therefore, be it

RESOLVED, That a committee of five, to be selected by the House if authorized and directed:

First. To investigate as to whether there are or are not combinations of financiers or financial institutions or corporate or other concerns who control the money and credits and, through that control, operate in restraint of trade and in violation of law.

Second. To investigate whether there are practices by which the spirit of the National Banking Laws is being violated in the organization of banks by the use of the kiting system of notes of the organizers or by the use of others' notes through the organizers or if any improper means are used to form the basis for any part of the capital of banks.

Third. To inquire into the deposit and use of the reserves by the banks and especially that portion of the reserves authorized to be kept in the reserve and central reserve banks, and also the effect of the reserve system on the finances of the country.

Fourth. To make report to Congress on their investigation on said subjects and those matters having direct connection therewith and make suggestions for further legislation if such seems to be necessary.

Said committee as a whole or by subcommittee is authorized to sit during sessions of the House and the recess of Congress, and the hearings shall be open to the public, and the committee as a whole or by subcommittee is authorized to employ clerical and other assistance, to compel the attendance of witnesses, to send for persons and papers, and to administer oaths to witnesses.

The Speaker shall have authority to sign and the Clerk to attest subpoenas during recess of Congress.[31]

In accordance with House procedures, Lindbergh's resolution on the Money Trust investigation went before the Committee on Rules, which had the power to decide whether the House would act upon the resolution. The Rules Committee held hearings on the resolution on December 15, and this meeting gave Lindbergh an opportunity to expand on the intent behind his Money Trust probe. Because his prepared statement was lengthy (together with discussion during the hearings, it totaled fifty-one pages), he read only portions of it and answered questions during the morning session. He reiterated many of the points he had made during his June speech on trusts, banks, and the Aldrich plan, but he was more explicit on this occasion. In addition, he developed lengthy arguments on national banking laws and bank reserves.[32]

Surprising no one, Lindbergh began his discussion by informing the committee that a Money Trust did indeed exist, and that the "money kings" and Wall Street were manipulating the public's feelings on banking reform to favor the pro–Money Trust Aldrich plan. He stressed that the Money Trust was the "father" of all other trusts, and, unlike the Steel, Oil, Tobacco, and Railway trusts, worked by indirection with government support. He commented that U.S. banking laws governing the opening of banks aided the founding and development of trusts. Citing the report of the comptroller of currency for 1910, he noted that although 50 per cent of capital was required to organize a bank, the law did not specify that incorporators needed cash. Furthermore, he charged, the current system of bank examining did not allow sufficient time for an examiner to evaluate the true reliability of a bank. Hence, intelligent and responsible though examiners might be, banks could now be started by insolvent parties. Lindbergh also criticized the common practice of note-kiting, particularly by such large financial institutions as Prudential Insurance Company and Equitable Life Insurance Company, and the inability of courts to control trusts.[33]

One of the major arguments in Lindbergh's presentation before the Committee on Rules was his contention that national banking laws discriminated unfairly against small country banks. There is little doubt about the validity of his charge. Later studies have clearly documented the favoritism of the system toward the eastern states, especially New York. Professor George L. Anderson, for example, in analyzing the inequities of bank note circulation under national banking laws, wrote:

Massachusetts received the circulation which would have been necessary to raise Virginia, West Virginia, North and South Carolina, Louisiana, Florida, and Arkansas to their legal quotas. . . . The little state of Connecticut had more national bank circulation than Michigan, Wisconsin, Iowa, Minnesota, Kansas, Missouri, Kentucky, and Tennessee . . . Massachusetts had more than the rest of the Union exclusive of the New England and Middle Atlantic states.

Even though passage of the free banking and resumption bill in January, 1875, legally removed any basis for the charge that the national banking system was a sectional monopoly, western hostility remained. As Anderson concluded: "The contractive tendencies of the system now became the foundation of much of the western criticism of the national banks and of the expansion and free coinage of silver." At the same time Lindbergh may have overlooked certain reasons why the flow of monies was naturally directed to the urban centers of the nation near the turn of the century. One important factor he did not mention was the revolution in communications, particularly the nationalizing and urbanizing effect of the Post Office Department and the railway system in relation to banking functions.[34]

To reinforce his point about national banking laws Lindbergh used the example of three banks within his home constituency: the German-American National Bank of Little Falls, the First National Bank of St. Cloud, and the First National Bank of Sauk Centre. On the basis of letters from each of the three banks, which he quoted in their entirety in his statement, he asserted that these local country banks were forced by current banking laws to invest approximately 75 per cent of their deposits outside the local community. In the case of the Little Falls bank, for example, figures for 1911 disclosed that approximately $300,-000 of the $400,000 under loans and discounts were invested in outside commercial paper. This practice, he stressed, was "the seed on which the Money Trust is grown and maintained." A major difficulty, said Lindbergh, was the national banking provision that prohibited country banks from extending long-term loans. This effectively prevented country banks from servicing most farm loans—that is, from doing business in their own back yards. The heads of all three banks, therefore, had encouraged Lindbergh to try to get the provision revoked.[35]

Equally illuminating with regard to Lindbergh's views on the farmer, long-term loans, and national banking laws was an exchange during the hearings with Representatives Martin D. Foster of Illinois and Matthew R. Denver of Ohio.

MR. FOSTER. You speak, for instance, of farmers. Is it your idea, then, that there ought to be a change in the national banking law permitting them to loan on long-time paper?

MR. LINDBERGH. Yes, a certain amount of their time deposits.

MR. FOSTER. How long a time?

MR. LINDBERGH. At least a year.

MR. DENVER. Do you mean by that they should be allowed to take mortgage loans?

MR. LINDBERGH. Mortgage loans. Of course, the time is a mere matter of detail. I would not have it too long a time, understand.

MR. FOSTER. What is your idea, that the amount of loans they could make is to be governed not in limited amount?

MR. LINDBERGH. In that way? Yes; limited to a certain per cent of their deposits.

MR. FOSTER. Yes.

MR. LINDBERGH. There should be a limit to it, such as experience shows would be safe. I have letters from probably 100 bankers, and they to a unit agree that it would be better for the banking business, and better for the communities in which they are doing business, if they were permitted to use a certain per cent of time deposits to make loans on securities and reasonable time on farms.

MR. FOSTER. You confuse time deposits there, I think, because they are all deposits subject to call.

MR. LINDBERGH. I understand; but the practical effect is time, and it is its practical effect that I consider in these matters.

MR. FOSTER. They are all subject to be withdrawn at any time.

MR. LINDBERGH. They are all subject to be withdrawn at any time, and this bank letter No. 1 that I have in the notes particularly defines the conditions with reference to those. The bankers generally, who have written to me, say they can convert their mortgage loans into cash quicker than they can convert the commercial paper; and that is my experience, too, in what I have observed. I have observed the operation of that business to a considerable extent. Depositors not needing to use their money would be glad in times of panics to get safely secured paper.[36]

At another juncture in the hearings, on December 15, 1911, Lindbergh emphasized to the committee that ordinary banks were not knowingly a part of the Money Trust, and answered further questions on the role of country banks, the nature of commercial paper, and the problems of reserves. In response to a query from Committee Chairman Robert L. Henry of Texas as to whether there was a nation-wide conspiracy of banks that formed the Money Trust, he stated: "I do not think there is a conspiracy of the banks in general." But, he continued, "I think there are a few banks in New York that form the backbone to a real Money Trust." Again Lindbergh explained that under present law small banks were forced to contribute to the trust by investing most deposits outside their own area. As the discussion turned to deposits, commercial paper, and reserves, the following exchange took place between Lindbergh, Irvine Lenroot of Wisconsin, and Finis J. Garrett of Tennessee:

MR. LINDBERGH. . . . Bankers generally are fair and accommodating in their business, as the business is done. But the banking laws make it impracticable for them to loan all their deposits in the localities of their origin. In large cities, where the money kings, gamblers, and speculators reside, it can be done. These are heavy borrowers from the banks and take all they can get.

MR. LENROOT. Right there, for information. Are what are termed as commercial loans loans of this character, commercial paper by stock gamblers, and so on?

MR. LINDBERGH. The country banks figure all short-time paper that they buy as commercial paper.

MR. LENROOT. I mean, as a matter of practice, are they that character of paper, or are they the paper of the large business houses, like Wanamaker and Marshall Field?

MR. LINDBERGH. That is the real, true commercial paper.

MR. LENROOT. What is the fact? That is what I am asking for.

MR. LINDBERGH. The fact is, they use all kinds of paper they buy as commercial paper, or short-time paper.

MR. LENROOT. I mean, what do they buy? What is the character of the paper they do actually buy?

MR. LINDBERGH. They actually buy paper of the character of Wanamaker & Co. and other companies like that. A large part of the paper is made by companies of that character. But they get paper that is made by speculators, men of means, you know, who buy for a rise in the market. They are satisfied if they get good paper.

MR. GARRETT. In regard to reserves, your country bank is required to retain 15 per cent?

MR. LINDBERGH. Six per cent in its vaults.

MR. GARRETT. Six per cent in its vaults and 9 per cent of it they put in a reserve. Then the bank in which it places that reserve is required to retain only 25 per cent of that 9 per cent?

MR. LINDBERGH. And if it is a reserve bank it may redeposit it in another reserve or central reserve bank.

MR. GARRETT. And so on; so that eventually it really works out to where there is almost only the 6 per cent that is really held?

MR. LINDBERGH. Not very much more; not any more in the bank of original deposit.[37]

Indeed, the whole manner in which reserves were handled bothered Lindbergh a good deal, for he considered it the weakest point in the banking structure. He commented extensively on the problem in his statement to the committee, and, as usual, strengthened his case by quoting statistics. According to the comptroller's report for 1910, said Lindbergh, the volume of money in the United States on June 30, 1910, was $3,419,500,000 of which $317,200,000 was in the Treasury, $1,414,600,000 in reporting banks, and $1,687,700,000 in actual circulation. At the same time, he noted, individual deposits in banks on June 30 totaled $15,283,396,284. Thus the cash in banks, or reserves ($1,414,600,000) was less than 10 per cent of the deposits ($15,283,398,284). In view of this, he said, any "unusual number of depositers" demanding money would start a panic, particularly since the law did not permit the use of reserves to satisfy such demand. Lindbergh accused reserve city banks of violating the law by using clearinghouse deposits to pay depositors during a period of panic, adding, "it is in the panics that the Money Trust gets in its deadly work of capturing the smaller concerns for its subsidiary trusts." Another factor he brought out in the 1910 statistical example was that "business as a whole is done on approximately 95 per cent credit, money used merely as a basis," which, in turn, meant that cash in circulation was not available as a base for the credit system. Yet the cash in reporting banks, he argued, was the small margin of free money which "easily enables the trust, through its banks, to control the money market."[38]

The statement on bank reserves promoted inquiries from several congressmen in the committee room, and Lindbergh, according to the record of *Hearings on House Resolution No. 314*, responded to Lenroot, Garrett, and William W. Wilson of Illinois in this way:

MR. GARRETT. It was a fact that during the fall of 1907 clearing-house certificates were used pretty generally over the country?

MR. LINDBERGH. In reserve cities; I mean they were used from reserve cities. It is a fact, as you state, but they grew out of reserve cities.

MR. LENROOT. That is, they started there?

MR. LINDBERGH. Yes.

MR. WILSON. But they extended quite generally, did they not?

MR. LINDBERGH. They extended generally; yes.

MR. GARRETT. In other words, your idea is that clearing-house certificates would not have been used in the country towns—the small agricultural districts like that which I represent?

MR. LINDBERGH. No; they could not be used there.

MR. GARRETT. They would not be used there if they had not been started in the reserve cities.

MR. LINDBERGH. No.

MR. FOSTER. Where would you keep enough money to pay these deposits if they should be called for, as they were in 1907? Suppose the people wanted their money; would you keep it in the vaults of the banks?

MR. LINDBERGH. No. I would use the reserves in a panic to stop the panic, in the place of piling up the reserves, as the banks now do as soon as a panic begins. In my district I know one bank that increased its reserves during a panic to a little over 60 per cent. You will readily see that when, instead of using those reserves for the purpose of their creation, you collect every cent you can from everybody and pile it up in the vaults of the banks, it is going to aggravate the panic instead of relieve it.

MR. LENROOT. Could you prohibit that in any way by law?

MR. LINDBERGH. Prohibit what?

MR. LENROOT. The piling up of the reserves. The bank certainly has the right to call in the loans if it feels that the interests of the depositors require it.

MR. LINDBERGH. Exactly. I do not question that right. But the Government should not, in the time of panic, compel the banks to keep their reserves in the bank. They should then permit the reserves to be used.

MR. WILSON. Is not that a selfish, you might say, a quite safe, thing for a bank to do in time of panic?

MR. LINDBERGH. What?

MR. WILSON. Get all the ready cash they can?

MR. LINDBERGH. They are forced to by the present system of banking.[39]

Lindbergh came down hard on the issue of concentrated wealth during his appearance before the Rules Committee. He had already alluded to New York as the center of the Money Trust in the early portion of his statement, but he gave more details as the report progressed. Lindbergh called attention to the fact that national banks deposited huge sums in the central reserve banks of New York City, Chicago, and St. Louis. As of March, 1911, these redeposits from national banks, including nonreserve banks, totaled $606,858,037.97. There was, moreover, a tremendous concentration of monies in the six principal banks of New York City—Hanover National, New York City National, National Park, National Bank of Commerce, First National, and Chase National. Lindbergh noted that as of March, 1911, these six banks had individual deposits amounting to $371,864,545, and a total figure of $445,104,431 due to other banks. In all, then, they held a combined total of $816,968,976.[40]

Lindbergh gave further evidence of this phenomenon by quoting liberally from an article by John Moody and George Kibbe Turner in *McClure's* magazine. The main point of the article, "Masters of Capital in America—The Seven Men," was to expose seven individuals with Wall Street connections who, the authors maintained, controlled a great share of the fundamental industries and resources of the nation. Two identifiable groups emerged: the Morgan group—J. Pierpont Morgan, James J. Hill, and George F. Baker, head of the First National Bank of New York; and the Standard Oil-City group—John D. and William Rockefeller, James Stillman, head of the National City Bank, and Jacob H. Schiff, of the private banking firm of Kuhn, Loeb, and

Company. Lindbergh obviously had come to similar conclusions about these capitalists, who in his opinion, represented the very core of the Money Trust. Included in his presentation were tables (based on the *McClure's* article) showing which industries were affected and the percentage of monopolistic control exercised by these "giants." From 61 per cent to 93.5 per cent under their control were railroads, Express and Pullman businesses, anthracite coal, steel, iron ore, natural gas, oil, cement, lead, copper, and electricity (particularly American Telephone and Telegraph).[41]

Lindbergh also impressed upon his audience the fact that the American public was concerned about the Money Trust issue. He indicated, for example, that his own office had received more than one thousand letters from all sections of the country, "giving information of wrongs practiced by the Money Trust." Although the public had innocently allowed themselves to be "robbed" by the Money Trust in the past, Lindbergh suggested that an aroused populace would not permit this situation to continue. He also read to the committee *Duluth News-Tribune* items favorable to his appeal for a Money Trust investigation. While one Duluth editorial described the railroads as "excellent evidence" of a Money Trust and "meat for Lindbergh," another column noted: "Maybe there is no Money Trust, but the people would like to know a few more details before they mark Mr. Aldrich's banking plan with their approval." In Lindbergh's opinion, the Duluth daily was "a live newspaper with an editorial writer who has a brain, a conscience, and a judgment enabling him to discriminate."[42]

In the later portions of his statement at the 1911 hearing Lindbergh commented directly on the most immediate issue, the Aldrich plan itself. He repeated most of the arguments he had introduced on the floor of the House, but now he was intent on showing the connection between his criticism of the Aldrich plan and the need for a congressional investigation of the Money Trust. In the first place, he charged, the National Monetary Commission itself was not getting all the facts for Congress. As evidence, he referred to a meeting of the Commission in his home state, Minnesota, at which only bankers and businessmen were consulted, thus excluding "the farmer, the wage earner, and thousands of small business interests." The Aldrich plan, he asserted, was "the greatest monstrosity ever placed before the American people," and he proceeded to attack provision after provision of the plan. At one point he referred to the stipulation providing for the government cash balance to be placed in the National Reserve Association without requiring the association to pay interest. "If the people asked the Government to furnish them money without interest," declared Lindbergh, "it would be charged by Aldrich . . . that they were Socialists." One of the most crucial flaws in the Aldrich plan, Lindbergh felt, was the nature of the provision for a governing body of forty-five directors. Because local associations were to be structured on a given capital base, he argued, urban areas would dominate the directorships, and, ultimately, control would go to the Wall Street interests. Lindbergh also questioned the wisdom of establishing one large national bank and giving the proposed reserve association extensive authority in matters relating to foreign currency, securities, and credit affairs.[43]

Concluding his address, Lindbergh summarized the general purposes of House Resolution 314. A Money Trust investigating committee, he urged, would assume specific fact-finding responsibilities, which would include ascertaining the ownership and management of principal banks and trust companies eligible to hold stock in the proposed National Reserve Association, and determining how much cash is legally tied up in "fixed reserves" in country banks, reserve banks, and the three central reserve city banks.[44] In a somewhat unusual move for Lindbergh, he ended his presentation on December 15 by quoting from an earlier political leader. Referring to the Civil War and the fight to eliminate slavery, he included this warning statement, attributed to Abraham Lincoln:[45]

Yes; We may all congratulate ourselves that this cruel war is nearing its close. It has cost a vast amount of treasure and blood. The best blood of the flower of American youth has been freely offered upon our country's altar that the Nation might live. It has been, indeed, a trying hour for the Republic; but I see in the future a crisis approaching that unnerves me and causes me to tremble for the safety of my country. As a result of the war, corporations have been enthroned and an era of corruption in high places will follow, and the money power of the country will endeavor to prolong its reign by working upon the prejudices of the people until wealth is aggregated in a few hands and the Republic is destroyed. I feel at this moment more anxiety for the safety of my country than ever before, even in the midst of war.[46]

To Lindbergh the Money Trust and the Aldrich plan were the fulfillment of this prediction. To counter what amounted to industrial and commercial slavery, he emphasized, all people in the nation must join to "accept the Money Trust challenge."[47]

Lindbergh's December, 1911, Money Trust resolution and an earlier July resolution were blocked by the Rules Committee. Still, perhaps due to growing public concern, congressional leaders admitted that some type of investigating committee was inevitable. Accordingly, Representative Robert L. Henry of Texas, a Democrat, introduced a resolution through the Rules Committee calling for a special investigating committee on the Money Trust. The Henry resolution of January 29, 1912, was, in turn, referred to the Democratic caucus of the House. When the question came before the caucus on February 7, a substitute resolution was offered in its place. This resolution, credited to Arsène Pujo of Louisiana, proposed that the investigation be conducted by the House Committee on Banking and Currency rather than by a special committee. The Democratic caucus upheld the Pujo resolution by a 115 (yea), 66 (nay), 47 (not voting) roll call, and the bill was sent on to the House.[48]

When the resolution came before the House on February 24, Lindbergh seized the opportunity to deliver a lengthy speech on the Money Trust question and the Aldrich plan. He was disgusted with the prospect of an investigating committee structured by the Pujo resolution, for, like other progressives, he knew that the Committee on Banking and Currency would be sympathetic to bankers. Addressing his colleagues, Lindbergh remarked that "the very absurdity of the phraseology of the Pujo resolution stamps upon those who are responsible for it a weakness that ought never to be shown in this House." He then went on to compare each provision of the Pujo resolution with each provision of his own House Resolution 314, to which he now added eighteen new provisions included in his own January 3 amendment to the original resolution. The main portion of Lindbergh's House presentation, however, was an almost verbatim transcript of his statement and discussion before the Committee on Rules the preceding December. Despite his efforts the Pujo resolution passed, and the Money Trust investigation was thus placed in the hands of the Committee on Banking and Currency. Of some comfort to Lindbergh was Nebraska representative George Norris' strong statement on the House floor that Lindbergh deserved the real credit for beginning the Money Trust investigation. The implication, of course, was that he should have chaired the special investigating committee.[49]

Three days later, on February 27, Lindbergh made another speech before the House on the topic of banking and currency. He reiterated many of the arguments he had used in earlier presentations, stressing again the unhealthy concentration of wealth in the United States and the dangers of the Aldrich plan. At one point, he likened the Money Trust and the attempt to gain the American people's support for the Aldrich plan to the child's tale about the spider and the fly. "Come into my parlor said the spider to the fly," went the verse, "I've the prettiest little parlor that ever you did spy." In Lindbergh's analogy the scheming spider, of course, was the Money Trust, while the unsuspecting public was the fly. Lindbergh charged that many members of the National Monetary Commission and the House Committee on Banking and Currency were closely associated with banks and owned bank stocks. Thus, he complained, they could not be impartial judges on the Money Trust and banking reform issues before them.[50]

Two questions discussed in some depth in the February 27 speech were currency issue and the National Citizens' League for the promotion of a Sound Banking System. On the first question, Lindbergh believed that the right to issue currency was clearly the province of the government. He explained his position to Representative Fred Jackson of Kansas, who had asked for clarification on the problem.

MR. LINDBERGH. Certainly it [the reserve association of the Aldrich plan] would be a private corporation. The banks forming this company are private corporations, and by the bill they would own it. To be sure, the banks serve business, and I am not opposed to them if they ask only what they are entitled to. I am opposed, as I believe you are, to giving them any special privileges.

MR. JACKSON. The banks being the stockholders of this central bank, whatever profit or benefit there would be in issuing the currency would in the end be distributed back to the banks again, and the issuance of currency is really one of the powers of the banking corporations, and they ought to have that right.

MR. LINDBERGH. The gentleman from Kansas and I usually agree on economic problems, but I differ with him if he says that banks ought to have that right.

MR. JACKSON. Does not the gentleman believe that if we could get an ideal system it would be that every bank of the country, State or National, should have a right to issue its bank notes upon its own credit? Would not that give us the most and best money that we could have if we could do that with safety?

MR. LINDBERGH. If we could do it with safety, and I will add if we could do it with justice, but I do not believe any private institution can do it with both. The issue of money is properly a function of government.

MR. JACKSON. The gentleman uses the word "money." He uses that term, of course, not accurately. It is understood that the notes are not legal tender.

MR. LINDBERGH. If the bill proposed is passed they will be legal tender by section 53. Everything is money that passes as money, when we speak in a practical sense. I agree with you that a bank note does not come within the technical meaning of money.[51]

Lindbergh made a full-scale attack on the subject of the second question, the National Citizens' League. He was convinced that the league, which vigorously solicited support for the Aldrich plan, was the work of Wall Street influences. "I believe in citizens' leagues," Lindbergh declared, "but I would like to see them started voluntarily by the people themselves." Obviously, the league, which began in Chicago and spread rapidly to most states of the union, was not being financed by the one-dollar membership fees it collected, Lindbergh explained. Those fees, he conjectured, probably did not cover 10 per cent of the sums being spent by the various branches of the league. One of the most deceptive features of the scheme was the manner in which Wall Street interests were able, with a degree of finesse, to enlist the aid of men of good character for their movement. These men, Lindbergh felt, were innocent of the true nature of the National Citizens' League propaganda. Lindbergh concluded his House speech quoting his own written statements and letters he had received on the league question. To his credit, his early assessment of the National Citizens' League was later proven accurate.[52]

Part of Lindbergh's general work on the Money Trust and monetary reform involved a plan to establish a National Bureau of Money Reform Literature. Correspondence between Lindbergh, George Wilson, and J. J. Streeter, editor of the *Vineland* (N.J.) *Independent,* reveals an initial burst of enthusiasm for the idea. The group's aim was to distribute literature to congressmen and the public on the money issue, and, of course, in the process expose the faults of the Aldrich plan. On February 8, 1912, Lindbergh confided to Streeter that he would be compelled to use discretion in conducting such a campaign, for "I must work in line with what is practical so as not to land outside of where I can do some actual good." He also pointed out to Streeter that, unfortunately, many parties favorable to the idea had not offered the necessary cash to back actual operation of the bureau. Ironically, the proposed Money Bureau failed to materialize for lack of funds. In any event, Lindbergh cooperated with the publicity campaign of the ill-fated bureau by distributing regular letters to the press in his home state, and, on one occasion, by mailing out thirty thousand copies of one of his speeches at a cost of one thousand dollars.[53]

Among the issues Lindbergh commented on during the Sixty-second Congress were the desirability of public financial statements by members of Congress, and general constitutional government and the recall of judges with respect to the proposed constitution of Arizona. He strongly favored a public declaration of personal financial holdings by congressmen, and he introduced a resolution to the House on April 9, 1912, to that effect. He was particularly adamant on this issue, and one point in his resolution called for a listing in the *Congressional Record,* "in type larger than the regular print of the proceedings," of House members who failed to comply with the rule. On the constitutional problem Lindbergh came out squarely in support of the recall principle for judges. It was in keeping with his broad and unflinching faith in reform in general, and, in particular, with his belief in the initiative, referendum, and recall. "I have no sympathy with all this talk about the sacredness of old instruments of government," he stated.[54]

Lindbergh also discussed issues affecting his home constituency, such as post office appropriations, a proposed canal and dam, and the rights of Chippewa Indians. Referring specifically to appropriations for country roads provided for in the Post Office bill, Lindbergh assailed the urban press and congressmen for not understanding these needs. Good roads are for all people, rich and poor, he stressed, and the provision would not, like some other bills, serve only the "special interests." On the proposed dam and canal between Lake Winnibigoshish and Leech Lake, which had been funded in 1910 by legislation aimed at improving reservoirs at the headwaters of the Mississippi, Lindbergh urged federal authorities to make a thorough investigation of construction site possibilities. Apparently a degree of local sentiment was aroused when Army engineers supported a recommendation to change the proposed canal route between the two lakes to one designated as the Pike Bay route. The new route, connecting Cass Lake and Leech Lake via Steamboat Lake, was favored by the communities of Walker and Cass Lake. Since additional funds were needed for the new canal route, no construction was started at this point.[55] During the summer of 1912 Lindbergh introduced a resolution providing for a congressional committee to investigate the living conditions and property rights of the White Oak Point band of Mississippi

Chippewa Indians. In Lindbergh's opinion this small band had been "grossly wronged," and he advocated taking measures to rectify this situation. "They parted with their property and have received little in return except broken promises," he asserted.[56]

One further issue raised by Lindbergh during the Sixty-second Congress, and which, like the Money Trust probe, provoked national comment, was his discussion of sweeping legislative reform on the federal level. Lindbergh's resolution, still in preparation at the time, outlined major changes in the functional procedures of the U.S. government, among which were: (1) Abolition of the Senate and the vice-presidency; (2) reduction of House membership to 315 members; (3) election of 300 House members for seven-year terms; (4) election of 15 House members by the country at large for terms ranging up to fifteen years, to form a committee-at-large that would have absolute control and veto power over House legislation; (5) succession to the presidency by the chairman of the committee-at-large in the event of the president's death or disability; (6) use of recall by the people to act as a check and balance for the 15 members of the special committee; and (7) calling of a constitutional convention to implement these changes. In response, *The Nation* lauded Lindbergh for his thoroughness, and wondered if the Senate really would be missed. The *New York Tribune* pointed out that Representative Victor Berger of Wisconsin, a Socialist, had introduced a resolution to eliminate the Senate, "but he proposed no such radical changes as are contemplated by Mr. Lindbergh." Realistically, Lindbergh could not have been optimistic about the enactment of such a bill, but he had given the matter serious thought. To his way of thinking, he informed the press, the Senate was "unresponsive" to public sentiment, the vice-presidency was an unnecessary office, and the House size was unwieldy and cumbersome. Furthermore, he told a friend, he anticipated that the press would accept the challenge of the proposal and ridicule him, but, he added, "I might just as well have a little fun out of this."[57]

Family matters were mainly routine for Lindbergh during

1911 and 1912 with one or two exceptions. He continued to deal with Carl Bolander on land and property dealings in the Little Falls area. His younger daughter, Eva, a graduate of Minneapolis East High School, had begun college studies at Carleton College in Northfield, Minnesota. It was a good school, said Lindbergh, noting that tuition and board for a regular annual session there cost $225. Lindbergh's older daughter, Lillian, after graduating from high school in Detroit and studying literature for two years at the universities of Michigan and Minnesota, married Loren B. Roberts, son of Dr. and Mrs. L. M. Roberts of Little Falls. The wedding, originally planned for December, 1910, was postponed due to illness of the bride, and Lindbergh, pressed with affairs in Washington, was unable to attend the ceremony. On November 14, 1911, Lindbergh suffered an attack of acute indigestion, and "for a time it was feared that he was mortally stricken." The attack occurred at noon in the Senate restaurant, and from there Lindbergh was taken to the committee room of Senator Clapp, where he was examined by a physician. According to the press report, he felt better at that point and wished to go to his apartments at the Hotel Driscoll; but the physician advised that he go to the hospital. Thus Lindbergh spent a day and night at Casualty Hospital, where he rested comfortably and was in no danger.[58]

Clearly Lindbergh's main congressional contributions in 1911 and 1912 were his efforts opposing the Money Trust and the Aldrich plan. Early in 1912 he wrote an associate that he was convinced that the Wall Street interests would attempt to push the Aldrich bill through Congress by the end of the regular session. "They are afraid to let that go beyond the coming election," observed Lindbergh. Ultimately, and in no small part due to Lindbergh, the Aldrich bill was delayed pending the outcome of the Money Trust investigation. As he claimed in his book: "The Aldrich plan was defeated for the time being by the influence of a positive public sentiment which developed to greater and greater proportions as I pressed the inquiry, and the press published articles about it."[59]

Chapter VI

Progressive Politics

For Lindbergh and other progressive Republicans, 1911 and 1912 were crucial years in presidential politics. Deeply apprehensive about the advisability of their party renominating William Howard Taft, the nucleus of the insurgent group in Congress began considering alternative candidates for the 1912 campaign. Although there existed a brief flicker of hope for cooperation between the progressive and conservative wings of the party during the Canadian reciprocity period, the potential for such cooperation quickly dwindled and progressive opposition to Taft solidified. The progressives lacked confidence in Taft's ability to further progressive reform and felt that his performance as chief executive amounted to a desertion of the old Roosevelt policies. They were encouraged in their anti-Taft movement by the apparent growing unpopularity of the president and the fact that progressive Republican candidates had done well in the 1910 elections. Thus, from the very beginning of the Sixty-second Congress, Theodore Roosevelt and Robert M. La Follette emerged as likely candidates to receive progressive support for the Republican nomination.

One early sign of progressive defection from Taft was the formation of the National Progressive Republican League in January, 1911. The initial meeting of the League was held in the home of Senator La Follette in Washington, with the ostensible purpose of promoting progressive legislation. More realistically, however, it was designed to prevent the renomination of Taft. The composition of its membership clearly illustrated the League's bond with Midwestern insurgency. Its officers included Senator Jonathan Bourne of Oregon, president; Governor Chase Osborn of Michigan and Representative George Norris of Nebraska, vice-presidents; and Charles Crane of Chicago, a wealthy industrialist, treasurer. Other members of Congress who joined the League were Senators Moses E. Clapp of Minnesota, Joseph Bristow of Kansas, Albert Cummins of Iowa, Norris Brown of Nebraska, and, of course, La Follette of Wisconsin. Included among the several congressmen who endorsed the League and its activities were Representatives Irvine Lenroot and John M. Nelson of Wisconsin, Elbert H. Hubbard of Iowa, Victor Murdock of Kansas, Miles Poindexter of Washington, William Kent of California, and significantly, C. A. Lindbergh of Minnesota. Representing the private sector were such prominent citizens as Gifford and Amos Pinchot, George Record, Frederic C. Howe, William Allen White, Ray Stannard Baker, and Louis D. Brandeis. The League also numbered among its members Governors Hiram Johnson of California, Walter R. Stubbs of Kansas, Francis E. McGovern of Wisconsin, Joseph M. Carey of Wyoming, and Chester H. Aldrich of Nebraska. Overall, twenty-three of the thirty governors and members of Congress who joined the League were Midwesterners.[1]

Immediately state leagues sprang up in Minnesota, Wisconsin, Michigan, Nebraska, South Dakota, and Washington. In Minnesota, where a progressive convention in Minneapolis actually predated the official founding of the national league, the new Progressive Republican League of Minnesota organized under the leadership of George S. Loftus, president; Paul W. Guilford, treasurer; and Frank T. Wilson, secretary. Its principles, similar to those of the national organization, outlined such proposed reforms as the initiative, referendum, and recall; the direct election of U.S. senators and presidential delegates; passage of a corrupt-practices bill; freeing the party from political bosses; securing "responsibility, economy, and efficiency" in public service; conservation of natural resources; and the restraint of "corporate greed." At the same time, however, the basic *raison d'être* of the state leagues, like that of the parent league, was to promote a progressive candidate for the presidency. In this effort the entire movement was aided by the formation of the Progressive Federation of Publicists and Editors, which included among its members Norman Hapgood of *Collier's* magazine, Howard Brubaker of *Success* magazine, H. K. McClure of *McClure's* magazine, and Lincoln Steffens.[2]

During the early months of 1911 League leaders tried to enlist the support of Theodore Roosevelt. Even La Follette, always suspicious of the true depth of Roosevelt's progressivism, asked him to lend his influence in their cause. Clearly Roosevelt's name would help the League movement, but, more important, many progressive Republicans hoped that he would accept their backing for the presidential nomination. But Roosevelt steadfastly refused to become involved with the League. According to George E. Mowry, in 1911, he reasoned that the Republican party would be compelled to renominate Taft and face defeat in 1912. Thereafter, he, Roosevelt, would be the one man to reorganize the party and lead it to success. The former president therefore feared alienating either wing of the party and "walked on eggs" between the two camps during 1911.[3]

When progressive Republicans met in the office of Senator Bourne on April 30, 1911, they were anxious that the League settle the matter of a presidential candidate. All were convinced that Taft could not be reelected. Gilson Gardner, a friend of Roosevelt, informed the group that Roosevelt would not allow his name to be used in connection with the candidacy. After a lengthy discussion, Senator Cummins stated simply that La Follette should be the Progressive candidate. Thus, after reassurances of personal support and funding, La Follette decided to enter the race for the Republican nomination. His formal announcement came in early summer, and on October 16 three hundred progressive Republican delegates from thirty states met in Chicago and endorsed his candidacy. Even so, La Follette remained wary of divided support within the League, and the

Wisconsin senator later wrote: "I could not wholly dismiss from my mind an apprehension regarding both Roosevelt and Cummins." As it turned out, La Follette's uneasiness was well founded.[4]

Lindbergh openly declared his support for Senator La Follette during League discussions in the spring of 1911. Other members of Congress who gave early encouragement to La Follette were Senators Bristow of Kansas, Coe I. Crawford of South Dakota, and John D. Works of California; and Representatives Murdock of Kansas, Henry Helgeson of North Dakota, Gilbert Haugen of Iowa, Kent of California, and Nelson, E. A. Morse, and William J. Cary of Wisconsin.[5] Indeed, as the year progressed, it became apparent that La Follette's main political base and accompanying public following were largely restricted to the agrarian states of the Midwest, where Republican insurgency flourished.

In Minnesota the signs were promising for La Follette. George Loftus, president of the state League, described public feeling for the Senator as strong in April, while executive committee chairman W. I. Nolan confirmed in early July that the Minnesota organization had become "a campaign committee for La Follette."[6] By early November Loftus was candidly optimistic about La Follette's success in the state. In a letter to progressive Lynn Haines he happily noted that "the movement within the state is progressing far beyond our expectations" and referred to a recent Rochester meeting as a "howling success." (Other meetings scheduled by the League in late 1911 were at Fergus Falls, Mankato, Faribault, St. Cloud, Montevideo, Duluth, and St. Paul.) Loftus wrote Haines: "There is no question but what La Follette sentiment prevails throughout the state." Gifford Pinchot informed La Follete that insurgent contacts in the state assured him that the senator would win the majority of delegates to the Republican National Convention. A few sources predicted that seven of the nine Minnesota congressional districts would give delegate strength to La Follette. Lindbergh, too, was optimistic about the La Follette candidacy in Minnesota and his own Sixth District. "La Follette sentiment is very strong," he wrote Walter L. Houser, national League officer, on October 6, 1911. He noted that a few stand-patters were for Taft, but that in general the public lacked faith in the man. "No other persons are talked of in connection with Presidency here," Lindbergh revealed, "with the exception of now and then a suggestion for Roosevelt."[7]

Elsewhere La Follette prospects were not as good. Eastern support was virtually nonexistent. To many businessmen the uncompromising nature of La Follette's progressivism was unacceptable. In contrast, Theodore Roosevelt seemed less dangerous to business interests, and by the later months of 1911 a trend toward Roosevelt was developing. Roosevelt's strongest appeal was the fact that he, unlike La Follette, appeared to have a chance of winning the nomination. The most serious challenge to La Follette during the preconvention campaign came from within progressive Republican ranks. Some Progressive League members, among them Gifford Pinchot, had never been overly enthusiastic about La Follette, and when a Roosevelt boom began, their transfer of loyalty was not surprising. But the major stumbling block in a switch to Roosevelt by the progressives was La Follette himself. It was inconceivable that the Wisconsin senator, who disagreed with Roosevelt on so many substantive issues, would willingly withdraw in favor of the former president. Furthermore, La Follette had made it clear when he entered the race that he would remain a candidate until he was nominated or defeated at the convention.[8]

The heightening La Follette-Roosevelt conflict reached crisis proportions during January and February, 1912. In late January western insurgent George Norris wrote that he feared the effect of such a division within the progressive ranks, warning that "we will be defeated if there is." Even though Norris admitted that La Follette probably could not win the nomination, he urged that progressive Republicans avoid a La Follette-Roosevelt fight for convention delegates. Instead, Norris suggested, La Follette backers could easily shift their support to Roosevelt at the convention if La Follette did not receive sufficient support to win. But Norris' hope was not realized, and open progressive desertions from La Follette began in late January and early February. Governor Chase Osborn of Michigan, for example, denounced La Follette and left the League, while difficulties surrounding La Follette's candidacy were compounded by false news releases concerning a Washington meeting of progressive leaders on January 29. Published reports indicated that La Follette was withdrawing from the presidential race, and, although the senator issued statements to the contrary, such publicity was damaging.[9]

The real turning point came, however, during the days following La Follette's appearance before the annual banquet of the Periodical Publishers Association in Philadelphia on February 2. Tired from campaigning, distraught by the uncertainty of his own progressive managers, and worrying about the serious illness of his daughter Mary, La Follette delivered a rambling, confused, late dinner speech lasting almost two hours. The distinguished press audience concluded that La Follette was near mental and physical collapse. La Follette himself later observed that he had "overtaxed" his strength and "did not at once get hold" of his audience. Within hours the press reported the incident, interpreting La Follette's condition as the end of his presidential campaign. Progressive Amos Pinchot later wrote that on the next day, February 3, he met personally with Governor Hiram Johnson, Senator Albert Beveridge, Mark Sullivan of *Collier's* magazine, and George Record, all of whom assumed that La Follette would withdraw from the race. During the next few weeks more defections to Roosevelt occurred, and, as Malcolm Moos states, La Follette's candidacy "was not taken seriously after this event." But La Follette refused to submit to pressure and resolutely remained in the running. Certainly there was an element of truth to his charge that many progressives used the Philadelphia episode as "a pretext for the desertion which it is now plain to be seen had been under consideration for a long time."[10]

Lindbergh was directly involved in the progressive Republican shift from La Follette to Roosevelt. For a short time after the banquet incident he did not waver in his support of La Follette. On February 10 he sent the Wisconsin senator a strong letter of appreciation for his progressive work, perhaps partly out of sympathy, but with unquestionable sincerity and admiration.

I have been an admirer for years of your noble work in behalf of the people in general. I have not bothered you with personal visits nor with letters of commendation because I realize the immense draft upon your time for all matters. However there are times when an acknowledgment of appreciation is proper even with the busiest. I now wish to express to you my appreciation as a citizen of the greatest work you have done. I trust and hope you will soon get rested up and will soon be in the harness again. One must bear in mind the necessity of conserving his energies for the great battles to be.[11]

Even more explicit in defining his position was the telegram Lindbergh sent George Loftus the same day. "La Follette rapidly recovering from his illness" and "will be in shape to take hold in a few days," he wired Loftus. Lindbergh also instructed the president of the Minnesota Progressive Republican League that La Follette's legislative record in Wisconsin was "the best material to show what can be done by a progressive executive." Lindbergh concluded the wire by saying that "I believe any shift at this time would weaken the progressive work generally."[12]

But Lindbergh did not rule out a shift in the future, and three days later he indicated that he was pursuing a possible alternative course of action. In a brief letter to Theodore Roosevelt at Oyster Bay, the Minnesota congressman outlined a tentative decision to back him for the nomination, probably assuming that La Follette would drop out and that he could make his own position public at that time.

I would like to have a little visit with you. I will give my reasons now. I expect you to succeed Taft. There are two reasons why the third term idea will not, in my opinion, cut much figure. One, that you were elected only once. The other, that there has been an intervening period, which I think really covers the spirit of the idea. Last summer I signed a memorandum with others, asking La Follette to

From *The Literary Digest*, February 17, 1912. Minnesota Historical Society.

"To Rescue the Survivors." De Mar in the *Philadelphia Record*.

become a candidate, and I would not now want to do anything to injure his chances, because I should feel that I was doing wrong to do so after signing as I did, but the conditions now are such that I look upon his candidacy as impractical. I have written some of my friends about the situation today.

Of course I would seek to avoid anyone knowing that I see you, if I do.[13]

The "impractical conditions" to which Lindbergh referred as reasons for changing his position were probably a combination of an honest belief that La Follette could not physically endure the campaign and a degree of political expediency to go with

Roosevelt as a more probable winner over Taft. The same day he wrote his letter of commendation to La Follette, Lindbergh wrote Roosevelt-backer Gifford Pinchot asking to meet with him. He may have been influenced by Hugh T. Halbert, a member of the executive committee of the Minnesota Progressive Republican League, who, on February 10, informed Roosevelt that he would attempt to persuade Minnesota La Follette men to come out for Roosevelt. At a stormy meeting of the state league in Minneapolis on February 12, Halbert argued that La Follette was too ill to continue in the race. Nevertheless, the Minnesota league pledged its support to La Follette, whereupon Halbert resigned and came out for Roosevelt. Lindbergh's letter to Roosevelt was dated February 13, the next day.[14]

Ironically, Lindbergh received a reply from La Follette one week after he had sent his letter to Roosevelt. La Follette expressed to Lindbergh: "It was good of you to give me assurance of your continued confidence and loyalty. I shall never forget it while I live." In the letter—marked "confidential"—La Follette complained of the "nagging strain" of dissension among his own supporters, correctly asserting that there were those "who were determined to make me a stalking horse, and convert my candidacy into a cover for that of another man." In characteristic fashion, the Wisconsin senator declared: "I never have played that kind of politics, and never shall." La Follette concluded by assuring Lindbergh that, after a few weeks of rest, he would be back on his feet and in the "thick of the fight."[15]

After his initial February contact, Lindbergh corresponded regularly and met on occasion with Roosevelt. Following the postponement of a meeting originally scheduled for mid-February, a Lindbergh-Roosevelt consultation took place in late February or early March. According to Lindbergh, another person from Minnesota was present at the meeting, and it seems safe to assume that Lindbergh's commitment to the former president was made either at the meeting or shortly thereafter. On February 27 a Washington news release, based on "public and private statements," included Lindbergh as one of six Minnesota Republican congressmen supporting Roosevelt (Senator Clapp headed the list; the other four were Davis, Anderson, Steenerson, and Miller). Representatives Nye and Stevens announced for Taft, while Senator Nelson (later a Taft supporter) and Representative Volstead did not commit themselves at this point. Lindbergh's shift from La Follette to Roosevelt was somewhat uncharacteristic of him; it is perhaps best explained by his personal admiration for Roosevelt.[16]

In a March 7 letter, Lindbergh told Roosevelt that he hoped to write a small volume on the "issues of the day" that might be used in the progressive cause, and explained his position on not campaigning for Roosevelt in North Dakota, where the first presidential primary of 1912 was to be held on March 19. Roosevelt had hoped that the Minnesota congressman could increase his strength in that state, but Lindbergh was reluctant to do so because he believed that stand-patters in North Dakota were supporting Roosevelt. As a progressive, he found this situation "rather awkward." Roosevelt was insistent, imploring that "it seems to me that in North Dakota a vote for Senator La Follette is a vote for Mr. Taft and will be so accepted by the country." But Lindbergh did not give in, noting, for one thing, that Senator Gronna's position as a La Follette supporter "would have made it a little embarrassing for me to have gone out there because I went out to help him in his campaign to become Senator." Reassuringly, though, he wrote Roosevelt that his sources indicated a "vast majority of people" for Roosevelt in North Dakota, and that he was encouraged by good reports from Minnesota and Massachusetts. Lindbergh's optimism about North Dakota was a bit premature, however, for the primary results gave La Follette a comfortable 9,000-vote margin over Roosevelt, with Taft receiving only token support.[17]

During the remaining weeks prior to the mid-June Republican National Convention in Chicago, Lindbergh continued to supply information and opinion to the Roosevelt camp. On March 21 he praised the former president for attacking the performance of the Taft administration, noting that Roosevelt had made a "bully good speech" in the process. Lindbergh was firmly convinced that Taft was opposed to the people, and he chided Roosevelt for imposing this man on the American public. As punishment, asserted Lindbergh, Roosevelt should be required to put in four years of "hard work" in an additional term as president in order to "repair the injuries." On the problem of delegate strength, Lindbergh urged that there be an understanding between La Follette and Roosevelt backers, so as not to give votes to Taft. "In my opinion," Lindbergh wrote Roosevelt, "any delegates elected for La Follette will come to you when they are needed."[18]

A few days later Lindbergh mailed Gifford Pinchot a copy of a long, informative letter about the political situation in Minnesota. Lindbergh reminded Pinchot that the letter's author, whose name he had deleted, had been present at a recent meeting between himself and Pinchot. The writer, said Lindbergh, was honest and a keen political observer. Put simply, the observer stated that there was considerable La Follette strength in the Sixth, Seventh, and Ninth congressional districts of Minnesota. The primary message of the letter was the advice that Roosevelt should avoid attacking La Follette and should stay close to the topic of progressive doctrine when campaigning in the state. On April 4, Pinchot replied to Lindbergh, thanking him for the advice and noting that "Colonel Roosevelt was particularly careful not to attack La Follette in any of his speeches." Apparently in response to the same letter, Roosevelt wrote Lindbergh on April 16. "That's a strong letter," Roosevelt remarked. But, he continued, "a vote for Mr. La Follette is a vote for Mr. Taft. There is just one way to beat the reactionaries, and that is for the Progressives heartily to support me."[19]

Before the Chicago convention, Lindbergh made it clear to Roosevelt that he would advocate and support his candidacy whether or not he received the Republican nomination. Neither the people nor the Republican party wanted Taft for president, Lindbergh insisted. In his opinion only the "official bosses" who utilized "fraud and steam roller" tactics were behind Taft. Without equivocation, Lindbergh declared: "I for one am in favor of your running for President notwithstanding if by high handed means and misconduct Taft should be nominated." As it turned out, Lindbergh's offer to back a third-party candidacy was in fact tested, for out of the drama of contested delegates and the Republican National Convention came the renomination of William Howard Taft. Expectedly, Roosevelt bolted both the party and the convention on the evening of June 22 and called for the formation of a new party, which became known as the Progressive or Bull Moose party. The Minnesota convention delegates—instructed to vote for Roosevelt since the La Follette league lost in this struggle—refused to support Taft and were among those recorded as "not voting" during the final roll calls. Bolstered by a number of Roosevelt primary victories throughout the country, the new Progressive party officially organized and endorsed its presidential candidate in early August.[20]

Meanwhile, the Democrats, viewing the Republican split with pleasure, selected former Princeton University president and New Jersey reform governor Woodrow Wilson as their 1912 presidential candidate. For Roosevelt's progressive supporters, it was an unfortunate choice. Wilson, a capable campaigner known for his reform position on such issues as the tariff and political corruption, appeared as an attractive candidate to a number of progressives. Governor Osborn of Michigan, for example, stated that no third party was now necessary, although he finally came around to support Roosevelt. Among the old progressives Works, Gronna, and Norris Brown chose Wilson; while Beveridge, Bristow, Dixon, Clapp, and the Pinchots stood by Roosevelt. Ray Stannard Baker, Louis Brandeis, Charles Crane, Herbert Quick, and others termed Wilson the "best fundamental democrat." Cummins, Borah, Bourne, and William Kenyon favored Roosevelt, but not a third party. La Follette would not support Roosevelt, and in the end he refused to endorse anyone for the presidency.[21]

Lindbergh remained true to his promise to back a third-party presidential bid by Roosevelt. Although, curiously, he was dis-

turbed when Eva received some publicity in connection with a
Roosevelt Club at Carleton College, Lindbergh openly supported
Roosevelt as he hit the campaign trail in the fall.[22] His willingness to shed party label, if and when a new political vehicle
seemed practicable, fit his philosophy of progressivism. Less than
a year after the 1912 campaign, he wrote:

> To be a true Progressive it is not sufficient to stand up and say that
> one believes in what one has promulgated as progressive principles.
> One must be progressive in heart and active in promoting the pro-
> gressive principles of today, tomorrow, and always. There is no resting
> point, for humanity is ever ascending to a higher and better goal. . . .
> Their [the progressives] aim is to take step after step toward higher
> and nobler purposes and the general elevation of mankind. . . .
> There is no monopoly of the principle by party or sect. It is open and
> free to anyone who wishes to embrace it, but if one becomes a party
> to a faction, even if the faction is called a party, and lets a majority of
> that faction take him away from the broader field of national activity,
> by that act he ceases to be a progressive.[23]

To Lindbergh, the Taft element within the Republican party
represented such an undesirable faction, and by supporting
Roosevelt he was merely acting in the interests of true progressivism. More revealing, however, is the independent role taken
by Lindbergh and other Minnesota politicians who, as candidates
for public office in later campaigns, identified with the Nonpartisan League movement and the Farmer-Labor party.

But political realism dictated Lindbergh's personal party
alignment in the congressional race of 1912, and he filed for
reelection on the Republican ticket. Like most progressive Republicans, Lindbergh apparently doubted whether the Roosevelt
appeal would be sufficient to establish a party on a permanent
basis. Furthermore, progressive sentiment was very strong in
Minnesota's Republican organization, so there was little desire
to desert it on the state level. Although Minnesota did field Progressive party candidates for top state offices and in two congressional races, the majority of progressive Republicans probably agreed with Missouri governor Herbert Hadley's comment
about his state that "a pronounced feeling of regularity existed"

within the party. Among the few progressives who actually ran on the new party ticket in 1912 were Senator Joseph M. Dixon of Montana, Representative Miles Poindexter of Washington, and Governor Hiram Johnson of California. In the stronghold of the original insurgent bloc in Congress, the upper Midwest and the prairie states, a clear pattern developed in 1912. Almost without exception, Lindbergh included, progressive leaders in the area strongly endorsed Roosevelt but refused to bolt the Republican party in their own political contests.[24]

During Roosevelt's Progressive party campaign Lindbergh remained in close contact with the former president and his managers. On August 6 he wrote Roosevelt that his recent speech (undoubtedly at the Progressive convention) was "the greatest that has been made on the present system of government and business management," praising him for calling for reforms within the present system rather than demanding a "new economic basis." A few days later Lindbergh assured Roosevelt in a brief note that the Progressive standard-bearer would have no difficulty in carrying Minnesota.[25]

One of Lindbergh's main contributions to the Roosevelt camp was his proposal to use Lynn Haines's book *Law Making in America* as campaign literature. At a personal meeting with Roosevelt on August 20, Lindbergh convinced the Colonel that use of the progressive-oriented volume was a good plan. Roosevelt immediately informed Gifford Pinchot of the idea, referring to Lindbergh as "one of the few Congressmen on whom we can absolutely count." Haines's book was an analysis of the 1911–1912 House, and Roosevelt emphasized that its chief purpose would be to reveal the reactionary record of the Democratic-controlled body. Lindbergh also wrote Pinchot, stressing that the book could be "a most potent factor in drawing the distinction between the so-called progressive Democrats and the true progressives—like La Follette, yourself, and others." Pinchot, agreeing with Roosevelt and Lindbergh, contacted Haines. They arranged to put out a condensation of about ten thousand to fifteen thousand words for general campaign distribution and to send copies of the regular book to Progressive congressional candidates.[26]

Regrettably, the scheme fell through. Due to Haines's illness, the scheduled mid-September publication date of *Law Making in America* was delayed to early October. Moreover, it is apparent that Haines was unable to complete a condensed version of the book. Because of its late publication, the volume had only limited impact on the campaign. As Lindbergh explained to Haines on October 11, "I am not going to use [the books] especially for campaign purposes, as that is pretty well in hand now." Nonetheless, he contributed $250 to aid distribution of the book, and mailed copies to a number of political contacts in his home district. Among them were Lester Bartlett of Cass Lake, P. P. Ornberg of Grove City, and Oscar Lindquist of Dassel, who, in turn, distributed copies. Lindbergh also asked Haines to send hardbound copies to all newspaper editors in his district. (Lindbergh handed out paperbacks only to those whom he expected "will not take care of them.") Hence, for Lindbergh, the slim volume did have a degree of propaganda value in 1912.[27]

Lindbergh's campaign for a fourth term as congressman from the Sixth District was virtually no contest. Pitted against him once again was Dr. A. J. Kilkinson of Osakis, his Democratic opponent of 1908. One Minnesota political observer had astutely commented in March that Lindbergh "had no opposition in sight," and in terms of a real challenge the statement held true in the fall. Lindbergh still nurtured aspirations to higher public office, however, and his friend M. N. Koll expressed the view in late 1911 that trying for direct election to the Senate might be more feasible for Lindbergh than seeking the governorship through the convention system. In late spring of 1912 Lindbergh announced that he would be a candidate for the U.S. Senate, but little more came of the matter, and he apparently dropped the idea. In the September 17 primary Sixth District voters automatically endorsed Lindbergh (12,019 votes) and Gilkinson (4,167 votes) as the Republican and Democratic nominees for Congress. The primary also saved machine-oriented Governor

A. O. Eberhart from defeat in 1912. In a five-way Republican race for governor, he won a plurality of the votes, with William Lee of Long Prairie as his closest challenger. To the dismay of progressives, Eberhart and political boss Edward E. Smith thereby retained control of state government.[28]

The Lindbergh–Gilkinson general election race was uneventful; understandably, the major attraction was the unusual presidential campaign. During an appearance at the Little Falls courthouse, Lindbergh offered the opinion that the current confusion in political parties was "one of the best signs of the times." He attacked party government and the caucus system and suggested that a people's government could be instituted with the passage of such reforms as the initiative, referendum, and recall. Although he expressed admiration for the "sterling qualities" of Woodrow Wilson and thought he would bring about desirable reforms, Lindbergh emphasized that Theodore Roosevelt was more "positive" in fighting for people's rule. After his speech, according to reports in the pro-Taft *Little Falls Transcript,* Lindbergh and most of the audience left, with only "10 bullmoosers" remaining. The Bull Moose party, quipped the *Transcript,* was little more than a "Democratic Aid" society.[29]

Meanwhile, the Democratic press in the district appealed to voters on the premise that Wilson would likely be elected president, pointing out that a hostile Congress would prevent passage of Wilson's reform legislation. The *St. Cloud Daily Times* attacked Lindbergh's position on Roosevelt, stressing that Lindbergh was seeking reelection as a Republican while he openly backed Progressive candidate Roosevelt. "A Dr. Jekyl [sic] and Mr. Hyde candidate," the *Times* informed its readers. Thus, the *Times* argued on another occasion, there was no Republican candidate in the Sixth District, for Lindbergh, it asserted, was clearly a deserter to his own party. In contrast, the *Little Falls Herald,* another Democratic sheet and nominally a supporter of Gilkinson, stated: "We would not believe it right, however, to criticize any Democrat who feels like voting for the present congressman."[30]

The outcome of the Sixth District race was no surprise. On November 5, district voters returned Lindbergh to Washington for the fourth time with a 62.5 per cent majority. The final tabulation in the 1912 congressional election was: Lindbergh—21,286; Gilkinson—9,920; A. W. Uhl (Public-Ownership candidate)—2,839. Minnesotans also reelected Republican A. O. Eberhart as governor and gave nine of ten congressional seats to Republicans, including the new congressman-at-large, progressive James Manahan. Apparently there had been some confusion between the candidacy of Manahan and other congressmen because the results of the state-wide Manahan race seemed to conflict with established congressional districts. Knute Nelson was returned by a substantial margin for another term in the Senate, while, in the presidential contest, Theodore Roosevelt was victorious in the state. The 1912 Minnesota vote for president was: Roosevelt—125,856; Wilson—106,426; Taft—64,334. Thus, in Minnesota at least, the Lindbergh logic of progressive Republicanism at home, together with allegiance to a third-party presidential candidate, was sound. The phenomenon, however, did not occur in other parts of the country, for Roosevelt suffered national defeat in 1912.[31]

Chapter VII

Banking and Currency Reform

With the election of Woodrow Wilson to the presidency in 1912, American politics during the progressive era entered a new phase. Prospects for the Democratic president's popularly espoused program of reform, the New Freedom, were promising, for Wilson would be working with a congressional majority.[1] One of the principal issues that the Wilson administration considered during its initial months in office, and even prior to the actual transfer of power, was congressional passage of a banking and currency bill. Although the need for such legislation had been demonstrated and generally accepted by Congress, proposed solutions differed. Three main alternative plans on monetary reform were put forward: (1) The Aldrich plan, which was supported by bankers and conservative Republicans, and which called for one large central bank controlled by banking interests; (2) a plan, backed by conservative Democrats, for a decentralized reserve system controlled by private interests and free of Wall Street domination; and (3) a plan, supported by progressives in both parties, calling for a reserve system and currency supply owned and supplied by the government. As expected, Lindbergh supported the third proposal and continued to voice his strong and specific opinions on the issue as the debate developed. As a member of the House Committee on Banking and Currency after June, 1913, he became directly involved in the construction of legislation ultimately known as the Federal Reserve Act.[2]

Lindbergh's allegations against the Money Trust as corroborated by the reports of the Pujo Committee were accepted as an
integral part of Wilson's New Freedom program. The Pujo
Committee, aided by counsel Samuel Untermeyer, concluded, as
Lindbergh had previously, that there was an astounding concentration of credit resources in the United States. Committee
reports during 1912 and early 1913 listed the following firms,
among others, as responsible for this concentration of money and
credit: J. P. Morgan and Company; the First National Bank
New York; National City Bank of New York; Lee, Higginson
and Company of Boston and New York; Kidder, Peabody, and
Company of Boston and New York; and Kuhn, Loeb, and Company. Public opinion was aroused as a result of the Pujo Committee releases, and Wilson became convinced that an alternative
to the Aldrich plan was mandatory.[3]

Wilson directly attacked the Money Trust in *The New Freedom,* which first appeared serially in *World's Work* from January to July, 1913, and during his campaign for the presidency.
"I take my stand absolutely, where every progressive ought to
take his stand, on the proposition that private monopoly is inde-
fensible and intolerable," he wrote. A trust, to Wilson, was "an arrangement to get rid of competition," and he emphasized that the
Money Trust in particular was no myth, but rather a glaring and
undesirable economic reality. With almost Populist zeal, Wilson
exposed the Wall Street interests as the greatest source of centralized credit control. Through progressive legislation, he believed, democratic institutions, as well as consumers and wage
earners, could be delivered from the power of the Money Trust.
Politics, as well, must be purified of its associations with these
privileged monopolies. Wilson's statements advocating the destruction of this system of financial monopoly were nearly iden-
tical to those made earlier by progressive Republican Lindbergh.[4]

Meanwhile, between the 1912 election and the actual con-
vening of the Sixty-third Congress, over which the Democrats
would retain control, Lindbergh and other congressmen con-

ducted regular business during the third session of the old Congress. The interim session allowed Lindbergh time to introduce two resolutions in December, 1912; one called for an investigation of trusts through the House Committee on Banking and Currency, and the second outlined a bill that would compel all members of Congress to file complete financial statements to be published regularly in the *Congressional Record*.[5] Both requests were issues that Lindbergh had presented to the House on previous occasions. In early February, 1913, Lindbergh, who had been elected to serve on the House Committee on Election of President, Vice-President, and Representatives in Congress in April, 1912, voiced his support before the House both for direct primaries and for the election of the president by a direct, popular vote. "I am unalterably opposed to the placing of any limit whatever upon the free choice of the people for the high office of President of the United States," Lindbergh stated. He was also opposed to the proposed amendment that would limit one man's tenure in the office of president to one six-year term. At another point in the session Lindbergh delivered a short eulogy about Judge Elbert H. Hubbard, one of few colleagues with whom he had formed a close friendship. Revealing a bit about himself and his tendency to be a "loner" in his work, Lindbergh remarked: "Those of us who try hard to meet the demands placed upon us get but little chance to make close personal acquaintances here."[6]

During the same period the two subcommittees of the House Banking and Currency Committee dealing with the Money Trust and banking laws continued their activities. The Pujo Committee's impact with regard to the danger of the Money Trust was clear, while the other subcommittee, charged with revision of banking and currency laws and chaired by Carter Glass of Virginia, held hearings in early 1913. Glass later revealed that Pujo had given him the choice of heading either subcommittee, and that he had selected the banking law revision subcommittee chairmanship. On the key issue of banking reform the Virginia congressman stood resolutely against the idea of a central bank, "but he was thoroughly conservative in his belief in private control of the banking system and the money supply."[7]

Even before Wilson's inauguration, Glass and subcommittee banking expert H. Parker Willis began drafting a tentative banking bill. The major feature of the draft was an outline for a decentralized, privately controlled reserve system, with the elimination of Wall Street control as its primary objective. After a meeting with Wilson, Glass and Willis reluctantly revised the proposal to include an overall Federal Reserve Board, composed of six public members and three bankers, which would control the entire reserve system. During these months, the inner circle made up of Wilson, Glass, Willis, and Secretary of the Treasury William McAdoo held almost completely secret discussions with private bankers; by May 1, 1913, the group thought it had completed the basic administration bill. But they had misjudged the demands made by progressives within the Democratic party and other so-called radicals like Lindbergh. The progressives in general were disturbed by the dominant role given bankers in the reserve system structure in the Glass bill, and included among the critics was the influential William Jennings Bryan. For a time it appeared that the crisis would destroy any hope of banking and currency reform at all. After consulting with Louis D. Brandeis, however, Wilson insisted "upon exclusive governmental control of the Federal Reserve Board and upon making Federal Reserve notes the obligation of the United States" as an absolute minimum in satisfying the progressives. Accordingly, these changes were made in the bill, and the crisis passed. On June 19 the Federal Reserve bill was made public, and on the following day Wilson conferred with Democratic members of the House Banking and Currency Committee. Wilson opened the administration campaign for the bill by appearing before a joint session on June 23, and thereafter he held meetings with Glass and other congressional leaders. In early July the Democrats on the committee began considering the legislation, and the congressional debate was on.[8]

Lindbergh was disturbed both with the proposed Federal Reserve bill itself and with the manner by which Democrats had drafted the measure in secrecy. As an outspoken and established critic on banking and currency matters and a member of the House Committee on Banking and Currency, Lindbergh was certain to raise penetrating questions about the banking bill. Carter Glass wrote President Wilson in mid-May that the probable members of the new session's Committee on Banking and Currency were "a pretty dependable list, with possibly a single exception." It seems likely that Lindbergh may have been the individual to whom Glass referred, for Lindbergh's reputation as an expert on financial issues and an unrelenting foe if necessary was well-known. On June 19 Lindbergh received a copy of the tentative Federal Reserve bill from Glass, a courtesy extended to all members of the Banking and Currency Committee.[9]

Two weeks later Lindbergh introduced a resolution calling for an investigation of the House Committee on Banking and Currency. Thoroughly incensed by the fact that Glass and other Democratic committe members were meeting frequently to frame the bill and barring Lindbergh and other Republicans from the meetings, the Minnesota congressman maintained that such action was in contravention of the Constitution and the rules of the House. His resolution, in part, read:

RESOLVED that a special committee of seven be appointed by the Speaker to forthwith ascertain the true state of facts and report immediately to the House whether a part of the members of the Banking and Currency Committee with the chairman of the Committee are holding secret or other meetings for the purpose of framing the said bill or to influence the same and are excluding a part of the membership of said committee.[10]

A point of order was raised by Representative John J. Fitzgerald of New York, who maintained that Lindbergh's resolution was not privileged, and the Speaker of the House sustained the point of order. A few days later Lindbergh, obviously still angry about the committee's behavior, introduced another resolution demanding a congressional investigation of the constitutionality of the Glass bill. It should be decided, the Lindbergh resolution stated, "whether or not the Glass bill, as introduced in the House, would, if enacted, create an inconsistent governmental practice by fostering on the one hand a monopoly to privately control (for selfish interest) the distribution of money and credit, and on the other prosecuting trusts and combinations under the Sherman Anti-Trust Act." The resolution apparently died in the Committee on Rules.[11]

Opportunely, Lindbergh's full-length study on banking and currency, *Banking and Currency and the Money Trust,* appeared in print in June, 1913, during the heat of the debate on the Federal Reserve bill. Lindbergh had been working on the project for some time, and one of his main purposes was to provide evidence to head off passage of an Aldrich-type central bank plan. Certainly Lindbergh must have obtained added satisfaction from the fact that the book's publication was a statement contrary to the majority membership of the House Committee on Banking and Currency in 1913. The 318-page volume, published by the National Capital Press, was the first in a proposed trilogy of books. The volumes would concern the three basic areas of needed change in human conditions, said Lindbergh, namely, banking and currency, industrial relations, and political relations.[12]

Lindbergh expected public censure for exposing conditions as they really were in *Banking and Currency and the Money Trust.* He stressed that his attack on the Money Trust and the banking structure was aimed at the system, not at individuals. Most bankers were not dishonest, he believed, but were merely caught up in a false and unfair economic system. By this system bankers, who, in Lindbergh's opinion, "possess no more intelligence than ourselves," accumulated substantial wealth. At the apex of this undesirable system was the Money Trust. Since its purpose was contrary to conserving and protecting humanity, said Lindbergh, it should be condemned and eliminated. His charge did not mean that all aspects of industrial and economic expansion were negative, however, for expansion did provide increases in the productive energies of the masses, and in the accumulation of real wealth. The rewards of the commercial struggle compared favorably with the traditional values of war and its legacy of destruction, he argued. The main point, then, was to distribute more equally the wealth coming from the rewards of the industrial system.[13]

A large segment of Lindbergh's book concerned the historical build-up of concentrated wealth by the Money Trust. The ultimate funneling of bank monies to trusts and "special interest" groups "will become as plain as the noonday sun on a clear day," he wrote. Portions of the volume reflected Lindbergh's statements in the House during the debate on the Aldrich-Vreeland bill. Speculative gambling between 1896 and 1907, the 1907 panic, the Aldrich-Vreeland bill and the accompanying National Monetary Commission, and the Aldrich scheme for final legislation on banking as steps toward a complete "money monopoly" were presented in detail. The Aldrich plan and the National Citizens' League were vigorously attacked. Lindbergh was also sharply critical of both the banker-oriented House Committee on Banking and Currency and its banker-chaired special subcommittee. In referring to the initial drafting of the Federal Reserve bill during early 1913, Lindbergh accused the Glass Committee of sending draft copies to a "selected list" of bankers and others, but excluding farmers, wage earners, many congressmen, and the people in general. Lindbergh cited a letter from Carter Glass dated February 12, 1913. In reply to Lindbergh's request for an early draft of the bill, Glass wrote: "I beg to say that we have not yet formulated a currency bill, but just as soon as we shall have done so, I will be glad to let you have one of the first copies of the measure."[14]

In another part of the book Lindbergh discussed socialism and the nature of money. In view of what he termed the economic slavery of the general populace to the trusts, he wrote: "We must make a choice and either accept absolute Socialism or establish Individualism with opportunity for all." Lindbergh believed in the theory of socialism, but he preferred to see people govern themselves justly under the present economic structure by eliminating the trusts. As he put it: "The remedy for our social evils does not consist so much in changing the system of government as it does in increasing the general intelligence of the people so they may learn how to govern." In a short chapter on money he presented a strong case, as he had done in 1911, that false money usurped the value of true money. Legal tender, he argued, should be based on commodities and the applied energies of men, not on a "rich man's money" of gold.[15]

The case made plain, Lindbergh said, reform must follow. All one had to do was enter the luxurious homes of wealthy capitalists and compare the conditions he found there with those of the farmer and wage earner. While the capitalists "revel in extravagance and waste" and have servants performing things that "healthy people ought to do for themselves," the average farmer or wage earner had no luxuries in his home. The farmer, "the mainstay and the balance wheel of humanity," according to Lindbergh, employed frugality and self-support, and the laborer, in many cases a tenant, often did not have the means to provide for the basic necessities of life. Hence in both cases people were living below the true value of their products and services.[16]

As Lindbergh envisaged it, a twofold remedy would be necessary to bring about reform. First, the old system of banking and currency should be amended to correct its most serious defects; second, "an entirely new system should be instituted which shall be founded upon the natural demands of commerce and trade and divorced from personal favor or property preference." For a time the systems would operate concurrently because legitimate business would need a transitional period in which to transfer to the new system.[17]

Under Lindbergh's plan, essentially the same one he discussed in 1911, the gold standard and the monetizing of metals would be discarded. In one section of his book, he praised a contemporary study by Professor Irving Fisher of Yale University for exposing weaknesses in the gold standard, but he disagreed with Fisher's conclusions about trying to reform the old system. In place of the gold standard, Lindbergh advocated a true medium of exchange based on "a commercial measure regulated by the service value of things." He hypothesized about such likely bases for this commercial value structure as wheat, corn, cotton, rice, wool, iron, wood, silver, land, and labor services. Gold could also be added to this list, but only as an "article of commerce." By this method, Lindbergh judged, the artificial demand for gold would be destroyed by removing it from circulation as legal tender, and its value "would not exceed 10 per cent of its present cost."[18]

Banks would still exist in Lindbergh's reformed banking and currency structure, but their role would be more limited. They would act primarily as clearinghouses, receiving payment for their services but having no control over industrial and social conditions in the country. Most interest charges would be eliminated, bringing greater equality for the average wage earner. According to Lindbergh, the system currently in use allowed bankers to exchange billions of dollars with very little cash in actual reserve, while the ordinary person had to pay interest to a bank if he could not meet the total cost of a particular commodity. Under the new plan, any actual money would be issued by the government, and only in amounts necessary to meet the demands of natural trade and exchange. There would be no room for "speculative parasites." In his last chapter Lindbergh wrote harshly about "party government" and its attempt to subvert the genuine spirit of the progressive movement. "The special interests are seeking to convert the progressive movement into another victory for themselves." Lindbergh thought of himself as an "original" progressive, and he warned of "spies and traitors" now in the movement. If necessary, he contended, party vehicles might have to be changed. He was proud that Minnesota, at least, had countered party identity by establishing a nonpartisan legislature. In general, the book called for broad reform, not merely specific banking and currency changes. Social justice was not served, Lindbergh emphasized, "when we make the main aim of our social existence the gaining of money."[19]

It is difficult to know the impact of Lindbergh's *Banking and*

Currency and the Money Trust in 1913. No circulation figures
for the long-defunct National Capital Press of Washington exist.
The book, published in both hardbound and paperbound editions, sold either for one dollar or for fifty cents. Lindbergh almost certainly lost money on the book, as he apparently did on
later publication ventures, which he also financed. Frank Dewey
of Little Falls remembered "probably hundreds of his books"
kept in storage at the old produce building for many years. Sales
may have been inhibited by Lindbergh's somewhat complicated
and awkward style of writing. But although he tended to use long,
involved sentences, there was no mistaking his principal meaning. Paramount is the fact that Lindbergh's book gave him an
outlet for his reform views, and he undoubtedly felt the volume
had political and advertising value in that specific sense. Lindbergh's House colleagues, for example, must have been aware
of his effort during the heated debates on the banking and currency issue. Lynn and Dora Haines further record that in Chicago Lindbergh was offered a bribe of $2,000,000 (Eva says
$35,000 is more accurate) to stop circulation of his book. Ac-
cording to the Haineses, Lindbergh responded to the offer by
saying: "The point is, *Banking and Currency* no longer belongs
to me. It is public property, and the public has a right to every
copy it can use."[20]

Meanwhile, the Federal Reserve bill continued on its uncertain
congressional path. Conservatives, both in and out of Congress,
feared that the bill would abandon all semblance of laissez faire
capitalism in the economy, while a group of Southern and Western agrarian congressmen (Democrats Robert L. Henry and
Joe U. Eagle of Texas, Otis T. Wingo of Arkansas, J. Willard
Ragsdale of South Carolina, and George H. Neeley of Kansas)
objected to private control by the regional banks and to the
bill's lack of provision for agricultural credit. In a manner
reminiscent of the old Populist hatred of Wall Street, they demanded that the legislation provide for the destruction of interlocking directorates, the real core of the Money Trust. Repeat-
edly, the agrarian leaders (all of whom were members of the

House Committee on Banking and Currency except Henry, who chaired the powerful Rules Committee) obstructed Carter Glass's efforts to secure approval from Democratic committee members. For a time it appeared that Glass was losing control of the committee. In view of the new danger, President Wilson moved quickly, persuading the agrarian critics to support the bill with a promise that the interlocking directorate matter would be taken care of in the administration's new antitrust legislation. Even the secretary of state, the influential reformer William Jennings Bryan, was satisfied with the promise. The Democratic members of the Banking and Currency Committee approved the Federal Reserve bill by a vote of 11 to 3 on August 5, and the Democratic House caucus approved the measure on August 28 by a vote of 116 to 9. The bill now had become a party measure.[21]

At this point Glass referred the bill back to the full Banking and Currency Committee of the House. Lindbergh used the opportunity in early September to offer a number of minor amendments, mostly changes in wording, to the proposed legislation. All his amendments but one, however, were defeated. The exception, which received the unanimous support of the committee, was a proposal to reduce from 25 per cent to 20 per cent of deposits the amount reserve city banks were required to have in reserves during the first sixty days after their establishment in the district. The minutes of the committee also reveal that Lindbergh, early in the summer, had offered a resolution making Banking and Currency Committee meetings open to the public. The resolution was referred to a subcommittee, which eventually won approval with the suggestion that a clerk of the committee keep a journal and make the proceedings public after each meeting. Clearly, the Democratic membership of the committee was in complete control of committee discussions in late August and early September. On September 4, the House Banking and Currency Committee approved the Federal Reserve bill, which then was reported to the House on September 9.[22]

On the same day, Report no. 69, a minority report on the action taken by the House Committee, was submitted by Chairman Glass. A two-page "Views of the Minority" section was signed by committee members E. A. Hayes, Frank E. Guernsey, James E. Burke, Frank P. Woods, and Edmund Platt; while a thirty-two page segment entitled "Minority Views" was authored solely by Representative Lindbergh. The "Views of the Minority" was essentially the conservative position on the Federal Reserve bill; in it objections were raised to such features as government responsibility for notes and the extensive powers given the Federal Reserve Board. Lindbergh's minority statement on the Glass bill (H.R. 7837), on the other hand, represented the other extreme of the political spectrum. His basic purpose in voicing his many criticisms, he said, was to offer amendments to the Glass bill and, hopefully, to win support for a totally new banking and currency bill. Thorough reform was his ultimate aim, but Lindbergh did admit that "with some few amendments the system that the Glass bill would put into operation, would be less severe on the people than our present system."[23]

Lindbergh's comments on the bill were harsh. "The Glass bill proposes to incorporate, canonize, and sanctify a private monopoly of the money and credit of the nation. . . . It violates every principle of popular, democratic, representative Government and every declaration of the Democratic Party and platform pledges from Thomas Jefferson down to the beginning of this Congress." Portions of Lindbergh's report, such as the section on gold and metals, were the same as his discussions in *Banking and Currency and the Money Trust.* In Lindbergh's opinion the Glass bill was distinctly a "banker's bill," and he warned of likely panics since the people were tied to banks under the system the bill provided for. Although the government printed money under the proposed law, Lindbergh argued, its distribution would be controlled by banks. Other points that he criticized were the Federal Reserve bill's provisions for excluding small banks from the system, for keeping all public funds on deposit in banks, for placing an agency between the people and the government that had "absolute control of the distribution of money and the use of credit that would be valueless without the guaranty of the Government," and for excessive interest charges.[24]

At another juncture in the report Lindbergh suggested changes

in the banking and currency system that certainly merited classification as progressive, perhaps even radical, in 1913. Ideally,
Lindbergh wrote, an entirely new system should be structured
under the direction of a fiscal department of eight members.
This group, he noted, "shall include the Secretary of the Treasury, who shall be member ex officio, but without voting power
except as specifically in this act provided, and seven others, nonpartisan, to be selected by the President, by and with the advice
and consent of the Senate, and whose term shall be for ten
years." The issue of currency was clearly the province of the
government (Lindbergh quoted the Progressive party platform)
and would take the form of public service certificates. But most
startling were Lindbergh's detailed comments calling for the proposed fiscal department (1) to allow states, municipalities, school
districts, and other political divisions to secure loans from the
Secretary of the Treasury; (2) to organize a system of national
public works and improvements to aid labor conditions; (3) to
adopt a plan "systematizing the production, storage, transportation, and distribution of agricultural and horticultural products";
and (4) to extend government loans to individuals for homes,
legitimate industries, and any source, of whatever character, that
would "promote the general welfare." Charges for repayment on
these government loans would be "the lowest rate of interest
consistent with the cost and integrity of the service." Thus the
activities of real estate speculators and the overcharges of loan
agencies would be stopped. For 1913, these views were indeed
unusual; they bear a striking similarity to New Deal legislation
enacted twenty years later.[25]

Lindbergh actively participated in the House debate on the
Federal Reserve bill between its introduction on September 9
and its passage on September 18. His longest appearance before
the House came on September 11, when he informed his listeners
that he had enough material for a six-hour speech. However, he
settled for one hour in this case. The main point of his speech
was that passage of the Glass bill would perpetuate the old
banking and currency system, which allowed a concentration of

wealth. The false system, he argued, allowed certain persons and companies to get rich on interest, dividends, and rent while the ordinary man who worked for a living just got by on his finances. This situation, Lindbergh said, was unjust. Profit as the incentive for production was all wrong, he asserted; production should rather be governed by necessity, "people's actual requirements." Credit, he felt, should be as nearly free as possible to all who could produce value on which credit is based. As always, Lindbergh used statistics to substantiate his generalizations throughout the speech. At one point, when his facts were challenged from the floor, Lindbergh replied: "I have not verified the figures named, but I claim absolute verity of the principles involved." The major portion of his speech was devoted to a restatement of extended segments of his "Minority View."[26]

The following week Lindbergh, like other Republicans, offered a series of amendments to H.R. 7837. Among the changes he wished to incorporate in the bill were provisions outlining the levying of an assessment on bank surpluses as well as capital (thus removing the unfair advantage given New York and other city banks over small banks in agricultural districts with small surpluses), the prevention of bankers from becoming directors in the system, and closely related amendments dealing with the needs of small banks and the outlawing of interlocking directorates. All of Lindbergh's amendments were rejected by the House. During one verbal exchange involving a Lindbergh amendment, the partisan nature of the Federal Reserve bill debate was clearly evident. On September 15, when Lindbergh offered his amendment denying bankers the right to be directors, Committee Chairman Glass, after some discussion, rose to be heard on the House floor. Replying to Lindbergh and Representative Victor Murdock of Kansas, Glass declared: "If either gentleman does not know why the amendment against interlocking directorates was not included in this bill, it is because he was not here Saturday night to listen to what I had to say." Such a provision, Glass maintained, was not pertinent to the bill under consideration. Furthermore, he contended, both Murdock

163

and Lindbergh obviously agreed with him, since Murdock had named Lindbergh to the House Committee on Banking and Currency, and two currency bills submitted by Lindbergh contained no provision against interlocking directorates. The Glass statement was followed by applause from the Democratic side of the House.[27]

Lindbergh responded with the explanation that he had not introduced an amendment in the committee to that effect "because the members of the committee stated in the official meeting of that committee that neither provision could be inserted in that bill in committee because the caucus had determined every material issue that could be placed in the bill." This statement was followed by applause from the Republican side of the House. Glass countered that Lindbergh could have offered other amendments to the bill, and once again Democrats sounded their approval. With finality on the interlocking directorate matter, Glass asserted: "That proposition is not pertinent to currency legislation." "Upon that question the gentleman and I disagree," Lindbergh retorted. "We do," stated Glass, adding threateningly, "and this side is going to beat you on that proposition." Glass's prediction was tested immediately, for the question was called on the Lindbergh amendment. The Chair announced that the noes "seem to have it," but Lindbergh and Murdock demanded a division of the vote. The results were: ayes—44; noes—71, and the amendment was rejected.[28]

On September 18, 1913, the House cast the crucial votes on the Federal Reserve Act. An amendment endorsing the gold standard passed by a 299 to 68 margin, while an amendment to recommit the Glass bill was defeated by a 266 to 100 vote. Lindbergh was among the losing minority on both amendments, voting against the gold standard and for recommittal of the bill. Surprisingly, in view of his criticism, Lindbergh voted for passage of the main bill, and it passed easily with a 287 to 85 House vote on the same day. Apparently Lindbergh felt that certain essential amendments had been made, and that the system outlined in the revised bill was at least better than the current system of banking and currency. He may also have hoped that the Senate would return the bill with further needed changes.[29] At any rate, Lindbergh was not the only progressive Republican to register an affirmative vote on September 18, for the congressional bloc was about evenly split in its support of the Federal Reserve bill.[30]

Lindbergh's qualified approval of the bill had changed by the time it returned from the Senate and conference committee in December, however, and from then on he resumed his sharp opposition to the legislation. Actually the Senate version of the bill, drawn up under the direction of Banking Committee Chairman Robert L. Owen of Oklahoma, encountered serious difficulties, including the threat of the counterproposed Vanderlip plan. Then, too, many bankers and businessmen throughout the nation made their dissatisfaction known. But once again President Wilson intervened to keep the bill moving, and after heated debate on the Senate floor, it was passed by a vote of 54 to 34 on December 19, 1913.[31]

When the bill was presented to the House out of conference committee on December 22, Lindbergh assailed the bill in yet another floor speech. The Federal Reserve Act, he exclaimed, "established the most gigantic trust on earth." Such a trust, he pointed out, would have been dissolved under the Sherman Antitrust Act. He stressed that the bill would create inflation, establish regional banks owned by member banks, put into operation a disguised Aldrich bill, establish a system that would incorporate the false gold standard, and discriminate against farmers and agricultural districts. On the last point, he referred to the portion of the bill that allowed national banks to extend loans on security of land in an amount only "equal to 25 per cent of their capital and surplus." This provision was grossly unfair, asserted Lindbergh, disclosing that under such a practice, for example, the thirty-three national banks in his home district could loan the majority percentage of farmers' deposits to any "Tom, Dick, or Harry," even to speculators, but not to the farmers themselves. "When the President signs this act," charged Lindbergh, "the invisible government by the money power, proven to exist by the Money Trust investigation, will be legalized." It was, he chided, a congressional "Christmas present to the Money Trust." The next day the *New York Times* reported that Lindbergh, the "father of the money trust investigation," had condemned the bill as "radically wrong in fundamentals."[32] Despite Lindbergh's vociferous objections, the House overwhelmingly approved the conference report by a 298 to 60 vote. On December 23, 1913, the Senate approved the conference report, President Wilson signed the bill, and the Federal Reserve Act became law.[33]

In the end the Federal Reserve Act was, as Arthur S. Link writes, "a compromise between what the bankers wanted and what the most advanced progressives said the country needed." It did give needed attention to establishing a workable reserve system, to giving the country an elastic currency, and to limiting the concentration of wealth in Wall Street. The bill was not perfect. As Lindbergh pointed out, it left the money supply largely in the hands of private bankers and deprived the government of the ability to prevent depressions. His predictions were accurate on these matters, and it was not until the 1930's that further legislation corrected these problems.[34] Lindbergh's disenchantment with the Federal Reserve Act was now complete, and he continued to blast the system throughout his remaining political career. Later in the Sixty-third Congress, for example, he expressed minority views against banking measures that would allow all bank reserves to be placed in the twelve Federal Reserve district banks, and which would provide government loans to banks at 3 per cent interest. Farmers could not borrow from the government at 3 per cent, Lindbergh noted, but were forced to borrow the same government emergency currency from the banks at 8 per cent interest.[35]

Despite his failure to prevent passage of the Federal Reserve Act, Lindbergh deserves much credit for bringing about banking reform in 1913. His early, penetrating questions about the banking and currency system, and his relentless campaign to expose its faults, were immeasurable factors in awakening Congress and the nation to the crisis. His desire for complete and fundamental reform, as well as his stubborn and vehement criticism, made him appear radical on the issue. His role among progressives was virtually unique in that he wanted banking reform that would improve the distribution of wealth in the country, not just satisfy the operative needs of a banking and currency system. Typically, Lindbergh had stood alone at various stages during the fight for reform. As fellow Minnesota congressman James Manahan later recalled: "There was, as it now seems, something prophetic in the tall figure of the lonely Lindbergh inviting the assaults of Wall Street by attacking single-handed the money system of the country." The provisions of the final version of the Federal Reserve bill were likely more responsive to the nation's needs than they might have been without Lindbergh's constant prodding. As economist W. Jett Lauck has described the bill, and Lindbergh's relation to it: "It was nevertheless far more desirable in its technical and democratic features than legislation which would probably have been enacted had he not made the attack on the Money Trust, and aroused an enlightened public opinion to influence the movement for banking reform."[36]

During early 1915, Lindbergh had the opportunity once again to make public his views on banking and currency, as well as on economic conditions in general, when he testified before the U.S. Commission on Industrial Relations in New York City. When he appeared as the last witness of the day on February 5, he told Chairman Frank P. Walsh that he had made a study of costs and prices with reference to industrial relations. In a well-prepared and concise statement, Lindbergh effectively summarized his basic approach to the whole problem. He emphasized that there existed an unfair distribution of wealth in the country, and that ordinary people were unknowingly paying part of the profits of speculation through various means, including interest and high prices. Using statistical examples, he argued that control of property by capitalists was largely due to the monopoly that bankers had over money and credit.[37]

In his testimony Lindbergh suggested that two remedies to

the situation were possible. One was pure socialism, but the people had refused to accept that solution. The other, which he advocated, was government action to take away money and credit control from the banks. One reason why this was not being done more quickly, Lindbergh said, was that there was a lack of political solidarity among "progressive Republicans, progressive Democrats, progressive Progressives, progressive Socialists, and others." But Congress, the legislatures, and the courts could and must be willing to work together to stop the favors of "special interests." The organization of farmers and industries might also be needed.[38] The main point, Lindbergh stressed in both his opening and final remarks to the commission, was simply that "no permanent reduction in the cost of living in favor of the masses can be secured as long as there is no relative rule for fixing a reasonable return for farm or other products and for labor, as compared with the so-called 'reasonable return' of capital." The *New York Times* carried the statement and on February 8 editorialized that Lindbergh's views on the relation between profits and wages was "a sort of economic trade unionism, or averaging returns to all who work either with their property, brains, or hands." Significantly, the findings of the commission validated certain of the criticisms, such as the concentration of wealth in the nation, that Lindbergh had persistently expressed throughout his congressional career.[39]

Lindbergh's involvement in other congressional matters during his fourth term from 1913 to early 1915 seem minuscule compared with his participation in the banking and currency controversy. Nonetheless, there were other political matters. He addressed the House for example, on such issues as the dominance of political party structure in framing the Underwood tariff bill (he opposed party government); the violation of the rights of Indians when whites seized their territories; the need for rural mail delivery reform; the inadvisability of requiring prospective immigrants to pass a literary test (Lindbergh said he knew Minnesotans who could not read who were more intelligent than those who could, and he feared discriminating against disadvantaged Europeans like the Poles; he would, however, vote for the overall immigration bill); the building of an Alaskan railroad that would involve government ownership of the railroad (which he favored); and public ownership of water power (which he also favored). On one occasion Lindbergh entered into the *Congressional Record* a speech about Swedish immigration by Nebraska congressman C. O. Lobeck. The Lobeck statement was both a brief statistical summary of Swedish-American population distribution in the United States and a laudatory résumé of Swedish-Americans' contributions to their adopted country in widely varying fields of endeavor. In 1913 and 1914 Lindbergh voted for the Underwood tariff bill, the repeal of Panama Canal tolls, and the Clayton Antitrust Act.[40] In early 1915, as a member of the House Committee on Banking and Currency, Lindbergh uncharacteristically joined Chairman Carter Glass in opposing President Wilson's inclusion of three administrative appointees on the proposed National Commission on Rural Credits. The committee voted three to one against the presidential appointees, and Lindbergh, according to the *New York Times,* played a "prominent part" in the action it headlined: "Congressman Lindbergh Gives President a Slap." In addition, there were Lindbergh resolutions and correspondence with constituents concerning post office boxes (he felt they should be free where there was no delivery); the construction of bridges across the Mississippi River; and the possibility of creating a reservoir on the Mississippi to control drainage in northern Minnesota.[41]

When the Mexican intervention crisis developed during the same period, Lindbergh expressed definite opinions concerning foreign affairs. Lindbergh, in this instance, believed that the United States had no business in Mexico. The Mexican troubles went back to the revolutionary overthrow of the Diaz regime and the eventual assumption of power by General Victoriano Huerta in 1913. This political instability caused numerous American investors in Mexico deep concern. The Taft administration had stayed fairly clear of the problem, but it had refused to recog-

nize the *de facto* government of Huerta. Wilson, inheriting the
Mexican problem, reasserted a policy of nonrecognition toward
Huerta. At this stage Lindbergh wrote both Taft and Wilson,
informing them that he spoke for his district in discouraging any
involvement or armed intervention in Mexico. "I do not think we
owe any protection to land speculations of our citizens in Mexico." Wilson was openly critical of Huerta, and United States–
Mexican tensions increased following the Tampico incident in
April, 1914. The incident involved the arrest and release of
American Marines by Mexican officers, after which Admiral
Henry T. Mayo demanded an apology and a twenty-one-gun
salute from Mexican officials. The request was denied, and President Wilson, anxious to see the end of the Huerta regime,
asked Congress for the authority to use force.[42]

During the House debate Lindbergh delivered a brief but
savage attack on those individuals who strived to promote war
between the United States and Mexico. He singled out speculative investors and jingoistic members of the press as the prime
agitators in this effort. Furthermore, Lindbergh argued, the
ritual involved in the twenty-one-gun salute incident was "an
exceedingly trivial thing as compared with the real problem of
war." In fact, he asserted, U.S. approval of Mayo's act, inconsistent with previous diplomatic posture, actually gave recognition to the Huerta government. Yet, Lindbergh conceded,
because of the president's announced desire for peace and the
constitutional rights of the office, he must vote for the resolution
on Mexico. It was the lesser of two evils. Still, Lindbergh warned,
"the final windup of this whole Mexican situation is likely to
lose us the respect of the world." In a letter to Eva, he explained
the Mexican affair another way. "The Mexican difficulty all arises
out of Wilson's telling another nation who not to elect as its
President." What if Americans were told by Germany, England,
or France that they could not elect Taft, Roosevelt, or Wilson,
he wondered. Said Lindbergh, "We cannot run the domestic
affairs of other countries without paying dearly for that sort of
fiddling."[43]

Lindbergh also made a strong statement condemning war in

general during his House appearance on April 20, 1914. War, he charged, impeded social progress at home and created huge debts, and people suffered as a result. In his opinion, the socialist view of war was the correct one. He presented these thoughts in his address:

War is paid for by the people. It is the slavery and drudgery that follows war that is more damaging than war itself. We glorify the soldier. We appeal to his pride and to his patriotism. The country treats him as a hero, and he is a hero. We call the country to honor him when he proves to be a hero. But what of those who drudge year after year all through life to make up for the destruction of war? They are the ones who are entitled to our sympathy, and more especially our consideration. I would rather die in action amid the thunder of cannon than by the drudgery that war brings to those who pay the cost. We are safe here in this House. The most of us are safe from the burden that war would bring. Are we therefore to be indifferent to the men and women who would really pay the toll? It would be taken out of their daily earnings for the rest of their lives and out of their children's earnings. And what are we to gain? An enormous debt and the loss of valuable lives.[44]

To anyone listening closely in 1914, Lindbergh's statement on Mexico would prove to be a preview of his forthcoming position on the European war. The immediate outcome of congressional action on Mexico, of course, brought American intervention that lasted until 1917.

Family and office matters underwent normal changes during Lindbergh's fourth term. His office staff was headed by Arthur Gorman, chief secretary and administrative assistant, throughout the period. In the spring of 1914 Lindbergh moved to new offices in the House office building. With two rooms and a storage area, he remarked that there would be a better chance of keeping the office tidy ("as long as some one else tidies it"), and that the new office would be cooler. The top-floor office also provided Charles, Jr. with some new challenges, including crawling about in the two- or three-foot space between the ceiling and the roof of the building (he could peer into offices around openings in the light fixtures), and running along a ledge walkway on the outside of the building. In the same year Senator

Clapp moved for Lindbergh's admittance as an attorney qualified to practice law before the Supreme Court of the United States. Also during 1914, Lindbergh made a trip to Minnesota to visit his mother during an illness from which she recovered. There is also evidence that Lindbergh, though a busy man, always found time whenever he could to devote to the affairs of his children.[45]

In 1913, for example, both Lindbergh and son Charles (aged eleven) learned to drive a car. Clifton Roberts, the brother of Loren Roberts (Lillian's husband), was the instructor. Charles later recalled that his father "had considerable difficulty learning to drive," a phenomenon not uncommon in 1913. Charles remembered on one occasion when his father, practicing a turning maneuver on a sand road on the farm, became confused by the foot pedals (there was no gear shift) in his 1912 Ford Model "T" touring car, and "backed hard into our sheep wire fence." Young Charles, riding in the back seat, said nothing, and afterward the elder Lindbergh never mentioned the incident. In general, Lindbergh had no particular aptitude for mechanics or working with tools, but he did master driving and used a car frequently after 1914. On young Charles's learning to drive, Lindbergh wrote Eva in July, 1913, that her brother may have been stretching the truth a bit when he told her that he had an automobile. "That is in his mind rather than in fact as he does not run it and it is for our work on campaigns." Lindbergh related that Charles had had the car out once, but, because of the sandy roads, someone had had to run it back for him. "He could run one in a city O.K.," stated his father. In any case, Charles did learn to drive that summer, and in the political campaigns ahead he would be a regular addition, as chauffeur, to Lindbergh's staff.[46]

Particularly noticeable in the Lindbergh correspondence during 1913 and 1914 is the beginning of an increasingly frequent exchange of letters between Lindbergh and his daughter Eva. This growing closeness between father and daughter would continue through the years ahead, and the letters are a valuable source of information on both the personal and public aspects of Lindbergh. Discussions in these years often centered around

Minnesota Historical Society

August Lindbergh and family in Minnesota, about 1873.
Left to right: August, Linda (in back), Juno, Charles, Louisa, Frank

August Lindbergh

Minnesota Historical Society

August Lindbergh homestead near Melrose, Stearns County, Minnesota.
Left to right: August, Louisa (on porch), Linda, Juno, Frank (with horse)

August Lindbergh (left) in bank at Melrose, Minnesota

Charles A. Lindbergh, Sr., about 1885

Charles A. Lindbergh, Jr.

Minnesota Historical Society

Captain Måns Olsson Lindbergh,
about 1865

Minnesota Historical Society and
Silker Studio, Little Falls, Minnesota

Eva Lindbergh Christie Spaeth

Mary ("May") La Fond Lindbergh

Eva (left) and Lillian Lindbergh,
ages eight and eleven, about 1900

The Lindbergh home at 608 Broadway East, Little Falls, Minnesota

Minnesota Historical Society

Mrs. Frank A. Lindbergh

Charles A. Lindbergh,

Frank Albert Lindbergh, about 1908

Charles A. Lindbergh, Sr., 1901

Evangeline Lodge Land Lindbergh
and Charles, Jr., 1902

Minnesota Historical Society

Minnesota Historical Society

Cabin on the west bank of the Mississippi River, where Charles A. and
Evangeline Lindbergh lived in 1901

Lindbergh house under construction, 1901

Minnesota Historical Society

Carl Bolander, about 1915

Magnus Bolander

Lindbergh family and friends on Lake Emily, near Brainerd, Minnesota, about 1907.
Standing, third from right, Charles, Sr.; seated, left to right,
Lillian, Evangeline, Charles, Jr., Eva

Minnesota Historical Society

Eva Lindbergh Christie Spaeth

Lillian Lindbergh, about 1905

Eva Lindbergh as a freshman
at Carleton College, 1911

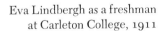

Eva Lindbergh Christie Spaeth

Minnesota Historical Socie

Representative Lindbergh and Charles, Jr. (see arrows) at the opening
session of the Sixtieth Congress, 1907

Lindbergh campaign poster, 1906

Lindbergh with Chippewa Indians at
Cass Lake, Minnesota, 1909

Minnesota Historical Society

Charles A. Lindbergh,

Minnesota Historical Society   *Minnesota Historical Society*

The Charles A. Lindberghs,
father and son, about 1910

Charles, Jr. with his dog Dingo

Charles, Sr. and Charles, Jr. hunting near Little Falls, about 1911

Minnesota Historical Society and Minnesota Division of State Parks

Minnesota Historical Society

Campaigning for Congress on the Minnesota-Canada border, 1914.
Lindbergh is in front of boat, at extreme right.

Lindbergh (center) with voters near Zippel Bay, in northern Minnesota, 1914

Minnesota Historical Society

Minnesota Historical Society

Charles A. Lindbergh, Sr., about 1915

Nonpartisan Leaguers boosting Lindbergh for governor
at Clarkfield, Minnesota, 1918

Lindbergh automobile caravan in rural Minnesota, 1918

Minnesota Historical Society

Lindbergh addressing a Nonpartisan League rally
near Cottonwood, Minnesota, 1918

A southern Minnesota example of
the bitterness of the 1918 campaign

Nonpartisan League support for reform
candidate Lindbergh, 1918

Minnesota Historical Society

Minnesota Historical Society

Minnesota Historical Society

Charles A. Lindbergh, Sr., about 1923

Eva's activities at Carleton College, where she was studying political economy and philosophy, and prospects for employment following graduation. At one point Lindbergh wrote his daughter about the problem of increasing world population. Those who write that the race is destroying itself because of population growth are pessimistic, he noted. He pointed out that intensive agricultural production could easily feed more people, and that "there is no danger of the food supply being exhausted within the next hundred years." But he did foresee trouble in the cities, and advised that some of its population "must return to the country." There were other, more personal observations in the letters, too. With regard to Eva's studies, Lindbergh emphasized, "I do not believe in overwork," but then he observed that she had never been worked very hard in terms of her abilities. In one note Lindbergh told Eva that he appreciated that she could make her own clothes, while in another letter he confessed that he did not like one particular picture of his daughter, because "I do not think it looks quite natural." Eva later explained that her father did not like the picture because it showed her dressed in evening clothes. On another occasion Eva was apparently unhappy because her father had not mentioned her good grades at school. In a revealing statement Lindbergh answered his daughter: "You need not think I failed to see your marks. The trouble with me is that I do not tell people when I am pleased. Unfortunately I tell them when I am not pleased."[47]

There are other glimpses of Lindbergh the man in these letters. The congressman related to his daughter, for example, his reactions, as well as those of others involved, when he encountered a twenty-seven-hour travel delay. During one thirteen-hour stop Lindbergh wrote a speech, while he "starved" and slept during other periods. He was amused that many people became quite nervous under these conditions. When one woman, recalling that she had seen his photograph in the newspapers, asked Lindbergh who he was, he told her that his name was Villa and that he was seeking recruits. Like most fathers of young women in college, Lindbergh sent notes about forgotten birthdays, the danger of impulsive spending (Eva had ordered a government book; it cost only $1.25, but some were $1.35, said her father), and, inevitably, the postscript, "I am enclosing you a small check."[48]

In 1914, as Eva neared graduation (Lindbergh did not attend the commencement exercises because of political commitments), she began the struggle of finding her first job. She relied heavily on her father's judgment, and he responded with patient and thorough advice although, significantly, he never dictated what she should do. "I want you," he wrote, "to be absolutely free to make your life what you wish it to be." The statement is profoundly characteristic in what it says about individual liberty and self-reliance. Lindbergh seemed pleased that his daughter would initially pursue a career, rather than marriage, since marriage, he maintained, "is usually the way to squelch a woman forever."[49]

Eva and two of her friends at Carleton, Hazel Aldrich and Eloise Gorman, decided to apply for teaching jobs at native Indian schools in Alaska during their senior year. As a result, Lindbergh examined prospects for new teachers in Alaska. He was not enthusiastic, and specifically objected to the plan to teach in native schools. He pointed out some of the realities of such a job to his daughter. Rough roads and poor food would be encountered. The fourth grade was the highest level in the native schools. Furthermore, "each teacher must practice as a doctor and nurse" for the children and often for the adults as well. In addition, said Lindbergh, "you will also have to take charge of a bunch of reindeer." At the same time, Lindbergh admitted that the young teachers would learn much about Indian life during such an experience, and he did write a letter to the governor of Alaska in their behalf. But Lindbergh's serious advice was to take jobs at white schools or none at all. Besides, in view of the Bureau of Education's reports of previous poor experience with young women fulfilling contracts, he doubted whether the three idealistic Carleton girls would receive any job offers at all.[50]

Lindbergh's prediction was correct, and Eva began to consider other job possibilities. For a time there was some discussion about Eva working with her father in the real estate business. Lindbergh's idea was to have Eva take charge of a quarterly journal on real estate and farms, with her pay consisting of a fixed salary plus an interest in the profits, to insure "enthusiasm." Eva also continued her search for a teaching position, making several contacts in Minnesota. By late summer, 1914, however, she still had not settled the job issue. At that point Lindbergh reassured his daughter that there would be work with him if a school did not materialize. "Remember there is nothing to worry about," he wrote, pointing out that within two weeks the matter would be settled. A few days later Eva accepted a teaching position at Akeley, a small community in the north central Minnesota lake country.[51]

When Eva began her first week of employment, Lindbergh sent his daughter warm and instructive letters of encouragement, telling her that he had great confidence in her success. He reminded her that teaching involved working with the minds of immature persons and required "an unusual amount of judgment as well as patience." He suggested the possibility of offering a five-minute discussion each day of some nation in the world, perhaps in Europe. He further advised:

There are two things that I caution you against, one is to steer clear of national prejudices, the other to steer clear of religious prejudices, and perhaps I should add a third, to steer clear of political prejudices. I do not mean to interfere with your privilege of having opinions upon these matters, but you are employed by the public to teach the children of that city, and they come from all sorts of homes so far as beliefs go, and it is a right of the parents that the school work be performed in such way as not to interfere with nationality prejudices, political prejudices, or religious prejudices, and when I say prejudices, I do so without any disrespect, but when you are out of school talking to the parents not in the presence of the children, if you wish to give your views on any subject, I would not discourage you from doing so, in fact, I don't believe in people tying themselves down, but merely exercising discretion as to when and where to give their views on these matters.[52]

Later that fall Lindbergh visited his daughter at Akeley, apologizing to his daughter prior to the trip that "by gorry, babe, I have not had time to get a suit." As Eva commented years afterward, "It was always a strenuous pull to get father to buy clothes." Eva wanted to use her first earnings to purchase a lasting gift for her father, and he suggested that a heavy watch chain or a plain gold ring would be good and not expensive. The gift was symbolic of the close bond between father and daughter, and Lindbergh felt strongly in these years that he would do all in his power to see more of his children in the future than his past years had allowed.[53]

Lindbergh's trip to Akeley in the fall of 1914 no doubt fitted into his campaign schedule for reelection as Sixth District congressman. Prior to his fifth congressional campaign, however, there had been another brief flirtation with the possibility of running for governor. In December, 1913, Lindbergh issued a somewhat nebulous public statement on the matter, pointing out that he was tied down with congressional duties but also noting that "I shall not say that I will not be a candidate." By late January, 1914, however, he had abandoned the governorship race. In a letter to one correspondent he stated simply: "My work does not permit me to be a candidate for any office at this time," explaining that he would actually prefer to work for the principles to which he was dedicated in private life, and that national jurisdiction, more than state affairs, affected the economic life of the people.[54]

Lindbergh's 1914 campaign was not as easy as his previous congressional contests of 1908, 1910, and 1912 had been. For the first time since the Lindbergh-Buckman primary of 1906, he faced genuine opposition. A strong feeling of regular Republicanism countering Lindbergh's maverick style of progressivism, plus the restructuring of the Sixth District, were the principal factors in this new challenge.[55] In the June primary, H. J. Maxfield of Wadena, a former state commissioner of immigration and a stand-pat Republican, filed against incumbent Lindbergh. Maxfield literature stressed what it considered the hypocrisy of Lindbergh running as a Republican candidate while his Congressional record indicated his repudiation of the Republican party. Lindbergh "'poses' as a Republican when he wants the votes and declares he is not a Republican just as soon as he has got the job," fumed the *Wadena Pioneer-Journal.* There was an element of truth in the charge, for at the beginning of the Sixty-third Congress Lindbergh, the only Republican to do so, had announced that he intended to attend Progressive party caucuses as a free agent and would not attend Republican party caucuses. The Bull Moose conference had approved his request, and Lindbergh had joined the eighteen other Progressive party members during the term. A Lindbergh brochure, meanwhile, emphasized his insurgent record in opposing Cannon, the Money Trust, the secret meetings of the Banking and Currency Committee, political bosses, and the "subsidized" press. Lindbergh also attended to local interests of the district and to farmers' wants, stated the literature. The progressive Republican approach still had appeal in the Sixth District, for the primary returns gave Lindbergh a 59.8 per cent majority. The election results in the June 16, 1914, primary were: Lindbergh—10,398; Maxfield—6,988. Of the eleven counties in the district, Maxfield carried only Beltrami (one of the two new counties in the district after reapportionment), Hubbard, and Wadena.[56]

The Democratic candidate in the traditionally Republican Sixth District in 1914 was Dr. J. A. Du Bois of Sauk Centre. His son Ben Du Bois recalled that his father entered the race because he felt that President Wilson would keep America out of war and needed Democratic support in Congress. Prohibition and Lindbergh's book on banking were not important campaign issues, the younger Du Bois noted, suggesting that his father probably agreed with many of Lindbergh's economic reform views. Candidate Du Bois, optimistic about success in 1914, spent ten thousand dollars of his own money in his campaign effort. The Democratic press eagerly supported him. Among anti-Lindbergh campaign arguments were statements that Lindbergh was a false Republican and had accomplished very little

in his eight years in Congress; that Du Bois, a "fearless progressive," would support President Wilson; and that votes for minor
candidates in the race would be lost. The *St. Cloud Daily Times*
divulged stand-pat Republican Franklin Eddy's criticism of
Lindbergh and outlined a partial record of bills introduced and
passed by Lindbergh.[57] According to the paper, this record included approximately two hundred bills, of which 141 were
private pension bills, introduced by Lindbergh during his eight
years in the House. Of these nearly two hundred bills, stated the
Times, only two bridge bills, two dam bills, two public building bills, and twenty-five pension bills had been passed.[58]

Although the Democratic campaign against him was unsuccessful once again in November, Lindbergh failed for the first
time in his political career to receive an absolute majority in a
Sixth District race. In the general election Lindbergh received a
plurality of 47.5 per cent, while Du Bois received a total of 35.2
per cent. Minor candidates Otto M. Thomason, a Socialist, and
Thomas J. Sharkey, a Progressive, received 11.6 and 5.7 per cent,
respectively, with Thomason showing strength in Aitkin, Beltrami, and Crow Wing counties. The splintering of votes, which
probably included some anti-Lindbergh Republican votes for
the other three candidates, accounted for the smaller percentage
given Lindbergh. The final tabulations of the November 3 election were: Lindbergh—15,364; Du Bois—11,409; Thomason—
3,769; Sharkey—1,836. Shortly after the election, Lindbergh
wired Eva: "I carried by a good majority all but Stearns
[County]. Everything O.K." In the same election Minnesotans
selected Democrat Winfield S. Hammond of St. James as their
governor over his Republican opponent, Long Prairie banker
William E. Lee. The European war, although front-page news,
was not a political issue in any of these campaigns. But the importance of the war in American politics, including the role of
Congressman Lindbergh, would change dramatically as Lindbergh began his fifth term in the nation's capital.[59]

Chapter VIII

Opponent of War

"It is true that Europe is ablaze and the destruction of life and property is tremendous; but nothing should be destroyed here as a result of the war, so why should we allow the European war to destroy our reason?"[1] Thus questioned Congressman Lindbergh on September 25, 1914, not long after the beginning of hostilities in Europe. The outbreak of World War I forced America to take a position with regard to European affairs, and President Woodrow Wilson responded with an immediate declaration of neutrality. But the degree and nature of the United States commitment to a neutral posture was far from settled, and the controversy that surrounded American neutrality and the European war from August, 1914, to April, 1917, was launched.[2] During this long debate Lindbergh remained firm in his objection to American involvement. Convinced that an "inner circle," composed chiefly of financial interests, was promoting American intervention,[3] Lindbergh became clearly identified as an opponent of war throughout the neutrality period. It was a courageous stand, but in the end his outspoken criticism on the war issue would bring him personal abuse and political defeat.

Lindbergh's comments on the war in the fall of 1914 were occasioned by discussion of the war revenue tax proposed by the Wilson administration. Because the European war had interrupted international trade, the federal government faced a sharp decline in its general revenue from customs receipts. Consequently, President Wilson and Secretary of the Treasury William

McAdoo decided that the most desirable course of action to meet this anticipated deficit was to levy new taxes. The basic bill called for $100,000,000 in additional revenue coming from increased taxes on beer and wine, tobacco manufacturers, bankers and brokers, and bonds, bills of sales, mortagages, and the like. Although some modifications were made in the bill during the congressional debate in September and October, its main tax thrust was aimed at the "wet" Northern and Midwestern cities and at the business community.[4]

In his House speech Lindbergh argued that there was no place for a war tax when the United States was not at war. "The only way we could get into a war would be to go around with a chip on our shoulder challenging other nations to knock it off." As Lindbergh analyzed the situation, Congress was being asked to vote on a war tax only "because our finances are run by speculators." In his opinion the economy was based on a "false system," and the war was a "mere excuse" for emergency legislation that would benefit the speculators. In a well-established Lindbergh line of thought, the Minnesota congressman pointed out that most Americans involved in productive work received only a portion of the value of what they produced. "The other part is taken by monopoly and becomes capital."[5]

Also characteristic of Lindbergh was his inclusion of several tables and charts in his September 25 speech. One table, used by Lindbergh several times during his congressional career, outlined the value of one dollar "invested for 100 years at compound interest computed by the method practiced by the bankers."

TABLE NO. 1[6]

6 per cent amounts to	$340
8 per cent amounts to	2,203
10 per cent amounts to	13,808
12 per cent amounts to	84,075
18 per cent amounts to	15,145,007
24 per cent amounts to	2,551,798,404

Thus, argued Lindbergh, those who own property and control money and credit possess an unfair advantage under the present economic system. In a second, more lengthy table, Lindbergh divided employed Americans into twelve classes according to range of income. According to his figures some 37,815,000 citizens earned average incomes of $601, while the remaining work force of only 425,000 persons had average income ranging from $4,500 to $1,500,000. (No date of sample or length of income period was given, but it is reasonable to assume that the figures were based on current data for yearly income.) As a result, said Lindbergh, most people were underpaid and overworked, and the condition "will increase instead of diminish as long as property—dead material—is socially and legally given a better status than human life."[7]

The crux of the problem, stated Lindbergh, was Wall Street. Unwilling to use $75,000,000 of government money which New York banks held as a basis for the credit system, they would force the $100,000,000 war tax on farmers and wage earners. Instead of the war tax, asserted Lindbergh, the secretary of the treasury should issue non-interest-bearing notes in an amount necessary for government needs and for use as legal tender. Because the tax bill had been handled in committee and secret caucus, without benefit of amendment, Lindbergh introduced an amendment concerning treasury notes directly on the House floor. But Lindbergh's maneuver made little impact, and the House approved the war tax measure the same day by a 234 to 135 vote. In the opinion of the Sixth District *St. Cloud Daily Journal-Press,* Lindbergh's views had a "greenback flavor." But the paper admired his ability to talk back to Wall Street and the subsidized press, "even if he does propose some joke admendments." The war tax bill experienced some opposition from the "cotton bloc" in the Senate, but it was finally passed by that body. On October 22, 1914, both houses approved the conference report and President Wilson signed the bill.[8]

During the early months of 1915 Lindbergh's thinking on the European war seemed to fit the mood of most Americans. Certainly there was an awareness of the war, but its horror somehow seemed remote. Strict neutrality was generally favored, particularly in the Midwest, and Lindbergh's views were not inconsistent with public opinion in his home area. At the same time, however, Lindbergh was openly concerned about the direction the war might take and about its possible effects on the United States. In February, 1915, he wrote Eva that "it looks like a long drawn contest, but in the spring it will be more fierce in all likelihood." More explicit were his statements labeling foreign loans and press propaganda as factors that would probably draw the United States into the conflict. "It is my belief that we are going in as soon as the country can be sufficiently propagandized into the war mania," he warned.[9]

Lindbergh's fears were compounded by the increase of German submarine operations and the attendant American difficulties on the high seas. With the sinking of the Cunard passenger liner *Lusitania* in May came a wave of public concern in the United States, due to the loss of 128 American lives. President Wilson sent strong notes to the German government about the incident, and subsequently pacific Secretary of State William Jennings Bryan resigned. In Minnesota and elsewhere there was a strong showing of unity in support of the president. Ironically, Minnesota senator Moses Clapp termed American involvement "inconceivable," for "it is foolish to talk of nations three thousand miles apart fighting each other, because it cannot be done." No specific comment on the *Lusitania* incident by Lindbergh is present in his extant letters, but it is safe to assume that the turn of events disturbed him. Although public opinion was still strongly in favor of neutrality, Americans, Minnesotans included, began to realize that the United States might become involved in the turmoil, and efforts for both peace and preparedness took on new meaning.[10]

Later in 1915, Lindbergh expressed further views on the European war in his new journal, *Real Needs: A Magazine of Co-ordination.* The first issue (there were two printings of the first 192-page issue; subsequently a less lengthy second, and apparently final, number, dealing with Lindbergh's familiar economic themes and including special articles on the labor question, was published in June, 1916)[11] was a pocket-sized volume containing articles on several topics ranging from "The Existing Capitalistic System" and "Do You Want to Lose Your Money?" to "Commercializing Sentiment at the Risk of War" and "The Invasion of the United States by Canada." Its purpose, said its editor, was to present material ordinarily "kept from the public." Although the regular subscription price was set at one dollar per annum, Lindbergh stated that many free copies would be mailed, and he suggested that readers pass on their copies to others who could also read its message. *Real Needs* also offered twenty- and ten-dollar prizes for the best articles submitted on "Farm Life" and "City Life." Lindbergh had expected to draw on the talents of economists for material, but the first volume of *Real Needs* revealed that virtually everything was written by its editor. In one section of the magazine, for instance, he printed the principal part of a lengthy congressional speech delivered in early 1915. The address was basically a restatement of his views on money and banking. Although Lindbergh wrote that "*Real Needs* is not published as a reform magazine," the material it aimed to present, generally suppressed by the metropolitan press, realistically included Lindbergh's reform thought. No documented circulation or cost figures for the little magazine, printed at the National Capital Press, exist, but Lindbergh claimed in the June issue of *Real Needs* that over fifty thousand copies of the March number had been distributed at a postage cost of nearly one thousand dollars.[12]

Real Needs attacked the Money Trust and the "subsidized" press for encouraging involvement in the European war. "Nothing but trouble to the United States will come out of the Money Trust speculation, with the foreign war nations," Lindbergh warned. He charged that the "Wall Street end of the Federal Reserve System" was aiding in the financing of the Allies, indirectly using treasury funds and depositors' money in the process. Already interest rates were higher than normal because of financial involvement with Europe, said Lindbergh, and he noted that his minority report on the Federal Reserve System had predicted such a development in the event of a European crisis. The "intermingling of finances," he argued, was the likely means by which the Money Trust sought to enter the United States into the war, which, he maintained, was itself the result of "commercial greed."[13] On the foreign loan matter, he wrote:

> The war loans, while they are not unlikely to be the means of involving us in war, will never be directly named as such. The subsidized portion of the press will be used in an attempt to trump up collateral incidents out of which to fan a blaze of public indignation to the extent of creating a war fever. The pretense that these war loans are to help the "poor farmer" and the "poor wage worker" is the limit. Examine what happened to the produce market, independent of what it would be influenced anyway by the war, and then examine what happened to the stock market and compare the two. Then you will see what the war loans were for. Both the produce and the stock markets will be found in the daily press.
>
> The war bonds are certain to be repudiated within a few years. No one should buy these bonds with the hope of collecting them in full.[14]

By late 1915 and early 1916 American thinking with regard to the European war began to change. With the sinking of the *Lusitania* and, later, that of the *Arabic,* support for strict neutrality lessened, and criticism of Germany's submarine operations increased. Most Americans still favored neutrality to the point of noninvolvement in the war itself, but there was a growing demand for unqualified insistence on the rights of neutrals at sea, and increasing public concern over the issue of military preparedness. For many people, even in Minnesota, the questions of different national sympathies, business opportunities, and the advisability of complete isolation were now overshadowed by the recognition of the European war as a phenomenon affecting the national honor and security of the United States. Thus attention was focused on the problems of neutral rights and an adequate defense system for the nation, and the military preparedness controversy was under way.[15]

Lindbergh and other congressmen were presented with a test of their views on neutral rights at sea and submarine warfare in March, 1916, with the debate and vote on the Gore-McLemore resolutions. When Secretary of State Robert Lansing indicated that the administration was withdrawing its support of the *modus vivendi* proposal to disarm merchant vessels, many congressional leaders, fearing that this abrupt shift in administration policy meant a greater possibility of war involvement, put forward opposing legislation. Jeff McLemore, Democrat of Texas, introduced a resolution in the House stating that Americans should refrain from traveling aboard armed vessels of belligerent nations, and Thomas P. Gore of Oklahoma proposed a similar resolution in the Senate. For a time it seemed unclear whether the president or the Congress was directing American foreign policy on the matter. President Wilson effectively countered the congressional revolt, however, noting that any abridgement of rights at sea would represent capitulation to the Germans and would disturb the rules of international law. The president emphasized that his diplomatic moves were guided by a desire to avoid war, not to promote it. Congress reacted positively to Wilson's explanation, and within days steps were taken to table the Gore-McLemore resolutions. On March 3 the Senate, by a 68 to 14 vote, tabled the Gore resolution in support of the president, while on March 7 the House of Representatives registered a 276 to 142 vote tabling the McLemore resolution.[16]

Lindbergh voted with the minority on the McLemore resolution. In doing so, he joined 101 other Republicans, 33 Democrats, 5 Progressives, 1 Independent, and 1 Socialist in voting against tabling; House members voting in favor of tabling included 128 Democrats, 93 Republicans, and 1 Progressive. The Democratic vote clearly reflected political pressure from the president and the nearness of fall elections, whereas the Republican vote revealed a substantial division of opinion on the issue. Most conspicuous was the sectional nature of the Republican split. The majority of House Republicans who voted against tabling came from the Midwest; they included the entire delegations from Wisconsin, Iowa, Minnesota, Nebraska, and North Dakota. Within this group were most of the original insurgents in the progressive wing of the party. Conversely the majority of Republicans voting for tabling came from Eastern states and were identified with the conservative wing of the party.[17]

Lindbergh's vote against tabling was no surprise, for he never deviated from his contention that "special privilege" groups were behind any movement that might involve the United States in the European war. In addition, he may have been influenced by the substantial German-American and Scandinavian-American populations in his home district. The ethnic identification with an isolationist position on foreign policy does not hold true in all cases, however, for Norwegian-born Senator Knute Nelson was the only Minnesotan in either house of Congress to vote for tabling the Gore-McLemore resolutions. Indeed, Nelson remained a strong advocate of preparedness and insisted on the rights of neutrals at sea throughout the period. Senator Moses Clapp and the nine Minnesota congressmen who voted against tabling were criticized for their action (the Democratic *Duluth Herald,* for example, referred to the vote as the "everlasting shame of Minnesota"), but in truth public opinion in the state was still divided on the armed neutrality and preparedness issues.[18]

Lindbergh explained his negative vote on tabling the McLemore resolution more fully in a presentation before the House on March 10. "Mr. Speaker," queried Lindbergh, "where did the edict come from that says all America may be juggled in order to protect foolhardy or designing speculators whenever they wish to travel on armed merchant ships controlled by nations at war?" Lindbergh vigorously attacked "special privilege" groups for promoting the war, stating:

At no period in the world's history has deceit been so bold and aggressive as now in attempting to engulf all humanity in the maelstrom of hell. The whole world is sizzling in the "melting pot." Sober men and women who measure the conditions with unselfish judgment and suggest sane action are pounced upon by the devils in command of the "hell-storm" in an attempt to have them labeled "cowards" and to force us into war over a standard of false national honor. Many of the highest officers of Government fail to sustain their moral courage for common sense, and add to the confusion of the excited by trying to support the demands of speculators.

Amid all this confusion the lords of "special privilege" stand serene in their selfish glee, coining billions of profit from the rage of war. They coldly register every volley of artillery, every act of violent aggression, as a profit on their war stock and war contracts. They commercialize every excitement, scalp in and out of the market alternately, taking a profit both ways on a fluctuating market.[19]

In Lindbergh's opinion, the American public had been "buncoed" on the war issue by "invisible organizers," and he warned that "special privilege" interests operated, often unknown to the public, through such agencies as the Rockefeller Institute, the Carnegie Foundation, the big-city press, and the U.S. Chamber of Commerce. On the surface, these organizations did beneficial work, said Lindbergh, but underlying that work were schemes carried out by the "inner circle" for selfish purposes. Lindbergh asserted specifically that the same "inner circle" that controlled the Chamber of Commerce was the busiest promoter of war armament propaganda, and he questioned whether it was patriotic to "insist on the right of a few Americans to travel on armed merchant ships, while a hundred million Americans who have not the means to travel, even if they wished, must take a chance to toil still more and secure less and drag out their existence on earth to support this claim in case we get into war over it."[20]

In the same speech, Lindbergh focused part of his antiwar attack on the general issue of preparedness. The word itself, he maintained, "according to its most frequent use, comes under the title 'deception as a fine art.' It was seized on by the war-munition lords as a substitute for 'armament,' because armament would suggest what was really meant." In Lindbergh's judgment, this was another instance of deception through wording. The same dishonest practice had been used when "special privilege" fooled the public on the meaning of "reciprocity," and when the phrase "Federal reserve banks" was publicized as referring to national banks "when, in fact, a more powerful Money Trust was created." Real preparedness, said Lindbergh, would involve abandoning false ideals and exercising common sense in dealing with actual conditions. War, he believed, was a violation of all law, and a total effort must be directed at stopping such conflagrations rather than adding to them. Emphatically, Lindbergh noted: "To seek to apply 'national honor' with no thought of existing conditions and without view of the general welfare is weakness instead of strength, foolhardy instead of brave, traitorous rather than patriotic."[21]

On foreign policy, he argued that the United States could not both follow the Monroe Doctrine and interfere with the affairs of Europe and Asia. In his opinion involvement in Europe was absurd, and "if we hold to it we will have to fight the world without a cause." Further, said Lindbergh, nations at war would utilize every possible means in attempting to destroy each other. Hence it was natural that merchant ships carrying war contraband would be attacked, and he asserted flatly that it was wrong for Americans or the citizens of other neutral nations to travel on these ships. The only possible way in which this might be allowed was to be certain the passengers clearly understood that they were traveling at their own risk. Lindbergh also charged that the production of war materials for export was contrary to the meaning of preparedness, for it furnished other nations with supplies that could be used against the United States. In short, it "is a crime not only against humanity but in contradiction to conservation." More sensible as a true step toward preparedness, he advised, would be an embargo. He also attacked private loans to belligerent nations, and he included a long segment from the "Commercializing Sentiment at the Risk of War" article from *Real Needs* in exposing speculator activity. If most of the money being absorbed by the profiteers could be kept in local regions, he observed, the defense needs of the country could be met by these funds alone—assuming, of course, that Americans did not want a regular professional army and navy.[22]

During late March and early April Lindbergh continued to assail the "speculators" in extended remarks before the House of Representatives. "Mr. Speaker, think of it!" he exclaimed at the outset of one speech. "Two per cent of the people own 60 per cent of all the wealth, while 98 per cent of the people own only 40 per cent." It was a familiar Lindbergh theme, and he referred to this "dollar plutocracy" as "the greatest foe to humanity." In his judgment, its presence was proof that the economic system was fundamentally a false one, and America's first responsibility was to correct this problem. "Our internal difficulties are many and acute, injustice prevails, and the actual danger is greater from within than from without." The immediate danger, of course, was that the "special interests" were the most active disseminators of war propaganda.[23]

Lindbergh offered an unusual and, at the time, radical idea as one important step toward solving the problem. He boldly advocated that the profit motive be totally removed from all business related to the production of war materials. "Let there be no profit in any war enterprise," he asserted. Then he pointed out that stockbrokers, munitions makers, and other contractors in war supplies had made a profit of two billion dollars in the preceding eighteen months. Obviously such profits helped to stimulate desires to expand and prolong war activities. Instead of this "commercialism" in war supplies, "let the Government immediately build all the factories and establish every agency to make its own preparations complete."[24]

His views on "Standing by the President" probably seemed unorthodox, too. He maintained that on most occasions citizens should back their president on major national decisions, and he cited his own support of Wilson's intervention in Mexico even though he did not think the action was wise. In a March 20, 1916, House statement, however, Lindbergh declared: "When a citizen has done all he can to reconcile his views with the President's action and is unable to do so he has a right to follow what he believes to be the right course, not only a right but a duty. This is not a monarch's country." Unless people were willing to stand by their own conviction, Lindbergh emphasized, "Our form of government would be a farce." Clearly, to Lindbergh, speaking out against the European war was one such duty.[25]

During his House presentations Lindbergh bemoaned the fact that economic preparedness was being overlooked in the rush of sentiment for military preparedness. He did believe that young men should learn the art of self-defense and that the nation should be strong against foreign invaders; his main argument concerned his own explanation of "true" preparedness. That preparedness lay with an equitable economic system and an independent people. Unless "special privilege" and the "subsidized press" could be stopped, he argued, such military preparedness efforts would make "industrial slaves" of the "plain people," the nation's consumers, producers, and "toilers." Already, for instance, the average price of gasoline had risen to between twenty-two and thirty cents per gallon, twice what it had been a year ago, and farmers' demands for rural credits had been undermined by urgent requests relating to the European war. Ultimately, predicted Lindbergh, this form of preparedness would create "disloyalty, weakness, and in the end [will] result in a fall of the Nation."[26]

By 1916 Lindbergh became convinced that America would enter the war, and, according to friends and biographers Lynn and Dora Haines, "that meant bigger, more vital struggles for him." Thus Lindbergh did not seek reelection to his seat in the House of Representatives, but instead considered the political possibilities of the governorship of Minnesota or a seat in the U.S. Senate, which "would give him a larger field for usefulness." Actually he had had political aspirations to higher office long before the European war, but his deep conviction on the issue probably influenced his desire to reach a wider political audience. His decision may also have been affected by his frustration at not getting progressive legislation through the House—a natural result, in part, of his ten years as a constant congressional critic— and by rumors that former congressman C. B. Buckman would try for his old Sixth District seat.[27]

Lindbergh was first mentioned in May, 1915, as a gubernatorial contender with prohibition-oriented support for the 1916 election. He explained to the press at the time that he "much preferred" the freedom of private life, "but that does not imply that I will or will not be a candidate." He officially announced his candidacy for governor on October 2, noting that he was not a candidate "in a personal sense," but that he sought the office because he had "political and industrial" plans that would bene-fit the general welfare of Minnesotans. His candidacy received diverse reactions from the press. The *Minneapolis Journal* re-ferred to him as "The Mysterious Lindbergh," noting that he had "deftly excited the public's curiosity" with his promise to solve all the political ills of the state. The conservative Republican *Journal*, declaring that junior senator Moses Clapp would have a problem running in the Republican primary because of his anti-Republican record, editorialized: "If Mr. Lindbergh could leave his test tubes, retorts, and bottles for a few minutes, he might out of his own rich experience give Moses a little help in solving that mystery." The *St. Cloud Journal-Press,* following the same anti-Lindbergh line, joshed that he "would have been a wonderful success as the leader of some occult society" and, while admitting that he was a "clever politician," charged that Lind-bergh "could not be induced to vote for a bill which he had not himself prepared and introduced in Congress." On the other hand, such papers as the *Little Falls Daily Transcript,* the *Alexandria Post-News,* the *Litchfield News Ledger,* and the *Mel-rose Beacon* came to Lindbergh's defense, praising his political independence, national reputation, and apparent ability to put a scare into the Republican press.[28]

The sudden death of Minnesota Governor Winfield S. Ham-mond in December, 1915, altered Lindbergh's plans. Hammond, a Democrat, was succeeded by Lieutenant Governor J. A. A. Burnquist, a Republican, and Lindbergh, receiving personal assurances that the principles and aims of the new governor were "in accord" with his own views, withdrew from the gubernatorial race on February 21, 1916. Encouraged by political associate Lester Bartlett, he then filed as a candidate in the Republican primary for the U.S. Senate. On January 13, Bartlett had written: "C A LISTEN HERE! When we know that the gangsters are making deals all the time to beat the people out of their rights what is wrong with our side making a deal if we can that will give the people what they want?" In Bartlett's mind such a "deal" would be support for a slate including Roosevelt for president, Lindbergh for senator, Burnquist for governor, and Dr. J. A. Du Bois of Sauk Centre for Sixth District congressman. The combination, he advised, would be "invincible." Bartlett also emphasized in his letter that Lindbergh's major work was really more suited to the national approach of the Senate than to the position of governor. "You can take care of your friends, lecture, travel, and edit your magazine and have a h--- of a time—do five times as much for the people as you can as governor and do it easier."[29]

Lindbergh apparently agreed with Bartlett, but it seemed strange that he should choose to run against the incumbent Senator Clapp of St. Paul. Clapp, who had served in the Senate since 1901, had a solid reputation as a progressive Republican. Like Lindbergh, Clapp had shown a certain disdain for party regularity in the Congress and had been unwavering in his support of such movements as the insurgent opposition to Taft in 1912. However, because he had never been elected by a direct popular vote and did not have total support from the progressives, Clapp was uncertain about his own candidacy.[30] Whether anti-Clapp forces exerted pressure on Lindbergh to enter the race is unknown, but there is the simple political fact that Lindbergh, committed to end his tenure as Sixth District congressman and obliged to bow out of the gubernatorial race, faced the choice of either running for the Senate or not running for anything.[31]

As the 1916 campaign developed, four well-known and well-qualified candidates entered the Republican senatorial primary race. In addition to Congressman Lindbergh and Senator Clapp, the candidates were A. O. Eberhart, former Republican governor of the state, and Frank B. Kellogg, a former St. Paul lawyer and nationally famous "trust buster" during the Roosevelt administration. A revealing commentary on the unusual primary race, but more important, on Lindbergh's own career and "behind-the-scenes" maneuvering by progressives, is a letter from Senator

La Follette to Minnesotan James Manahan supporting Clapp over Lindbergh:

I understand Lindbergh has announced as a candidate and that Clapp will be opposed by him, Eberhart, and Kellogg. Out of this mess Jim Hill will get either Kellogg or Eberhart and probably the later. . . . I write in a friendly way to give you my view.

It seems to me it would be a mistake for our friends to divide their strength between Clapp and Lindbergh. Such division can only result in turning that seat in the Senate over to the Steel Trust. It will divide the people who ought to stand together and in all probability Eberhart would slip in. He would not have the ability of Kellogg, but his vote would count the same.

Realizing the uselessness of talking with Lindbergh as he has his head set, I am writing to you, to ask, if you are to be a candidate yourself, and as no announcement has been made, I take it you are not. If that is the situation will you not do what you can to hold our friends back of Clapp.

The Senator has often disappointed you and he frequently takes a course which provokes all of us, but on the whole he has made a good record. On the basic issue he is right. No man in the Senate has during the past six years given his time on the stump more unselfishly than Clapp for the extension of democracy, through his advocacy of the initiative, referendum, recall of officials, the direct primary, direct election of Senators, Presidential primary law, woman suffrage, and all the kindred subjects affecting the right of the people to govern themselves. . . .

In service and ability he is superior to any of the announced candidates. On some questions he is not as radical as Lindbergh, but as a Senator he has such standing as makes it possible for him to render greater service than any of the candidates. If he is defeated by any of the men in the field other than Lindbergh, his defeat would rightly be regarded by the country as a set back to our cause, if by Lindbergh, our enemies would rejoice because the later would not have Clapp's rugged fighting strength. Clapp can get a hearing in the Senate. He can accomplish more for the general movement than any of the announced candidates.[32]

In essence, what La Follette says about Lindbergh is simply that his effectiveness in Congress was limited, whereas from the view of practical politics Clapp could do more for the progressive cause. Certainly Lindbergh supported all the reforms that La

Follette mentions in connection with Clapp, but his role as constant critic had taken its toll. La Follette may also have been
miffed at Lindbergh's support of Roosevelt in 1912; however,
Clapp had backed Roosevelt, too. La Follette's remark that Lindbergh was more "radical" than Clapp on some issues in all likelihood refers to Lindbergh's economic positions. Manahan's reply
to La Follette is unknown, but, in view of an earlier experience
involving Clapp, it seems likely that his enthusiasm for Clapp
would be limited. Ultimately, he supported Kellogg.[33]

During the brief spring campaign the preparedness question
emerged as a major political issue. Lindbergh and Clapp remained firm in their opposition to expanded military preparedness. Eberhart was identified with traditional Republicanism and
was the least vocal of the candidates on preparedness, while
Kellogg waged a vigorous campaign in support of preparedness,
stressing that Americans "should immediately prepare this country for defense" and "maintain the national honor and the high
standard of protecting American rights." In a May 25 letter to
Edmund Pennington, Kellogg expressed the opinion that "Lindbergh and Clapp represent nothing except all the follies and
absurdities of every 'ism' imaginable" and that Eberhart was
simply "straddling" on the issue to gain votes. In late May there
was also a brief stir in the newspapers over the fact that Magnus
Martinson, a former Lindbergh secretary and supporter on the
temperance issue, came out for Kellogg because of the candidate's stand for "Americanism."[34]

During the later stages of the campaign, Lindbergh and Kellogg exchanged several personal letters dealing with the preparedness issue. Lindbergh initiated the correspondence on
May 29, 1916, requesting that Kellogg join him in an open meeting to discuss political and economic questions and to give the
public an opportunity to question the candidates directly. Obviously disturbed by Kellogg's position on the preparedness issue,
he told him: "Your campaign statements make it appear that you
are a militarist." Lindbergh then explained his own views on
preparedness, singling out such themes as the need for basic

economic reform to counter the Money Trust, the need to take profits out of war-materials production, and the clear lesson to be learned from European militarism and its resultant war. In true preparedness, argued Lindbergh, since the "plain people" would drill and man the armed services, the "rich" should contribute all the necessary funds. As Lindbergh informed Kellogg: "I favor safe and sane preparedness to protect us against unfriendly nations if they attack us, but I oppose turning our country into a military camp."[35]

Kellogg replied to Lindbergh on June 5, declining the offer to join Lindbergh in a public meeting. His reasons were twofold: (1) It was late in the campaign and his speaking engagements were "practically all arranged for"; and (2) he had already brought his views before Minnesotans, so such a meeting would add little to "enlighten" the public. Kellogg agreed with Lindbergh on the need to defend America against foreign attack, but he further elaborated on his interpretation (which Lindbergh had misconstrued, he said) of the full meaning of preparedness. That included, Kellogg maintained, the necessity "to protect our borders against invasion; to protect American citizens on the high seas and in foreign countries; to protect American commerce, and to maintain the national honor and stability and permanency of our institutions."[36]

In early June, Lindbergh, invited to present the commencement address at Gustavus Adolphus College in St. Peter, used the opportunity to express his views on preparedness and the war. Although the sword may determine for a time "how and by whom nations shall be ruled," Lindbergh stated, "it can never determine how people shall live. . . . These are problems of the mind and their solution is written into the forms of national and international law by the force of public opinion." He challenged the graduates to work for this necessary change in the fields of government and business. Lindbergh questioned whether the national honor of the United States was at stake in a European war, and he made a major point of emphasizing the depletion of natural resources fostered in wartime by the trusts (especially the Copper, Steel, Oil, and Shoe trusts), which, in turn, created higher prices for American consumers. That, he stressed, "constitutes waste, not conservation."[37]

An interesting view of Lindbergh's 1916 campaign, and of one aspect of his son's early teen-age years, may be found in a short diary that Charles, Jr. kept during the campaign. Fourteen-year-old Charles was given the task of driving the new Saxon car during the campaign, and his entries reveal something of their day-to-day activities from April 22 through June 8, during which time they covered more than three thousand miles. According to the diary, Lindbergh's campaign was based in Minneapolis and the St. Cloud-Little Falls area, with periodic swings through southern, northeastern, and central Minnesota. At times young Charles and Gust Raymond, a Lindbergh associate, traveled together distributing literature and making contacts, while Lindbergh himself, because of unreliable roads, was forced to take the train. For young Charles the campaign meant listening to speeches on some occasions and handing out literature to farmers or at the steelworks at Duluth, but any real interest or understanding on his part of political issues was limited. At one point he did note the specific reason for a campaign stop at Heron Lake. "That is where a banker is that is down on us and Father gave it to him in the money trust book so we distributed some there."[38]

One incident during the 1916 senatorial campaign made a particular impression on the elder Lindbergh, and young Charles recorded the event.

When we were about 16 miles from Duluth the gas got low and we didn't know if we had enough to last us or not and there were no side stations before West Duluth so when we got to the top of one of the many hills which surround Duluth we would turn off the gas and let the machine coast down. This went all right until we got to the top of the highest hill looking over West Duluth and we started to coast down but the hill got steeper and steeper and as it curved around a lot we could not see the end of it. Then I put on brakes that stopped the progress until they got loose and the hill got steeper. We were going so fast that the gear wouldn't go in and then in front of us down the steepest part of the hill was the railroad track and a freighter in the middle. The gate was down and there was no way to stop. A slight rise in the ground (about 50 ft. from the track) slowed us down a little but the gate was right in front of us. We were going from 15 to 20 miles per and if we went through the gate we might hit the train beyond. There was a slight opening (about the width of the car) between the gate and the track and full of deep clay. I turned into that and as there was nothing could go through it we stopped in about ten feet. Nothing was hurt but there was no getting out of that hole so we got a grocery team but both it, ten or so men, and the power of the car couldn't get us out. Then the yardmaster came along and offered us a tow out with a locomotive that was near by. When it got on the cable it just lifted the car right out and we went on.[39]

After the incident was over, Lindbergh told his son that it was only "proper" that they should have been pulled out by the locomotive, because the freight train had been occupying the tracks longer than the legal time limit. But Lindbergh, who had applied the emergency brake to no avail on the downhill ride, was most concerned as to whether "there couldn't be an emergency arrangement whereby a metal rod, like a crow-bar, could be dropped down through the center of the car as a quick stop in case the brakes failed." Years afterward, Charles, Jr. wrote that his father "had no concept of the effects of inertia or of the stresses that would be involved in such a device," adding that "this was the only time I knew him to suggest a mechanical invention."[40]

Minnesotans handed Lindbergh his first political defeat on June 19, 1916. Kellogg, carrying fifty-four of the eighty-six counties in the state, easily outdistanced his opponents and emerged victorious in the four-way race for the Senate. The results in the Republican primary were: Kellogg—73,818; Eberhart—54,890; Clapp—27,668; Lindbergh—26,094. Lindbergh carried only eight counties, five of which were in the Sixth Congressional District. It is clear that the preparedness theme drew support from Minnesotans, for the number of votes given preparedness advocate Kellogg was roughly 20,000 more than the combined total given antipreparedness candidates incumbent Senator Clapp and Congressman Lindbergh. Yet it seems equally clear that the campaign emphasis on preparedness was, in part, a deliberate propaganda effort by the state's urban press following the strong noninterventionist vote by Minnesota congressmen on the Gore-McLemore resolutions. Furthermore, the impact of Kellogg's victory is lessened by the fact that, with Eberhart's vote, the total support given the three other candidates exceeded Kellogg's total by 35,000 votes. Without doubt Kellogg's national fame and general popularity contributed to his victory. Reaction to his general antipreparedness stand was certainly a factor in Lindbergh's first political defeat in 1916, but perhaps just as important were the unusual nature of the four-cornered race and the simple fact that it was his first attempt in campaigning for public office on a state-wide level.[41]

In the November general election that followed Republicans Kellogg, Governor Burnquist, and Harold Knutson, a St. Cloud newspaperman, were elected to the positions of senator, governor, and Sixth District congressman (replacing Lindbergh). In the senatorial race, Kellogg, who received support from deposed Republican Senator Clapp, registered only a plurality of 185,159 votes, defeating Democrat Daniel W. Lawler, a former St. Paul mayor and a perennial losing candidate, who polled 117,541 votes, and Prohibitionist candidate W. G. Calderwood, who, in a surprising show of strength, received 78,425 votes. Unlike Clapp, Lindbergh revealed the resoluteness of his antipreparedness stand and a looseness in his Republican ties by supporting Prohibitionist Calderwood in the general election. Burnquist was easily elected governor by a strong two to one margin over Lawler, while Knutson won handily over his Democratic opponent in the Sixth District.[42]

The presidential vote cast in Minnesota was exceedingly close. Republican Charles Evans Hughes won the twelve electoral votes of the traditionally Republican state, but he received only 392 more popular votes than Democrat Woodrow Wilson, who was reelected president by the nation. Without question, Wilson, campaigning on the slogan "He kept us out of war," picked up a good deal of regular Republican support in the state. The press attributed the unusually high Democratic vote in Minnesota to the peace and prosperity issues, pointing out Wilson's strength in prosperous farming regions, areas with a sizable Scandinavian population, and urban centers and centers of organized labor. Many Minnesotans were swayed by Wilson's promise to keep the United States from becoming physically involved in the European war, but this attitude did not lessen the considerable support for "reasonable" preparedness and a reluctant backing of American rights at sea.[43]

Back in Washington after the rigors of the 1916 campaign, Lindbergh resumed his regular congressional activities and continued to voice his strong noninterventionist attitude toward the European war. In early September, for example, he charged that the Money, Transportation, and War trusts were the powers behind the political machines that were forcing America to build a navy and create an army. The military power, said Lindbergh, would be used for "wars of conquest" rather than for the defense of the nation. It was once again the work of organized wealth, for "nothing but an inordinate fear for the safety of the country can justify those who believe in 'America First' to stand for the program." Rear Admiral Emory Scott ("Jerry") Land, a cousin of Evangeline, attested to Lindbergh's opposition to an expanded navy and increased spending on national defense. As a young naval officer, Land was put in charge of the construction of the U.S.S. *New Mexico* in 1916, and he also did some lobbying in Congress for the Navy during wartime. He "got nowhere" with his cousin-in-law, Land said; the two just "didn't click." Lindbergh, observed Land, "thought all evils emanated from Wall Street."[44]

In December Lindbergh offered resolutions in the House advocating special committees to examine the effect of international commerce on agricultural supplies and to pursue with the president plans for a conference to bring about peace negotiations among the nations at war. In both resolutions he emphasized that great quantities of the nation's natural resources were being used to supply warring European countries, to the detriment of the general welfare in the United States. He referred to the unnecessary rise of prices affecting American consumers, the higher interest rates on loans, and the inexcusable "speculator" loans to foreign nations. The foreign loans prevented a proper reduction of interest to American borrowers of credit, said Lindbergh, and that credit now represented a total indebtedness in America— by the nation as a whole, by individual states and municipalities, and by private concerns—of over $100,000,000. In the event that plans made by the president and the House and Senate committees involved with foreign affairs failed to secure action that would end the war, stated Lindbergh in House Concurrent Resolution 64, "Congress may then proceed to inaugurate an industrial plan for the regulation of the commerce and business among the people of this nation on such basis, that the people will not by force of the existing circumstances, be longer made to contribute to the expense of carrying on the inhuman and senseless wars now raging." The Lindbergh resolutions, however, died in the House committees on Rules and Foreign Affairs.[45]

Any hopes for a negotiated peace in the European war ended abruptly when, on January 31, 1917, the Imperial German Government proclaimed a policy of unrestricted submarine warfare. The new German policy stated in unequivocal terms that *all* ships, including American, would be attacked if located within stipulated war zones. Startled by the suddenness and forcefulness of the action, President Wilson responded on February 3 by severing diplomatic relations with Germany. It was an ominous sign, and, with the apparent proximity to a state of war, the break in diplomatic relations prompted anew the national debate over war and peace.[46]

According to Lynn and Dora Haines, Lindbergh visited their Washington office shortly after the diplomatic break with Germany. "There isn't any such thing as a war for democracy," Lindbergh declared during that discussion. The real democrats and the movement toward good government in the United States, he believed, would suffer if America entered the war. Someone pointed out that a war would result in more government control, thus stimulating action toward progressive reform. But Lindbergh was pessimistic, explaining that, although the theory was logical on the surface, "war-born things" never work out. Instead, he predicted, there would be less political and industrial democracy and "dictators will spring up, perhaps even here."[47]

As further evidence of his total commitment to nonintervention in the European war, Lindbergh introduced a bill calling for an advisory referendum vote before an actual declaration of war was made. In the event that the president should sever diplomatic relations with any foreign government without previous consent of Congress, stated Lindbergh's H.R. 20998 on February 20, 1917, "the Director of the Bureau of the Census shall ascertain and report to Congress the number of persons voting for and against a declaration of war as hereinafter provided." Included in the bill was a sample ballot; the voter was to sign his name, give his local address and state and congressional districts, and indicate a yes or no on the declaration of war question. According to provisions, the Public Printer would forward all ballots (one original and one duplicate) through the regular post offices within eight days of any such severance of diplomatic relations. According to the bill, any citizen of the United States eighteen years of age or over, regardless of sex, should be allowed to cast a ballot in the referendum. Actually, Lindbergh was not the first to suggest a war referendum during the neutrality period, and it seems possible that his views, perhaps indirectly through La Follette, were influenced by Socialist writer and 1916 presidential candidate Alan Benson. But Lindbergh's hope that a referendum vote might counter the trend toward war never had a chance to be realized, for his bill apparently died in the Committee on Foreign Affairs.[48]

In Minnesota public response to the question of American entry into the war remained divided. Conservatives, the press, the Minneapolis business community, and various organizations proclaimed their intention to "Stand by the President." In a speech before a Loyalty League meeting of several thousand persons in early February, 1917, Cyrus Northrop, president emeritus of the University of Minnesota, declared: "We all want peace—but peace without dishonor. . . . And let the united voice of the whole American people cheer and encourage [President Wilson] as he does his best to keep us out of war, or if in spite of his best efforts war should come." Strong Minnesota support for Wilson also came from the state legislature, where both houses passed resolutions indicating "consecrated patriotism" in following the president's leadership. The one dissenting House vote on the resolution was cast by Ernest Strand of Two Harbors, a small northern Minnesota community with some Socialist strength. Indeed it was the Socialists, together with organized labor, many German-Americans, and a growing agrarian bloc distrustful of Wall Street's interest in the war, who were the State's major proponents of nonintervention. Peace meetings were held, too, as exemplified by a February 10 gathering of several thousand in Minneapolis featuring the city's Socialist mayor, Thomas Van Lear, as an antiwar speaker.[49]

There was evidence of divided opinion in the Sixth District. On February 9, 1917, Lindbergh read into the *Congressional Record* an offer to the War Department from the Commercial Club of Aitkin, Minnesota. To be placed at the government's immediate disposal, stated the telegram, was the "Red River Lumber Company's sawmill plant, consisting of five factory buildings, over 2,000-horsepower engines, and equipment located on ideal site with ample trackage and yards." Lindbergh prefaced the entry by referring to his constituents as "practically all" opposed to war but ready to support their government right or wrong in case of conflict. On the other hand, a protest against President Wilson's action was indicated by the decision of a mass meeting of railroad workers at Brainerd on February 7. Included in the resolution that was passed and sent to the president was the statement that the group opposed American entry into war "for any course other than to repel the invasion of our shores." The workers also emphasized that living costs had already increased because of the war, and, unless the government would keep the peace, they favored a "General Strike" to prevent war.[50]

In Congress the question of war or peace focused on the debate over armed neutrality. With the publication of stories about the *Laconia* sinking on February 27 and the Zimmermann note suggesting a German-Mexican alliance on March 1,[51] excited congressmen engaged in expressions of patriotism and denunciations of Germany. When the House of Representatives voted on the armed ships bill on March 1, 1917, the results were an overwhelming 403 to 14 majority in favor of the legislation. Lindbergh, however, unswayed by the emotions of the moment, cast one of the fourteen negative ballots. He was one of nine Midwestern congressmen in that tiny minority, which could be identified, in most cases, with German-American or Scandinavian-American constituencies.[52] Certainly both ethnic groups were present in Lindbergh's district and may have had some impact on the congressman, but it is clear that his main reason for voting against the bill was to continue his battle against the "special interests." On the day of the House vote Lindbergh pointedly and succinctly stated his position:

No action toward starting war was taken till the submarine warfare stopped the munition makers sending their goods across the ocean. Americans had, without notice, been killed upon belligerent ships, also upon neutral ships and upon our own ships, but no step toward war was taken until the ships carrying munitions of war were being held in American harbors, because the owners could not afford to take the financial risk incident to sending them through the war zone. . . . None of us dispute the law or the right of free travel and commerce upon the high seas; and no one would surrender any right essential to our national independence, but we should see the necessity of civilization, and that it can not come out of the existing law unless we make different rules of application.[53]

Not long after the vote on the bill Lindbergh wrote Eva: "I am certain that I would not change my vote if I had it to do over again." He observed that the newspapers and the country in general were "going wild" on the war issue, but on March 21, he optimistically noted that he had received approximately one thousand letters in the last twelve days "saying that people are now getting their eyes opened." Meanwhile the armed ships bill ran into difficulty in the Senate, receiving sharp criticism from Senator Clapp during the debate. But the main opposition, by filibuster, came from Senator La Follette, and eventually President Wilson used executive authority to arm merchant ships for defense purposes.[54]

In early April, 1917, spurred by news of the sinkings of three American merchant vessels by German submarines on March 16, 17, and 18, the irrevocable decision for war came. President Wilson delivered his war message to the Congress on the second day of the month, and Congress responded by passing resolutions for war on April 4 and April 5. The Senate vote was 82 to 6, while the margin of victory in the House was 373 to 50. Included in the fifty House votes against entry into the European war were those by Minnesota congressmen Charles Davis, Carl Van Dyke, Ernest Lundeen, and Harold Knutson, who had replaced Lindbergh as Sixth District representative on March 4, 1917. The Minnesota antiwar votes were generally attributed to the sizable German and Scandinavian population in these constituencies, but more specific reasons included the need for a referendum, entanglement in the affairs of Europe beyond the submarine question, and, in keeping with Lindbergh's line of thought, the tremendous economic cost to future generations. There is no doubt whatever that Lindbergh would have voted against the war resolution on April 6 had he been a member of Congress at the time.[55]

One substantive matter about which Lindbergh has been misunderstood was his position on the European war after American entry in April, 1917. Many people believed that Lindbergh, in view of his bitter attacks during the neutrality period, remained opposed to the war, and in a later campaign in Minnesota, his position was interpreted by political opponents as disloyalty. But the evidence suggests otherwise. Obviously Lindbergh was not pleased with American entry into the war, yet, as he wrote his daughter just before the war declaration: "If we get in war, we will have to support it right or wrong." After the declaration came, even though he considered the beginning of the war the "height of folly," Lindbergh simply believed that "it is best not to do any thing now to discourage, for the thing has been done, and however foolish it has been, we must all be foolish and unwise together, and fight for our country."[56]

Clearly Lindbergh's congressional efforts during American neutrality from 1914 to 1917 were primarily devoted to the cause of nonintervention in the European war. There were, however, other congressional issues, and Lindbergh supported such measures as the extension of rural credits to farmers; government control of water power; reform of House rules, including making all committee meetings open to the public; an investigation of the Federal Reserve Bank at Chicago; reform of the postal savings bank system; and economic and governmental reform to counter the corruptive influence of big business—the "invisible government"—on the political system. Basic reform was necessary in this latter area, he argued, for it did no good to follow political leaders because they were often bribed by the business interests. Lindbergh also gave attention to Sixth District matters, particularly water levels on the upper Mississippi and government reservoirs, and the construction of bridges in Aitkin and Beltrami counties.[57]

Prohibition and woman suffrage were two other issues that Lindbergh discussed during the period. Although he emphasized that he was not opposed to the manufacture, sale, and use of liquor in a "reasonable way," the evidence convinced him that this was probably impossible. Experience has shown, he noted in a short House speech, "that the manufacture and sale of liquors is attended with practices that are extremely detrimental to good government, very bad in its effect on many drinkers, and especially their families, causes much suffering and crime, and serves no sufficient requirement of men and women to offset the damages it causes." Furthermore, he asserted, the industry's expenditure of manpower and materials was a pure waste of the nation's resources.[58] Lindbergh was even more emphatic in his views on woman suffrage. Unlike some progressives, who supported woman suffrage because it would enhance their prospects for election, he believed it to be a basic human right. In his opinion, to exclude half of the population from voting rights was not even a debatable question—it was "simply a wrong." Therefore, he said, he had not felt it necessary to argue the case in his debates or his writing. The exclusion of women, Lindbergh further claimed, was analogous to suggesting that New Yorkers could cast ballots for the presidency, but Pennsylvanians could not. Included in one of Lindbergh's books was a brief statement on the subject by his daughter Lillian, who encouraged women to advance the cause by becoming interested and knowledgeable in local, state, and national politics. When Lindbergh made a public statement in the House on January 12, 1915, he forthrightly declared: "There is an absolute fundamental right in the women to vote." Only selfishness on the part of men had prevented women from being allowed to exercise this right, Lindbergh claimed, and he noted that politics would be "improved and purified" with the extension of suffrage to women.[59]

Lindbergh also commented on the concept of socialism and the nature of the Roman Catholic church during 1915 and 1916. Pure socialism, Lindbergh believed, was desirable, but it could not be attained until people stopped being "personally selfish." Part of the problem, of course, was the fact that under the current economic system people were forced to act with a degree of selfishness in order to survive. As a result, stated Lindbergh, "we are not prepared for complete socialism." Yet, reflecting a degree of idealism, he was optimistic about the future, and noted that, within certain limitations, socialism had already been adopted in certain areas of human affairs. "Evolution will eventually bring us to it." Meanwhile, until pure socialism might be reached, Lindbergh believed that the next best remedy for economic problems was to take away from the banks the privilege of controlling money and credit. It was a familiar Lindbergh theme, and it explains the broad context of the short-range goal served by his repeated attacks on the Money Trust and the banking and currency system.[60]

Lindbergh's interest in the Roman Catholic church was prompted by reports from the Free Press Defense League,[61] a Kansas organization that accused the Papal system of attempting to destroy free institutions in the United States. These institutions, claimed the League, included public schools, the free press, free speech and assembly, freedom of thought, and separation of church and state. Additional League charges against the Roman church cited its demands for blind obedience to the church by the laity, its "pernicious" involvement in American politics, its position backing war between Mexico and the United States, and its role "in carrying out the conspiracy to bring the United States of America under the complete domination of the Pope of Rome and the Catholic hierarchy." Lindbergh outlined the charges in a House speech and in a July, 1916, resolution requesting a "true and impartial investigation" of the matter. In his statement Lindbergh referred to the "founding fathers" of the nation and the wisdom of the principle of separation of church and state. His need to open the question of the role of the Roman church arose, he said, as did other issues during his political career, "without prejudice of party, rationality, church, or anything else, because I realize that prejudice is the enemy of good government and defeats the exercise of the rights of the people." Lindbergh's character would substantiate the sincerity of his motives, but in a sense it seemed politically naive to introduce such a controversial resolution. Though an investigation was never conducted, reaction against Lindbergh could be expected, and it occurred not in 1916, but in 1918. In the opinion of his friends and biographers, the Haineses, "There is nothing that more surely brought about his political defeat."[62]

In the fall of 1916 Lindbergh demonstrated his concern for labor when he spoke out during the debate on the Adamson eight-hour bill. Some 400,000 trainmen were demanding a workday of eight hours instead of ten hours, no reduction in pay, and time and a half pay for overtime work, and the railroad brotherhoods threatened a strike unless the demands were met. President Wilson offered a compromise that included enlargement of the

Interstate Commerce Commission, with the assumption that new appointments would be favorable to management, but Congress refused to endorse the plan. Lindbergh saw the compromise as dangerous because he felt that the new commissioners would take the part of "organized wealth" in adjusting railroad rates. Lindbergh supported the eight-hour day, declaring that the request by labor was an "absolute right" and noting that the railroads feared any discussion of comparative pay between railroad workers and other workers. He also approved of the right to strike. Though strikes were not justified under normal circumstances, Lindbergh explained that in view of the unjust control of government by party politics and wealthy interests, "strikes are not only excusable when orderly, but are sometimes necessary." As he had written in the June issue of *Real Needs:* "Looking back over the industrial history of the last quarter-century, the industrial disputes which have attracted the attention of the country and which have been accompanied by bloodshed and violence have been revolutions against industrial oppression, and not mere strikes for the improvement of working conditions." Ultimately the amended Adamson bill passed the House, with Lindbergh's approval, by a 239 to 56 vote on September 1, 1916. Lindbergh's position during the controversy was in keeping with his general belief that "special interests" were intent on making "industrial slaves" out of the "masses." Like his unsuccessful attempt to have the House study industrial relations and his campaign to make public the report of the U.S. Commission on Industrial Relations in 1915, it indicated Lindbergh's deep concern that something be done about the inequitable distribution of weath in the nation.[63]

During his last weeks as a congressman, Lindbergh spoke directly and provocatively on another domestic issue of constant interest to him, the nation's banking and currency system. Lindbergh struck dramatically at the Federal Reserve Board, which he considered to be at the core of the alignment between the Money Trust and the system. On February 12, 1917, he probably startled his colleagues when he presented on the floor of the House articles of impeachment against five members of the Board. Stated Lindbergh:

I, upon my responsibility as a Member of the House of Representatives, do hereby impeach the said W. P. G. Harding, governor; Paul M. Warburg, vice governor; and Frederick A. Delano, Adolph C. Miller, and Charles S. Hamlin, members, and each of them as members of the Federal Reserve Board, and also impeach all of them collectively as the five active working members of the Federal Reserve Board, of high crimes and misdemeanors in aiding, abetting, and conspiring with certain persons and firms hereinafter named, and with other persons and firms, known and unknown, in a conspiracy to violate the Constitution and the laws of the United States and the just and equitable policies of the Government.[64]

He named several specific firms, including J. P. Morgan and Company; Kuhn, Loeb, and Company; Lee, Higginson, and Company; Kidder, Peabody, and Company; and the National City Bank of New York, as major conspirators in the plan to devise a new banking scheme which they could control. Actually Lindbergh had made attacks on most of the same groups in his earlier public statements on the Money Trust, but his comments in 1917 were by far his most caustic. He outlined fifteen major facts about the board, the last of which included an appeal to Congress to declare the Federal Reserve Act void and unconstitutional. Lindbergh's articles of impeachment were referred by the House to the Judiciary Committee, where they were subsequently shelved. Lindbergh expected that no action would be taken. "Don't worry if the press slams me," he wrote Eva on February 17. "I hit the board a hard blow, and they are sore. My real aim was to block some bad legislation—now they have not dared to bring it out." In a matter-of-fact fashion, he added: "Of course I don't expect the committee to do anything—it is stacked."[65]

As he always had, Lindbergh took time when possible during his last years in Congress for personal and family affairs. In June, 1915, he and Charles, Jr. took a boat trip of several days down the Mississippi River from Itasca to Cass Lake. The trip allowed Lindbergh to view the water system as a part of his congressional work, but more important, it provided a chance for father and son to be alone with nature. There was also a constant flow of letters between Lindbergh and Eva, with concern expressed when Eva went into quarantine at Akeley to nurse a friend with scarlet fever, when she considered leaving teaching, and when she discussed marrying a newspaperman. After spending the winter of 1915 and 1916 doing research and office work in her father's Washington office, Eva married the journalist, George W. Christie, in the summer of 1916. The young couple, consulting with Lindbergh, selected the northwestern Minnesota community of Red Lake Falls, with its *Red Lake Falls Gazette,* as the place to pursue their journalistic careers.[66]

But there were unhappy moments, too. The death at twenty-nine of his elder daughter Lillian in November, 1916, deeply saddened Lindbergh. In a last fight against tuberculosis Lillian, accompanied by her husband Dr. Loren Roberts, her daughter Louise, Eva, and Lindbergh, had gone to her uncle Perry's ranch in California, where the climate might aid her recovery. The disease had already progressed beyond that point, however, and Lillian, always somewhat frail, was taken to a hospital, where she died. Tenderly, Lindbergh recorded his last journey and vigil with his daughter in 1916.[67]

Shortly after the end of his official duties in March, 1917, Lindbergh underwent surgery in Washington for a hernia caused by a slight accident in the summer of 1916. During the operation, which he had without benefit of an anesthetic, the former congressman discussed international banking with his friend Lynn Haines. The recovery period took a bit longer than expected, and as Eva later observed: "Father had a more serious time with his operation than he expected or would admit. He was alone as none of the family were in Washington, too." Interestingly, many of Lindbergh's notes to Eva in early 1917 were written on long white scratch paper, heavy brown paper, and, on occasion, old envelopes or cardboard. "These days when paper is a million per pound we can use up the old scrap paper," he explained. "That's what I do for the paper trust." That same spring, fearing that "we will be mixed up in the war in a short time" and predicting that "interest notes will go up and bonds will go down for a while," Lindbergh encouraged his associate Carl Bolander to "put the sale across" on farm land in the Little Falls area.[68]

During the months between the 1916 campaign and his departure from Washington in the late spring of 1917, Lindbergh
was also busy with another project, the publication of his second
major book. According to one of his later publishers, Lindbergh
picked the title, *Why Is Your Country at War and What Happens
to You After the War and Related Subjects,* because he was
writing "for the people." The small, 220-page volume, published
by the National Capital Press in July, 1917, was designed to be
easily carried in one's pocket and thus more widely read. "The
object of the book," Lindbergh wrote, "is to emphasize *independence.*" And that independence was based on a willingness to
counter what Lindbergh believed to be the real causes of the war,
the chief one being, of course, the existence of an "inner circle"
of business interests involved in promoting the war for commercial purposes. Most of the book, therefore, was devoted to a
summation of the major political and economic positions Lindbergh took as a congressman. The attack on "special privilege"
and Wall Street interests, the unfairness and corruptness of the
political system, a discussion of the Federal Reserve system and
the inadvisability of foreign loans, and other excerpts from the
Congressional Record and his writings were included. Lindbergh
also made brief statements on science and technology, and conservation, in his new book. In his opinion it was unfortunate that
as science and technology had progressed and "multiplied the
products of human energy," "the masses" had become more, not
less, "dependent." Although with a different emphasis, it was a
statement broadly similar to those his aviator son would later
make about the dangers to the environment and to humane values
posed by the uncritical acceptance of whatever "progress" ad-
vances in science and technology made possible. In both cases
the general human welfare suffered from a poorly conceived use
of technology. On the question of preserving natural resources,
Lindbergh stated very simply that the "European war threw conservation to the four winds."[69]

Lindbergh pointed out in *Why Is Your Country at War* that
in stating his position on the war he was impartial as to whether

the truth of his work favored the Central Powers or the Allies. He indicated that he would support the war now that the United States had entered, but he also encouraged the right to honest disagreement with government policy.

Our highest representative is Congress and the President. Whether we believe their official acts right or not in this matter, we must support them with all our power. There are two sides involved internationally, and we are for America. Whether in battle, in industry or elsewhere—everywhere and wherever really needed or required, we will respond patriotically. . . .

We should stand by the President and Congress as well, in the execution of their official duties, but until their acts become law, it is our right to direct them as we believe right and to determine their authority. Even after they have officially acted, we are still at liberty to seek to have officially undone what has officially been done—that is, to change and officially amend. There is much which they have done which should be repealed and amended. Any attempt under the guise of war or otherwise to prevent this being done in the legal way is revolutionary, and invites revolution in opposition.[70]

In Lindbergh's judgment war was the most "senseless" of all follies, and "has the least prospect of doing justice in any way." In a pointed attack, Lindbergh charged that: "It feeds upon vanity—false personal egotism, and a false so-called 'patriotism' that would destroy millions to avenge wrong to an individual when to avenge that wrong by war begets thousands of other wrongs, and secures no reform, that could not in most cases have been more honorably secured and permanently established by natural means." In the case of the European war "speculative interests" had provoked violations on the high seas to satisfy their own greed and egos, and now as a result "we must fight to the limit of our capacity until we get an agreement that does not put us at a disadvantage."[71]

Ultimately, though, he felt that the only true victory would come with "an economic victory for the masses of the world." If won, he argued, this battle would make actual military conflict "dwindle into insignificance." To bring about this economic freeing of the "industrial slaves," Lindbergh suggested that the operation of communication facilities, transportation facilities, the finances of the country, and other services all be charged at cost only. This would ensure the absence of a profit motive. These circumstances, asserted Lindbergh, "would result in *an equal opportunity to all and special privilege to none.*"[72]

Lindbergh's antiwar stance during the 1914 to 1917 period was thus closely related to his progressive economic reform perspective. The judgment of historians on the general relationship between nonintervention and progressive reform has varied, but in the case of Lindbergh the thesis that there was a direct relation between the two is valid.[73] His opposition to war can be traced to the primary factor of his domestic reform goals, as well as to sectional, partisan, and ethnic considerations. Clearly he stands as a major contributor to the tradition of economic opposition to war, which emerged again during the 1930's with the Nye Committee investigation of the munitions industry, and in the revisionist thinking of such historians as Charles A. Beard. Indeed, Senator Nye stated that Lindbergh was "solidly sound" on his position of "noninvolvement in other people's wars and hates." Said Nye, "I found support in his position on these issues, and confirmed my thinking that his thinking on World War I was a smart stand, an American stand." It has therefore been argued that the bases for World War I isolationism reemerged as the foundation for similar opinion in the period prior to World War II.[74] But Charles Lindbergh, Jr., an America First supporter during the late 1930's, disagrees with those who attempt to draw specific comparisons between his views and those of his father. (It should be noted that the younger Lindbergh was associated only with the pre–World War II America First Committee. He joined "partly to support the Committee and partly because the Committee gave me reliable and easily available speaking platforms." He had complete freedom "to say what [he] wished" and placed "great confidence" in committee spokesman General Robert E. Wood. After the declaration of war the prewar committee disbanded immediately, and Lindbergh "had no connection whatever with the post-war America First Committee" [headed by

Gerald L. K. Smith].) Although, like his father, Lindbergh, Jr. strongly believed in avoiding physical participation in a European war, he did not share the same fear of the "special interests" as did his father, for "in regard to my opposition to World War II, the question of financial 'vested interests' never entered my mind to the extent of influencing my position." The elder Lindbergh's idealistic belief in the possibility of a society without war is not shared by his son. On this issue, he recently wrote: "I believe that wars *can* be reduced in frequency and intensity (and that this is what we should concentrate on doing); but I doubt that war can be eliminated."[75]

By the summer of 1917, then, Congressman Lindbergh had wound up his affairs in the nation's capital. A friend, Representative Caleb Powers of Kentucky, was to move into his old House office,[76] and Lindbergh now looked to the familiar associations and political challenges in Minnesota. As an opponent of preparedness and war, he had tasted political defeat. A new campaign would soon absorb his attention, and though he could hardly know it as he left Washington, so would the grueling experience of personal vilification.

Chapter IX

Nonpartisan League Candidate
for Governor

During my service as a Member of this House I have been a close observer of events during three different presidential administrations. I have seen the progressive tendencies of legislation under a Roosevelt, inspired by the logic, eloquence, and candor of La Follette, strangled by the stand-pat proclivities of a Taft, and the power of a great party, which had controlled the country for 16 years, dwindle until it was able to carry only the electoral votes of two of the smallest States in the Union. I have seen another great party ride into power on the strength of roseate promises to the people, and I expect to see it go out of power, because it has been abundantly proved that those promises were merely statements to catch votes. The plain truth is that neither of these great parties, as at present led and manipulated by an invisible government, is fit to manage the destinies of a great people, and this fact is well understood by all who have had the time and have used it to investigate.[1]

This damning speech on the floor of the House in July, 1916, is saturated with an informed disillusion with national party politics. In view of this fact, and keeping in mind Lindbergh's earlier remark that a real progressive should not become a "party to a faction,"[2] it is not a complete surprise that he soon found it necessary to break with major party politics. Upon his return to Minnesota, within less than a year after making the House statement, Lindbergh became actively involved with the Nonpartisan League, the focus of an agrarian protest movement in the upper Midwest; and, as if to reconfirm his analysis of the moral poverty of the two major national parties, he joined the Farmer-Labor party, which eventually was to modify the two-party system in Minnesota. Lindbergh was entering the twilight of his political career, and it was not going to be tame.

The Nonpartisan League, a farmers' political organization, originated in North Dakota.[3] The League was formed in 1915 through the efforts of a disenchanted "Flax King" in the state, Arthur C. Townley. Its initial program involved a protest by small wheat farmers against existing grain-marketing practices. One leader of the movement, Henry G. Teigan, has singled out the American Society of Equity and the Socialist party as the economic and political antecedents of the National Nonpartisan League.[4] The League's primary aim was to see that the farmer received adequate compensation for his products, which led to the formation of a plan involving elimination of the middleman. Senator Edwin F. Ladd of Fargo, North Dakota, put it simply in his maiden speech before Congress in 1921, when, in clear concordance with the views of Lindbergh, he stated that the farmers ask for "legislation which shall insure justice to all and special privilege to none." In order to correct inequities, the League platform called for such bold reforms as state ownership of terminal elevators, flour mills, packing houses, and cold storage plants; state inspection of grain and grain dockage; tax exemptions for farm improvements; state hail insurance; and rural credit banks operated at cost. The League spread rapidly throughout North Dakota, and it soon expanded to include the general wheat-growing area of the northern plains. In Minnesota, organizing began during the summer of 1916 and the League, desirous of a central location from which to extend its program into other states, moved its national headquarters from Fargo to St. Paul in early 1917.[5]

Lindbergh's association with the Nonpartisan League apparently began in late 1915, when he had agreed to write several articles on the money and currency question for the *Nonpartisan Leader*. In January, 1917, he wrote the League that his new book on the war might "help the NPL in its campaign." His direct involvement with the League began almost immediately upon his return to Minnesota from Washington. In early July, 1917, Henry Teigan wrote Lindbergh that League president Townley "would like to have an interview with you as he feels that you are in thorough sympathy with this organization." Of such sympathy there can be little doubt, for the League's attack on Eastern interests and its championing of the small grain farmer fit well with Lindbergh's public record. In addition, the former congressman embraced the more radical notions of the League involving expanded government ownership. League leaders were hopeful that Lindbergh might help their work both in Minnesota and on the national level. In a July 25 letter to Eva, Lindbergh revealed that he and Townley had traveled to Washington on League business. She was concerned about her father's new relationship with the League, but Lindbergh assured her that, although the League was not always popular, "they have a real plan whereas the other fellows have none—except to let a few get the dough and run away with it." Even if it meant being called a radical, he insisted, he would not change his course. "I am a radical because I oppose the few and stand for the masses." Lindbergh also told Eva that on his recent trip he had helped a new man "to get into trouble" and "to get started along the line of radical [politics], as they call it."[6]

Meanwhile the League, already suspect in business and political circles because of its radical stand on domestic reform, and because of its rapid growth as a political force, found itself under severe attack as a disloyal organization following American entry into the European war. The League, which had roughly 25,000 members in Minnesota by mid-1917, was vulnerable on the war issue, for its leaders had continually assailed the "war profiteers" as the culprits behind U.S. involvement and now demanded that the government take over the industries they controlled. Reaction to the League in Minnesota was split. The Minneapolis-St. Paul press, the metropolitan business community, and even many small-town leaders, breaking tradition in aligning with Twin City interests, joined in responding to the threat of "Townleyism" by opposing the League. Urban newspapers such as *Commercial West* and the *Minneapolis Tribune* were openly hostile to the League, while small-town businessmen feared it as an economic competitor. Farmers, on the other hand, formed the core of League strength, with growing support from organized labor.[7]

A meeting of producers and consumers, called by Townley and the League in September, 1917, provided its enemies with the occasion for a stepped-up anti-League campaign focusing on the disloyalty issue, and for a general venting of emotions on the war. The purpose of the League convention, held on the first day at Fargo and on the next three days at St. Paul, was to discuss the problems of regulated prices and food products during wartime. Several prominent Midwestern politicians, including senators, congressmen, state and local officials, as well as federal government representatives, were among the speakers. On the evening of September 20, Lindbergh addressed the overflow audience of eight thousand at the St. Paul auditorium on the topic "Profits of Finance in the High Cost of Living." It was a typical Lindbergh attack on the "special interests," emphasizing the unequal distribution of wealth in the nation. Sixty-five per cent of the wealth, he stated, was owned by only 2 per cent of the population. As he zeroed in on Wall Street, and then discussed free speech and the need to remain loyal to the United States by supporting the nation in the war, the responsive audience frequently interrupted with applause. "I think I am as loyal as any man can be, and I stand for the institutions of our country according to the spirit in which our constitution was adopted." Again there was applause when Lindbergh declared that it was not disloyal to speak out on the problems of the nation while the war was going on. He concluded his speech by asserting that the war must be paid for while it was being carried on, and he called for the structuring of a true economic order with money as a measure of exchange only, the elimination of interest in the handling of money, and the elimination of profits and dividends in the transportation of the nation's commerce.[8]

The real high point of the conference came, however, with a

speech by Senator La Follette later that evening. Warned by League leaders to avoid the explosive issue of American involvement in the war, La Follette initially planned to limit his speech to a discussion of war finance. But "Fighting Bob" could not resist responding to the tremendous enthusiasm of the huge crowd. La Follette, one of the holdouts against voting for American entry into the war, declared: "For my own part, I was not in favor of beginning the war." The comment was met by continued applause. Then he explained that "I don't mean to say that we had not suffered grievances, we had, at the hands of Germany . . . they had interfered with the right of American citizens to travel upon the high seas on ships loaded with munitions for Great Britain." Again there were yells and applause. When La Follette noted it was poor judgment that allowed Americans to travel on belligerent vessels, he was interrupted by cries of "Yellow!" and "Put him out!" The senator, however, was able to control the emotionally aroused audience and went on with his speech. At another point a heckler challenged La Folette on the *Lusitania* sinking. The senator responded that Secretary of State Bryan had appealed to President Wilson to stop Americans from traveling on the ship. The last portions of La Follette's speech concerned war taxation, and his performance ended with heavy applause.[9]

The reaction of the press and certain officials to La Follette's speech, however, was vicious. An Associated Press release, for example, quoted La Follette as saying "We had *no* grievances against Germany," when, of course, he had stated just the opposite. In addition, his comments on the *Lusitania* incident were branded as sympathetic to German submarine warfare. "La Follette Defends *Lusitania* Sinking," glared a *New York Times* headline. Even more drastic was action taken at a September 25 meeting of the Minnesota Commission of Public Safety. The Commission, a wartime state agency created in April, 1917, with broad and sweeping powers to insure public safety and to promote the war effort, passed a resolution demanding that proceedings be undertaken "looking to the expulsion of the said Robert M. La Follette from the Senate, as a teacher of disloyalty and sedition giving aid and comfort to our enemies." On September 29 Senator Kellogg introduced the resolution, in the form of a petition, to the Senate. The resolution, which threatened La Follette's political life, went to committee, where it sat shelved for the duration of the war.[10]

The La Follette incident was damaging to the Nonpartisan League. Since it had provided the forum for La Follette's speech, there was an assumption that its views were equally "seditious." Most of the official League resolutions at the St. Paul convention, however, outlined the need for food production and government control of industry during the war, as well as stressing loyalty in the entire war effort. One portion of the resolutions, for instance, stated: "We, the members and delegates of farmers' organizations, representing sixteen states, and the members and delegates of fourteen labor organizations, representing eleven states, do hereby reaffirm our unalterable loyalty and allegiance to our fellow citizens and our government in this world struggle and in their every need." Nonetheless, the Public Safety Commission moved quickly against the League. President Arthur Townley was questioned before a secret meeting of the Commission on September 25, where most of the testimony concerned the purposes and leaders of the League. Later reports said that Townley had repudiated La Follette's speech as seditious, but an examination of the existing testimony (presumably complete) revealed no reference to La Follette. From the time of the St. Paul convention, however, League activity was under constant surveillance by state officials. The convention, furthermore, had drawn the attention of the national administration; as a result George Creel, head of the Committee on Public Information, President Wilson, and Food Administration director Herbert Hoover met with Townley in Washington. Out of these conferences came the report that Townley and the League were loyal, but this official approval did little to cleanse the smeared image of the League.[11]

Inevitably, Lindbergh drifted back into active politics. In August, 1917, he wrote Eva that he had no current intention of getting "into politics again for myself, but can't tell but what I might get in just the same." He was convinced that the League was the only organization "except the socialists" which offered any real remedy to the nation's problems, and by early 1918 he felt the League was on its way to becoming a national power. League leaders were pressing Lindbergh to become a candidate for governor, and on February 1, 1918, he wrote Eva: "I have concluded that I am likely to run for Gov, for if elected there is a chance to do something for the state, and I find that B. [Burnquist] is not doing anything except to take things as they come." Eva encouraged her father to run for his old seat in Congress, but Lindbergh argued that he could not be effective in that body unless there were forty or fifty progressives with whom to work. At the same time he had not entirely given up the idea of Congress, and he was likely waiting for the results of the Nonpartisan League State Convention.[12]

The League convention, held in St. Paul on March 19, 1918, selected Lindbergh as its choice for governor in the June 18 primary, and his decision to run for the highest state office was made. Among other candidates endorsed by the League to join Lindbergh were: for lieutenant governor, State Representative R. E. Crane; for attorney general, Hibbing mayor and union sympathizer Victor Power; for auditor, Yellow Medicine County farmer S. J. Tjosvold; for secretary of state, State Representative Henry Holmes of Big Lake; for treasurer, Preston banker Thomas Meighan; and for railroad and warehouse commissioner, St. Paul railroad engineer Fred E. Tillquist, endorsed by organized labor. All the candidates except Democrat Meighan were Republicans, which reflected the general division of delegate strength at the convention. There were, in addition, a few Socialists and Prohibitionists present. Technically, the Nonpartisan League did not offer its own candidates as a political party; rather, as a farmers' organization, it merely endorsed the candidates of its choice regardless of party. Thus Lindbergh, even after his selection as the League-endorsed candidate, could write former California congressman William Kent that "I am not a member of the League." However, he informed Kent, who had given the League a check for one thousand dollars made out specifically to Lindbergh, that the principles for which the League was working "in my judgment are absolutely right."[13]

The St. Paul League convention sponsored a two-day rally at which more than seven thousand persons heard speakers including Kent, Socialists Walter T. Mills and Mayor Thomas Van Lear of Minneapolis, League president Townley, and Lynn Frazier, League-supported governor of North Dakota. Governor Burnquist, who inexplicably had been invited to address the rally and who would be Lindbergh's opponent in the gubernatorial primary, declined either to speak or attend. Although his refusal to speak did not ingratiate Burnquist with the farmer and labor interests represented, it should have been expected. For one thing, the governor had probably already lost a good deal of labor support through his crude handling of an iron range strike in 1916; and then in late 1917, he alienated the entire labor movement when the Safety Commission, with his support, intervened with almost dictatorial power in the Twin City Rapid Transit Company strike. In declining the League invitation, Burnquist saw an opportunity to attack the League. In a statement to Executive Secretary Arthur Le Sueur, he charged that the League was a party of discontent and was closely aligned with the pro-German element in the state, the "lawless I.W.W.," and the "Red Socialists." For him it was enough to say that the only "two parties" in Minnesota were "one composed of the loyalists and the other of the disloyalists."[14]

Lindbergh formally received the League gubernatorial endorsement at the St. Paul gathering. In his acceptance speech, Lindbergh spoke on the war issue, asserting that the most important factor in gaining victory lay with proper economic management. Anticipating probable charges in the campaign and referring to Governor Burnquist's criticism of the League, Lindbergh discussed the loyalty question. Burnquist had divided all citizens into two classes, the loyalists and the disloyalists, he said, but what is the real difference between the two? "The difference is that a few would destroy democracy to win the war, and the rest of us would win the war to establish democracy." President Wilson had said that the United States went to war to win world democracy, but it was apparent that the governor of Minnesota had failed to grasp that point. In Lindbergh's judgment most people were loyal, but where overt disloyalty did exist it should be prosecuted. However, he noted, a false issue of loyalty had been raised in Minnesota because "these profiteers and politicians, pretended guardians of loyalty, seek to perpetuate themselves in special privilege and in office."[15]

Meanwhile the League platform was drawn up, outlining such goals as an economic program of public ownership, several state programs to help labor, the vigorous prosecution of the war, and a demand that something be done to curb the lawlessness of state officials. In early April Lindbergh officially filed as candidate for governor in the Republican primary, and on April 25 he opened his campaign in Willmar. He discussed the commercial causes behind the European war, the need to raise food and to support the Red Cross and Liberty Loans in order to win the war, and the League platform of state ownership. The strategy of the Lindbergh–League campaign became clear. A strong dose of League domestic reform, emphasizing its significance in carrying on the national war effort, would be a basic theme. Government takeover of all industry during the war was advised, and demands were made for higher taxes on large incomes and corporations in order to pay for the war. The League appeal for both farmer and labor support was a powerful one, and without question it had the potential for national influence.[16]

In Minnesota regular Republican politicians and businessmen were well aware of the threat posed by the League. An all-out effort to defeat Lindbergh was made, particularly since he, more than any other League candidate, was widely known and experienced in politics. The *Nonpartisan Leader*, the national organ of the League, later corroborated this when it came into possession of correspondence that revealed that a major anti-League movement had been organized by a group of influential Twin Cities bankers and commercial leaders. Guy Stanton Ford of the University of Minnesota, who worked closely with the Creel Committee during World War I, described the anti-League forces as a "combination of old-line Democrats and old-line Republicans" who were out to "crush" the League. It was clear that the Burnquist administration and anti-League forces, working through the Public Safety Commission in 1918, were mainly concerned with utilizing the disloyalty issue against the NPL as a means to thwart a major political competitor.[17]

Governor Burnquist announced that he would not campaign in the primary because he did not believe that "this is a time to go into politics." Assuming the guise of the hard-working wartime executive, Burnquist said that he would not discuss the policies of his administration but would instead appeal to Minnesotans on the basis of his "loyalty." In reality, Burnquist waged a vigorous campaign by making frequent speeches at "loyalist" meetings scheduled through the Public Safety Commission. The state organ of the League, the *Minnesota Leader*, smoldered at this duplicity, labeling Burnquist's tactics as "unscrupulous and damnable." In its opinion the "shameless political activity" of the governor in using taxpayers' money to publish campaign literature and finance meetings through the Commission was unforgivable. Furthermore, charged the *Leader*, the daily papers of the state "DO NOT EVEN DARE GIVE STRAIGHT NEWS REPORTS OF WHAT BURNQUIST AND HIS GANG ARE DOING, LET ALONE PROTEST AGAINST IT."[18] This turn of events put Lindbergh and the League on the defensive, and the campaign centered on the loyalty issue. Attacks against Lindbergh also made reference to League socialism, anti-Catholicism, and Lindbergh's book *Why Is Your Country at War*.

The charge of a conspiratorial identity between socialism and the Nonpartisan League was nothing new in the spring of 1918. The League program for state ownership, together with later developments including comment on the Russian Revolution and the activities of the Industrial Workers of the World in the Midwest, had already given opponents sufficient evidence to lambaste the League on the issue. They reiterated the charges throughout the 1918 campaign. The vehemently anti-League *Minneapolis*

HE WON'T MAKE ANY POLITICAL SPEECHES

From the *Minnesota Leader*, June 8, 1918. Minnesota Historical Society.

"Flag in hand and wires to his political dummies in the rear the Hon. J. A. A. Burnquist is touring the state delivering 'patriotic' addresses. The Pioneer Press said this was the best method of electioneering that Governor Burnquist could adopt—but from the astounded expressions of these listeners, there seems to be something wrong.

"You can guess it first shot—they can't discover the 'loyalty,' it is so badly mixed with 'vote-for-me-ism.' They have seen so much flag-waving and so much wire-pulling that they recognize both. One of these listeners is pointing to the hand the governor is trying to hide. Another is hiding a snicker behind his hand. In fact all Minnesota is looking on in amazement that Governor Burnquist could be so blind as to think the people do not see through his thin veil of would-be deception."

Journal, for example, noted a statement by American Federation of Labor president Samuel Gompers indicating that socialism was a part of German propaganda; hence, it concluded, Townleyism was pro-German. The Democratic *Duluth Herald* stated that Minnesota was in danger of being "Russianized" and "Kaiserized" by Townley and Lindbergh. The League membership was probably not disloyal, admitted the *Herald,* but virtually all their leaders were "red card socialists." Moreover, it warned, "every element of Bolshevist tendencies, I.W.W., Socialists, seditionists, pro-German intriguers and all, is for Lindbergh for governor." Echoed the *Hibbing Daily Tribune:* "There is not an American fibre in their [Townley and Lindbergh's] being. . . . They are ultra radical socialists of the Bolsheviki stripe. . . . Acute anarchy is their sole aim."[19]

Less strident in its wording against Lindbergh and the League was the *Svenska Amerikanska Posten,* but its message was the same. It warned that Lindbergh was associated with Townley, received support from Socialists, and opposed the war. Actually the *Posten,* one of the largest Swedish-language papers in the nation, had taken a position sympathetic to Germany during the early stages of neutrality. This attitude, typical of most Swedish papers and probably of their readers, was justified in their opinion because of the racial and religious ties between Germany and Sweden. By 1916, however, the Minneapolis-based *Posten,* now under the editorship of Swan Turnblad, had begun to support the Wilson administration. From the spring of 1917 its support of the president and the war was complete. The *Posten's* position favoring the war and attacking the League was not typical of the entire Swedish-American press, but, in Minnesota at least, it had definite impact. Although the *Posten* had a repuatation for objective reporting and usually did not "defend political candidates," one week before the Lindbergh-Burnquist primary its editorial headline proclaimed: "Vote For Governor Burnquist."[20]

Lindbergh's 1916 House resolution calling for congressional investigation of the Roman Catholic church was also used against him in 1918. The *Catholic Bulletin,* a St. Paul weekly that had suggested in 1916 that the Lindbergh resolution be relegated to

Minnesota Historical Society

Vociferous anti–Nonpartisan League comment in *The Red Flame*
(Bismarck, North Dakota), January, 1920.

the "waste basket," now gave the resolution front-page space
and published the entire resolution just prior to the election. The
Bulletin, which normally took no part in political affairs, could not
stand by while, in its judgment, such an obviously anti-Catholic
candidate was a strong contender for high public office. The gist
of the Lindbergh resolution, which was based on charges made
by the Kansas Free Press Defense League, it pointed out, was
that Catholic prelates "in all lands and at all times have been the
ally of oppression." The charge was untrue, asserted the Catholic
weekly, and in rebuttal it singled out such church activities as
religious orders during the Middle Ages and opposition to slavery.
Lindbergh's assumption that there was a close alliance between
the Roman church and big business was misguided, said the
Bulletin, and it summarized his position as "unmistakable evidence of anti-Catholic prejudice, based, as usual, upon misinter-

Minnesota Historical Society

A reflection of gubernatorial attitudes according to
The Red Flame, January, 1920.

pretation of history." The St. Paul paper insisted that his candidacy
should not be given support, for such a man is "un-American,
irreligious, and a sure menace to the peace of the community
which he may seek to control." There was other comments, too,
as in the case of Bishop Joseph E. Busch, who, in speaking at the
commencement exercises at St. Benedict's Academy on June 7,
counseled "the good Sisters of the Academy and all women to
throw their whole soul into the prayer, 'Lindbergh shall not be
governor.'" Lindbergh's true intention in introducing the original
resolution had been to investigate both the Defense League and
"the high dignitaries of the church to see if the latter were seeking
to interfere with the free exercise of governmental rights under
the Constitution." He simply wished to determine "the effect of
human conduct upon economic operations," he said, a phenomenon that need not involve people's religious beliefs. Despite Lind-

bergh's level of argument, there was little doubt that discussion of the resolution in 1918 would hardly improve his chances to be governor.[21]

Perhaps even more damaging to his campaign, however, was the constant publicity given to Lindbergh's book *Why Is Your Country at War*. Ironically enough, Lindbergh's purpose in writing the little volume had been to clarify his views on economics, politics, and the war, which, he believed, had been started by an "inner circle" of business interests. With the help of the propagandizing anti-League press, however, his efforts in that direction failed monumentally. Time and again the press (particularly in the Twin Cities) misquoted, distorted by elision, or quoted out of context from Lindbergh's *Why Is Your Country at War*. The attacks began during the early stages of Lindbergh's candidacy in March, when a *Minneapolis Journal* headline declared that "Nonparty Governor Candidate Author of Antiwar Book," and they continued until the election. Invariably their principal message was that Lindbergh was disloyal. Indeed, Lindbergh gave no quarter in naming those Americans he believed responsible for U.S. participation in the war, but in no way could the book fairly be labeled a piece of seditious or disloyal literature.[22]

One segment of the book that provoked comment and accusations of disloyalty concerned the Red Cross. In Lindbergh's opinion it was humiliating to see how the "wealth grabbers" and "big press" attempted "to drive the people as if we were a lot of cattle, to buy bonds, subscribe to the Red Cross, to register for conscription and all other things." This "vindictive statement," except for its "clear malice," editorialized the *St. Paul Pioneer Press*, might be put down "as a piece of driveling idiocy." But the main theme of the response to Lindbergh and to *Why Is Your Country at War* was disloyalty. The Twin Cities press periodically called Lindbergh's book "a disgraceful performance," "disloyal bolshevism," "an ignominious book," and "a political mistake." On June 4 the *Minneapolis Journal* quipped "O, that mine enemy would write a book." Three days later the *Pioneer Press* noted that a misdrawn flag in a Lindbergh campaign poster "comes just as close to being the flag of our country as the author of 'Why Is Your Country at War' comes to being a patriotic American."[23]

Lindbergh was not without press support, however, for the League's state organ, the *Minnesota Leader,* vigorously defended its candidate and his book. The *Leader* asserted that the metropolitan press was despicably dishonest in reprinting only isolated sentences and portions of paragraphs from *Why Is Your Country at War.* Frequently the League publication used some of the same quotations presented in the anti-League papers. On the Red Cross item, for instance, the *Leader* included the statement from Lindbergh's book that immediately followed the one reprinted by the *St. Paul Pioneer Press:* "THE PEOPLE WILL DO THEIR DUTY WITHOUT BEING HECTORED IN ADVANCE BY THE BIG INTEREST PRESS." On another occasion, discussing a Lindbergh statement declaring the right to question presidential and congressional policies, the *Leader* emphasized that he had further written: "WE MUST SUPPORT THEM WITH ALL OUR POWER. There are two sides involved internationally and WE ARE FOR AMERICA." In all cases the complete statements from the book had been left out in coverage by the Twin Cities dailies.[24]

The real reason for the attempts to discredit Lindbergh and his book, asserted the *Leader,* was that the "hired press" and "politicians" were directly threatened by the "sweep of the people's movement." Thus, argued the paper, the political opposition was merely utilizing the book as a side issue to divert attention from real issues in the campaign. In its judgment, the core of the campaign was Lindbergh's position as a potent political power, and "THE FACT THAT HE IS RUNNING FOR ELECTION ON A PLATFORM THAT WILL RESTORE THE GOVERNMENT OF THE STATE TO THE PEOPLE AND THAT WILL DRIVE CROOKS AND GRAFTERS FROM THEIR HIGH PLACES." Furthermore, declared another editorial, citing Woodrow Wilson, Lindbergh, and even Theodore Roosevelt, "ALL GREAT MEN write books." However, "Burnquist never a wrote a book," chided the *Leader.* "It takes brains to write a book." In early June Lindbergh made a public statement about his book, citing portions of the text and stressing that he supported Liberty Bonds, the Red Cross, and other war aids. Moreover, he informed the public that he had offered his services to Governor Burnquist in May, 1917, in connection with the war. The distortions of *Why Is Your Country at War* and the general misrepresentation of his views, Lindbergh stated, were "a political scheme to deceive the people."[25]

Lindbergh's book drew national attention when, in May, the Military Affairs Committee of the U.S. Senate conducted hearings that focused on the leadership of the Nonpartisan League. League president Townley, after introducing loyalty statements by League members from Thief River Falls and New Ulm, stated directly that he supported Lindbergh as the NPL candidate for governor of Minnesota. Then he was confronted by Senator John W. Weeks of Massachusetts and Senator James A. Reed of Missouri with several quotations from Lindbergh's book. In reply to questioning on a Lindbergh statement that "conscription is intended to raise, by force, if necessary, armies to take across the seas to fight in foreign lands," Townley replied: "I do not know whether that is a part of the book. I could not express an opinion. I do not know the context. I have not read it." Townley's point was well taken, because the book was difficult to assess unless the whole text were read. As the discussion continued it was clear that Townley would not be trapped on the disloyalty issue. He told the committee that he "did not know whether he had seen the book or not" and that Lindbergh was not a leader of the League, but only "a man endorsed for governor." Questioned on a Lindbergh quotation suggesting America had been "dragged into the war by the intrigue of speculators," Townley unconvincingly parried that the speculators may have been German. Further quotations from the book concerning the role of "wealth" in promoting the war were answered by Townley with such comments as "I would have to make a study of that." The senators then quoted a number of Townley speeches which curiously sounded much like the statements in Lindbergh's book, but Townley was equal to the challenge, countering that he was often misquoted.[26]

In late May the *New York Times* publicized *Why Is Your*

Country at War when it responded sympathetically to anti-Lindbergh activity in Duluth. The principal question in the Minnesota campaign, it said, was to determine the sincerity, or lack thereof, of Lindbergh's patriotism. This "may be best judged," editorialized the *Times,* "by a few dips into his little book." One of the statements they singled out was Lindbergh's declaration that although the violation of international rights on the high seas made U.S. entry into the war "just," he still felt that participation was unwise. The focus of Lindbergh's statement (from page 6 of the book), and indeed of his attitude about the war, was most clear in this portion of the quotation: "Our purpose is humane, nevertheless I believe that I have proved that a certain 'inner circle,' without official authority and for selfish purposes, adroitly maneuvered to bring about conditions that would make it particularly certain that some of the belligerents would violate our international rights and bring us to war with them." Although Lindbergh was "careful," said the *Times,* he could not hide his "animus" against the "moneyed" interests. Certainly Lindbergh would not have argued with that assessment, but the *Times* obviously viewed such sentiments as disloyal. The New York paper suggested that Lindbergh's economic views put him in the category of "a sort of Gopher Bolshevik." Later in the campaign another *Times* editorial reiterated its anti-League position. "Many Socialists and extreme radicals" were a part of the movement, it warned, and although most of its members were loyal, its leaders were another matter. Lindbergh, it pointed out, was clearly a "pacifist, nonviolent Bolshevik," and he "specifically approves" of La Follette, who was under investigation by the U.S. Senate. Many League leaders, like Townley, were under indictment for disloyalty, the *Times* stressed, and further suggested that these same leaders, with a League membership of 200,000, might be out for financial gain. "Even without 'special privilege,' Mr. Lindbergh's favorite bogey," it observed, "substantial financial results may be achieved."[27]

Not long after the Senate hearings and the *Times* May 29 editorial, the Duluth *Labor World* raised a valid point about the controversy surrounding Lindbergh's book. Why, it asked, had government officials not taken action against the book long ago? The volume had been in circulation for almost a year, and only after Lindbergh's candidacy for governor had the question of the "seditious" nature of the book become a major issue. "Are there two standards of gauging loyalty," it asked, "one set by the federal government and the other by the press and petty politicians?" In fact, the labor-oriented Duluth paper, which took an anti-Burnquist and pro-Democratic position on the gubernatorial race, correctly pointed to a deliberate anti-League strategy; namely, an attempt to utilize national governmental agencies in attacking the League. Safety Commissioner Charles W. Ames, for example, had advised Governor Burnquist in February that "my effort has long been to shift the burden of [the NPL] investigation to the Federal government." Ames, who was convinced that the League was "planning a social revolution" under the leadership of "anarchists and criminals," admitted that he was "hampered and baffled" when Justice Department officials viewed his interest in the matter as "politics."[28]

Later investigation reveals that the 1918 response to Lindbergh's *Why Is Your Country at War* went beyond the heated rhetoric of a political campaign. Indeed, it approached hysteria. When a reprint of the book appeared in 1934, Walter Quigley, a Lindbergh associate, stated in the introduction that all the original plates of the book were destroyed by "government agents" during the spring of 1918. Gordon Dorrance of Dorrance and Company, Philadelphia, the publisher of a later Lindbergh book, *The Economic Pinch* (1923), and of the reissued war book, noted that only about three hundred copies of *Why Is Your Country at War* had been printed when the plates were destroyed. Furthermore, according to these same reports, plates for the first 128 pages of Lindbergh's volume attacking the Money Trust, *Banking and Currency and the Money Trust*, were also destroyed.[29]

Absolute proof of such government action against Lindbergh's books is unavailable. If there was official suppression, there is the question of what the legal charges against the book were—sedition or something else. In attempting to validate the role of government agencies against *Why Is Your Country at War,* the author experienced no success. Burrill Peterson, assistant to the director of the Secret Service, wrote simply: "The Secret Service does not have a file on Charles A. Lindbergh, Sr." After an interview with an agent at the Federal Bureau of Investigation, assurance was given that a file on Lindbergh did indeed exist; but what it contained is unknown, for in a letter dated May 9, 1966, Director J. Edgar Hoover stated: "A review of material in FBI files fails to reflect any information pertinent to the subject of your inquiry."[30]

Yet other records suggest that unusual activity with respect to Lindbergh's book was taking place. Most explicit is correspondence in the Department of Justice which reveals that a number of copies of *Why Is Your Country at War* were placed with the department for safekeeping between 1918 and 1921. According to Justice Department officials, Lindbergh turned the books over to the department voluntarily in 1918, and they were returned at his request in 1921.[31] If the plates were in fact destroyed, and it seems likely that they were, then there were very few copies of the book circulating during the 1918 campaign in Minnesota. Nonetheless, the press obviously made it an issue. Many of the copies that were in circulation seem to have suffered from another malady resulting from the emotion of the campaign—the removal of pages 173 through 178. Significantly, those pages contained Lindbergh's resolution and commentary on the Roman Catholic Church.[32]

The conduct of the Lindbergh-Burnquist Republican primary campaign in 1918 was bitter. It ranks as one of the most acrimonious contests in Minnesota political history. Thanks to the efforts of the staunch anti-League judge John F. McGee, the dominant influence on the Commission of Public Safety, numerous League meetings were forbidden by local officials on the grounds that they constituted disloyal activity. Of some 250 meetings scheduled for the winter and spring of 1917 and 1918,

40 were cancelled because of these local actions, while nineteen
of Minnesota's eighty-six counties outlawed public appearances
by members of the Nonpartisan League. McGee, who in testimony before the Senate Military Affairs Committee had stated
that "A Nonpartisan League lecturer is a traitor every time . . .
no matter what he says or does, a League worker is a traitor. . . .
The disloyal element in Minnesota is largely among the German-
Swedish people," considered Lindbergh "an anarchist and a
Bolsheviki [sic]." As the campaign progressed, some Minnesota
towns greeted League parades with fire hoses, ripe tomatoes, and
yellow paint. Throughout these months League leaders trod
precarious ground as local courts, county attorneys, and grand
juries leveled indictments against them ranging from "discouraging enlistments" to "conspiracy." Townley and organizer Joseph
Gilbert were indicted in several counties and ultimately jailed
in Jackson County. The civil liberties of a number of Leaguers
were violated during what amounted to a reign of terror against
the movement.[33]

Personal abuse and actual physical danger became common-
place for Lindbergh during the campaign. He was run out of
town, stoned, pelted with rotten eggs, hanged in effigy at Red
Wing and Stanton, and refused permission to speak in a number
of places throughout Minnesota. Even a major city, Duluth,
barred Lindbergh from a public platform. Local chapters in
Duluth of both the Shriners and the Woodmen denied Lindbergh access to their halls, despite the fact that rent had been
paid in advance and that literature announcing the appearance
had been distributed. The *Duluth Herald* wholeheartedly supported the action, declaring that "free speech that prospers a
seditious element is a travesty" and that "Duluth need make no
apologies to anybody for having refused a public hearing to
Lindbergh." A later *Herald* editorial, "Traitor or Ass," attacking
Lindbergh's book, and a pamphlet, *The Poison Book of Lindbergh*, containing critical comments on *Why Is Your Country at
War* by Congressman Clarence B. Miller of Duluth, also contributed to anti-Lindbergh sentiment in the Duluth area. The *New*

York Times gave the incident and the Miller charges prominent coverage. The *Labor World,* however, suggested that denial of the halls was the "worst piece of asinine politics ever played here," for it would give Lindbergh and the League an opportunity to brand Duluth a "fief" of the Steel Trust.[34]

As it turned out, the *Minnesota Leader* reacted in just such a manner. It roundly denounced the "foul methods" and threats of violence used by anti-Lindbergh forces in Duluth, and specifically accused the Steel Trust, with its "special domain" on the iron range, of being the main instigator of anti-League activities there. The *Leader* also ran portions of Lindbergh's intended Duluth speech, which he eventually delivered in June, 1918, to a crowd of ten thousand farmers at Osakis. As he had done throughout the campaign, Lindbergh stressed loyalty to one's country. "We are at war . . . and every true American should insist that we fight this through to victory with the least possible delay," he asserted. "The security of democracy itself depends on continuing this conflict until Prussian autocracy is overthrown." The traditional foe of the Money Trust also got in some verbal blasts at the "war profiteers." In his opinion they were the "real disloyalists" in wartime, for "even the pro-German in our midst is actuated by a mistaken sentiment for his fatherland, but these scoundrels, who stab our boys in the back, are moved by selfishness alone." In concluding his speech at Osakis, Lindbergh praised the Nonpartisan League as the only organization that had both a wartime and postwar program, as the true representative of both farmers and laborers, and as an enlightened movement supporting legislation comparable to that of the British Labour party and progressive economic programs in Australia and Scandinavia.[35]

The most intense response to the Nonpartisan League's 1918 campaign developed in southern Minnesota. The League had substantial support from the farmers in the area, primarily those of German, Norwegian, and Swedish ethnic backgrounds, but it also encountered a wave of irrational superpatriotism in the same counties. Henry Martinson, for example, recalled that as a

League organizer in southern Minnesota he was often confronted with refusals to hold meetings, and as a result he resorted to unused pigpens and barns as meeting sites. Frequently, he said, local officials, citizens, and Leaguers were "roughed up" in the process. Martinson, a North Dakotan who had been a member of the Socialist party and editor of its controversial newspaper, *The Iconoclast,* stressed that one of the main purposes of League meetings was simply to disseminate literature. He noted that payment for his work for the League consisted of a salary of thirty-five dollars per week, the use of a Ford car, a Liberty bond, and a copy of Woodrow Wilson's *The New Freedom.* Socialists and Leaguers were "damn good salesmen," he emphasized, adding, "I could talk Norwegian, and that helped like hell."[36]

Lindbergh himself observed in a letter to his son on June 12, about a week before the primary election, that "the south half of the state is afire with excitement." He related to Charles one incident involving a woman with three children who "poked a man 3 times in the nose and face" because he had torn a Lindbergh banner off her car. On another occasion, he said, there was the possibility that he might be physically mobbed, "but I spoke to 6000 people in a grove, and no one interfered." Even more exciting for Lindbergh must have been an incident that occurred in Rock County, near the South Dakota and Iowa borders. According to Congressman John Baer of North Dakota, who was campaigning with Lindbergh at the time, the Lindbergh campaign party was fired on by someone with a shotgun. The blasts were first fired into the air, but later shots hit the campaign car as the party drove away. Baer, who had scrambled to the floor of the vehicle, told the author that "C. A. sat up straight" and instructed the driver: "Don't drive so fast, Gunny, they will think we are scared."[37]

To make matters worse, Lindbergh was arrested near Fairmont, Minnesota, in Martin County, on June 8, 1918, nine days before the election. According to the *Fairmont Daily Sentinel* the arrest, which took place while Lindbergh was trying to con-

IN THE NAME OF PATRIOTISM!

From the *Nonpartisan Leader*, March 25, 1918. Minnesota Historical Society.

"—Drawn expressly for the Leader by John M. Baer. Nineteen out of 87 [sic] counties in Minnesota have barred meetings of the Nonpartisan league. These counties have decided that the farmer has no right in politics; that he has not the right to organize. Congressman Baer shows in this cartoon what is happening in these counties. The farmer is being tied and gagged by the profiteers, the parasites and the politicians. How much longer will the constitution and laws of the state of Minnesota be suspended in 19 of 87 of its counties. Ask Governor Burnquist."

duct a Nonpartisan League meeting on a local farm near Monterey, was based on two charges—unlawful assembly and conspiracy to violate the law interfering with enlistments. Eric Olson, a League member who was at the meeting and ran into trouble with officials when defending the right to hold the meeting, later recalled that the indictment against Lindbergh by County Attorney A. R. Allen singled out Lindbergh's participation in writing and distributing a League pamphlet. Obviously Olson's comments would suggest that county officials considered the pamphlet seditious.[38] The only extant record of the arrest, however, simply lists the one-word charge "conspiracy" against Lindbergh, Townley, and G. H. Griffith. The same Register of Criminal Actions for Martin County reveals that the individuals cited were arraigned and then released on a one-thousand-dollar bond on June 8, with hearings to be held on June 20, three days after the primary election. Lawyer Conrad Gaarenstroom of Fairmont recalled that Rollor Ruble of Fairmont, a League member, signed the bond for Lindbergh.[39]

The Martin County incident was not a complete surprise to either Lindbergh or the *Minnesota Leader*. Both had been suspicious that the political opposition might employ such a tactic in the later stages of the campaign. As early as April 12 Lindbergh had written Eva: "They may even try to convict me to make a hit. They are desperate." In another letter on May 18 he had revealed that "they are getting scared now and trying to make me trouble," but he had also indicated that he would easily win any case brought against him.[40] About a week before the incident took place Lindbergh wrote his daughter once again, reassuring her:

Don't worry about indictment. It would do no good for them and would not succeed. They know now that they are beated [sic] and are crazy. They may turn the scale, but it now stands strong for us. The desperate acts they try will either beat them still worse or turn things their way, can't tell which, but I think the first.[41]

Meanwhile a *Leader* headline on May 25 exclaimed: "BURN-QUIST SUPPORTERS HATCH BLACK PLOT." According to *Leader* sources, early hesitation by the Burnquist "gang" as to whether or not they should bring "trumped-up charges" against farmer-labor candidate Lindbergh had now been removed. This "diabolical eleventh-hour trick to swing the state," warned the *Leader,* would be attempted during the last ten days of the campaign. In its opinion the state was already won by Lindbergh, yet the *Leader* admonished: "WARN YOUR FRIENDS AND ACQUAINTANCES THAT THIS PLOT IS BEING HATCHED." The *Leader* prediction of an indictment, of course, came true, and expectedly the League organ said, in a sense, "I told you so." Just after the Lindbergh arrest, a *Leader* story headlined "RING IN DESPERATION SEIZES LINDBERGH" claimed that Lindbergh had been "thrown in jail." Countering the *Leader* report, however, was a front-page release in the *Fairmont Daily Sentinel* which clarified that Lindbergh had been in court only five or six minutes and was then "free to go his way." Obviously, judged the *Sentinel,* " 'thrown in jail' of course is good political stuff, but it isn't true."[42]

One case in which the "thrown in jail" phrase was true, although it did not involve a political candidate, was that of Eric Olson. A few months after the Martin County affair, Olson wrote former Minnesota governor John Lind about the sequence of events on that fateful day. The Lindbergh-League meeting, he said, was immediately confronted by about one hundred "voluntary guards" who intended to force the assembled crowd to disperse, and Olson protested. Whereupon, he reported, "I was kidnapped by Sheriff W. S. Carver's order, placed in an automobile forcibly in the front seat with a guard chauffeur and two deputy sheriffs in the back seat . . . and . . . taken 25 miles to Fairmont and locked up in the county jail with a person on an Insanity charge." Olson's case had gone through court, and he appealed to Lind that he be given an acquittal and damages for false arrest. Understandably, Olson was bitter toward County Attorney Allen, whom he labeled an "anarchist" and a "terrorist," a view shared by Claude N. Swanson of the *Fairmont Daily Sentinel.*[43] There was no question of Allen having any sympathy for the Nonpartisan League, as evidenced by his statements in

February, 1918, that it was "disloyal and unlawful," and that he would not permit League meetings in Martin County. Lindbergh, in commenting on the incident, agreed with Olson that approximately one hundred deputies were "on hand to arrest me, and did not wait until I began to speak." After being "spirited" to Fairmont, said Lindbergh in a letter to Charles, Jr., "I had over a dozen invitations to go out to supper with different prominent families who before thought I had bristles made in Germany on my back."[44]

Throughout the vituperative campaign of 1918 Lindbergh displayed remarkable courage. A lesser man would not have exposed himself to the conditions of that campaign. Understandably Eva worried about her father, and Lindbergh constantly reassured her that he was taking it well. "I am absolutely immune from anxiety." He pointed out that it did not matter to him "personally" whether he won or lost, and that in his judgment it was indeed patriotic to discuss the "bad and false things about ourselves." He knew that his son-in-law had strong reservations about the Nonpartisan League, and he advised Eva that, "unless vital in their own thinking," family members should not take a position that might interfere with their own business success. "Don't let the boys squabble over me, or my running," he urged. "I know that I am loyal—and more loyal than those who pretend to be 100 per cent loyal." In one reflective letter during the campaign, Lindbergh noted that his purpose in the whole effort was "to do right in the interest of the human family," explaining that "this thing is bigger than anyone's life, and I am not so cowardly as to be afraid for myself." In the same letter he included a portion of text from Mark Twain's *The Mysterious Stranger*, which vividly outlined the rapidity with which war fever could build among the people. "It tells life about as it runs," said Lindbergh, noting how "silly" it was that no one really knew what we were fighting about in the war. "You must prepare to see me in prison and possibly shot," he wrote his daughter, "for I will not be a rubber stamp to deceive the people." But he emphasized that he was at his "happiest" when fighting battles "for the right and for the weak," and he further advised that Eva be philosophical about any "unexpected things" that might happen. Despite these reassurances at the time, Eva later observed about her father that "the campaign of 1918 hurt him psychologically, although he would never admit it." It was, she said, a "blow" to his implicit trust in people.[45]

Although the general tone of the 1918 gubernatorial primary was highly charged and even dangerous, there were also good moments for Lindbergh. Particularly among the farmers of the state, huge and thoroughly sympathetic crowds turned out to hear the League candidate. Clearly Lindbergh was their man. At Wegdahl, for example, it was estimated that fourteen thousand people turned out for an all-day picnic to hear Lindbergh on June 14. He wrote Eva at one point that requests for appearances were coming from counties all over the state, and "I can't hold many." During the late stages of the campaign, the Lindbergh camp staged impressive automobile parades, the vehicles festooned with banners and flags. As the campaign group traveled, these parades grew spontaneously, for farmers would join along the route between towns. One such parade in Meeker County was said to have been twelve miles long. In the opinion of the anti-League *Fargo Forum*, however, the Lindbergh parades were probably composed of the same League organizers on a constant journey.[46]

There were other times during the campaign, reported participant John Baer, when Lindbergh successfully won over crowds at meetings where the local law officials were hostile to the League. Often, said Baer, Lindbergh would ask the crowd how many wished to hear him speak. In most cases, it was easily a majority of those present, and Lindbergh would then turn to the sheriff or other officials and ask if they wished to oppose the voters of the county. Usually he won his point. League president Townley remembered Lindbergh as a "pretty good" campaigner and stated that the people liked him because "they believed he understood what he was talking about." On the other hand, Townley observed, Lindbergh was not a very "clear talker," for he would generally give the same kind of speech to a group of farmers that he might deliver before Congress. "And he talked too long," said Townley. Interestingly, John Baer confirmed that a good relationship existed between Lindbergh and the League president, noting that "Townley thought the world of Lindbergh."[47]

Shortly before the primary election, the League-sponsored *Minnesota Leader* made a last appeal to its readers for Lindbergh support at the polls, based on his congressional record against the trusts, his true loyalty, and his clear concern for farmers and organized labor. Pointing to the Fairmont incident, Townley editorialized on June 15: "[Lindbergh] was shaking hands with the farmers when arrested! County Attorney Allen, who caused Lindbergh to be arrested, WAS APPOINTED BY GOVERNOR BURNQUIST." In the *Leader's* opinion "A VOTE FOR LINDBERGH" was "A VOTE AGAINST TAR AND FEATHERS," "A VOTE FOR DEMOCRACY," and "A VOTE AGAINST JUDGE MCGEE." Lindbergh also made a statement to the Minnesota public by means of a brief circular during the last days of the primary. The two issues of the campaign, said Lindbergh, were to "win the war for democracy" and to "preserve democracy at home." He stressed his farmer-labor orientation, attacked the Public Safety Commission for its activities in Minnesota, and declared his loyalty to the nation. "Let the people rule in Minnesota," Lindbergh implored.[48]

On June 17, 1918, Minnesotans turned out in record numbers as they renominated Burnquist over challenger Lindbergh in the Republican primary election. The final totals were: Burnquist—199,325; Lindbergh—150,626. All things considered, Lindbergh did well, carrying thirty counties, mainly along the North Dakota border, and receiving total votes equal to three times the number of League members in Minnesota at the time. In a normal year he might have won; 1918, however, saw an abnormally large voter turnout and a great deal of bipartisan balloting. The Democrats, who had received 38,840 votes for governor in the 1916 primary, received 32,649 votes in the 1918 primary, but the Republicans, who had polled 179,077 in the 1916 primary, received an unprecedented total of 349,951 in 1918. Clearly the loyalty issue had drawn many people, normally not classified as Republicans, to participate in the 1918 Republican primary.[49]

The disloyalty campaign against Lindbergh had taken its toll. Without question the bitter attack on Lindbergh had been a political move to stop the League, and as Peterson and Fite conclude: "Charges of disloyalty proved to be an excellent means of keeping the Nonpartisan League from extending power from beyond the bounds of North Dakota." Furthermore, serious questions were raised in 1918 as to whether improper procedures in counting the vote deprived Lindbergh of victory. Lindbergh wrote Eva that he estimated "from things I have learned" that about 25,000 votes cast for him had been counted in Burnquist's tally. Usually, he said, this was accomplished by having the judge read Burnquist's name instead of Lindbergh's; the poll worker would then simply write it down. Leaguer John Baer later declared that the Burnquist forces "stole" the election in 1918. There is no evidence of a recount, however, and the results stood.[50]

Further evidence of political motivation behind the disloyalty campaign against Lindbergh and the League is the fact that about a month after the election the charges pending against Lindbergh in Martin County were dropped. The entry on the justice docket merely states "case dismissed." County Attorney Allen announced that the dismissal was based on recent Minnesota Supreme Court action clearing League officers Townley and Gilbert of indictments against them. Dismissal of charges against Leaguers after the election in July, of course, did the League little good. The damage had already been done.[51]

Press reaction to the primary was predictable. While the League-sponsored *Minnesota Leader* was disappointed with Lindbergh's defeat, it emphasized that his "astonishing" vote total was a victory in one sense, for it would put the "enemies" on "thin ice." It attributed the election outcome to a large crossover of Democratic votes. Papers hostile to the League, such as the *Minneapolis Tribune,* were pleased with Burnquist's reelection, of course, as a "LOYALTY WINS IN PRIMARIES OF MINNESOTA" headline indicated. Moreover, the *Tribune* judged, this nation "is going to stay a democracy in spite of all the A. C. Trotzkies of the Nonpartisan League." The *New York Times* was relieved at Lindbergh's defeat, too, editorializing on June 20: "It is a satisfaction to loyal men everywhere to hear that Governor Burnquist has beaten Mr. Lindbergh by more than 75,000 [sic] votes."[52]

Lindbergh's defeat in the gubernatorial primary put the Nonpartisan League in a difficult position. Although the *Minnesota Leader* was encouraged by the 150,000 votes given Lindbergh, there was the question of where this strength would fall in the general election. The main options open to the League were to "sit out the election," to support the Democratic party, or to run candidates on an independent ticket. While the *Leader* blamed the state Democratic machine for contributing to Burnquist's victory, there was some comment favoring a coalition between the Democrats and League-labor forces—a suggestion later realized with the formation of the Minnesota Democratic–Farmer-Labor party during the 1940's. But attempts in 1918 to woo the Democrats failed, in part because the party's gubernatorial nominee, Fred E. Wheaton, was a conservative and rejected any moves in that direction. Thus the League-labor forces, choosing not to forfeit their political impact, decided to file candidates on an independent basis. Perhaps because of the emotional nature of the Burnquist–Lindbergh primary contest and the fact that he had been defeated once, Lindbergh was not seriously suggested as a repeater in the governor's race. Named at an August convention in St. Paul were hardware merchant and farmer David H. Evans of Tracy, formerly a Populist and now a Democrat, as candidate for governor; and Tom Davis of Marshall, an insurgent Republican, as candidate for attorney general. Originally the petitions for Evans and Davis stated that they would file as "independent" candidates, but because of a ruling by the state attorney general that the name of a party be entered on the ballot, the label "Farmer-Labor" was used for the first time.[53]

The disloyalty campaign against the League continued during the general election campaigning in the state, but with less intensity than in the primary. As the war neared an end in Europe, national comment began to criticize the overzealous "patriots," and there was some evidence of similar feelings in Minnesota. Still, when the votes were in on November 5, Governor Burnquist won reelection over Evans and Wheaton, although he did not receive a majority of the total vote. The returns for governor were: Burnquist—166,611; Evans—111,966; Wheaton—76,836. Farmer-Labor candidate Evans, a lesser-known figure than Lindbergh but as a Wilson Democrat not as vulnerable on the war issue, carried twenty-one counties in northwestern, central, and west-central Minnesota, all of which had given majorities to Lindbergh in the primary. Knute Nelson, no friend of the NPL, easily won reelection to another term in the U.S. Senate, although W. G. Calderwood, the old Prohibitionist, made a substantial showing as a candidate of the National party, receiving 137,000 votes to Nelson's 206,000. Calderwood undoubtedly received Democratic support to bolster the announced Progressive, Prohibitionist, and Socialist base of the ticket. Nelson forces were angered when, at the urging of John Lind, the Wilson administration came out for Calderwood.[54]

League-labor candidates Lindbergh and Evans both did well in the primary and general elections with three groups in the state: (1) The farmers of the Red River Valley and of central and west-central Minnesota, largely Scandinavian-American in ethnic background; (2) the German-American population throughout the state; and (3) the labor element in the Twin Cities. The good showing in the Valley could be expected, for agrarian protest had found a solid base there during the Populist days of the late nineteenth century, and Townley's NPL program likewise appealed to the same rural sentiment and grievances as it swept across from North Dakota. More surprising was the League support in German-American counties, for they had no previous history of sympathy for liberal or radical politics. A case in point was Democratic and German-settled Stearns County, which Lindbergh, as Sixth District congressman, had consistently failed to carry. In 1918, however, Lindbergh defeated Burnquist by a solid 4,966 to 3,807 vote, while Evans, with 3,454 votes, won a plurality over Burnquist (2,647) and Democrat Wheaton (1,414). As further evidence, Republican Congressman Harold Knutson, who voted against American entry into the war, carried Stearns by three to one. In view of its consistent antiwar voting pattern, beginning during the World War I period and extending through the World War II era, Samuel Lubell has gone so far as to suggest that "Stearns County is in many ways the classic isolationist county in the whole United States." In heavily German-American Brown County, in southern Minnesota, Lindbergh won by more than two to one, and Evans carried the county by a clear majority. Although some German farmers probably agreed with the Nonpartisan League domestic reform program, the major factor in determining German-American voting behavior in 1918 was clearly the war issue. This contention is reinforced by the fact that German-American support for the League was not noticeable until after American entry into the war in 1917.[55]

Though Lindbergh and Evans failed to win majority support in urban Hennepin and Ramsey counties, their strong showing in labor wards in the Twin Cities was encouraging to those who favored a League coalition with labor. In contrast to a general pattern throughout the state, where Lindbergh received more votes than Evans, Evans outpolled Lindbergh in certain precincts in St. Paul. Apparently the anti-Catholic campaign had borne fruit in the home constituency of the *Catholic Bulletin.* The war record of the Burnquist administration and a conservative Democratic gubernatorial candidate also contributed to the election results in Minneapolis and St. Paul. In contrast, Lindbergh and Evans did poorly in northeastern Minnesota labor areas. In St. Louis County, for example, which includes Duluth and the Mesabi and Vermillion iron ranges, Lindbergh lost to Burnquist by a disappointing two to one margin in the primary, and Evans came in a weak third to victor Burnquist and Democrat Wheaton in November. Lindbergh's defeat on the iron range, as some political analysts pointed out at the time, was in part attributed to a strong feeling of distrust among the large southern European population, mainly Slavic-American, toward the League and its leaders, who had been accused of being pro-German. Moreover, because Germany's position seemed to favor the "white" faction in the Finnish Civil War, radical Finnish-Americans there were similarly suspicious of the League. Another factor was the lack of a viable League organization in the range area at the time. In 1918, as a part of the somewhat complex protest movement in range politics, William L. Carss narrowly defeated Congressman Clarence Miller in his bid for reelection in the Eighth District. Miller, a harsh critic of Lindbergh and the League during the primary, ran as a Republican, while Carss won on the Union Labor ticket. The *Minnesota Leader* termed the political upset an NPL victory, but the disparity between the Lindbergh and Carss results suggests that the *Leader's* assumption was too simplistic.[56]

Two counties in southern Minnesota, Martin and Rock, showed a more consistent relationship between anti-League campaign activity and voting patterns. In Martin County, where Lindbergh had been arrested, Burnquist won by a convincing 2,445 to 1,136 vote over Lindbergh, and the combined vote total given Burnquist and Wheaton was more than six times that given Evans. In Rock County, where anti-League violence had occurred, including shotgun blasts at Lindbergh's campaign car, the returns were equally devastating. In both races Lindbergh and Evans lost to the opposition by a margin of almost four to one.[57]

The 1918 election clearly represented a shift in Minnesota politics. From what Carl H. Chrislock has termed a bipartisan political "consensus" based on progressive goals among "moral reformers, small-town business and professional men, and farmers"[58] during the early twentieth century, there emerged a new coalition of political forces prompted by division over the war issue and the domestic reform policies of the Nonpartisan League. This change in 1918, initially accented by the Lindbergh–Burnquist confrontation, now drew on radical progressives, organized labor, and German-Americans to add to the NPL voting base of farmers and Scandinavian-Americans. Meanwhile the conservatives also gained a new solidity as the more moderate progressives, apprehensive about the League program, joined stand-patters as their main supporters. Professor Chrislock describes the two new coalitions in this way:

> The Townley movement attracted groups whose complaints against the status quo were acute—notably grain farmers, trade unionists, left-wing progressives, and pragmatic Socialists—as well as those who harbored resentful memories of the wartime "loyalty" crusade. The Republican party commanded the support of defenders of the established order along with that of former progressives who feared Nonpartisan League radicalism more than they welcomed change.[59]

Without question the war record of the Burnquist administration and the Safety Commission were the most important catalysts in the forming of the new political alignments. Organized labor, additionally frustrated by the weakness of the Democratic party in Minnesota, made a commitment in the summer of 1918 to pursue independent political activity. There was no new third party as yet, but the crucial elements of the Farmer-Labor movement had been formed and would mature during the 1920's and 1930's.

For Lindbergh, 1918 was truly a turning point in his political career. Although he had met defeat before, in 1916, the stigma of the "loyalty" crusade against him, despite its lack of justification, would be difficult to erase or forget. Time and his participation in the emerging Farmer-Labor movement in Minnesota would help to heal the political and personal wounds of the traumatic 1918 election, but never again would Lindbergh approach his 1918 vote total in later attempts to win public office.

Chapter X

Farmer-Labor Politics

"The Farmer-Labor party is the lifeboat that shall save the best of those that are yet upon the two big ships that have both been shipwrecked upon the rocks of 'legislation for special interests.'"[1] Thus spoke Farmer-Labor congressman Knud Wefald of Hawley in 1923, indicating the hope and purpose of the third-party movement in Minnesota. Indeed Wefald, Magnus Johnson, Henrik Shipstead, Ole J. Kvale, and C. A. Lindbergh were among the first political figures around whom the independent Farmer-Labor movement[2] rallied during its formative period, 1918–1922. In 1923 and 1924, following Farmer-Labor success at the polls in 1922, the commitment was made to fulfill the role of a national third party, and Floyd B. Olson headed a state ticket for the first time.[3] During these years Lindbergh, whose controversial 1918 gubernatorial campaign had provided a major impetus to the concept of a farmer-labor coalition, remained politically active, running for Congress in 1920 and the U.S. Senate in 1923. He lost both races, managed the Nonpartisan League state campaign in 1922, and, shortly before his death in 1924, emerged as the probable Farmer-Labor candidate for governor.

Prior to this political activity in Minnesota, and not long after the 1918 primary race, Lindbergh briefly became involved in national politics when he received an appointment from President Woodrow Wilson to serve on the War Industries Board in August, 1918. In reply to a telegram of August 23 from Bernard M. Baruch, chairman of the board,[4] asking him to serve,

Lindbergh wired on August 26 that he was willing to "serve anywhere for the general cause."[5] Lindbergh was optimistic about the nature of his assignment with the war agency, for he wrote Eva: "I have gotten the work to do that I can do best and am free lance, my own boss to look into things from an economic view and deal direct with the Chairman of the Board." He was pleased with Baruch, noting that he was a "broad good man and progressive" and "about 1000 per cent more satisfactory than I expected." Lindbergh emphasized that Baruch would not ask him to do anything that "is not consistent with my views." In early September, Lindbergh was sworn in for government service with the WIB, and after two long conferences with Baruch, he was prepared to proceed with a "special matter" assigned to him by the chairman.[6]

Lindbergh's appointment received strong endorsement in the Wilson administration from George Creel, head of the Committee on Public Information, who, in fact, claimed that he personally persuaded Baruch to make the appointment. Although Lindbergh himself denied that Creel had anything to do with the WIB position,[7] there is clear proof that Creel persistently defended the Nonpartisan League during the war. Actually Creel's involvement with the League went back to 1917, when he had furnished administration speakers at the controversial St. Paul-La Follette convention. Furthermore, he had been a prime mover behind the Washington conferences between President Wilson, Townley, Lindbergh, and other figures involved in the League movement. Wilson, however, became worried lest the administration become too closely tied to the League, and he warned Creel in April, 1918, that "we had better pull away from them." But Creel did not budge in his own thinking, replying in the heat of the Lindbergh–Burnquist campaign that the League was "absolutely loyal" and that the "Safety Commission is willing to drive it into disloyalty in order to further its own mean political end." Later in the year, Wilson indicated that he was disturbed by incidents of mob violence against the League and other groups and instructed Attorney General Thomas Gregory to take appropriate action. He warned Gregory, however, that there was a danger of "playing into the hands of some violently and maliciously partisan Republicans." The Lindbergh appointment seemed to be an overt sign of administration confidence in League loyalty, though the choice of Lindbergh appears to have been more the act of Creel than Wilson.[8]

But the War Industries Board appointment was short-lived for Lindbergh. As soon as news of the appointment was released, it touched off a storm of protest in Minnesota, and within two weeks Lindbergh, at the request of the board, volunteered his resignation. "CAPITAL STUNNED OVER MYSTERY OF LINDBERGH BERTH" exclaimed a *Minneapolis Tribune* headline on September 8, 1918. The *Tribune* named Creel and Minnesota Democrats as those to blame for the appointment, and it wondered how anyone could accept the choice of Lindbergh, a man who had written *Why Is Your Country at War* and voted for the McLemore resolution. Predictably, the anti-League *Minneapolis Journal* also strongly denounced Lindbergh's appointment, again isolating Creel, Lindbergh's war book, and "the disloyal character of Mr. Lindbergh's record" as factors in the case. Anti-Lindbergh sentiment was expressed in many letters to Senator Knute Nelson, who himself had declared shortly after the 1918 primary that Lindbergh was "as disloyal as can be." It is safe to assume that Nelson exerted congressional pressure to reverse the administration appointment, and, as he wrote one correspondent about the board investigation of the matter, "I do not think there is any danger of the matter culminating in Mr. Lindbergh's appointment."[9]

Lindbergh's letter of resignation to Baruch, dated September 10, 1918, reveals a remarkable tolerance on the part of the former congressman, given the immediacy and harshness of the events that had precipitated it. Noting that the "forces of opposition" in the state had had their effect, Lindbergh stated: "I realize how difficult it is for the Administration to meet the emergencies created by conditions such as these, and it is not so important that I should have the honor of serving my country in a responsible position." Lindbergh did point out that his own supporters were truly loyal to the nation, in contrast to those individuals who now threatened to cease work on the Liberty Loan program unless his appointment was revoked. "I shall express no spirit of resentment against the objectors," concluded Lindbergh, "and will say to you that whenever there is an opportunity for me to serve the nation in its crisis, I shall be ready to do so."[10]

Even more explicit in explaining the sequence of events and the emotion surrounding the whole War Industries Board affair is a long letter Lindbergh sent to Eva. Among the many erroneous statements released about the appointment, he wrote, was the suggestion that the publication of *Why Is Your Country at War* forced the administration to change its decision. In addition, neither Creel nor the Nonpartisan League "had any influence with my appointment," nor did the offer come from any "solicitation" by himself. In Lindbergh's judgment the administration could not be charged with making a mistake either in appointing him or in withdrawing that appointment, "if for reasons, political . . . or otherwise, it found itself hampered in the prosecution of the war . . . it was not its duty to insist upon my service, nor my duty to complain."[11] Of these "political" reasons and the response in Minnesota to the appointment Lindbergh concluded:

When my appointment was announced in Minnesota it raised a storm of protest from certain well understood forces, who were willing to subvert their loyalty to selfish personal ends. Prominent among these objectors, as suggested by the press, were the Federal Reserve Bank of the 9th District, as well as the Reserve Banks in other sections of the country.

Certain of these interests, by virtue of their positions as heads of Liberty Loan Committees were willing to block the success of the Liberty Loan, and (even) to obstruct the National Administration in its war program, in order to have me removed from any position where I might be able to deal effectively with economic and industrial problems.

This inspired campaign was aided by the malicious attacks of certain newspapers, and could be made effective through the power of certain U.S. Senators to embarrass the President in hampering his war policies and thereby obstructing the National Administration in its war work.[12]

Once again the combined phenomena of organized political opposition and war hysteria succeeded in defeating Lindbergh. Significantly, George Creel demanded that Lindbergh be retained on the Board. In a letter to President Wilson on September 18, Creel asserted that Lindbergh was "absolutely" loyal and charged that the real truth of the matter was simply that both Republicans and Democrats feared the political power of the Nonpartisan League. To condone the removal of Lindbergh, "a single act of cowardice," stated Creel, could only be interpreted as a concession to reactionary politics. For Lindbergh the whole affair must have been a trying experience, coming as it did so soon after the emotional 1918 campaign. As Eva later observed: "I am positive that the machinations which brought about Father's release by the War Board were some of the meanest ever employed in Minnesota—the whole thing was disgraceful and I *know* it hurt Father keenly, though he would not admit it."[13]

A few weeks after his political ordeals in 1918, Lindbergh joined his friend James Manahan, the NPL counsel, at his lake cottage north of St. Paul for several days of needed rest. According to Manahan, it was during this retreat that their friendship deepened. Lindbergh's reserve was formidable, Manahan noted, and "it took me many years to get down beneath [it]." Manahan, assessing Lindbergh's character after many years of association, singled out his "fine sense of justice" as his "predominant" trait. "The sorrow of human beings, the greed, the dishonesty, had all been magnetized by his innate sense of honesty until he had constantly before his eyes a great mosaic of human wrongs." During their brief stay at the lake the two men were undisturbed, cooking their own meals and enjoying the beauty of the late autumn season. What surprised Manahan most was to see Lindbergh strip and jump into the cold water of a Minnesota lake in November. When the two friends were ready to leave the cabin, Lindbergh took a slow last look around, and said: "There isn't any better medicine for the mind or body than we have just enjoyed."[14]

Shortly thereafter, Lindbergh faced the important question of what project or work he might next pursue. He did not wish to practice law, nor did he intend to run for public office. Nevertheless, it would have been unrealistic to expect that so stubborn a reformer as Lindbergh would be satisfied with any work not somehow connected with the public interest, and thus it was that he opted for a career as editor and publisher of a new journal, *Lindbergh's National Farmer*. Ignoring requests from Eva that he relax and enjoy a few months of world travel before plunging into the new project, Lindbergh went ahead with his plan to establish a farm paper that would feature editorials by Lindbergh; articles by voluntary contributors on dairying, stock raising, sheep, poultry, hogs, and other items; and discussions on economic problems in general. Set up in Minneapolis, Lindbergh was optimistic and insistent that his monthly would have a circulation of 25,000 within a year and would eventually reach 50,000 to 100,000. He did not fear the possibility of journalistic and political attacks on his writings; in fact, he welcomed them, counseling Eva to "put on [her] Lindbergh grit," for "really would you not be ashamed of your father if he went into a hole and pulled the hole in behind him?"[15]

The first issue of *Lindbergh's National Farmer*, financed largely by Lindbergh himself, appeared in March, 1919. In format it was a large, handsome magazine, roughly 11 by 15 inches, with a bold, impressive front-page heading and large, readable headlines throughout the sixteen-page issue. It represented a "new era" in the publication of farm magazines, its editor and publisher wrote, for it was a "challenge" to the press serving "special interests," and a "protest against injustice and wrongs, not only to the farmers, but to all people everywhere." Politically the new magazine was independent, and its purpose in addressing economic and world problems was to aid the "welfare of the workers."[16]

As the monthly issues came out from March to December, 1919, it became evident that the journal was both a farm magazine and a vehicle for the expression of reform thought. Stories and reports on farm production, shipping quotas, and care of livestock and crops were regularly printed, but there also appeared long editorials attacking the officers of corporations ("the destroyers of industrial liberty"), endorsing the radical approach to government control taken by the 1919 North Dakota legislature, and discussing such world issues as the nature of capitalism and the role of President Wilson at the Treaty of Versailles. On the latter issue Lindbergh wrote in early 1919 that he approved of the president's personal participation at Paris, that he saw hope in Wilson's views concerning self-determination of nations and the cessation of secret diplomacy, and that the League of Nations might help in the reorganization of the world. But, he warned, the League was not the real solution to the problem of economic injustice; furthermore, he was displeased that the workers had no "controlling representation" at the peace conference. Within a few months, Lindbergh found he had to take a thoroughly critical position on the Versailles Treaty. "Wilson has his pay now for trying to tie us to a world war machine," he wrote in early 1920. "Nothing ever done in my judgment was so un-American as to try to hitch us to that treaty."[17]

Lindbergh's National Farmer, however, was but a brief episode in the history of American agrarian journalism. In the January, 1920, issue, Lindbergh announced that because of increased costs the journal would now be published as a small, pocket-sized pamphlet. Refunds for subscriptions to the original journal would be made. One more issue of *Lindbergh's National Farmer*, its final issue, appeared in March, 1920. In view of the emerging farm depression in 1920, it would seem that a farm magazine might have had appeal, since people in trouble need a forum, and indeed journals like *Wallaces' Farmer* survived.[18] For Lindbergh, however, the mixed style of his journal plus a lack of promotional organization combined to force its collapse. According to letters between Lindbergh and his printer, *Svenska Folkets Tidning* publisher A. G. Johnson, printing runs of *Lindbergh's National Farmer* varied between 1500 and 5000 copies. Unquestionably, Lindbergh lost money on the project, probably about two thousand dollars on printing alone, not to mention his office, travel, staff, and any promotional or contributor costs he may have incurred. Subscription rates of one dollar per year certainly did not offset the deficit.[19]

Meanwhile political developments in Minnesota during 1919 and 1920 centered on the unprecedented farmer-labor coalition formed during the 1918 campaign. Although there was an unwillingness to unite into a single political organization, the Minnesota State Federation of Labor established the Working People's Nonpartisan Political League during its meeting at New Ulm in July, 1919, thus providing a strictly political vehicle whose activities would parallel those of the farmer-oriented Nonpartisan League. The Working People's League, representing a membership of 45,000 in the state and headed by William Mahoney, president of the St. Paul Trades and Labor Assembly, supported most of the same issues as the parent League, including the eight-hour day, workmen's compensation, equal rights for women, and public ownership of railways, steamships, banks, packing plants, grain terminals, and telegraph and telephone companies.[20]

On March 24, 1920, the two Nonpartisan Leagues held endorsing conventions, which, by prearrangement, were scheduled in the same hotel in St. Paul. There was speculation as to whether Lindbergh, the "central figure" and "sterling leader" (in the words of later Farmer-Laborites Ernest Lundeen and Elmer Benson) around whom the farm-labor element initially formed ranks in 1918, might wish to head the state ticket again. But Lindbergh was not interested. On March 18 he notified League officer William Lemke of North Dakota: "I ask you to act for me to tell the delegates, that I refuse to be a candidate for Governor, and would not accept endorsement to run." Lindbergh felt it necessary to take this action prior to the convention because he had information from several sources that delegates wanted him as the standard-bearer, and "it will avoid embarrassment to make an advance refusal." His decision not to run is probably one indication of the cumulative effects of the 1918 campaign. Subsequently, the League conventions selected a ticket headed by Glenwood dentist and unsuccessful 1918 congressional

From the *Minnesota Leader*, June 1, 1918. Minnesota Historical Society.

"Hand to hand and shoulder to shoulder, the awakened people of the cities and farms are marching towards victory—JUNE 17. Mechanic, toiler, and the small business man realize with increasing clearness as the great fight surges forward that Lindbergh is their only hope, that they must uphold him in order to uphold themselves, that he is the one man in Minnesota who today stands Lincoln-like above the boiling mud of 'politics' and strikes for freedom with swift and telling blows. Lindbergh! calm, powerful, unbeatable as the ocean tides! Lindbergh! whose popularity outruns that of any former candidate since the great people's uprising of the early '90s! He stands today as the connecting link between laborer and farmer, who were strangers for so many years. They grip his hand with the intensity of men aflame with enthusiasm and confident of victory. They have actually been doing that in many a grove and town auditorium throughout Minnesota for four weeks. He is their choice, their champion, and they will follow him over the top on primary election day in a charge that will sweep autocracy before it—both in Europe and in Minnesota."

candidate Henrik Shipstead as candidate for governor in the Republican primary. They also took the precaution of preserving the third-party label by filing additional candidates with Farmer-Labor designation.[21]

The main race in the Minnesota primary campaign of 1920 pitted Shipstead against the Republican nominee for governor, Jacob A. O. Preus. Preus, experienced as insurance commissioner, state auditor, and secretary to Senator Knute Nelson, had been selected by the Republicans after Governor Burnquist announced that he would not seek reelection. Anti-League strategy during the campaign of 1920 changed from the disloyalty issue of 1918 to vigorous attacks on the League involving international socialism. Emotions were still high regarding the League, but, unlike 1918, League speakers were not barred from speaking in Minnesota towns in 1920. Fergus Falls and St. Cloud, for example, communities that had refused League president Townley permission to speak in 1918, welcomed him in 1920. On June 21, Preus defeated Shipstead in the Republican primary by a vote of 133,832 to 125,861. Despite the setback, Shipstead had done well, carrying fifty-four of the state's eighty-six counties, thus adding twenty-four to the thirty won by Lindbergh in 1918. The League candidate for attorney general, Tom Sullivan, proved to be the closest contender for a major state office, losing to incumbent Attorney General Clifford Hilton by only 1,133 votes. Oscar Keller, a Republican, and William Carss, a Democrat, won renomination as League candidates in the Fourth and Eighth congressional districts, while in a bizarre development in the Seventh Congressional District, League-endorsed candidate O. J. Kvale, a Lutheran minister, won over Andrew J. Volstead by 2300 votes, only to be later disqualified in a court suit for having stated during the campaign that his opponent was an atheist.[22]

Between the primary and general election campaigns of 1920 Lindbergh was drawn back into Minnesota politics. Reluctantly, after being approached by several committees, Lindbergh agreed to run for his old seat as Sixth District congressman if a sufficient number of signatures were obtained on filing petitions. "They will file me as independent," he wrote Eva. "It is no cinch to be elected though, for the present man [Harold Knutson] is a very smooth duck—not right but that is not known by many of the voters." By late August the Lindbergh movement had secured the needed signatures, and Lindbergh was once again a candidate for Congress.[23]

The Lindbergh candidacy evoked little excitement in the Sixth District. Campaign publicity from the Knutson camp stressed the incumbent congressman's responsiveness to his home district, his opposition to socialism and radicalism, and his alignment with the Republican party. As declared, Lindbergh ran in the 1920 race as an independent, stating in his campaign literature: "I emphasize *independent*, because I belong to no political party, but seek to help organize the progressive forces in them all for the general good so far as I am able." He campaigned in a great many towns in the district throughout October, but perhaps indicative of the last-minute nature of the campaign was the fact that one of his main pieces of promotional literature had first been written for his abortive farm journal. In the pamphlet, "The Voter and the Economic Pinch," Lindbergh concentrated on the familiar topics of political machines and problems within the economic structure.[24]

On November 2, 1920, Lindbergh lost his first race in the Sixth District, receiving only 31 per cent of the vote and carrying no counties. The final results were: Knutson—47,954; Lindbergh—21,587. No Democratic nominee was entered in the congressional race, which helped Knutson, as evidenced by his three to one vote margin over Lindbergh in Democratic Stearns County. Generally it was a Republican landslide in Minnesota in 1920, with Warren G. Harding winning by four to one over Democrat James M. Cox in the presidential contest and Republicans easily winning all state office races. Preus once again defeated Shipstead, who had filed as an independent during the general election, for the governorship of the state. His margin of victory was 415,805 to 281,402, with Democratic nominee Laurence Hodgson polling 81,293 votes. The only League candidate to win a congressional race in 1920 was Republican Oscar Keller in the Fourth District. In the Seventh District, Republican Volstead narrowly defeated repeat challenger Kvale, who had filed as an independent. Thus Minnesota reflected the national Republican trend, and in addition showed a strong negative response to the Nonpartisan Leaguers that was indicative of the intense fear of radical politics during the postwar "Red Scare." There was also evidence of Democratic crossover to the Republicans in the gubernatorial race once again. Finally, the general concensus was that the expanded vote to women aided conservative forces in 1920 since the feminine turnout was strong in the cities and weak in the rural areas. All of these factors contributed to Lindbergh's defeat in 1920, but equally as significant was the simple fact that he waged a late, probably underfinanced, campaign as an "independent" candidate against the incumbent congressman. Farmer-Labor failures in the Minnesota election of 1920 signaled the end of the first period of the insurgent movement. Its leaders were now ready to abandon the old strategy of capturing the Republican party in the state.[25]

From the end of the 1920 campaign until mid-1922 Lindbergh devoted most of his time to nonpolitical matters. He increasingly became involved in the development of real estate properties in Florida, the beginning of a bank in Shakopee, Minnesota, and work on a new book-length manuscript. Actually Lindbergh made initial contacts on the Florida and bank matters during the winter of 1919–1920, while the writing project, a study of economic conditions, probably began in late 1921 or early 1922. William Agard, an Eastern businessman and an important new Lindbergh associate on the Florida and banking projects, invested substantially in both ventures. Other investors in the newly chartered People's National Bank of Shakopee included Carl Bolander, A. M. Opsahl, a number of Eastern business friends, and Congressman Volstead, who, with Lindbergh, owned half the stock in the bank.[26]

What influence may have prompted Lindbergh to investigate the opportunity in Florida real estate is unknown, but he clearly forecast the development boom that was to hit the Miami area.

Operating out of Little River, Florida, just a few miles north of Miami, Lindbergh began purchasing property as funds and time permitted. "Think I can make a few thousand by hustling," he wrote Eva in February, 1920. Later he constructed a rough cottage with rooms to rent, keeping a garage for his Buick car (equipped with tent-type camping equipment, which he used frequently in parks or out in the open) and himself. Obviously he liked the Florida winter climate and the new setting, and he pointed out to his daughter that he even enjoyed "batching" rather than eating out all the time. Agard was a key factor in the Florida venture, and Lindbergh periodically received funds from him for extending loans and making property purchases. Businessman Lindbergh warned Agard that there were unsafe properties and many more "deadbeat" loan applicants than usual in the Florida area, but he was supremely confident that investment opportunities on loans or property would yield "better returns than anywhere else I know of." The citrus industry, he felt, was risky—the poultry business was better—but he predicted "a great future" for Miami. Furthermore, he liked the climate so well that on one occasion he declared that in "ten years or so" he would settle in Florida permanently.[27]

There were personal and family changes affecting Lindbergh during these years, too. In 1921 his mother, Louisa, died, and he reflected in a letter to his daughter that he had pleasant memories of the period on the farm when his mother was the "big factor" in his life. "Mother and father were good to us," he wrote Eva. "They were with us more than you and Lillian had of your father and mother." A year later, on a more happy note, Eva and George Christie became the parents of a baby boy, George, Jr. During the same period, Charles, Jr.'s experiences varied from Morrison County farmer to University of Wisconsin student to aviation trainee. From mid-1918 to the fall of 1920 he operated the home farm, concentrating on Guernsey cattle, sheep, hogs, and chickens, as well as taking on the Empire Milking Machine agency for the area. Like his father, Charles, Jr. loved the land, although, unlike C. A., he enjoyed actual farming and working with machinery.

C. A. had begun to stock the farm with cattle and sheep after the war broke out in 1917 and the need for increased food production was obvious. The same need and simultaneous expansion of the armed services resulted in a drastic shortage of farm workers, a situation that enabled Charles, Jr. to stop attending Little Falls high school in the late winter of 1918 and still receive his diploma in the spring. The brief tenure of the younger Lindbergh as a farmer was never an economic success, however, for the limitations of a 120-acre farm, the expenditures for a tractor, machinery, and livestock, and the generally depressed state of agriculture after the war were hard obstacles to overcome. C. A. occasionally wrote Evangeline about the problem, noting that he had little success in convincing Charles to sell his stock, and, finally, that "this farm game will have to be given up, for I have been near ruined by it and tried to quit but Chas begged to take it on and now it is pinching him."[28]

Lindbergh was pleased in 1920 and 1921 when Charles studied mechanical engineering at Wisconsin and felt that many jobs would be open to him. At one point he worried that, since Charles was on the school rifle team, in time of war he might be made "leader of a squad of sharp shooters." At no time did young Charles wish to follow his father's career in law and politics, and Lindbergh, realizing this fact, never imposed his will on his son concerning a choice of profession. By the summer of 1921, Lindbergh wrote Evangeline that he would have no money to contribute to Charles's schooling for the coming year. The following spring young Lindbergh, not particularly enchanted with college anyway, headed his motorcycle for Lincoln, Nebraska, where he entered flying school at the Nebraska Aircraft Corporation. He completed a course of instruction in 1922 and began his career as a mechanic, wing walker, and barnstorming pilot. His father was not overly pleased with the vocation, for he kept thinking of the short duration of a pilot's life aloft during World War I.[29] A year or so later he discussed Charles's activities in a letter to Evangeline. He worried a bit that Charles "seems to live within himself so much," but then he reflected that "he gets that from me at least in part, for I am living as if the rest of the world gets along by itself." Charles may get interested in "things on earth" soon, he thought, but "he is tied up at present with roving and I sort of envy him."[30]

Meanwhile the Farmer-Labor movement in Minnesota entered a crucial period in its development during 1922, for out of that campaign and election came the solidification of the third-party approach. It was not an easy transition for the new party, and in its struggle for direction Lindbergh was drawn into active Farmer-Labor politics. There had been some discussion of a possible fusion between the Democrats and the two Nonpartisan Leagues when all three groups held simultaneous conventions in Minneapolis on March 31, 1922. But agreement could not be reached, primarily because of the innate ideological base of the League, which saw both the Republican and the Democratic parties as vestiges of the "special interests," and because of the anti-Catholic prejudice felt toward the Democratic party by a large segment of Scandinavian and Lutheran Leaguers. Although League president Townley still favored a "balance-of-power" concept in swinging League support to candidates of any party, he was outvoted at the conventions, and the decision to back a full slate of Farmer-Labor candidates was made. In the major contests League delegates endorsed their 1920 gubernatorial candidate, Henrik Shipstead, for the Senate, and, as their choice to run for governor, Magnus Johnson, a Swedish-born Meeker County farmer.[31]

During the same period the Nonpartisan League itself, influenced by the general economic depression of the early 1920's, experienced serious difficulty. After a brief business boom during the months immediately following the war, the depression took hold about mid-1920. The effect on agriculture was particularly severe, and, although the farm crisis was a definite stimulus to the farmer-labor coalition and the new party, the economic consequences of the depression, along with the disloyalty and radicalism charges, contributed to the demise of the parent League. By 1922, paid memberships, the crux of League support, had dwindled severely, even though well-meaning farmers had sent in postdated checks totaling $1,200,000 to the national organization. Many of the state and county League newspapers, effective propaganda organs for the movement, were forced to cut back or liquidate. President Townley resigned his position with the League in May, and for all practical purposes the old leadership and operative features of the League were dead.[32]

In 1922, Lindbergh's role in Farmer-Labor affairs was to serve in party offices for the first time, rather than to be an actual candidate for public office. During the year he served variously as counsel and general manager to the state executive committee of the Nonpartisan League, as treasurer of the state central committee of the Farmer-Labor party, and, in connection with the latter office, as state campaign manager. Significantly, among those serving on the twelve-man state committee of the Farmer-Labor party with Lindbergh were Working People's Nonpartisan League leader William Mahoney and Nonpartisan League officer Henry G. Teigan, both of whom were strong advocates of the third-party point of view and principal contributors to the founding of the new party.[33]

In a revealing letter of September 7, Lindbergh recounted his activities as counsel to the NPL state committee, spelling out its difficulties with Townley and ultimate disintegration. The five-member committee was given a twofold task by the League—to promote business efficiency in the organization and to aid the general political cause. In a series of committee votes, usually three to two, Townley, who had agreed to remain as head of League organizational activity following his resignation as president, convinced the committee that all state organization and newspaper fees were to be turned over to him. Lindbergh advised the committee to break its agreement with Townley, but the former League president persuaded them to defer action. Not long afterward Ole Langhaug and Henry Arens resigned from the committee, and, in a short time, Lindbergh tendered his resignation as counsel. At the time he quit, said Lindbergh, the committee still had no funds to implement its program, and there had been no business accounting of state League records. Lindbergh also pointed out that he had offered his services at considerable personal expense for four months and thus far had received no salary or compensation for his work. In his judgment, the major cause of the League crisis was Townley himself, for as an administrator he did not have adequate control over his office. Moreover, Lindbergh asserted, "The League should not be dominated by one man." Instead members should be in close touch with League affairs through "a carefully prepared democratic system." He also maintained that his statements were not appearing in the *Minnesota Leader* during the campaign because the paper was under the direct control of Townley. Lindbergh, however, felt that these conditions need not hamper the farmer-labor coalition, for the political burden would be carried on by the Farmer-Labor party, and therefore he would continue to participate in the 1922 campaign as a member of its state central committee.[34]

Although it is difficult to document Lindbergh's part in the direction of the 1922 campaign,[35] it is clear that the Farmer-Labor campaign strategy was effective. The major race in 1922 was the U.S. Senate contest between Republican incumbent Frank Kellogg, League-labor candidate Henrik Shipstead, and Mrs. Anna Dickie Olesen of Northfield, the Democratic nominee. Kellogg was the real target of the Farmer-Labor forces, and Shipstead attacked the senator's apparent affiliation with big business interests. Kellogg, in turn, stressed his trust-busting record and his general sympathy with the farm bloc. But the farmers were more inclined to believe that their interests might be better served by Shipstead, who set about convincing them of his worth with a homespun campaign that was often laced with serious two-hour speeches on economics. Many farmers wondered whether Senator Kellogg, who traversed the state in a Pierce-Arrow automobile, was their man. Both candidates enlisted outside help, as Senator La Follette, an adamant foe of Kellogg, came to Shipstead's aid, and Senator Arthur Capper of Kansas campaigned for Kellogg.[36]

In the gubernatorial campaign, Farmer-Laborite Magnus Johnson faced incumbent Republican Governor Preus and Democratic nominee Edward Indrehus, a Benton County farmer and state legislator. Johnson's pronounced Swedish accent, unusually loud voice (the result, in part, of his training as a professional glass-blower in Sweden), and earthy campaign style evoked mixed responses. Referred to as the "magnavox" by some observers, Johnson could literally be heard for blocks. But Johnson's credentials also included political experience in state and local government, a deep concern for the farmer, and support for the basic reform ideas of the old Nonpartisan League.[37]

The results of the general election clearly demonstrated acceptance of the Farmer-Labor program in Minnesota. In the senatorial race, Farmer-Labor candidate Shipstead won a decisive victory over Senator Kellogg and Mrs. Olesen, carrying sixty-eight of the state's eighty-six counties. Although defeated, Farmer-Laborite Magnus Johnson yielded only a 14,277-vote margin to victor Governor Preus in the gubernatorial race, with Democratic candidate Indrehus receiving approximately 12 per cent of the total vote cast. Farmer-Labor backed candidates Oscar Keller, O. J. Kvale, and Knud Wefald won election in the Fourth, Seventh, and Ninth congressional districts, although only Wefald, a small-town lumber dealer described by his son as "hand-in-glove" with the Nonpartisan League, officially ran on the Farmer-Labor ticket. Farmer-Labor candidates, in addition, won seventy seats in the Minnesota house and senate in 1922, thereby increasing the legislative strength of the new party.[38]

The positive response to the Farmer-Labor campaign of 1922 represented the fruition of the work done by the old Nonpartisan League over the preceding six years. Minnesota farmers, facing disastrous potato prices and selling wheat for less than the cost of production, were unwilling to accept Republican promises of prosperity. In the Shipstead race special attacks on the Esch-Cummins Transportation Act and the Federal Reserve system contributed to the favorable Farmer-Labor response. In addition, the appeal to labor, based on such issues as wages, prices, public ownership, and political reform, produced results when Farmer-Labor candidates carried the three major urban centers in the state. Farmer-Labor's success in the 1922 election established it as Minnesota's second party and accelerated the already pronounced decline of the Democratic party. Yet, as Arthur Naftalin writes: "It remained for the events of 1923 and 1924 to shape the movement into a party formally committed to integrated political activity."[39]

In addition to his political activity during 1922, Lindbergh spent a good deal of time finishing the manuscript for his third major book, *The Economic Pinch*. On November 14 he sent the completed manuscript, a study of current economic conditions, to his publisher, Dorrance and Company of Philadelphia. Lindbergh hoped that the book might come out while the Minnesota legislature was still in session during the winter and spring of 1923, for "there will be much activity during that period." He sent a list of four thousand names for possible distribution and was concerned that the publisher do his part in promoting the volume; he also reserved the right to purchase copies himself at a reduced price. After some discussion, Dorrance and Lindbergh settled on a list price of $1.50 per hardbound copy, with no photographs.[40]

Actual publication of *The Economic Pinch* was in April, 1923, later than its author had hoped. Lindbergh's first concern was that the book be used to promote the Farmer-Labor movement. He asked that a number of copies be sent quickly to members of the "association," and an initial 1,600 books were sent out. According to Lindbergh, five movement organizations were out soliciting buyers for the book. At one point he inquired if a cheaper edition for a run of 5,000 copies might be printed, for "eleven friends," including two candidates for public office, who wished to promote the Lindbergh book. W. H. Dorrance replied that a paper edition of the book could be printed for fifty cents per copy, but no further discussion of that possibility appears in Lindbergh's letters. Without question Dorrance agreed with Lindbergh's economic views, telling him so and giving extra help from his home office on the book. For instance, more than 150 copies were sent for review to newspapers (more than the usual number, said Dorrance), and, on one occasion, the publisher offered to absorb the charge for a special order of 200 books. Lindbergh refused to accept the special treatment, however, and on one occasion he mailed a check to cover costs and set up a royalty arrangement to cover a portion of the amount. If all else failed, he revealed: "I can always borrow when no one pays me, even if I do lambaste the banking system."[41]

The book was a detailed monograph on existing economic conditions. It was careful to point out those in political office whose service to the "interests" was responsible for the plight of the farmers, the laboring man, and small businessmen. Some of the familiar themes—trusts, banks, and the war—were treated, but Lindbergh also updated the new study with further commentary on the development of the Federal Reserve system, problems of transportation, deflation, and Congress. In his judgment, the basic crisis in the capitalistic system, as it was practiced in the United States, was due to the fact that three "useful" groups and one "useless" group made up the economic structure. The three desirable, or "useful" elements were: (1) Farmers for agriculture; (2) wage workers for industries, and (3) legitimate business to manage exchange and distribution. The fourth group, the "profiteers," charged Lindbergh, were "useless," and merely exploited the other three groups through administrative and legislative action. Lindbergh then compared these "profiteers" of capitalism to the old European nobility, who had refused to share the tax burden with the peasantry. Unless changes were made, he warned, the United States might well face revolutionary activity, as European nations had at an earlier date.[42]

Lindbergh also touched on the problem of racial prejudice within the broad context of reform in *The Economic Pinch*. In his view, it was a major obstacle to implementing necessary change. Although he still had a strong faith in the Darwinian approach, it seems that his specific position on race, confirming Eva's comments, had changed somewhat by the 1920's. For one thing, Lindbergh, like other progressives, was influenced by the experience of World War I and the attendant display of racial feeling. "To subdue any self-respecting people by war simply intensifies racial prejudices and makes the world worse to live in," he wrote. It was a new dimension, but Lindbergh stated that the ultimate goal of one "national human family" of all people in the world would not work at this time, for, as he saw it, "too much racial prejudice exists."[43]

Nevertheless, there was hope for America. The key to bringing about economic and political change lay with the mind, emphasized Lindbergh. Honest thinking and a concern for political and industrial justice must prevail. In order to accomplish this, Lindbergh went on, people would have to show as much interest in making progress in the "game of life" as they now displayed in a prize fight or other popular sports. At the same time, he warned, "blind following of leaders is pitiful" and must be avoided. Major areas of the economy that needed reform were finance, transportation, coal, oil, iron, timber, water power, packing and storage agencies, the private press, and politics. It was a tall order, and Lindbergh warned that too many "progressives" in politics had sold out. Even the Populists, the Bull Moosers, and now the Nonpartisan League had failed to gain sufficient support for lasting success. The actual people of Main Street in American politics and economics, Lindbergh asserted, were even more ludicrous than the unsophisticated characters of Gopher Prairie in Sinclair Lewis' *Main Street*. Government control, of course, was one answer to some of the economic crises, Lindbergh argued, but until constructive change occurred hard times would continue. In his opinion change was inevitable, but, he warned, "That change will be orderly, or chaotic, according to the way we use or fail to use our heads."[44]

On April 28, 1923, within less than a month after the appearance of Lindbergh's *The Economic Pinch*, senior Minnesota senator Knute Nelson died. His death created a Senate vacancy, which ultimately led to the last active political campaign in Lindbergh's life. Shortly after Nelson's death, Governor Preus, whom Nelson had considered his protégé and heir to his Senate seat, discussed the prospect of resigning and permitting Lieutenant Governor Louis T. Collins to become governor. Collins, in turn, would then appoint Preus to the Senate. But unfavorable comment in the state forced Preus to change his strategy, and he subsequently called a special election to fill the vacancy. Primaries were scheduled for June 18, and a fight for party nominations ensued. Results of the primary contests in the Republican and Democratic parties gave the respective nominations to Governor Preus and State Senator James Carley of Plainview. Preus received about 34 per cent of the vote in a field of nine Republican candidates, while Carley won easily against one opponent in a light Democratic vote.[45]

Lindbergh, Magnus Johnson, and New Ulm mayor and physician L. A. Fritsche filed for the senatorial nomination in the Farmer-Labor primary. In a note of May 19, 1923, Lindbergh assured Eva: "Elected or not this is my last in politics." Lindbergh was not overly optimistic about his chances in the primary, for he told Eva that he was taking some time to "shape up" things for a line of work he might do in case of defeat. He emphasized that his candidacy was mainly intended "to scare those who thought they had rubbed out my existence by lies." According to Francis Johnson, son of Magnus, Lindbergh approached his father prior to the Senate race, suggesting that Magnus run for governor again in 1924 and leave the Senate seat to him. Lindbergh argued that since Johnson had already been defeated by Preus his chances of winning now were poor, but Johnson disagreed. Johnson's political potential was actually much better than Lindbergh's in 1923, for, although both had suffered previous defeats at the polls, Johnson a year earlier had come within fourteen thousand votes of being governor. Fritsche was expected to do well among German-Americans. An NPL sympathizer, he had been removed as mayor in 1917 by the Safety Commission, thereby receiving some unwanted publicity. According to T. R. Fritsche, his father was encouraged to run because he believed that Lindbergh, whose antiwar views he admired, could not win. On May 25 Benjamin Drake wrote Lindbergh's old progressive friend Lynn Haines that he expected Magnus Johnson to win the Farmer-Labor primary "by a large margin."[46]

As the Farmer-Labor primary campaign progressed, it was apparent that there was little difference between Lindbergh, Johnson, and Fritsche on substantive issues. All were in favor of the basic reform outline put forward by the old Nonpartisan League. Greater government control, the rights of free speech and assembly, the abolition of monopoly, the graduated income tax, and the institution of the iniative, referendum, and recall were among the reforms advocated by the Farmer-Labor candidates. Labor seemed pleased, too, for the *Minnesota Union Advocate* revealed that the "rank and file" would have "no embarrassment" in choosing between the three candidates. It pointed to Lindbergh's attack on the Money Trust, Johnson's "100%" record, and Fritsche's stance as a "prominent progressive." On one occasion all three candidates spoke from the same platform in New Ulm to a rather small audience of 150 persons. Lindbergh's address at New Ulm, which was longer than he intended because Johnson was delayed by automobile trouble, consisted of a discussion of the transportation question, attacks on the Federal Reserve system and on war profiteers, and a statement opposing all "entangling alliances" with European or other countries. At one point in his speech Lindbergh was interrupted by a question about his position on liquor. The *New Ulm Review* was unhappy about the question, warning that "it is this tendency on the part of the public in minor matters that the politicians take advantage to obscure real issues." The liquor question was actually not a serious campaign issue in the 1923 primary. T. R. Fritsche, who drove his father's campaign car, described Lindbergh as "not a very forceful speaker" and more of a "scholar" than his father; he noted that later "solidarity" campaigning involved Fritsche and Johnson only. In some quarters there was a feeling that Johnson was not qualified to be a Senator, as evidenced by Lindbergh's position and by Ole Langhaug's letter to Congressman Knud Wefald urging him to "boost" Lindbergh's candidacy. He felt that Lindbergh would have a better chance to defeat Preus in the general election since Johnson had been defeated by Preus for the governorship. Wefald responded on June 15, indicating that unfortunately he had been on a trip and thus there was no time left to campaign, but that he would vote for Lindbergh and felt that he would do well in the Ninth District. "But, of course," Wefald added, "I shall support the Farmer-Labor nominee, whoever he is."[47]

One interesting aspect of the 1923 Lindbergh campaign was a plan to have the candidate fly with Charles, Jr. in his government surplus Curtiss "Jenny" from town to town. Young Lindbergh was actively pursuing a barnstorming career with his plane at the time, and the intention was to combine campaigning with barnstorming. On May 17, a day before filing for the senatorial nomination, Lindbergh wrote Charles that he should come as soon as he was sure that the plane was "working O.K.," adding, "I think you can make some spondulix at the same time." Perhaps passengers could be taken up for cash on the farms where they landed, he suggested, while he went to town on campaign activities.[48]

Charles joined his father's campaign at Marshall, Minnesota, where, in short order, the elder Lindbergh experienced his first airplane ride. Armed with a bundle of hundreds of sheets of campaign literature, Lindbergh climbed into the open-front cockpit of the "Jenny." As was customary in the early biplanes, Charles, Jr., the pilot, took his place at the controls in the cockpit behind his father. By prearrangement, Lindbergh was to throw out the bills when his son rocked the plane and nodded. He did so when the signal was given, but instead of throwing the leaflets a few at a time, Lindbergh threw out the whole stack of literature at once and the bundle sharply hit the plane stabilizer. Fortunately, no damage was done, but as Charles, Jr. observed many years later, "the distribution of the literature in the town wasn't very broad." He recalled that "My father's face was quite serious when he looked back at me after the thud."[49]

The airplane campaign strategy was short-lived. On June 8, in an attempted takeoff from a pasture landing field on the Miley farm, west of Glencoe, the plane "swerved into a ditch," causing the propeller and landing gear to break. Curiously, two area papers reported conflicting accounts of the accident. The *Litch-field Saturday Review* stated that the mishap occurred during takeoff, but the *McLeod County Republic* at Glencoe reported that it took place during an attempted landing. There was evidence that someone had tampered with the rudder on the aircraft, causing the difficulty. Fortunately, neither C. A. nor Charles was injured in the mishap, but since repairs had to come from Minneapolis, Lindbergh proceeded to Litchfield by automobile and Charles remained with his plane. Eva was disturbed by reports of the accident, and Lindbergh assured his daughter that the plane would not be in shape to fly anymore during the campaign, "even if I wanted to fly." He also wrote that the plane had been "munked with," but, he noted, "I figure it was not a plot, just some boys." Although Townley, for one, had used an airplane in Minnesota in his 1920 campaign, the Lindbergh air episode in 1923 was a novel idea and certainly one of the earliest examples of airplane campaigning in the state.[50]

The returns in the Farmer-Labor primary race of 1923 gave Magnus Johnson a clear-cut victory over Fritsche and Lindbergh. The totals were: Johnson—57,570; Fritsche—38,393; Lindbergh—21,811. Johnson carried sixty-two counties in the state, while Fritsche carried sixteen counties, largely in the southern and German-settled part of Minnesota, and Lindbergh carried only eight counties, spotted throughout the central and northwestern part of the state. Although he accepted the results stoically, the returns must have been disheartening for Lindbergh, for in many ways the essence of certain of his reform ideas appeared to be reaching a moderately high degree of circulation within the new third-party movement. Yet, as one editor who talked with him during that campaign observed, Lindbergh was always forgiving to his opposition and retained a strong faith in the positive side of human nature. From a political standpoint, Lindbergh's 1923 primary showing was, in part, the price paid by a man who had been a two-time state-wide loser at the polls. Certainly the endorsement of Johnson by the Nonpartisan League and a number of labor unions strengthened the Johnson vote. Finally, the unpleasant memories of 1918 may have been a factor, for both Lindbergh and Burnquist were soundly defeated in the 1923 primaries.[51]

During the 1923 general election campaign the momentum toward Magnus Johnson continued. Even though Governor Preus, the Republican nominee, had instituted cooperative laws and other reforms as governor, he was assailed for his conservatism and for imposing the cost of the special election on Minnesotans. Johnson had his own folksy touch, and members of the farm bloc in the Senate—Shipstead, La Follette, Lynn Frazier of North Dakota, and Burton Wheeler of Montana—came to Minnesota and wrote articles in the *Minnesota Leader* in his behalf. In the opinion of the *New York Times* the Farmer-Labor campaign was simply a case of the "radicals" pressing the "old guard" in the state. Another national publication, *Labor*, actively supported the Johnson candidacy. Lindbergh, however, had had enough of Johnson, and he refused to support him even though he was the Farmer-Labor nominee. In doing so he departed from the position taken by such party colleagues as Shipstead, Wefald, and Fritsche, all of whom came out for Johnson. According to Governor Preus, Lindbergh had approached him the day after the primary election and stated: "I'll do anything you want me to do to put you in the United States Senate." In his judgment Johnson was "not prepared" to be a good senator. To this statement Preus responded: "Charlie, I want you to do nothing but to vote for me. You can speak to your friends if you want to, but since you were in the primary I don't think I should ask you to come out openly and support me."[52]

Most Minnesotans did not agree with Lindbergh, however, for on July 16, 1923, they selected Magnus Johnson as their second Farmer-Labor senator. The margin of victory was substantial, with the following vote totals: Johnson—290,165; Preus—195,319; Carley—19,311. Johnson quickly reaffirmed his allegiance to the Farmer-Labor cause by announcing the appointment of Henry Teigan, the influential NPL officer, as his secretary. Clearly, Johnson's election was another morale lift for the fledgling

Farmer-Labor party, and leaders of the movement now turned their attention to improving the party machinery and to the question of a possible national third party.[53]

Although Johnson was a popular vote-getter, it should be pointed out that Lindbergh's earlier campaign, in 1918, had not only provided the focus for the original farmer-labor coalition, but his thinking and writing were an important part of the ideological base which existed during that era of upper Midwest protest politics. This was particularly true within the Farmer-Labor party. Certainly more than any other early political figure, he set down his reform ideas in words and impressed these often maverick views on subsequent leaders. William Lemke of North Dakota, a key NPL figure and 1936 Union party presidential candidate, for example, owed much to Lindbergh in his views on money and banking. Edward Blackorby notes that "Lindbergh had the most influence on Lemke in this field of thought," a fact validated by an examination of Lemke's book, *You and Your Money.* Ernest Lundeen, Minnesota Farmer-Labor congressman and U.S. Senator of Swedish extraction, revealed a close association with Lindbergh's philosophies in his isolationist stand during both World War I and World War II, and openly attested to his admiration for Lindbergh. Senator Gerald Nye was similarly influenced on isolationism by Lindbergh's views. Another Farmer-Laborite, Elmer Benson, Minnesota governor and U.S. senator during the late 1930's, stated that he had read two of Lindbergh's books and "may have been influenced by him." At the same time the former Appleton banker referred to Lindbergh as a "funny money man," a common description probably used partly in jest and partly in earnest. Of some interest is the fact that, according to Benson biographer James Shields, Benson's father, a Norwegian immigrant, successful merchant, and ardent NPLer, considered Lindbergh "his great hero." Although Eva was totally opposed to Governor Benson during the 1930's and felt that her father would not have approved of his administration, the two men were alike in at least one respect. Both were unusually uncompromising in whatever views they held, a characteristic that probably hurt them politically and enhanced the possibility of their being called "radical."[54]

Farmer-Labor leaders like O. J. Kvale, Magnus Johnson, Knud Wefald, and Floyd B. Olson are more difficult to pinpoint with respect to Lindbergh's influence, but there was clearly contact with, and appreciation of, Lindbergh and his views. Farmer-Laborite Conrad Gaarenstroom stated that Kvale and Lindbergh were known to be friends, Francis Johnson stated that his father had been influenced on banking issues by Lindbergh, and Magnus Wefald indicated that his father had had a great deal of respect for Lindbergh. Congressman Wefald's son and onetime secretary also noted that Lindbergh was more of a "student and scholar of politics" than his father had been. After Charles, Jr.'s transatlantic flight, Knud Wefald was prompted to write a poem entitled "The Lindbergh Name," a eulogy to the senior Lindbergh with particular reference to his courage in attacking the Money Trust and opposing the European war. In his fight, he wrote, the elder Lindbergh was "an untamed polar bear." According to close friend Gaarenstroom, Olson, the principal figure in the Farmer-Labor movement during the 1930's, considered Lindbergh a "martyr" to the Farmer-Labor cause. Olson believed that Lindbergh had "devoted his life to those issues which he [Olson] believed most important." Olson and Lindbergh knew each other only a brief time, but in a 1924 meeting Lindbergh told Gaarenstroom that Olson "had a future in politics" and "speaks well." Admittedly the Nonpartisan League, the war issue, the labor situation, and the weakness of the Democratic party were more crucial factors in the formation of the new Farmer-Labor party in Minnesota, but insofar as a body of specific reform thought is concerned, Lindbergh emerges as one of the key figures to offer its reform solutions to the people through his writings and campaigns.[55]

From the end of the 1923 campaign until his fatal illness in early 1924, Lindbergh devoted his efforts to business activities at his Minneapolis office. His contacts with Agard on Florida properties continued, as did those with Bolander on Little Falls real

estate and Shakopee bank activities. In view of the general economic difficulties during the early 1920's, it is doubtful that Lindbergh made much money on his business deals during this period.
Lindbergh and Agard, for example, worried about the bank
venture. As early as November, 1922, Lindbergh had advised
getting out with a 5 per cent loss, but he was more optimistic by
February, 1924. Yet he had cut down his own stock to twenty
shares, and was also liable for two thousand dollars to depositors.
The outlook was even bleaker on his Florida and Minnesota real
estate properties, for land values had declined sharply after the
boom broke. Lindbergh summarized the situation in March, 1924,
when he wrote Evangeline that he was in debt on his land holdings, explaining: "You see land has tumbled so that the mortgages
that I guaranteed are coming back on me and the taxes will
swamp me so I don't know where I am at. It may change but just
now land is not selling for enough to pay mortgages, and things
are uncertain."[56] In any case, the economic depression, together
with Lindbergh's personal investments in his publishing activities
and his political campaigns, seriously decreased his liquid assets
and total net worth as compared with earlier years.[57] Ultimately,
the Lindbergh home and farm property on the Mississippi River
was deeded by the Lindbergh family to the state of Minnesota.[58]

In late 1923, Lindbergh also launched a new reform project related to business activity, principally involving the role of insurance companies in the economy. According to Lindbergh,
large insurance companies took huge amounts of capital out of
the upper Midwest and invested at least 75 per cent of it in
Money Trust banks in the East. To expose this situation a group
of farmers from Minnesota, North and South Dakota, Iowa, and
Nebraska held a conference at the West Hotel in Minneapolis on
November 27, 1923. Expressing confidence in Lindbergh's theories,
the conferees authorized him to publish a small pamphlet on the
subject. *Who and What Caused the Panic and Who Can Stop
the Panic* appeared in early 1924 as a pocket-sized volume, selling for ten cents per copy and including Lindbergh's comments
on the insurance problem and its relationship to the general

economic crisis of 1921–1923. In essence, Lindbergh said that "Mr. and Mrs. Plain Citizen" must do something about the situation themselves. He outlined two major areas of change—a "concrete financial remedy" to bring immediate relief to industry, and a broader economic program to coordinate the industrial relations of various industrial groups in the nation. Although details on the actual procedural steps of his program were limited and generalized, Lindbergh clearly meant the focus of his new plan to be the use of local banks as the basis for a system of credit insurance, thereby stabilizing finances at home and curbing the inflationary effect of Eastern companies. The sixty-one-page pamphlet included a list of the names and addresses of approximately three hundred farmer supporters of the program, which, said Lindbergh, actually had a following of about three thousand individuals. The reliability of the new scheme was never tested, however, as Lindbergh's illness cut short its development.[59]

During the last several weeks of his life, in early 1924, Lindbergh, characteristically, was once again involved in reform politics. Urged by friends and political associates to enter the competition for the Farmer-Labor nomination for governor of Minnesota, Lindbergh reluctantly agreed that he would not "shirk it" if there were an opportunity to change "panicky" conditions to prosperity for the people of the state. Obviously, to act simply as other governors had done would not be sufficient, but Lindbergh felt that through the unofficial influence of the office people could be induced to carry out needed economic changes. Although the Lindbergh backers no doubt hoped that their candidate might be endorsed at the Farmer-Labor convention, such hopes were altered by a serious split in the Farmer-Labor ranks. The main problem was the attempt by labor forces in the party to take control of the state organization and promote a national third party in 1924; the farmer element in the party reacted with some hostility to this effort. A compromise was reached at the St. Cloud convention in March, 1924, and the Farmer-Labor Federation was formed. The compromise consisted of an agreement that candidates would be chosen by a primary election rather than party endorsement. Within a short time seven candidates announced for the Farmer-Labor gubernatorial nomination, and Lindbergh and Tom Davis of Minneapolis emerged as the major contenders. Lindbergh campaign literature was circulated during these weeks, emphasizing his congressional record as a foe of the trusts and "boss politics," his stand against the war profiteers, his support of laborers and farmers, and his championing of the "cause" in 1918.[60]

The campaign had barely begun when Lindbergh became seriously ill. In late April he was taken to the Mayo Clinic in Rochester, where doctors diagnosed the illness as a deep-seated brain tumor. Dr. Alfred W. Adson performed exploratory surgery and "found a glioma so far advanced as to be inoperable." Actually, Lindbergh had had either a premonition or some warning of his developing condition, for almost a year before his death he had written a letter to Eva to be opened only in the event of his death. She recalled that at a later visit to her home he had commented that "he would rather be dead than handicapped." Eva was with her father at all times during the final illness, and Charles, Jr., now in flight training as an Army flying cadet in Texas, hastened to see his father at Rochester. Meanwhile, the press and others were insistent on knowing whether Lindbergh would withdraw from the gubernatorial race. Eva recalled with some bitterness the incessant demands from the press and the lack of privacy during this time of personal tragedy. Her anguish was compounded by the actions of certain Lindbergh associates, who, she said, took "cruel advantage" of her father during his illness. By the end of April Lindbergh's name was withdrawn from the gubernatorial race, although, because he could not sign an affidavit, his name remained on the ballot. Lindbergh's removal from the race improved the chances of Hennepin County attorney Floyd B. Olson, for, with the help of the Lindbergh managers, much Lindbergh rural support went to Olson. Olson lost the general election of 1924 as the Farmer-Labor nominee, but in the 1930's he became governor and emerged as the unquestioned leader of the Farmer-Labor movement.[61]

Lindbergh's condition did not change, and when it was apparent that nothing more could be done for her father at the Mayo Clinic, Eva asked that he be moved to St. Vincent's Hospital in Crookston, Minnesota, nearer to her own home and family at Red Lake Falls. There C. A. Lindbergh died on May 24, 1924. Funeral services were held at the First Unitarian Church in Minneapolis, with Reverend J. H. Dietrich officiating. At Lindbergh's request, his remains were cremated. A few years later, again honoring his earlier request, and certainly symbolic of the character of the man, his ashes were distributed by his son, Charles A. Lindbergh, Jr., from an airplane over the old Lindbergh homestead near Melrose.[62]

Chapter XI

The Measure of the Man

C. A. Lindbergh could be nothing but what he was. His career clearly demonstrated the depth of his convictions and the absence of merely personal ambition. Time and again he opposed the way things were and proposed specific change without a thought to what it would do to his own political future. In so conducting his public life, Lindbergh made fundamental contributions to the history of American protest politics from 1906 to 1924. He spoke most directly to the issues of money and banking, insurgency, the war, and the farmer's plight, while in a party sense he contributed variously to the make-up of the progressive wing of the Republican party, to the Nonpartisan League, and finally to the Farmer-Labor party.

A reserved, serious, lawyerlike person, Lindbergh was an unlikely prospect for political success. He was not a spellbinding speaker. His campaign style was not flamboyant. The image of the stubborn Swede was true for Lindbergh as a politician. His adamant refusal, for example, to compromise on issues and policies no doubt inhibited his political career somewhat. The total commitment of the man to his views and his people, however, more than offset any disadvantages. People would listen to his long discourses for two hours in the hot sun, probably not understanding the meaning of all his words, yet convinced that he knew what he was talking about and that he had a good plan for the common people. To some, Lindbergh's disregard for party regularity during the latter part of his career was almost inexplicable. In examining Lindbergh's beliefs, however, one can only conclude that his basic outlook on issues did not change—he merely changed political vehicles to better implement what he felt should be done through the legislative process. It was natural for him therefore to join those in revolt against the autocratic House Speaker Joe Cannon; later it was equally natural, when his efforts to reform the Republican party failed, to move on to the Nonpartisan League and Farmer-Labor movements in Minnesota. Another consideration was the simple fact that Lindbergh, during his ten years in the House, sat with Democratic majorities three times, while, even during his first two terms, he moved away from the stand-pat philosophy of the Republican majority. Lindbergh was always independent in action. Witness his decision, though a Republican congressman, to caucus with the Progressive party bloc in 1913; his support of Prohibitionist W. G. Calderwood in 1916; and his refusal to support Farmer-Laborite Magnus Johnson in 1923.

He was equally independent as a national legislator, for, unlike current practice, he was not dependent upon a staff nor were his views shaped by aides or advisers. He familiarized himself with the legislation he supported and became a recognized expert on specific reform issues. The nature of his campaign activities was another example of his independence. Lindbergh was simply not inclined to work with committees or the party machinery, preferring to reach the people directly through his speeches and writing. The one exception was the 1918 gubernatorial campaign, when he benefited from the organizational talent of the Nonpartisan League. Many Sixth District voters probably met Lindbergh for the first time when, using a favorite ploy, he would stop on the road by a farmer's field, get out of the car, and strike up a conversation by asking: "What's land worth around here?"[1]

As a progressive reformer Lindbergh made his main contributions in banking, currency, and credit developments. He acted as a major catalyst in drawing the attention of Congress and the nation to certain of the economic ills in these areas. His demand for a Money Trust investigation, his attack on the Aldrich plan, and his criticism of the Federal Reserve system were detailed and effective. He was instrumental in preventing the bankers and political compromisers from making the Federal Reserve law a totally inadequate reform. Although Lindbergh himself later questioned whether his crusading attacks had in fact done any good,[2] the degree of change that did take place in these specific areas was a step forward. For Lindbergh, who wanted fundamental and basic change, these laws did not go far enough.

Other aspects of Lindbergh's reform activities reveal a heritage from the old Populist ideology, a strong belief in evolutionary progress and government control, and a practical faith in the printed word. There is a basic similarity between the grievances and reform thought of the Midwestern agrarian revolt of the late nineteenth century and the reform views and attacks on Wall Street that characterized Lindbergh's career during the early twentieth century. Lindbergh's concern for the farmer and his dislike of big business were not mere political expediency; they were based on study of, and experience with farm prices, mortgages, and land values. At times his attacks may have revealed an unwillingness to examine the other side, but there were absolutely no grounds for questioning the basic truth of his charges. In terms of the literature of American progressivism, Lindbergh stands as an example most closely substantiating the traditional interpretation of the movement,[3] which emphasizes its nineteenth-century egalitarian and rural origins. Although he admitted that many progressives were banker-oriented, Lindbergh's own career would counter the recent thesis that depicts progressive reformers, whether they knew it or not, as capitalists at heart and intrinsic conservatives.[4] Unlike many progressives, Lindbergh saw the danger that reform policies and mechanisms might become the property of the "special interests," and he fought to prevent this from happening. The only situation that seems uncharacteristic in this respect was Lindbergh's failure to perceive that Theodore Roosevelt was capable of "playing ball" with individual capitalists and with politicians whom Lindbergh would consider unsavory. But his obvious commitment to real reform, a commitment held in common with many early Wisconsin progressives,[5] places his career as a progressive politician in direct opposition to the recent revisionist thesis.

Lindbergh's confidence in evolution was great. In political terms, he viewed the need for greater government control as part of the broad evolutionary process, and he therefore advocated government control of banks, and government ownership of transportation and communication facilities, public utilities, and basic industries related to power. He did not favor pure socialism, however, for he believed it would not work; furthermore, he placed considerable value on competition among individuals and groups within society and within the economic structure. Neither did he believe in violent revolution as a means to achieve reform or any political end. Interestingly, though, in view of the economic crisis of the early 1920's in America, Germany, and elsewhere, he predicted that the United States would experience a kind of revolution within twenty years. "I do not think it will be a war," he wrote Eva in 1924, "but I do think it will be a revolution in law and administration."[6]

Lindbergh's various journalistic ventures were typical of one phase of the American reform movement. Obviously, he learned from, and admired, the efforts along those lines by his friend Lynn Haines. Lindbergh's published works were not the polished products of a professional journalist, however, and on his magazine endeavors, such as *Lindbergh's National Farmer* and *Real Needs*, he was naive about what it took to make such ventures succeed. But the progressive reform message of his writings was unmistakable. They reflect the thorough, even scholarly, approach Lindbergh took in investigating economic and political conditions in America and were essential in his career as a reformer. Significantly, Lindbergh's views were presented to a broader public through his books and magazines. And, to a degree, they were effective. Although they were not profitable, Lindbergh clearly felt he had made a substantial contribution to the reform cause with their appearance. Politically, these efforts often coincided with periods when he was either out of office or felt restricted in his effectiveness as a congressman.

In regard to the progressives and World War I, Lindbergh's

career was significant because he was among the first to voice economic reasons for opposition to involvement in war. Ethnic, partisan, and geographic factors were definitely peripheral to his broadside against the "war profiteers." His position, like that of many Midwestern Republican congressmen, is therefore contrary to the thesis that most progressives were imperialists on foreign policy.[7] Lindbergh's early antiwar stand, emphasized by the fact that he wrote a book about it, made him one of the most harassed and persecuted public figures during the intolerant wartime era.

The origins of Lindbergh's reform thought lie in the liberal tradition of his father's Swedish career, the challenges and lessons of growing up on the frontier, and exposure to the ideas of law professor Thomas Cooley. Influences during the Little Falls years included continued reading of Darwinian literature and the experiences surrounding the farm crisis of the 1890's. Through his observations and experience in land and real estate, Lindbergh concluded that the producer was not getting a just reward for his labors. He was also appalled at the flow of monies out of the Midwest to the Eastern capitalists. Whether a particular experience in his personal involvement with banking procedures created an indelible impression on Lindbergh is not known, but his almost obsessive interest in money and banking, prompted, in part, by the panic of 1903, was stirred during these years. His early commitment to reform is evident with his abortive cooperative and magazine ventures in Little Falls. His views took more solid shape when his Congressional seat provided a more satisfactory forum from which to present his reformist ideas. Further incensed by certain endemic features of government and the political party system, his dedication to change was strengthened as a congressman. Even among the progressives, Lindbergh could be described as an iconoclast. Whatever terms are used, Lindbergh sincerely wished to "reshape society," and his role as an almost irreverent critic was directed to the fulfillment of that goal.

As a man Lindbergh was honest and forthright. He was a person of strong character. He was trusted. People around him responded to, and respected, his stability and sense of purpose. There were times, however, when his single-mindedness on issues diverted him from personal affairs. Yet his love of family was palpable and great. Children, without fail, took to "Uncle Charlie," and there was a strong Lindbergh family tradition. For Lindbergh, the man, there was also a deep appreciation of nature, and he loved to roam and think in the wilds. Here, on occasion, a bit of the poet and philosopher in Lindbergh emerged. In a sense this desire to be close to the soil and water sharpened both the competitiveness and the gentleness of the man. Most demonstrative of the human side of Lindbergh in his political career, however, was the courage he revealed during the 1918 campaign. His unflinching response on the hustings in the face of continual personal abuse was indeed a measure of the man. He met every campaign commitment. The fact that the odds were stacked against him did not frighten him. This sure courage was characteristic not only of C. A., but also of his father, Ola Månsson, who challenged majority opinion in the Swedish Riksdag during the 1850's, and of his son, Charles, Jr., who met the challenge of the Atlantic in 1927.

Above all, Charles A. Lindbergh was a democrat and a humanitarian. In all of his extensive statements and writings on economic conditions, his true purpose was to bring political and industrial democracy to the average citizen. Although knowledgeable in the details of economic theory, his primary interest was always the relationship of economics to the basic freedoms of the people. For Lindbergh the most fundamental need of society was to eliminate the existence of "economic slavery" under the rapacious form of capitalism his society knew. "The whole social system," he wrote in *Why Is Your Country at War*, "has seared my soul. . . . I see in many cases, thoughtless, glad faces, made so by the possession of riches wrested from the toil of others, magnify the sad faces of those put in distress by the 'system.'"[8] Perhaps the weakest aspect of his reform thought, like that of many other reformers, lay in the vagueness of the programs outlined for his

beneficent socialist-capitalist system. There were, of course, concrete suggestions like government ownership, but there were also
tantalizingly undefined programs such as a "national association
of all producers and consumers." In his fight for political and industrial justice, Lindbergh was described by some contemporaries
as a radical, and in the sense of wanting bold and deep change,
he was radical. As Farmer-Laborite Knud Wefald saw it, however, Lindbergh was "the most sanely radical man I ever met."[9]
While other observers called him the "funny money man," he
was more accurately the ever-active champion of the common
man. Lindbergh's determination to arrive at truth and to help
humanity was real, even painful. He hated "privilege" because he
knew "privilege" as the trusts used it was a corrupt license to
steal from the farmer and the working man a great portion of
what little they had. His rage at such greed, however legalized,
was complete, all the more so because he knew in his bones that
there was enough wealth in America to provide a secure and
decent life for all. He summarized much of his basic political life
when he wrote in *The Economic Pinch:* "We must substitute
reason for tradition—if we are ever to unshackle ourselves from
the arbitrary domination of property privilege over human right."[10]

Appendix A

Campaigns of Charles A. Lindbergh, Sr.: Election Results

Year	Candidate	Results	%	Year	Candidate	Results	%
Morrison County Attorney							
1890	Lindbergh	1,379	54.7				
	Lyon	1,143	45.3				

U.S. House: Sixth Congressional District

	Republican Primary Returns				*General Election Returns*		
1906	Lindbergh	9,962	53.4	1906	Lindbergh (Rep.)	16,752	56.1
	Buckman	8,709	46.6		Tifft (Dem.)	13,115	43.9
1908	Lindbergh (unopposed)	11,152	100	1908	Lindbergh (Rep.)	22,574	63.1
					Gilkinson (Dem.)	13,174	36.9
1910	Lindbergh	13,415	73.2	1910	Lindbergh (Rep.)	25,272	100
	McGarry	4,923	26.8		(unopposed)		
1912	Lindbergh (unopposed)	12,019	100	1912	Lindbergh (Rep.)	21,286	62.5
					Gilkinson (Dem.)	9,920	29.1
					Uhl (Public Ownership)	2,839	8.4
1914	Lindbergh	10,398	59.8	1914	Lindbergh (Rep.)	15,364	47.5
	Maxfield	6,988	40.2		Du Bois (Dem.)	11,409	35.2
					Thomason (Socialist)	3,769	11.6
					Sharkey (Progressive)	1,836	5.7
				1920	Knutson (Rep.)	47,954	69.0
					Lindbergh (Ind.)	21,587	31.0

Election Results

Year	Candidate	Results	%
	Governor of Minnesota		
	Republican Primary		
1918	Burnquist	199,325	54.0
	Lindbergh	150,626	40.8
	(NPL-endorsed)		
	Other	19,147	5.2
	U.S. Senator		
	Republican Primary		
1916	Kellogg	73,818	38.0
	Eberhart	54,890	28.2
	Clapp	27,668	14.2
	Lindbergh	26,094	13.4
	Other	11,930	6.2
	Farmer-Labor Primary		
1923	Johnson	57,570	48.8
	Fritsche	38,393	32.6
	Lindbergh	21,811	18.5
	Other	166	0.1

Sources: Data based on statistics and computations from Abstract of Votes Polled: Election Returns, 1890 and 1906, Secretary of States' Collection, Minnesota State Archives; and *Legislative Manual of Minnesota,* 1907–1925.

Appendix B

Partial Congressional Voting Record of Charles A. Lindbergh, Sr., 1907–1917

	Lindbergh Vote	House Vote
Aldrich-Vreeland emergency currency bill, 1908	No	Yes (185–145)
Republican gag rule, 1909	No	Yes (195–178)
Vote to investigate Department of Interior under Ballinger, 1910	Yes	Yes (149–146)
Vote to restrict Speaker's power (Norris amendment), 1910	Yes	Yes (191–156)
Vote to unseat Cannon as speaker, 1910	Yes	No (192–155)
Vote to recommit Mann-Elkins bill on railroad rates, etc., 1910	Yes	No (176–157)
Mann-Elkins bill, 1910	Yes	Yes (201–126)
Vote to recommit bill increasing House membership to 433, 1911	Yes	No (177–99)
Direct election of U.S. senators, 1911	Yes	Yes (296–16)
Vote to conduct full Money Trust investigation, 1912	Yes	Yes (241–15)
Lindbergh amendment to postpone Canadian reciprocity agreement, 1912	Yes	No (voice vote)
Canadian reciprocity bill, 1912	No	Yes (268–89)
Underwood tariff bill, 1913	Yes	Yes (281–139)
Lindbergh amendment to Federal Reserve bill, denying bankers right to be directors, 1913	Yes	No (71–44; call for division on voice vote)
Amendment to Federal Reserve bill, endorsing gold standard, 1913	No	Yes (299–68)

Partial Congressional Voting Record

	Lindbergh Vote	House Vote
Vote to recommit Federal Reserve bill, 1913	Yes	Yes (287–85)
Federal Reserve bill, 1913	Yes	No (266–100)
Approval of final conference report, Federal Reserve bill, 1913	No	Yes (298–60)
Naval bill, favoring one battleship instead of two, 1914	Yes	No (202–106)
Clayton antitrust bill, 1914	Yes	Yes (275–54)
War revenue tax bill, 1914	No	Yes (234–135)
Woman suffrage amendment, 1915	Yes	No (204–174)
Vote to table McLemore resolution, 1916	No	Yes (276–142)
Adamson labor bill, 8-hour day, 1916	Yes	Yes (239–56)
Child labor bill, 1916	Yes	Yes (337–46)
Cooper amendment to armed ships bill, preventing munitions shipments, 1917	Yes	No (293–125)
Armed ships bill, 1917	No	Yes (403–14)

Sources: *Congressional Record*, 60th–64th Congresses. For statistical comparison of a broader range of progressive voting patterns on domestic reform and foreign policy, see *The Searchlight on Congress* (October 1916), published by the National Voters' League, Lynn Haines, executive secretary; and the appendixes in Jon Wefald, *A Voice of Protest*, pp. 81–84, and John Milton Cooper, Jr., *The Vanity of Power*, pp. 220–40.

Appendix C

Some Lindbergh Resolutions, Bills, and Proposals That Failed in Committee or in the House

H. Res. 314, 4 December 1911	Congressional investigation of the Money Trust
Cong. Record, 62nd Cong., 2nd sess., 2 April 1912	Framing resolution abolishing the U.S. Senate, the vice-presidency, and reducing House membership. Creation of Committee of Fifteen with veto power.
H. Res. 484, 9 April 1912	Personal financial accounting by congressmen
H. Res. 720, 2 December 1912	Money Trust investigation by House Committee on Banking and Currency
H. Res. 192, 2 July 1913	Investigation of secret meetings of House Committee on Banking and Currency
H. Res. 201, 12 July 1913	Investigation of constitutionality and monopolistic tendencies of Glass bill
H. Res. 71, 17 December 1915	Whenever one-fifth of members present in Congress demand a roll call on amendments, it shall be taken
H. J. Res. 264, 13 July 1916	Investigation of activities of the Roman Catholic Church and the Free Press Defense League of Kansas
H. Con. Res. 64, 6 December 1916	Presidential peace conference to be called, formulating negotiations among nations at war

Some Lindbergh Resolutions, Bills, and Proposals that Failed

Cong. Record, 64th Cong.,
   2nd sess., 12 February 1917

Articles of impeachment introduced against members of the Federal Reserve Board

H.R. 20998, 20 February 1917

Advisory national referendum to be called before congressional declaration of war

Sources: House Originals, RG 233, National Archives, Washington, D.C.; *Congressional Record,* 62nd and 64th Congresses.

Notes

Code:

LP—Charles A. Lindbergh, Sr., and Family Papers, Minnesota Historical Society, St. Paul, Minn.
LP (Yale)—Charles A. Lindbergh, Jr., Papers, Sterling Library, Yale University, New Haven, Conn.
LF—Little Falls (in *LF Daily Transcript, LF Herald, LF Transcript,* and *LF Weekly Transcript*)
MinnHS—Minnesota Historical Society, St. Paul, Minn.
MinnSA—Minnesota State Archives, St. Paul, Minn.
RG—Record Group (in National Archives, Washington, D.C.)

Chapter I: Swedish Immigrants on
the Minnesota Frontier, pp. 3–17

1. The best sources on Lindbergh family background may be found in LP. Useful books and articles are Lynn and Dora Haines, *The Lindberghs* (New York, 1931), a sympathetic biography of Charles A. Lindbergh, Sr. (undocumented, but still an important published source); Grace Lee Nute, ed., "The Lindbergh Colony," *Minnesota History* 20 (September 1939): 243–58; Charles A. Lindbergh [Jr.], *The Spirit of St. Louis* (New York, 1953) and *Boyhood on the Upper Mississippi: A Reminiscent Letter* (St. Paul, 1972). Brief comments are found in James Creese, "Charles Augustus Lindbergh," *American-Scandinavian Review* 15 (August 1927): 488–92; and Adolph B. Benson and Naboth Hedin, eds., *Swedes in America, 1638–1938* (New Haven, 1938), pp. 538–39. Much material has been published on the Lindberghs since the 1927 New York-to-Paris flight of Charles, Jr. Many of these studies are informative but highly inaccurate on specific details. Examples

are Kenneth S. Davis, *The Hero* (New York, 1959); and Walter S. Ross, *The Last Hero: Charles A. Lindbergh* (New York, 1968). See also Richard L. Neuberger, "The Hero Had a Father," *Esquire*, March 1937, pp. 35, 206–09. Further research in Swedish sources is needed to document fully the history of Månsson's career; data here is from Reminiscences, LP; *LF Daily Transcript*, 15 October 1893; *St. Cloud Journal-Press*, 16 May 1889; Creese, "Lindbergh," p. 491; Nute, "Lindbergh Colony," p. 243.

2. For Sweden and its immigration movement, consult Florence Janson, *The Background of Swedish Immigration, 1840–1930* (Chicago, 1931); George M. Stephenson, *The Religious Aspects of Swedish Immigration* (Minneapolis, 1932); Ingvar Andersson, *A History of Sweden* (London, 1956); Eli F. Heckscher, *An Economic History of Sweden* (Cambridge, Mass., 1963); and the files of *Swedish Pioneer Historical Quarterly*.

3. See Andersson, *Sweden*, pp. 324–62; Haines and Haines, *The Lindberghs*, p. 7.

4. No records on Månsson exist in either the household registers or the migration registers for the parish of Smedstorp (his native area in the province of Skåne, including the village of Gårdlösa) after 1859, and "he apparently emigrated in secret." According to Charles, Jr., Månsson personally endorsed a number of notes for individuals indebted to the Bank of Sweden, "which would have been all right had he not been an officer of the bank from the standpoint of Swedish law." Information supplied by Bengt Olof Nilsson, Provincial Archives of Southern Sweden, Lund, and cited in Nilsson to the author, 3 August 1972; commentary by Charles, Jr., 17 October 1971; interview with Eva Lindbergh Christie (now Mrs. G. Howard Spaeth) and Charles, Jr., 16–20 April 1966 (Russell W. Fridley, director of the Minnesota Historical Society, also participated in the interview), hereafter cited as Minnesota interview; Nute, "Lindbergh Colony," p. 243.

5. There is confusion on the minor point of Lindbergh's middle name. It was August, not Augustus. Discrepancies do appear in print, partially because Charles, Jr.'s middle name is Augustus. Primary sources that validate the name August are the family Bible (signed by August Lindbergh) and commencement program for University of Michigan Law School, 1883, both in LP; and interview with Eva Lindbergh Christie Spaeth, 22 June 1972.

6. Haines and Haines, *The Lindberghs*, pp. 3–9; Nute, "Lindbergh Colony," pp. 243–44; *LF Daily Transcript*, 24 May 1924; family Bible, LP; Andersson, *Sweden*, p. 358; *St. Cloud Journal-Press*,

16 May 1889; H. L. Mencken, *The American Language* (New York, 1963), p. 587.

7. Haines and Haines, *The Lindberghs*, pp. 3–4, 11–12.

8. *Ibid.*, pp. 4, 14, 37, 40.

9. *St. Cloud Democrat*, 8 August 1861; extract from C. S. Harrison to the American Home Missionary Society, 22 November 1861, LP; Harrison, *Adorning the Beulah Land of the Hither Shore and How to Become an Extinguished Minister* (n.p., 1911), pp. 42–43; Haines and Haines, *The Lindberghs*, pp. 15–17; Lindbergh, *Spirit of St. Louis*, pp. 221–22.

10. Nute, "Lindbergh Colony," pp. 243–58; Haines and Haines, *The Lindberghs*, pp. 17–18; family Bible, LP. Måns Olsson Lindbergh's personal account of the emigrant journey with his planned colonists is in Nute, "Lindbergh Colony," pp. 249–58. The best analysis of the colonization project is in Lars Ljungmark, *For Sale—Minnesota: Organized Promotion of Scandinavian Immigration, 1866–1873* (Chicago, 1971), pp. 96–100, 111–16.

11. Theodore C. Blegen, *Minnesota: A History of the State* (Minneapolis, 1963), p. 282. On the uprising, see also William Watts Folwell, *A History of Minnesota* (St. Paul, 1924), vol. 2; and Kenneth Carley, *The Sioux Uprising of 1862* (St. Paul, 1961).

12. Haines and Haines, *The Lindberghs*, pp. 22–23, 29–31; Lindbergh, *Spirit of St. Louis*, pp. 219–22.

13. Reminiscences, LP; *St. Cloud Journal-Press*, 16 May 1889; statement by August Lindbergh, 2 May 1871, Edwin Clark Papers, MinnHS; minutes, Village Council Proceedings, 1881–97, and Book of Financial Records, 1887–96, Village of Melrose, Minn., in possession of City of Melrose; William Bell Mitchell, *History of Stearns County, Minnesota* (Chicago, 1915), vol. 2, p. 1432; Evelyn Hoeschen, *History of Melrose* (n.p., n.d.).

14. Record Book A, Naturalization Record, p. 472, Stearns County, St. Cloud, Minn.; Haines and Haines, *The Lindberghs*, p. 10; Village of Melrose minutes and Book of Financial Records.

15. Haines and Haines, *The Lindberghs*, pp. 36–37; Minnesota interview; commentary by Charles, Jr. on the Minnesota interview, 7 April 1967; family Bible, LP.

16. Haines and Haines, *The Lindberghs*, p. 37; Charles, Jr. commentary, 1967; Lindbergh, *Spirit of St. Louis*, p. 218.

17. Minnesota interview; Charles, Jr. commentary, 1967; Haines and Haines, *The Lindberghs*, p. 37; Lindbergh to sisters, 21 April 1921, LP.

18. Mitchell, *Stearns County*, 2:1380; interview with Eva Lindbergh Christie, 1 April 1967; Haines and Haines, *The Lindberghs*, pp. 32–36.
19. Haines and Haines, *The Lindberghs*, pp. 37–41, 44–46; interview with Mrs. P. W. Huntemer (niece of Charles A. Lindbergh, Sr., and daughter of Mrs. Linda Lindbergh Seal), 27 April 1967.
20. Sauk Centre Academy and Business College, *Catalogue and Circular, 1890–1892;* entry on Cogan in Warren Upham and Rose Barteau Dunlap, comps., *Collections of the Minnesota Historical Society,* vol. 14, *Minnesota Biographies, 1655–1912* (St. Paul, 1912), p. 131; Ivy Louise Hildebrand, "Sauk Centre: A Study of the Growth of a Frontier Town" (master's thesis, St. Cloud State College, 1960); Gust Levorson to Pope County Historical Society, 27 November 1939, and N. K. Strande to Edward Karrigan, 21 December 1939, Pope County Historical Society, Glenwood, Minn.; clippings, Linda Lindbergh Seal scrapbook; Haines and Haines, *The Lindberghs,* pp. 57–58.
21. Useful studies on political and economic conditions during the 1860's and 1870's, in addition to the general histories of the state by Blegen and Folwell, include Solon J. Buck, *The Granger Movement: A Study of Agricultural Organization and Its Political, Economic, and Social Manifestations, 1870–1880* (Cambridge, Mass., 1913); Merrill E. Jarchow, *The Earth Brought Forth: A History of Minnesota Agriculture to 1885* (St. Paul, 1949); Martin Ridge, *Ignatius Donnelly: The Portrait of a Politician* (Chicago, 1962); and Earl W. Hayter, *The Troubled Farmer, 1850–1900: Rural Adjustment to Industrialism* (De Kalb, Ill., 1968).
22. *St. Cloud Journal-Press,* 16 May 1889; O. Fritiof Ander, "Swedish-American Newspapers and the Republican Party, 1855–1875," *Augustana Historical Society Publications,* vol. 2 (Rock Island, Ill., 1932), pp. 64–78; Andersson, *Sweden,* pp. 357–62. Portions of the August Lindbergh letter appear in Haines and Haines, *The Lindberghs,* pp. 54–55; and Nels Hokanson, *Swedish Immigrants in Lincoln's Time* (New York, 1942), p. 15. A recent study which argues that there was an identifiable relationship between the folk heritage of one Scandinavian country, Norway, and the reformist political tradition of many of its immigrants in America is Jon Wefald, *A Voice of Protest: Norwegians in American Politics, 1890–1917* (Northfield, Minn., 1971). While Lindbergh's Swedish origins seem to confirm this thesis, his reform thought nonetheless was also substantially shaped by his self-education and by political and economic conditions in America.

23. Although Lindbergh himself used the term "pheasant" in referring to these birds, evidence of the existence of pheasants in Minnesota in 1880 and 1881 is inconclusive. According to Thomas S. Roberts, the Asian pheasant was first successfully introduced to North America (Oregon) in 1881, but its appearance in Minnesota was primarily a twentieth-century development. Challenging this view is the content of a Minnesota law in 1877 that used both the terms "ruffed grouse" and "pheasant" in setting up a fall hunting season. The question of the likelihood of his father's quarry being pheasant was raised with the author by Charles, Jr., the twentieth-century conservationist son. Data from *Nonpartisan Leader,* 3 June 1918; Thomas S. Roberts, *The Birds of Minnesota* (Minneapolis, 1932), vol. 1, pp. 417–18; *General Laws of the State of Minnesota* (St. Paul, 1877), chap. 57, p. 92, sec. 4; interview with Charles, Jr., 22 March 1971.

24. *Nonpartisan Leader,* 3 June 1918; Spaeth interview, 22 June 1972.

25. Haines and Haines, *The Lindberghs,* pp. 58–59.

26. The best source on the University of Michigan Law School is Elizabeth Gaspar Brown's detailed institutional history, *Legal Education at Michigan, 1859–1959* (Ann Arbor, 1959). Information here is from pp. 102–04, 181, 192, 273, 429–30, 716, 740; and interview with Elizabeth Gaspar Brown, 7 July 1969. Records indicating that Lindbergh began studies on September 27, 1881, and again on September 19, 1882, are in Department of Law records, University of Michigan, Ann Arbor. See also James Gray, *The University of Minnesota, 1851–1951* (Minneapolis, 1951), pp. 88–89; and Walter A. Donnelly, Wilfred B. Shaw, and Ruth W. Gjelsness, eds., *The University of Michigan: An Encyclopedic Survey* (Ann Arbor, 1958), vol. 2, pp. 1015–34.

27. Brown, *Legal Education,* pp. 694, 700.

28. *Ibid.,* pp. 467, 469, 489, 670; Donnelly, Shaw, and Gjelsness, *Michigan,* 2:1021–24; Howard H. Peckham, *The Making of the University of Michigan, 1817–1967* (Ann Arbor, 1967), p. 79; Brown interview; interview with Roy F. Proffitt, associate dean of University of Michigan Law School, 7 July 1969.

29. Brown, *Legal Education,* p. 469; Brown interview. A listing of 182 Michigan alumni who served in Congress from 1858 to 1947 may be found in Earl D. Babst and Lewis G. Vander Velde, eds., *Michigan and the Cleveland Era* (Ann Arbor, 1948), pp. 320–34.

30. Alan Jones, "Thomas M. Cooley and 'Laissez-Faire Constitutionalism': A Reconsideration," *Journal of American History* 53 (March 1967): 751–71. See also Jones, "Thomas M. Cooley and the Michi-

gan Supreme Court, 1865–1885," *American Journal of Legal History* 10 (April 1966): 97–121.

31. Jones, "Cooley and 'Laissez-Faire Constitutionalism,'" pp. 766, 770.

32. Charles I. York, *History of Law Class of 1883 of Michigan University* (Ann Arbor, 1883), p. 10. See also Elizabeth Gaspar Brown, "Student Conduct and Misconduct: The Uproarious Past of the Law School," *Michigan Alumnus Quarterly Review* 66 (Winter 1960): 153–62.

33. Haines and Haines, *The Lindberghs*, pp. 59–60; Minnesota interview; Evangeline Lodge Land Lindbergh notebook, LP (Yale), a copy of the notebook, as well as copies of LP (Yale) letters relating to Charles, Sr., in LP; York, *Law Class of 1883*, preface.

34. Matriculation, nonresident, and diploma fees for the two terms totaled $120. Living costs probably varied, but one law student's diary reveals average total expenditures of approximately $27.50 per month in 1881. See Brown, *Legal Education*, p. 708; and Austin Mires Diary, Michigan Historical Collections, University of Michigan, Ann Arbor.

35. Faculty record of Lindbergh's graduation, University of Michigan, *Proceedings of the Board of Regents*, January 1881–January 1886, p. 320; commencement program, 28 March 1883, LP. Issues of the *Calendar of the University of Michigan* for 1881–82, 1882–83, and 1883–84 list Lindbergh as a law junior, senior, and graduate on pp. 172, 167, and 146 of each volume, respectively.

Chapter II: Little Falls Lawyer, pp. 18–40

1. Haines and Haines, *The Lindberghs*, p. 62; Hiram F. Stevens, *History of the Bench and Bar of Minnesota* (Minneapolis and St. Paul, 1904), vol. 2, pp. 179–80; Mitchell, *Stearns County*, 1:506, 209; *LF Transcript*, 16 May 1884.

2. On the history of Little Falls and Morrison County, see Clara Fuller, *History of Morrison and Todd Counties, Minnesota* (Indianapolis, 1915), vol. 1; Warren Upham, *Collections of the Minnesota Historical Society*, vol. 17, *Minnesota Geographic Names: Their Origin and Historic Significance* (St. Paul, 1920), pp. 350–58; Agnes M. Larson, *History of the White Pine Industry in Minnesota* (Minneapolis, 1949); and anniversary editions of *LF Daily Transcript*, 4 April 1942 and 4 April 1967.

3. Upham, *Minnesota Geographic Names*, pp. 352–53; *Legislative Manual of the State of Minnesota, 1891* (St. Paul, 1891), p. 580.

4. Upham and Dunlap, *Minnesota Biographies*, p. 56; *LF Transcript*, 16 May 1884, 18 September, 20 November 1885.
5. Interview with Frank A. Lindbergh, 26 June 1964; Stevens, *Bench and Bar of Minnesota*, 2:193; *University of Michigan Law School Alumni Directory, 1860–1950*, pp. 101, 232.
6. *LF Transcript*, 12 September 1884; Frank Lindbergh interview.
7. No records from Lindbergh's law practice exist. Evidence of his legal cases in the 1880's may be found in Register of Actions, Book B (1857–88) and Book C (1882–92), and Judgment Record, Book A (1881–87), Morrison County, Little Falls. Certificate of Lindbergh's admittance to the Circuit Court of the United States is in LP. See also Haines and Haines, *The Lindberghs*, pp. 78–80.
8. Information on the La Fond family is from Upham and Dunlap, *Minnesota Biographies*, p. 416; "Biography of Mrs. Mary La Fond Lindbergh," WPA Project 3870, Biography 430, Morrison County Historical Society, Little Falls; *LF Transcript*, 8 April 1887; Christie interview, 1 April 1967; Haines and Haines, *The Lindberghs*, pp. 62–63. Lindbergh data is from Haines and Haines, *The Lindberghs*, pp. 62–68; *St. Cloud Journal-Press*, 16 May 1889; interview with Eva Lindbergh Christie, 12 July 1965; Minnesota interview; Huntemer interview; interview with Mrs. G. V. Butler (niece of Charles A. Lindbergh, Sr., and daughter of Juno Lindbergh Butler), 19 June 1965; *LF Daily Transcript*, 16 October 1893.
9. Fuller, *Morrison and Todd Counties*, 1:93–94; Articles of Association, First National Bank of Little Falls, Minnesota, 17 April 1889, in possession of First National Bank, Little Falls; Haines, Stone and Company, *Little Falls City Directory for 1892* (Little Falls, 1892), p. 5; Articles of Incorporation, Transcript Publishing Company, Miscellaneous, Book D-4, pp. 416–17, Morrison County, Little Falls.
10. Thomas Pederson, "Charles Augustus Lindbergh, Sr. As I Knew Him," LP (hereafter cited as Pederson reminiscences); Frank Lindbergh interview; interview with Carl Bolander by Sarah Thorp Heald, WPA Project 3870, June 1937, Morrison County Historical Society, Little Falls; interview with Martin Engstrom, 22 June 1967.
11. Bolander interview.
12. *Ibid.*
13. Frank Lindbergh interview; interview with Gladys M. Brown (niece of Arthur P. Blanchard), 21 June 1967; Stevens, *Bench and Bar of Minnesota*, 2:179–80, 193; Register of Actions, Book

C (1888–92), Book D (1892–95), Book E (1895–99), Book F (1899–1904), Morrison County; Lindbergh to Moses E. Clapp, 18 November 1891, 22 August 1892, Attorney Generals' Papers, MinnSA; L. A. Rosing (private secretary) to Lindbergh, Blanchard, and Lindbergh, 9 May 1899, and Rosing to Lindbergh and Blanchard, 15 May 1899, John Lind Papers, Governors' Archives, MinnSA.

14. Stevens, *Bench and Bar of Minnesota*, 1:193; *LF Weekly Transcript*, 25 October, 28 October, 4 November 1898; Upham and Dunlap, *Minnesota Biographies*, pp. 442, 808.

15. *Legislative Manual, 1891*, p. 475; Abstract of Votes Polled: Election Returns, 1890, Secretary of States' Collection, MinnSA. Representative correspondence is Lindbergh to Clapp, 15 October, 17 October, 18 November, 24 November, 27 November, 23 December 1891, 22 August, 3 October 1892, and Clapp to Lindbergh, 16 October, 28 November, 26 December 1891, 25 August 1892, Attorney Generals' Papers, MinnSA.

16. Affidavits (23 March and 11 April 1891) and Lindbergh statement (23 April 1891) are in Case 3228, Seventh Judicial District Court of Minnesota, Morrison County; *LF Transcript*, 12 August 1892; Eva Lindbergh Christie to the author, 26 February 1967.

17. Butler interview; Minnesota interview; Christie to the author, 26 February 1967; Haines and Haines, *The Lindberghs*, p. 70; Register of Actions, Book C (1888–92), Book D (1892–95), Book E (1895–99), Book F (1899–1904), Book G (1904–07), Morrison County.

18. Larson, *White Pine Industry*, pp. 234–35, 353; Val E. Kasparek, "Great Industry, Logging and Lumbering, Morrison County" (18 April 1948), Morrison County Historical Society, Little Falls; *Little Falls City Directory for 1892*, cover, p. 11; *Legislative Manual, 1907*, p. 519.

19. Kasparek, "Great Industry," p. 6; interview with John C. Patience, 22 June 1967.

20. Minnesota interview; Christie interview, 12 July 1965; Pederson reminiscences; Howard P. Bell to Lindbergh, 5 May 1898, LP.

21. Bell to Lindbergh, 21 January, 26 March 1903, LP.

22. Bell to Lindbergh, 31 March 1906, LP.

23. Minnesota interview; Butler interview; *LF Weekly Transcript*, 19 April 1898; Christie to the author, 26 February 1967; Charles, Jr. commentary, 1971.

24. Land family data is from Evangeline Lindbergh notebook; Charles, Jr. commentary, 1967; Charles, Jr. to the author, 1 April 1971;

Minnesota interview; interview with Emory Scott Land (first cousin of Evangeline Lodge Land), 11 May 1970. On Charles H. Land's career, see L. Laszlo Schwartz, "The Life of Charles Henry Land (1847–1922)," *Journal of the American College of Dentists* 24 (1957): 33–51; and Robert M. Warner, *Profile of a Profession: A History of the Michigan State Dental Association* (Detroit, 1965).

25. Evangeline Lindbergh notebook; marriage announcement, LP; Lindbergh, *Boyhood,* pp. 2–3; Charles, Jr. commentary, 1967; Christie interview, 1 April 1967; Bolander interview.

26. Bell to Lindbergh, 20 May 1901, LP (Yale); Bolander interview; Charles, Jr. commentary, 1967.

27. *LF Daily Transcript,* 7 August 1905; Charles, Jr. commentary, 1967; Charles, Jr. commentary, 1967 and 1971; Huntemer interview; Lindbergh, *Boyhood,* p. 5; Lindbergh, *Spirit of St. Louis,* p. 372; Charles, Jr. to the author, 23 October 1972.

28. Minnesota interview; Charles, Jr. commentary, 1967; Christie interviews, 12 July 1965, 1 April 1967; Evangeline Lindbergh notebook.

29. Charles, Jr. commentary, 1967; Eva Lindbergh Christie Spaeth commentary, 1971. Correspondence between C. A. and Evangeline, indicative of their feelings toward one another, in LP (Yale). See also Case 24994, State of Minnesota, *In Supreme Court* (Respondent's Brief and Appellant's Brief) regarding the estate of C. A. Lindbergh, and statements and correspondence on the estate in LP (Yale).

30. Interview with Elmer Benson, 21 February 1970; Land interview; Mrs. A. M. Opsahl reminiscences, LP; interview with Fred Larson, 10 September 1967, and periodic discussions in June and July 1966; Charles, Jr. to the author, 1 April 1971; Grace Van Sickle to Lindbergh, 30 September 1900 (only part of the letter is intact, but content is sufficient to assume it was written to C. A.), LP (Yale); Christie interview, 12 July 1965; Pederson reminiscences.

31. "Lindbergh Library" list, LP; Minnesota interview. Only part of C. A. Lindbergh's library remains, as books were lost in the fire of the first house, and, after Charles, Jr.'s 1927 flight, a number of volumes were stolen or lost.

32. "Lindbergh Library" list, LP; Minnesota interview; Charles, Jr. to the author, 1 April 1971.

33. Minnesota interview; Bolander interview.

34. Christie to the author, 26 February 1967; Minnesota interview; Charles, Jr. commentary, 1967; Lindbergh, *Spirit of St. Louis,* pp. 308–10; Bolander interview.

35. Christie interview, 12 July 1965; Lindbergh to Eva, 16 March 1917, LP; interview with Frank Dewey, 23 June 1967; Opsahl reminiscences; Charles, Jr. commentary, 1967.
36. Lindbergh to "Im" (Evangeline Lindbergh), 17[?] December 1905, LP (Yale). Many of the handwritten letters between C. A. and Evangeline are dated by the envelope only. In this case the postal marking is very unclear.
37. Lindbergh statements and speeches, *LF Transcript*, 3 June 1887, 1 January 1894, copies in LP. Evidence of Lindbergh law firm foreclosure cases is in Deeds, Book 12 (1895–99), Morrison County, Little Falls.
38. *LF Transcript*, 2 November 1900, copy in LP.
39. *Ibid.*, 17 March, 21 March 1903.
40. For the racial question with respect to Roosevelt, the progressives, and Darwinism, see Seth M. Scheiner, "President Theodore Roosevelt and the Negro," *Journal of Negro History* 47 (July 1962): 169–82; I. A. Newby, *Jim Crow's Defense: Anti-Negro Thought in America, 1900–1930* (Baton Rouge, La., 1965); David W. Noble, *The Progressive Mind, 1890–1917* (Chicago, 1970), pp. 81–116; C. Vann Woodward, "The Negro in American Life, 1865–1918," in John A. Garraty, ed., *Interpreting American History: Conversations with Historians* (New York, 1970), pt. 2, p. 59; and John S. Haller, Jr., *Outcasts from Evolution: Scientific Attitudes of Racial Inferiority, 1859–1900* (Urbana, Ill., 1971).
41. Spaeth interview, 22 June 1972. Eva was shocked to learn that her father had made these statements on the racial question, and said they were not in keeping with his later views. She also recalled that later, when traveling in the South, he often extended kindnesses openly to Negroes. There are no comments on the racial issue in the *Congressional Record* during Lindbergh's tenure as congressman. This is not totally surprising, since he represented a rural and Northern district. See also Belle Case La Follette and Fola La Follette, *Robert M. La Follette: June 14, 1885–June 18, 1925* (New York, 1953), vol. 2, p. 1120; and Dewey W. Grantham, Jr., "The Progressive Movement and the Negro," in Barton J. Bernstein and Allen J. Matusow, *Twentieth-Century America: Recent Interpretations* (New York, 1969), pp. 59–74.
42. The Industrial Adjustment Company was incorporated on 28 February 1905, although it was not officially on record until 4 June 1907. Incorporations, Book H-9, pp. 319–21, Morrison County, Little Falls.
43. Carl Bolander to Dora Haines, 15 November 1930, Lynn Haines and Family Papers, MinnHS.

44. Haines and Haines, *The Lindberghs*, pp. 89–97; *LF Herald*, 10 March 1905.
45. *The Law of Rights: Realized and Unrealized, Individual and Public* 1 (March 1905): introduction page, p. 20; Haines and Haines, *The Lindberghs*, pp. 90–95.
46. Haines and Haines, *The Lindberghs*, pp. 89–91; Bolander to Haines, 15 November 1930, Haines Papers; Dewey interview; Walter E. Quigley, "Like Father, Like Son," *Saturday Evening Post*, 21 June 1941, p. 34.

Chapter III: Sixth District Congressman, pp. 41–68

1. *LF Daily Transcript*, 22 August 1906.
2. Pederson reminiscences; Haines and Haines, *The Lindberghs*, p. 98; Frank Lindbergh interview; *Minneapolis Evening Star*, 14 July 1913, copy in LP.
3. Bell to Lindbergh, 5 March 1906, LP.
4. Bell to Lindbergh, 14 April, 16 April 1906, LP.
5. Lindbergh to Evangeline, 17 April 1906, LP (Yale); Bell to Lindbergh, 17 April 1906, LP.
6. Bell to Lindbergh, 24 April 1906, LP; Lindbergh to Evangeline, 6 May 1906, LP (Yale); Minnesota interview.
7. Compiled from statistics in *Legislative Manual*, 1907, pp. 510–12, 514, 519–23.
8. *Ibid.*, p. 105.
9. *Ibid.*, p. 504. On Minnesota politics consult the state histories by Blegen and Folwell; Harlan Page Hall, *Observations* (St. Paul, 1904); James H. Baker, *Collections of the Minnesota Historical Society*, vol. 13, *Lives of the Governors of Minnesota* (St. Paul, 1908); Martin W. Odland, *The Life of Knute Nelson* (Minneapolis, 1926); Theodore Christianson, *Minnesota: A History of the State and Its People* (Chicago, 1935), vol. 2; George M. Stephenson, *John Lind of Minnesota* (Minneapolis, 1935); Charles B. Cheney, *The Story of Minnesota Politics* (Minneapolis, 1947); and G. Theodore Mitau, *Politics in Minnesota* (Minneapolis, 1960).

   Published material on Populism is extensive, but especially useful in examining traditional and recent interpretations are John D. Hicks, *The Populist Revolt* (Minneapolis, 1931); Richard Hofstadter, *The Age of Reform* (New York, 1955); Norman Pollack, *The Populist Response to Industrial America* (Cambridge, Mass., 1962); Walter Nugent, *The Tolerant Populists* (Chicago, 1963); and O. Gene Clanton, *Kansas Populism: Ideas and Men* (Lawrence, Kans., 1969). See also James C. Malin, *A Concern About Humanity: Notes on Reform, 1872–1912 at the National and Kansas Levels of Thought* (Lawrence, Kans., 1964), which stresses the importance of reform prior to the 1890's.

10. *Legislative Manual, 1907,* pp. 504–05. See also Winifred G. Helmes, *John A. Johnson, the People's Governor: A Political Biography* (Minneapolis, 1949).

11. Upham and Dunlap, *Minnesota Biographies,* p. 88; *Biographical Directory of the American Congress, 1774–1961* (Washington, D.C., 1961), p. 621. Information on newspapers in the Sixth District in *Legislative Manual,* 1907, pp. 609–19; and *N. W. Ayer and Son's American Newspaper Annual* (Philadelphia, 1906), pp. 424–55. Pro-Buckman comment in *Wadena Pioneer-Journal,* 6 September 1906; and *Brainerd Arena,* 22 August 1906.

12. *Litchfield Saturday-Review,* 15 September 1906; *Long Prairie Leader,* 6 September 1906; *LF Daily Transcript,* 6 September, 10 September, 17 September 1906.

13. *Buffalo Journal,* 31 August, 14 September 1906; *Todd County Argus,* 6 September, 13 September 1906; *Hubbard County Enterprise,* 6 September 1906. Statements from *Akeley Herald* and *Sebeka Review* in *LF Herald,* 3 August 1906.

14. Helmes, *John A. Johnson,* pp. 133–35, 146–49, 151–52, 190–94; *Brainerd Daily Dispatch,* 14 June 1906; Upham and Dunlap, *Minnesota Biographies,* pp. 132, 134, 191, 195, 367.

15. *St. Cloud Daily Times,* 20 September 1906; *Alexandria Citizen,* 30 August 1906; Upham and Dunlap, *Minnesota Biographies,* p. 491; *Brainerd Dispatch,* 14 September 1906; *LF Daily Transcript,* 13 September 1906.

16. Nelson to Heen, 22 August 1906, Knute Nelson Papers, MinnHS; *Long Prairie Leader,* 13 September 1906; *Pine Tree Blaze,* 17 September 1906.

17. Speech reprinted in *LF Daily Transcript,* 6 July 1906; *Hubbard County Enterprise,* 13 September 1906; Haines and Haines, *The Lindberghs,* p. 101.

18. "To the People of the Sixth Congressional District of Minnesota, 1906," quoted in Haines and Haines, *The Lindberghs,* pp. 102–03; *LF Daily Transcript,* 6 July, 3 September 1906.

19. *Alexandria Citizen,* 6 September 1906; *LF Daily Transcript,* 3 November 1906.

20. Minnesota interview; Christie interview, 12 July 1965; Christie to the author, 26 February 1967; Charles, Jr. commentary, 1967.

21. Frank Lindbergh interview; interview with Mrs. Frank A. Lind-

bergh, 7 April 1971; Butler interview; Pederson reminiscences; Elmer Benson interview; Fred Larson interview; interview with John M. Baer, 24 August 1965; Charles, Jr. commentary, 1967; Minnesota interview.

22. *Hubbard County Enterprise,* 13 September 1906; *Todd County Argus,* 13 September 1906; Frank Lindbergh interview; *Litchfield Saturday-Review,* 15 September 1906. The *Review* labeled the statement a "characteristically Buckman reply."

23. *LF Daily Transcript,* 10 September 1906; *Wadena Pioneer-Journal,* 13 September 1906; Deeds, Book 12 (1895–99), Morrison County; Fred Larson interview; Frank Lindbergh interview.

24. *LF Daily Transcript,* 19 September, 22 September 1906; *Buffalo Journal,* 28 September 1906.

25. Edward M. La Fond to Mrs. Dora Haines, August 1930, Haines Papers; Pederson reminiscences.

26. Based on statistics in Abstract of Votes Polled: Primary Election Returns, 1906, Secretary of States' Collection, MinnSA; interview with Nina Hollister Sullivan, 2 August 1970; Christianson, *Minnesota,* 4:336–37.

27. *Cass Lake Voice,* 3 November 1906; *Hubbard County Enterprise,* 4 October 1906; *LF Daily Transcript,* 1 November 1906; *Litchfield Saturday-Review,* 29 September 1906.

28. *Hubbard County Enterprise,* 18 October 1906; *Osakis Review,* 25 October 1906; *Dassel Anchor,* 1 November 1906.

29. *St. Cloud Daily Times,* 22 October, 29 October, 3 November 1906; *LF Herald,* 26 October, 21 September 1906; *Der Nordstern,* 25 October 1906. On St. Cloud newspapers, see *Legislative Manual, 1907,* pp. 609–19.

30. Buckman won the Sixth District seat in the general election of 1902 by 4,189 votes; in 1904 he won by 2,879 votes. *Legislative Manual, 1903,* p. 517; *ibid.,* 1905, p. 511.

31. Based on statistics in *Legislative Manual, 1907,* pp. 484–87, 491. Certificate data in Office of the Governor to Lindbergh, 27 December 1906, 25 January 1907, John A. Johnson Executive Letters, Governors' Archives, MinnSA. Although there are some exceptions, there is a general correlation between Lindbergh's political following in the Sixth District and those counties with the highest proportion of Scandinavian-Americans. This may be seen especially in Aitkin, Cass, Crow Wing, Douglas, Hubbard, Meeker, Sherburne, and Wright counties. With a combined Swedish, Norwegian, and Danish foreign-born population between 9.1 per cent and 17.7 per cent in these counties in 1910, the average vote

given Lindbergh in these counties during the general elections of
1906, 1908, 1912, and 1914, with one exception, ranged from
60.9 per cent to 72.3 per cent. Lindbergh was unopposed in 1910,
and he received 56.1 per cent of the vote in Aitkin County in
1914, when it was added to the district. Even in his later weak
congressional race, in 1920, Lindbergh generally did better in
these counties than his overall total of 31 per cent in the district.
The significant exception in 1920 was Sherburne County, which
gave him only 17 per cent. Statistics and computations are from
Thirteenth Census of the United States: Population, 1910; and
Legislative Manual, 1907–21.

32. Lindbergh to Bolander, 15 October 1906, LP; Dewey interview;
Bradstreet report, 23 March 1908, LP (Yale).

33. It should be noted that most of Lindbergh's incoming official
correspondence, and virtually all of his outgoing mail for the
congressional years, has been either destroyed or lost. There are
four boxes of valuable primary letters in the Lindbergh Papers,
mostly with selected correspondents and his daughter Eva. But
the Papers must be supplemented with material from other collections, his writings, and other public and private documents.
One unpublished source is Harald P. Christensen, "The Political
Ideas of Charles A. Lindbergh, Sr." (master's thesis, State University of Iowa, 1940).

34. Lindbergh to Nelson, June 1907, and Nelson to Lindbergh, 28
June 1907, Knute Nelson Papers.

35. *Biographical Directory of the American Congress,* pp. 289, 291,
1000; Lindbergh, *Spirit of St. Louis,* pp. 311–12; Charles, Jr. commentary, 1967; Haines and Haines, *The Lindberghs,* p. 106. See
also W. F. Toensing, comp., *Minnesota Congressmen, Legislators,
and other Elected State Officials: An Alphabetical Check List,
1849–1971* (St. Paul, 1971).

36. Haines and Haines, *The Lindberghs,* pp. 107–15; *Congressional
Record,* 60th Cong., 1st sess., pp. 427–28.

37. Lindbergh to Nelson, 1 August, 6 May 1907, 18 August 1908,
2 June 1907, Nelson to Lindbergh, 24 September 1908, Eddy to
Nelson, 25 September 1908, and Bartlett to Nelson, 13 October
1908, Knute Nelson Papers; Lindbergh to Williams, 16 March
1908, and Lindbergh to Koll, 12 February 1908, LP; Upham and
Dunlap, *Minnesota Biographies,* pp. 198–99; Bell to Lindbergh,
22 May 1907, LP (Yale).

38. Lindbergh telegram to secretary of war, 29 May 1907, and W. P.
Duvall (acting chief of staff) memorandum, 31 May 1907, RG 94,

Records of the Adjutant General's Office, 1780's–1917, National Archives, Washington, D.C. (the War Department argued that space and facilities were not adequate at the forts); *Congressional Record*, 60th Cong., 1st sess., p. 2033.

39. Theodore Roosevelt to Nelson Aldrich, 20 January 1907, Theodore Roosevelt Papers, Library of Congress, Washington, D.C. Milton Friedman and Anna Jacobson Schwartz, *A Monetary History of the United States, 1867–1960* (Princeton, 1963), pp. 168–71. See also Henry Pringle, *Theodore Roosevelt: A Biography* (New York, 1956), p. 339; and William Henry Harbaugh, *The Life and Times of Theodore Roosevelt*, rev. ed. (New York, 1963), pp. 301–02.

40. *Congressional Record*, 60th Cong., 1st sess., p. 2899.

41. *Ibid.*, p. 2900.

42. *Ibid.* Portions of Lind'.rgh's speech, somewhat changed in wording, are in Charles A. Lindbergh, Sr., *Banking and Currency and the Money Trust* (Washington, D.C., 1913), pp. 177–81.

43. *Congressional Record*, 60th Cong., 1st sess., pp. 2900–2901.

44. *Ibid.*, pp. 2901–05.

45. *Brainerd Daily Dispatch*, 31 January 1908; *Congressional Record*, 60th Cong., 1st sess., pp. 6563–64, 3861–64, Appendix, p. 58; Friedman and Schwartz, *Monetary History*, pp. 170–71; George E. Mowry, *Theodore Roosevelt and the Progressive Movement* (Madison, 1946), p. 27.

46. W. Jett Lauck, unpublished manuscript, two handwritten chapters, W. Jett Lauck Papers, Alderman Library, University of Virginia, Charlottesville (hereafter cited as Lauck MS). See also W. Jett Lauck, *Political and Industrial Democracy, 1776–1926* (New York, 1926). On Populism, see Pollack, *Populist Response*.

47. Haines and Haines, *The Lindberghs*, pp. 105–06, 130–31; Lindbergh to Evangeline, 20 April 1907, LP (Yale); Minnesota interview; Charles, Jr. commentary, 1967; Evangeline Lindbergh notebook; Lindbergh to Bolander, Summer 1908, LP.

48. Lindbergh to Koll, 12 February 1908, Lindbergh to M. M. Williams, 2 March, 4 April 1908, and Lindbergh to Bolander, Summer 1908, 24 May 1908, LP; *Legislative Manual, 1909*, p. 541.

49. *St. Cloud Daily Times*, 28 September 1908; *Long Prairie Leader*, 25 September 1908; *Brainerd Dispatch*, 28 September 1908.

50. *LF Daily Transcript*, 21 October 1908; *Osakis Review*, 29 October 1908; *Hubbard County Enterprise*, 29 October 1908; *Brainerd Daily Dispatch*, 22 September 1908; *Long Prairie Leader*, 13 October 1908.

51. *LF Daily Transcript,* 30 September, 29 October, 31 October 1908; *Brainerd Daily Dispatch,* 31 October 1908.
52. *Legislative Manual, 1909,* pp. 528, 544, 557; *LF Daily Transcript,* 5 November 1908.

Chapter IV: Republican Insurgent, pp. 69–98

1. Interview by Kenneth Hechler with John M. Nelson, 5–7 February 1939, John M. Nelson Papers, Wisconsin State Historical Society, Madison.
2. The best studies on the insurgent revolt are Kenneth W. Hechler, *Insurgency: Personalities and Politics of the Taft Era* (1940; reprint ed., New York, 1970); and James Holt, *Congressional Insurgents and the Party System, 1909–1916* (Cambridge, Mass., 1967). Briefer treatments are found in Mark Sullivan, *Our Times: The United States, 1900–1925* (New York, 1937), vol. 4; Henry Pringle, *The Life and Times of William Howard Taft: A Biography* (1938; reprint ed., Hamden, Conn., 1964), vol. 1; George E. Mowry, *The Era of Theodore Roosevelt and the Birth of Modern America, 1900–1912* (New York, 1958); Mowry, *Theodore Roosevelt and the Progressive Movement;* and Horace Samuel Merrill and Marion Galbraith Merrill, *The Republican Command, 1897–1913* (Lexington, Ky., 1971).
3. Hechler, *Insurgency,* pp. 12, 14, 16–20; Holt, *Congressional Insurgents,* pp. 1–6; Minnesota interview.
4. Hechler, *Insurgency,* p. 22.
5. *Ibid.,* pp. 14–15; Holt, *Congressional Insurgents,* p. 3; John Nelson interview.
6. Hechler, *Insurgency,* p. 14; Sullivan, *Our Times,* 4:378–79.
7. Pringle, *William Howard Taft,* 1:408. The following statement from House records clarifies the rule of recognition prior to 1879: "In the early history of the House, when business proceeded on presentation by individual members, the Speaker recognized the Member who arose first; and in the case of doubt there was an appeal from his recognition." The rule changed in 1879, when the Committee on Rules, in order to direct discussion on bills before the House, reported that "in the nature of the case discretion must be lodged with the presiding officer," and this development, in turn, led to the eventual exercise of arbitrary power by the Speaker. U.S. Congress, House, *Constitution: Jefferson's Manual and Rules of the House of Representatives of the United States, Ninetieth Congress,* 89th Cong., 2nd sess., 1967, H. Doc. 529, sec. 753, p. 379.

8. John Nelson interview. See also Hechler, *Insurgency,* pp. 13, 52; and Mowry, *Era of Theodore Roosevelt,* pp. 239–40.
9. John Nelson interview; Hechler, *Insurgency,* pp. 13, 46–49; Holt, *Congressional Insurgents,* p. 17; statement by several national editors opposing Cannonism, John Nelson Papers; *Congressional Record,* 60th Cong., 2nd sess., p. 3572.
10. John Nelson interview; Hechler, *Insurgency,* pp. 40–41; *St. Cloud Daily Journal-Press,* 10 March 1909.
11. John Nelson interview. Quotation also in Hechler, *Insurgency,* p. 41.
12. Interview with Grace L. Nelson, 31 October 1970; Grace L. Nelson to the author, 9 November 1970; interview with Fola La Follette, 5 May 1966; interview with Gerald P. Nye, 16 July 1969; Victor Murdock to Mrs. Lynn Haines, 30 September 1930, Haines Papers; Minnesota interview; Charles, Jr. commentary, 1971.
13. *Daily Star and Standard* (Anama, Panama), 31 December 1908, and *Pilot* (Norfolk, Va.), 10 January 1909, LP; Lindbergh to Evangeline, 17 December 1908, LP (Yale). On Roosevelt, see Mowry, *Era of Theodore Roosevelt,* pp. 149–50, 153–54.
14. Haines and Haines, *The Lindberghs,* pp. 123–24.
15. Theodore Roosevelt to Lindbergh, 16 January 1909, LP.
16. The bills are H.R. 26624, H.R. 26730, and H.R. 28016, in House Originals (including House Bills, House Reports, House Concurrent Resolutions, House Joint Resolutions, and House Resolutions), RG 233, Records of the United States House of Representatives, National Archives (hereafter cited as House Originals, RG 233, National Archives).
17. *Congressional Record,* 60th Cong., 2nd sess., pp. 3555, 3683–84.
18. Edward M. La Fond to Dora B. Haines, 26 November 1930, Haines Papers; *St. Cloud Daily Journal-Press* [1909], in clippings, LP, and 30 January 1909; *LF Daily Transcript,* 25 February, 17 March, 19 March 1909; Lindbergh to M. M. Williams, 22 March 1909, LP; Haines and Haines, *The Lindberghs,* pp. 120–23.
19. Hechler, *Insurgency,* pp. 49–56; John Nelson interview.
20. *Congressional Record,* 61st Cong., 1st sess., pp. 18, 33; Hechler, *Insurgency,* pp. 56–59; Mowry, *Era of Theodore Roosevelt,* pp. 240–41.
21. "On the Nation's Roll of Honor," *La Follette's Weekly Magazine,* 10 April 1909; *LF Daily Transcript,* 19 March 1909.
22. *Congressional Record,* 61st Cong., 1st sess., p. 827. Portions and discussion of Lindbergh's tariff speech appear in Haines and Haines, *The Lindberghs,* pp. 133–38.

23. *Congressional Record,* 61st Cong., 1st sess., p. 827.
24. *Ibid.,* p. 828.
25. *Ibid.,* pp. 827–28.
26. *Ibid.,* pp. 828–29.
27. *Ibid.,* p. 831.
28. On the Senate tariff struggle, see Hechler, *Insurgency,* pp. 92–145, 131 (Nelson's statement); and Carl H. Chrislock, *The Progressive Era in Minnesota, 1899–1918* (St. Paul, 1971), pp. 43, 52–53. Chrislock's study is the best published source on the general history of early-twentieth-century Minnesota politics.
29. *Congressional Record,* 61st Cong., 1st sess., Appendix, pp. 88–89; Hechler, *Insurgency,* pp. 139–45.
30. Lindbergh to Evangeline, 18 June 1909, LP (Yale); *Winona Republican-Herald,* 18 September 1909; *Minneapolis Tribune,* 19 September 1909; Lindbergh to M. M. Williams, 2 February 1910. On the Winona speech, see Pringle, *William Howard Taft,* 1:451–56.
31. Hechler, *Insurgency,* pp. 64, 154–58; *Congressional Record,* 61st Cong., 2nd sess., p. 404; minutes of insurgent meetings, 10 January, 12 January, 31 January 1910, John Nelson Papers. On the Ballinger-Pinchot controversy, see James Penick, Jr., *Progressive Politics and Conservation: The Ballinger-Pinchot Affair* (Chicago, 1968); and Elmo R. Richardson, *The Politics of Conservation: Crusades and Controversies, 1897–1913* (Berkeley, 1962).
32. Hechler, *Insurgency,* pp. 65–78; *Congressional Record,* 61st Cong., 2nd sess., pp. 3436, 3438.
33. John Nelson interview; Hechler, *Insurgency,* pp. 78–82; Holt, *Congressional Insurgents,* pp. 19–28. For representative comment on the varying interpretations of the Progressive movement in American history, see Benjamin Parke De Witt, *The Progressive Movement* (New York, 1915), and Hicks, *The Populist Revolt,* which stress the traditional approach of democratic reform and identify the connection between Populism and Progressivism; Hofstadter, *The Age of Reform,* and George E. Mowry, *The California Progressives* (Chicago, 1963), which challenge the first interpretation and its emphasis on the agrarian and economic origins of the movement; and Gabriel Kolko, *The Triumph of Conservatism: A Reinterpretation of American History, 1900–1916* (New York, 1963), Robert H. Wiebe, *The Search for Order, 1877–1920* (New York, 1967), and James Weinstein, *The Corporate Ideal in the Liberal State, 1900–1918* (Boston, 1968), which, in the latest revisionist school of thought, deny the old democracy-versus-privilege concept of Progressivism, emphasizing rather its func-

tional nature in adjusting to new social and economic conditions and its close alignment with, and even deliberate promotion by, big business.

34. Russel B. Nye, *Midwestern Progressive Politics: A Historical Study of Its Origins and Development, 1870–1958* (New York, 1965), p. 247; *Washington Herald,* 3 February 1910; *Current Literature* 48 (February 1910): 129; *Record-Review* (Madison, Wis.), July 1910.

35. See Hechler, *Insurgency,* pp. 163–77; and Mowry, *Theodore Roosevelt and the Progressive Movement,* pp. 94–103.

36. *Congressional Record,* 61st Cong., 2nd sess., p. 5170.

37. *Ibid.,* p. 5171.

38. *Ibid.,* pp. 5173–74.

39. *Ibid.,* p. 5172; Minnesota interview.

40. *Congressional Record,* 61st Cong., 2nd sess., pp. 5170, 5175–76.

41. *Ibid.,* pp. 5173–74.

42. *Ibid.,* p. 5172.

43. *Ibid.,* p. 5175.

44. Hechler, *Insurgency,* pp. 173–76.

45. *Congressional Record,* 61st Cong., 2nd sess., pp. 8271–72, 8274.

46. *Ibid.,* p. 8273.

47. *Ibid.,* pp. 8273–76; Hechler, *Insurgency,* p. 177. For further discussion on discriminatory railroad rates and the history of the Mann-Elkins bill, see Gabriel Kolko, *Railroads and Regulation, 1877–1916* (Princeton, 1965), pp. 177–95; Edward C. Kirkland, *Industry Comes of Age: Business, Labor, and Public Policy, 1860–1897* (Chicago, 1967), pp. 97–101; K. Austin Kerr, *American Railroad Politics, 1914–1920: Rates, Wages, and Efficiency* (Pittsburgh, 1968), pp. 14–17; and Robert H. Wiebe, *Businessmen and Reform: A Study of the Progressive Movement* (Chicago, 1968), pp. 85–90.

48. H.R. 18591, House Originals, RG 233, National Archives; M. N. Koll to Lindbergh, 28 February, 7 March, 5 December 1910, Mathias N. Koll Papers, MinnHS (copies of Koll items have been placed in LP).

49. Lindbergh statement to Koll, December 1910, Koll Papers; Folwell, *A History of Minnesota,* 1:307.

50. Account of C. A. Lindbergh v. Carl Bolander, Debits and Credits, 1910–11, LP (Yale); *LF Daily Transcript,* 24 February, 14 April, 15 April 1909; Lindbergh to Evangeline, 28 June, 19 July, 11 June, 2 July, 17 July, 1 November 1909 LP (Yale).

51. Upham and Dunlap, *Minnesota Biographies,* p. 467; *Hubbard*

County Enterprise, 15 September 1910; *Minneapolis Tribune,* 21 September 1910.

52. *St. Paul Pioneer Press,* 1 September 1910.
53. C. A. Lindbergh, *Progressive Republican Candidate for Congress,* campaign pamphlet, 1910, LP (Yale).
54. *Ibid.*
55. *Legislative Manual, 1911,* pp. 482, 484–86, 488, 636; *Minneapolis Tribune,* 21 September 1909. See also Roger E. Wyman, "Insurgency in Minnesota: The Defeat of James A. Tawney in 1910," *Minnesota History* 40 (Fall 1967): 317–29; and Holt, *Congressional Insurgents,* pp. 40–43.
56. Koll to Lindbergh, 5 December 1910, Koll Papers; *LF Daily Transcript,* 22 September, 23 September 1910; *Brainerd Dispatch,* 30 September 1910; *Long Prairie Leader,* 29 September 1910; *Duluth News-Tribune,* 28 October 1910.

Chapter V: Canadian Reciprocity and the Money Trust, pp. 99–132

1. Ida M. Tarbell, "The Hunt for a Money Trust," *American Magazine,* May 1913, p. 11.
2. General discussion of the Canadian reciprocity issue may be found in Pringle, *William Howard Taft,* 2:582–602; L. Ethan Ellis, *Reciprocity, 1911: A Study in Canadian-American Relations* (New Haven, 1939); Mowry, *Era of Theodore Roosevelt,* pp. 282–86; and D. Jerome Tweton's treatment of Minnesota and North Dakota response to reciprocity, "The Border Farmer and the Canadian Reciprocity Issue, 1911–1912," *Agricultural History* 37 (October 1963): 235–41.
3. Pringle, *William Howard Taft,* 2:586–88; Mowry, *Era of Theodore Roosevelt,* p. 283; Tweton, "Border Farmer," p. 235; William Howard Taft to Nelson Aldrich, 29 January 1911, Nelson Aldrich Papers, Library of Congress.
4. Tweton, "Border Farmer," pp. 236–37.
5. P. V. Collins to Knute Nelson, 5 June, 15 June 1911, Knute Nelson Papers.
6. Tweton, "Border Farmer," p. 236; James J. Hill to William Howard Taft, 25 February 1911, William Howard Taft Papers, Library of Congress.
7. *Congressional Record,* 61st Cong., 3rd sess., pp. 2538–39.
8. *Ibid.,* p. 2539.
9. *Ibid.,* pp. 2539–40.

10. *Ibid.*
11. *Ibid.*, p. 2539.
12. *Ibid.*, pp. 2540–41.
13. *Congressional Record*, 62nd Cong., 1st sess., pp. 557, 559–60; Tweton, "Border Farmer," pp. 237–38.
14. Pringle, *William Howard Taft*, 2:593–602; Tweton, "Border Farmer," pp. 238–39; Holt, *Congressional Insurgents*, pp. 45–47; Mowry, *Era of Theodore Roosevelt*, pp. 284–86.
15. Charles, Jr. commentary, 1967.
16. Friedman and Schwartz, *Monetary History*, p. 171; A. Barton Hepburn, *A History of Currency in the United States*, rev. ed. (New York, 1967), p. 395; Arthur S. Link, *Wilson: The New Freedom* (Princeton, 1956), p. 200; Haines and Haines, *The Lindberghs*, p. 163.
17. Hepburn, *Currency*, p. 396; Link, *Wilson: The New Freedom*, p. 201; *Congressional Record*, 62nd Cong., 1st sess., pp. 1992–93. See also the extensive comparison between provisions of the Aldrich plan and those of the later Federal Reserve system in Paul M. Warburg, *The Federal Reserve System: Its Origin and Growth* (New York, 1930), vol. 1, pp. 178–406.
18. Lindbergh, Sr., *Banking and Currency*, pp. 94–96.
19. *Ibid.*, p. 97.
20. *Ibid.*, pp. 33, 75–76, 83–85; Haines and Haines, *The Lindberghs*, p. 185.
21. *Congressional Record*, 62nd Cong., 1st sess., pp. 1989–90.
22. *Ibid.*, pp. 1991–92.
23. Lindbergh, Sr., *Banking and Currency*, p. 45.
24. *Congressional Record*, 62nd Cong., 1st sess., pp. 1992–94.
25. *Ibid.*, pp. 1992, 1994.
26. *Ibid.*, p. 1994.
27. *Ibid.*, pp. 1994–95.
28. *Ibid.*, pp. 1997–98.
29. *Ibid.*, p. 1999; *Congressional Directory*, 61st Cong., 3rd sess., p. 210; *Congressional Directory*, 62nd Cong., 1st sess., p. 189.
30. Lynn Haines, *Law Making in America: The Story of the 1911–1912 Session of the Sixty-second Congress* (Bethesda, Md., 1912), pp. 18–20.
31. H. Res. 314, House Originals, RG 233, National Archives.
32. U.S. Congress, House, Committee on Rules, *Hearings on House Resolution No. 314*, 62nd Cong., 2nd sess., pp. 1–51.
33. *Ibid.*, pp. 3–9.
34. Quotations are from George L. Anderson, "The National Banking

System, 1865–1875: A Sectional Institution" (Ph.D. dissertation, University of Illinois, 1933), pp. 111–13 and "Western Attitudes Toward National Banks, 1873–1874," *Mississippi Valley Historical Review* 23 (September 1936): 216. See also U.S. Congress, National Monetary Commission, *History of Crises Under the National Banking System*, by O. M. W. Sprague, 61st Cong., 2nd sess., S. Doc. 538, *Reports* 5 (Washington, D.C., 1910), pp. 15–35; Irwin Unger, *The Greenback Era: A Social and Political History of American Finance, 1865–1879* (Princeton, 1964); and Anderson, "Banks, Mails, and Rails, 1880–1915," in John G. Clark, ed., *The Frontier Challenge: Responses to the Trans-Mississippi West* (Lawrence, Kans., 1971), pp. 275–307; and Anderson, *Essays on the History of Banking* (Lawrence, Kans., 1972).

35. Committee on Rules, *Hearings on House Resolution No. 314*, pp. 10–15.
36. *Ibid.*, p. 13.
37. *Ibid.*, pp. 16–17.
38. *Ibid.*, pp. 19–20.
39. *Ibid.*, p. 20.
40. *Ibid.*, pp. 22–25.
41. *Ibid.*, pp. 26–33.
42. *Ibid.*, pp. 26, 36–38.
43. *Ibid.*, pp. 38–47.
44. *Ibid.*, pp. 48–50.
45. There is reasonable doubt as to whether the Lincoln statement that Lindbergh used is authentic. While Archer H. Shaw, *The Lincoln Encyclopedia: The Spoken and Written Words of A. Lincoln Arranged for Ready Reference* (New York, 1950), p. 40, attributes the statement to a letter of 21 November 1864 from Lincoln to William F. Elkins, it is not included in the definitive work on Lincoln's writings, Roy P. Basler, ed., *The Collected Works of Abraham Lincoln*, 9 vols. (New Brunswick, N.J., 1953–55). Furthermore, Benjamin P. Thomas, in his *Abraham Lincoln: A Biography* (New York, 1953), p. 530, writes that the Shaw volume "not only quotes inaccurately but includes a number of known forgeries." Lindbergh probably got it from a printed source, though which source has not been determined.
46. Committee on Rules, *Hearings on House Resolution No. 314*, p. 51.
47. *Ibid.*
48. *Congressional Record*, 62nd Cong., 2nd sess., p. 2395; Haines, *Law Making in America*, pp. 11–12, 34–35, 75–77; Haines and Haines, *The Lindberghs*, pp. 182–83.

49. *Congressional Record,* 62nd Cong., 2nd sess., pp. 2395–2410; Haines and Haines, *The Lindberghs,* pp. 182–83.

50. *Congressional Record,* 62nd Cong., 2nd sess., Appendix, pp. 55–69.

51. *Ibid.,* p. 58.

52. *Ibid.,* pp. 61–69; Haines and Haines, *The Lindberghs,* pp. 176–77; Link, *Wilson: The New Freedom,* p. 201; Lauck MS. See also Lindbergh, Sr., *Banking and Currency,* pp. 107–37.

53. Lindbergh to J. J. Streeter, 8 February, 9 February, 11 February, 5 March, 15 March, 27 March 1912, and Lindbergh to George Wilson, 5 March 1912, LP; Wilson to Lynn Haines, 22 January 1928, Haines Papers.

54. H. Res. 484, House Originals, RG 233, National Archives; *Congressional Record,* 62nd Cong., 1st sess., pp. 1517–18.

55. *Congressional Record,* 62nd Cong., 2nd sess., Appendix, p. 151; Lindbergh to secretary of war, 2 May 1912, W. M. O'Neil to Knute Nelson, 8 June 1912, Lindbergh to W. H. Bixby, 22 June 1912, and John C. Scofield to Lindbergh, 13 August 1912, RG 77, Records of the Office of the Chief of Engineers, National Archives.

56. H. Res. 564, House Originals, RG 233, National Archives; *Congressional Record,* 62nd Cong., 2nd sess., p. 10226, Appendix, pp. 432–36.

57. *Congressional Record,* 62nd Cong., 2nd sess., p. 4198; Haines and Haines, *The Lindberghs,* pp. 138–41; *New York Tribune,* 22 March 1912, commentary in Haines Papers; *Washington Herald,* 23 March 1912, clippings in LP.

58. Carl Bolander to Lindbergh, 14 January 1911, LP (Yale); interview with Eva Lindbergh Christie Spaeth, 12 October 1972; *Congressional Record,* 61st Cong., 3rd sess., p. 52; *LF Weekly Transcript,* 3 February 1911, clippings in LP; *LF Daily Transcript,* 15 November 1911.

59. Lindbergh to J. J. Streeter, 8 February 1912, LP; Lindbergh, Sr., *Banking and Currency,* p. 99. See also Haines, *Law Making in America,* pp. 75–76; and Lauck MS. Examples of national coverage on Lindbergh and the money issue may be found in *Washington Herald,* 23 December 1911, clippings in LP; *American Review of Reviews,* 45 (February 1912): 138–39; and Tarbell, "Hunt for a Money Trust."

Chapter VI: Progressive Politics, pp. 133–149

1. Nye, *Midwestern Progressive Politics,* pp. 261–62; Holt, *Congressional Insurgents,* pp. 49–50; Richard Lowitt, *George W.*

Norris: *The Making of a Progressive, 1861–1912* (Syracuse, 1963), p. 201; La Follette and La Follette, *Robert M. La Follette,* 1:314–19.

2. Nye, *Midwestern Progressive Politics,* p. 262; F. T. Wilson to W. I. Nolan, 30 December 1911, James Manahan Papers, MinnHS; Mowry, *Theodore Roosevelt and the Progressive Movement,* pp. 172–73.

3. La Follette and La Follette, *Robert M. La Follette,* 1:315; Nye, *Midwestern Progressive Politics,* pp. 262–63; Mowry, *Theodore Roosevelt and the Progressive Movement,* pp. 172–77.

4. Robert M. La Follette, *La Follette's Autobiography: A Personal Narrative of Political Experiences* (Madison, 1911), pp. 516–29; La Follette and La Follette, *Robert M. La Follette,* 1:329–31, 352–53; Lowitt, *George W. Norris,* pp. 216–17; Nye, *Midwestern Progressive Politics,* pp. 262–63.

5. La Follette, *Autobiography,* pp. 520–21.

6. George F. Loftus to John Hannan, 29 April 1911, Robert M. La Follette Papers, Library of Congress (copies of several letters from the La Follette Papers, including those cited in this study, have been placed in LP); W. I. Nolan to James Manahan, 1 July 1911, James Manahan correspondence, private collection in possession of James H. Manahan (grandnephew of James Manahan), Mankato, Minn.

7. Loftus to Lynn Haines, 2 November 1911, and Lindbergh to Walter L. Houser, 6 October 1911, La Follette Papers; Gifford Pinchot to Robert M. La Follette, 31 August 1911, Gifford Pinchot Papers, Library of Congress.

8. See Nye, *Midwestern Progressive Politics,* pp. 263–66; Holt, *Congressional Insurgents,* pp. 50–54; La Follette, *Autobiography,* p. 526; M. Nelson McGeary, *Gifford Pinchot: Forester-Politician* (Princeton, 1960), pp. 213–25.

9. George W. Norris to F. P. Corrick, 24 January 1912, George W. Norris Papers, Library of Congress; Nye, *Midwestern Progressive Politics,* p. 265; La Follette and La Follette, *Robert M. La Follette,* 1:394–96.

10. La Follette and La Follette, *Robert M. La Follette,* 1:398–414; La Follette, *Autobiography,* pp. 608–09, 612; Amos Pinchot, *History of the Progressive Party, 1912–1916,* ed. Helene M. Hooker (New York, 1958), pp. 27–28, 134–36; George H. Mayer, *The Republican Party, 1854–1964* (London, 1967), p. 324; Malcolm Moos, *The Republicans: A History of Their Party* (New York, 1956), p. 271.

11. Lindbergh to Robert M. La Follette, 10 February 1912, La Follette Papers.
12. Telegram from Lindbergh to Loftus, 10 February 1912, copies in La Follette Papers, LP, and Manahan Papers.
13. Lindbergh to Theodore Roosevelt, 13 February 1912, Roosevelt Papers.
14. Lindbergh to Pinchot, 10 February 1912, and Pinchot to Lindbergh, 13 February 1912, Pinchot Papers; Hugh T. Halbert to Theodore Roosevelt, 10 February 1912, Roosevelt Papers; La Follette and La Follette, *Robert M. La Follette*, 1:420–21.
15. La Follette to Lindbergh, 20 February 1912, La Follette Papers.
16. Frank Harper (Roosevelt office) to Lindbergh, 17 February 1912, Lindbergh to Harper, 19 February 1912, and Lindbergh to Roosevelt, 27 February, 7 March 1912, Roosevelt Papers; *LF Daily Transcript*, 27 February 1912; Spaeth interview, 12 October 1972.
17. Lindbergh to Roosevelt, 7 March, 12 March, 16 March 1912, Roosevelt Papers; Roosevelt to Lindbergh, 11 March 1912, LP; Elwyn B. Robinson, *History of North Dakota* (Lincoln, 1966), p. 268.
18. Lindbergh to Roosevelt, 21 March 1912, Roosevelt Papers.
19. Unsigned letter to Lindbergh, 12 March 1912, copies in Pinchot Papers and LP; Lindbergh to Pinchot, 25 March 1912, Pinchot Papers; Pinchot to Lindbergh, 4 April 1912, and Roosevelt to Lindbergh, 16 April 1912, LP.
20. Lindbergh to Roosevelt, 5 June 1912, Roosevelt Papers; Mayer, *Republican Party*, pp. 326–29; Christianson, *Minnesota*, 2:328.
21. Mayer, *Republican Party*, p. 330; Nye, *Midwestern Progressive Politics*, p. 270; Holt, *Congressional Insurgents*, pp. 64–70.
22. Lindbergh to Roosevelt, 16 August 1912, Roosevelt Papers; Eva Lindbergh Christie interview, 12 July 1965; Ernest Lundeen to Eva Lindbergh, 27 September 1912, LP; *LF Daily Transcript*, 28 September 1912.
23. Lindbergh, Sr., *Banking and Currency*, pp. 277–78. The Darwinian influence on Lindbergh's thought seems evident in this statement.
24. *Legislative Manual, 1913*, pp. 506–07, 512–13; Holt, *Congressional Insurgents*, pp. 64–70.
25. Lindbergh to Roosevelt, 6 August, 16 August 1912, Roosevelt Papers.
26. Lindbergh to Pinchot, 21 August 1912, Pinchot Papers; Roosevelt to Pinchot, 21 August 1912, and Pinchot to Roosevelt, 24 August 1912, Roosevelt Papers.

27. Haines to Lindbergh, 9 October 1912, and Lindbergh to Haines, 11 October 1912, Haines Papers.
28. Unsigned letter to Lindbergh, 22 March 1912, Pinchot Papers; Koll to Lindbergh, 30 December 1911, Koll Papers; Lindbergh to Roosevelt, 29 May 1912, Roosevelt Papers; *Legislative Manual, 1913*, p. 360. On the Minnesota political situation, see Chrislock, *Progressive Era*, pp. 47–58; and Cheney, *Minnesota Politics*, pp. 32–33, 39–43.
29. *LF Daily Transcript*, 28 September, 5 October, 30 October 1912.
30. *St. Cloud Daily Times*, 22 October, 4 November 1912; *LF Herald*, 6 September 1912.
31. *Legislative Manual, 1913*, pp. 500–503, 506, 512–13; Lindbergh to Manahan, 19 October 1912, Manahan to A. J. Opsahl, 28 October 1912, and La Follette to Loftus, 15 September 1912, Manahan Papers. Manahan, a Bryan Democrat turned progressive Republican, was a St. Paul lawyer and a close colleague of George Loftus. Both were La Follette holdouts during the La Follette-Roosevelt controversy over delegates in 1912. Manahan served one term in Congress (1913–1915), and he came to know Lindbergh fairly well. Many of Manahan's maverick political views were similar to Lindbergh's, and later he, like Lindbergh, identified with the Nonpartisan League. See night letter from Loftus and Manahan to La Follette, 23 April 1912, Charles W. Bryan to Manahan, 20 August 1912, William Lemke to Manahan, 26 April 1916, and A. C. Townley to Manahan, 3 July 1916, Manahan correspondence; and James Manahan, *Trials of a Lawyer* (Minneapolis, 1933).

Chapter VII: Banking and Currency Reform, pp. 150–178

1. Observer Lynn Haines records the Sixty-third Congress as: 290 Democrats, 120 Republicans, and 25 Progressives. See Haines, *Your Congress: An Interpretation of the Political and Parliamentary Influences That Dominate Law Making in America* (Washington, D.C., 1915), p. 60.
2. *Journal of the House of Representatives*, 63rd Cong., 1st sess. (Washington, D.C., 1913), p. 171; Link, *Wilson: The New Freedom*, pp. 199–240. A useful compilation of selective bills, reports, speeches, and other comment concerning the creation of the Federal Reserve bill may be found in Herman E. Krooss, ed., *Documentary History of Banking and Currency in the United States* (New York, 1969), vols. 3–4, pp. 2083–2473.

3. Link, *Wilson: The New Freedom*, p. 202; Haines and Haines *The Lindberghs*, pp. 187–88; Lauck MS.

4. Woodrow Wilson, *The New Freedom: A Call for the Emancipation of the Generous Energies of a People*, intro. William E. Leuchtenburg (Englewood Cliffs, N.J., 1961), pp. ix, 11, 105, 109. See also Lauck MS; and Haines and Haines, *The Lindberghs*, pp. 189–90.

5. H. Res. 720 and H. J. Res. 367, 62nd Cong., 3rd sess., House Originals, RG 233, National Archives.

6. *Journal of the House*, 62nd Cong., 2nd sess., p. 536; *Congressional Record*, 62nd Cong., 3rd sess., pp. 2878–79, Appendix, pp. 46–47; Haines and Haines, *The Lindberghs*, p. 206.

7. Carter Glass to George W. Norris, 17 September 1920, Carter Glass Papers, Alderman Library, University of Virginia, Charlottesville; Link, *Wilson: The New Freedom*, p. 202. On the role of Glass with regard to the Federal Reserve bill, see also Rixey Smith and Norman Beasley, *Carter Glass: A Biography* (New York, 1939).

8. Link, *Wilson: The New Freedom*, pp. 203–20. See also H. Parker Willis, *The Federal Reserve System: Legislation, Organization, and Operation* (New York, 1923).

9. Glass to Woodrow Wilson, 15 May 1913, and Glass to Lindbergh, 19 June 1913, Glass Papers; Smith and Beasley, *Carter Glass*, pp. 119–20.

10. H. Res. 192, 63rd Cong., 1st sess., House Originals, RG 233, National Archives.

11. *Journal of the House*, 63rd Cong., 1st sess., p. 202; H. Res. 201, 63rd Cong., 1st sess., House Originals, RG 233, National Archives.

12. See Lindbergh to Eva, 13 April, 24 May 1913, Lindbergh to George Wilson, 22 April 1913, and George Wilson, "Lindbergh Data," 1928, LP; Lynn Haines to Stiles P. Jones, 26 May 1913, Haines Papers; Lindbergh, Sr., *Banking and Currency*, pp. 5–7.

13. Lindbergh, Sr., *Banking and Currency*, pp. 37–38.

14. *Ibid.*, pp. 50, 75–137.

15. *Ibid.*, pp. 144–48, 183–94.

16. *Ibid.*, pp. 195–96.

17. *Ibid.*, pp. 220.

18. *Ibid.*, pp. 208–71. See also Lauck MS.

19. Lindbergh, Sr., *Banking and Currency*, pp. 245–46, 272–88.

20. *Ibid.*, p. 4; Christie interview, 12 July 1965; Frank Dewey interview; Charles, Jr. commentary, 1967; Haines and Haines, *The*

Lindberghs, pp. 191–92, 211; Eva Lindbergh Christie Spaeth commentary, 1972.

21. Link, *Wilson: The New Freedom,* pp. 215–22.
22. The minutes of the House Committee on Banking and Currency are sketchy. During the crucial period of the Federal Reserve bill discussion brief minutes exist for meetings on June 6, July 9, and September 2, 3, and 4, 1913. Minutes, House Committee on Banking and Currency, 63rd Cong., 1st sess., RG 233, National Archives. See also *New York Times,* 5 September 1913; and Link, *Wilson: The New Freedom,* p. 227.
23. U.S. Congress, House, Committee on Banking and Currency, *Changes in the Banking and Currency System of the United States,* 63rd Cong., 1st sess., 1913, H. Rept. 69, p. 135.
24. *Ibid.,* pp. 135–50.
25. *Ibid.,* pp. 150–54.
26. *Congressional Record,* 63rd Cong., 1st Sess., pp. 4733–53.
27. Discussion of Lindbergh amendments to the bill may be found in *ibid.,* pp. 4968–73, 4983–84, 4988–89, 5014–15, 5018, 5049–50, 5058–60, 5066.
28. *Ibid.,* p. 4989.
29. *Ibid.,* pp. 5127–29; Committee on Banking and Currency, H. Rept. 69, p. 147.
30. Holt, *Congressional Insurgents,* pp. 107–08; Link, *Wilson: The New Freedom,* p. 227.
31. Link, *Wilson: The New Freedom,* pp. 227–37; Kolko, *Triumph of Conservatism,* pp. 237–42.
32. *Congressional Record,* 63rd Cong., 2nd sess., pp. 1445–54; Link, *Wilson: The New Freedom,* p. 239; *New York Times,* 23 December 1913.
33. *Journal of the House,* 63rd Cong., 2nd sess., pp. 86–87; Link, *Wilson: The New Freedom,* pp. 237–38. The final bill may be found in Krooss, *Documentary History,* 4:2436–70.
34. Link, *Wilson: The New Freedom,* pp. 238–40. Lindbergh's view of the Federal Reserve system as a "banker's bank" is corroborated by Gabriel Kolko's later analysis of banking reform and progressivism. Lindbergh's overall career, however, is contrary to the Kolko thesis' description of progressives as conservative and business-motivated. See Kolko, *Triumph of Conservatism,* pp. 242–54.
35. *Congressional Record,* 63rd Cong., 2nd sess., p. 13169; H.R. 1166, H.R. 1173, and H.R. 18875, 63rd Cong., 2nd sess., House Originals, RG 233, National Archives.
36. Manahan, *Trials of a Lawyer,* pp. 196–97; Lauck MS.
37. U.S. Congress, Senate, Commission on Industrial Relations, *Final*

Report and Testimony Submitted to Congress by the Commission on Industrial Relations Created by the Act of August 23, 1912, 64th Cong., 1st sess., 1916, S. Doc. 415, pp. 8304–09. Lindbergh's testimony before the Commission was entered in the *Congressional Record,* 10 February 1915, by Representative John I. Nolan of California. See *Congressional Record,* 63rd Cong., 3rd sess., Appendix, pp. 353–55.

38. Committee on Industrial Relations, *Final Report,* pp. 8305–09.
39. *Ibid.,* p. 8305; *New York Times,* 6 February, 8 February 1915. For a complete discussion on the Commission, see Graham Adams, Jr., *Age of Industrial Violence, 1910–15: The Activities and Findings of the United States Commission on Industrial Relations* (New York, 1966).
40. *Congressional Record,* 63rd Cong., 1st sess., pp. 752–54, 1386, 2429; 63rd Cong., 2nd sess., pp. 2124–25, 2131, 2610–11, 3633–35, 6323, 10745, 12894, Appendix, pp. 723–26.
41. *New York Times,* 7 February 1915; H.R. 6855, 63rd Cong., 1st sess., H.R. 9830 and H.R. 20244, 63rd Cong., 2nd sess., House Originals, RG 233, National Archives; Lindbergh to M. N. Koll, 29 November 1913, and Lindbergh to W. A. Perrin, 25 July 1914, LP.
42. Lindbergh to William Howard Taft, 17 February 1913, Taft Papers; Lindbergh to Woodrow Wilson, 8 August 1913, Woodrow Wilson Papers, Library of Congress; Arthur S. Link, *Woodrow Wilson and the Progressive Era, 1910–1917* (New York, 1963), pp. 107–44.
43. *Congressional Record,* 63rd Cong., 2nd sess., pp. 6951–53, 6957; Lindbergh to Eva, 27 April 1914, LP; Haines and Haines, *The Lindberghs,* pp. 198–205.
44. *Congressional Record,* 63rd Cong., 2nd sess., p. 6952, quoted in Haines and Haines, *The Lindberghs,* p. 204.
45. Arthur Gorman to Eva Lindbergh, 6 February 1914, Lindbergh to Eva, 8 March 1914, and statement of admittance as a practicing lawyer of the Supreme Court of the United States, 19 January 1914, LP; Charles, Jr. commentary, 1967.
46. Charles, Jr. to the author, 25 January 1966; Minnesota interview; Charles, Jr. commentary, 1967; Lindbergh to Eva, 10 July 1913, LP; Lindbergh, *Spirit of St. Louis,* p. 246.
47. Lindbergh to Eva, 17 September 1912, 13 January, 10 February 1913, 11 June, 9 July 1914, LP.
48. Lindbergh to Eva, 1913 (undated), 26 February 1913, 8 June, 28 August, September 1914, LP.
49. Lindbergh to Eva, 20 May, 3 July, 9 July 1914, LP.

50. Lindbergh to Eva, 18 November, 31 December 1913, 2 January, 15 January, 23 January 1914, and Lindbergh to J. F. A. Strong, 2 January 1914, LP; Haines and Haines, *The Lindberghs*, pp. 153–54.

51. Lindbergh to Eva, 1914 (undated), 13 March, 11 June, 1 July, 3 July, 26 August, 28 August, 29 August, 15 September 1914, LP.

52. Lindbergh to Eva, 4 September, 8 September 1914, LP, quoted in Haines and Haines, *The Lindberghs*, pp. 154–55.

53. Lindbergh to Eva, 23 September, 15 November, 17 November, 12 December, 22 December 1914, LP.

54. *Minneapolis Journal*, 4 December, 5 December 1913; Lindbergh to unknown, 23 January 1914, and Lindbergh to M. M. Williams, 24 January 1914, LP.

55. Reapportionment by the state legislature changed the composition of the Sixth District between the 1912 and 1914 elections in this way: Douglas, Meeker, and Wright counties were dropped from the district, and Aitkin and Beltrami counties were added to it. See *Legislative Manual, 1915*, p. 192; and map on p. 45 of this book.

56. *Wadena Pioneer Journal*, 26 June 1913, 30 April (Maxfield brochure), 21 May 1914; *New York Times*, 5 April 1913; Lindbergh campaign brochure, 1914, LP; *Legislative Manual, 1915*, p. 192.

57. Interview with Ben Du Bois, 24 October 1972; see *LF Daily Transcript*, 28 September 1914; *LF Herald*, 23 October 1914; *St. Cloud Daily Times*, 17 October, 31 October, 2 November 1914; *St. Cloud Journal-Press*, 17 October, 23 October 1914.

58. *St. Cloud Daily Times*, 17 October 1914. Although the author kept no statistical count on bills passed, and there are no Lindbergh records, the *Times* estimate seems reasonable. Except for local patronage bills, Lindbergh had almost no success with his bills and resolutions in the House.

59. *Legislative Manual, 1915*, pp. 536, 543; Minnesota state canvassing board reports, 1914; *St. Cloud Daily Journal-Press*, 23 October 1914; telegram from Lindbergh to Eva, 4 November 1914, Lindbergh to Eva, 6 November 1914, and Lindbergh to Gust Raymond, 4 December 1914 (original in Ernest Lundeen Papers), LP.

Chapter VIII: Opponent of War, pp. 179–214

1. *Congressional Record*, 63rd Cong., 2nd sess., p. 15708.

2. Among the general studies on American neutrality are Charles

Seymour, *American Neutrality, 1914–1917* (New Haven, 1935); Charles Tansill's revisionist account, *America Goes to War* (Boston, 1938); and two valuable recent works: Ernest R. May, *The World War and American Isolation, 1914–1917* (Chicago, 1966); and John Milton Cooper, Jr., *The Vanity of Power: American Isolationism and World War I, 1914–1917* (Westport, Conn., 1969). See also volumes 3, 4, and 5 of *Wilson* by Arthur S. Link.

For discussion on Minnesota and Lindbergh during American neutrality, see Franklin F. Holbrook and Livia Appel, *Minnesota in the War with Germany* (St. Paul, 1928), vol. 1, pp. 1–66; Haines and Haines, *The Lindberghs*, pp. 212–21, 236–57, 265–70; Christensen, "Political Ideas of Lindbergh," pp. 83–94; Bruce L. Larson, "Northern Minnesota and the World War, 1914–1917" (master's thesis, University of North Dakota, 1961); and Chrislock, *Progressive Era.*

3. Charles A. Lindbergh, Sr., *Why Is Your Country at War and What Happens to You After the War and Related Subjects* (Washington, D.C., 1917), p. 6.
4. Arthur S. Link, *Wilson: The Struggle for Neutrality, 1914–1915* (Princeton, 1960), pp. 102–04.
5. *Congressional Record*, 63rd Cong., 2nd sess., pp. 15708–09.
6. *Ibid.*, p. 15709.
7. *Ibid.*, pp. 15709–10.
8. *Ibid.*, pp. 15710–12, 15772; Link, *Wilson: The Struggle for Neutrality*, p. 104; *St. Cloud Daily Journal-Press*, 26 October 1914.
9. Lindbergh to Eva, 25 February 1915, LP; Haines and Haines, *The Lindberghs*, p. 213; Larson, "Northern Minnesota," pp. 26–42.
10. See Thomas A. Bailey, "The Sinking of the *Lusitania*," *American Historical Review* 41 (October 1935): 54–73; *Ada Norman County Herald*, 30 June 1915.
11. Although the magazine is dated March 1916, Lindbergh himself related that it was published in late 1915. See *Real Needs: A Magazine of Co-ordination*, no. 1 (March 1916); *Real Needs*, no. 2 (June 1916); and *Congressional Record*, 64th Cong., 1st sess., Appendix, p. 498.
12. *Real Needs*, no. 1, pp. 1–4, 39–88, 189–92; *Real Needs*, no. 2, p. 4. See also *Congressional Records*, 63rd Cong., 3rd sess., pp. 1979–97.
13. *Real Needs*, no. 1, pp. 27–28, 90.
14. *Ibid.*, p. 102.
15. Arthur S. Link, *Wilson: Confusions and Crises, 1915–1916* (Princeton, 1964), pp. 15–54, 142–94.

16. Link, *Woodrow Wilson and the Progressive Era*, pp. 205–14; Link, *Wilson: Confusions and Crises*, pp. 167–94; *Congressional Record*, 64th Cong., 1st sess., pp. 3465, 3720.
17. *Congressional Record*, 64th Cong., 1st sess., p. 3720; Link, *Wilson: Confusions and Crises*, p. 193; Cooper, *Vanity of Power*, pp. 113–15; Holt, *Congressional Insurgents*, p. 128.
18. Cooper, *Vanity of Power*, p. 115; Mitau, *Politics in Minnesota*, pp. 112–13; George M. Stephenson, "The Attitude of Swedish-Americans Toward the World War," *Proceedings of the Mississippi Valley Historical Association* 10 (1918–19): 70–94; *Duluth Herald*, 8 March 1916. Two recent studies that include comment on Scandinavian-American attitudes toward World War I, including opposition, are Sture Lindmark, *Swedish America, 1914–1932: Studies in Ethnicity with Emphasis on Illinois and Minnesota* (Chicago, 1971); and Wefald, *Voice of Protest*.
19. *Congressional Record,* 64th Cong., 1st sess., Appendix, p. 497.
20. *Ibid.,* pp. 497, 506.
21. *Ibid.,* pp. 497–98.
22. *Ibid.,* pp. 498–506.
23. *Ibid.,* pp. 665–67, 739.
24. *Ibid.,* p. 666.
25. *Ibid.*
26. *Ibid.,* pp. 665–67, 739–41. See also Haines and Haines, *The Lindberghs,* pp. 236–42; Lindbergh to William S. Davis, 22 October 1915, LP.
27. Haines and Haines, *The Lindberghs,* p. 265; *Minneapolis Tribune,* 4 October 1915.
28. *LF Daily Transcript,* 6 May, 2 October, 7 October 1915; *Minneapolis Journal,* 5 October 1915; *St. Cloud Journal-Press,* 6 October 1915; *Alexandria Post-News,* 7 October 1915; *Litchfield News Ledger,* 7 October 1915; *Melrose Beacon,* 21 October 1915.
29. Christianson, *Minnesota,* 2:354; *St. Cloud Daily Journal-Press,* 21 February 1916; Lester Bartlett to Lindbergh, 13 January 1916, LP (Yale).
30. In 1907 Clapp, an admirer of Roosevelt, was mentioned as a possible vice-presidential running mate with William Howard Taft. See clippings from several Minnesota and Washington newspapers in Moses E. Clapp Papers, MinnHS.
31. One theory has been advanced by Millard Gieske that Lindbergh was prompted to run for the Senate by political forces close to candidate Frank B. Kellogg, with the purpose of further dividing the non-Kellogg vote. Gieske's evidence is based on Kellogg correspondence which indicates that a meeting with the "adversary"

took place shortly before Lindbergh's announcement to run, that a close association existed between this same candidate and Senator La Follette, and a reference by one contact advising that a "Norwegian" run since several Swedes were in various races. But, in light of the latest available sources, Lindbergh seems an unlikely prospect for this role in a "conspiracy candidacy." More plausibly, it may have been Clapp. Factors working against Lindbergh's identification would be his harsh attack on Kellogg during the primary campaign, the fact that Senator La Follette supported Clapp over Lindbergh in the race, and the minor point that Lindbergh was Swedish, not Norwegian. Finally, in the general election, Clapp endorsed Kellogg, while Lindbergh, significantly, broke with the party and supported Prohibitionist candidate W. G. Calderwood. See Gieske, "The Politics of Knute Nelson, 1912–1920" (Ph.D. dissertation, University of Minnesota, 1965), pp. 290–99.

32. La Follette to Manahan, 17 April 1916, Manahan correspondence.
33. During the early days of the Progressive Republican League in 1911, Manahan became apprehensive about the thoroughness of Clapp's progressive activities. On April 1 he had discovered "nine full mail bags" containing Progressive literature that had been piled in Clapp's back office in St. Paul "for months." In the fall of 1910, when progressives "were clamoring" for such literature, Manahan charged in a letter to Senator La Follette, the Minnesota senator had obviously been negligent. Manahan blamed the suppression, in part, on Lee Warner, Clapp's secretary who, he pointed out, was the son of Eli Warner, "a reactionary and system politician." La Follette replied to Manahan that this news presented "a rather serious and delicate question," but that he would "find a way to let Senator Clapp know." See Manahan to La Follette, 1 April 1911, and La Follette to Manahan, 6 April 1911, Manahan correspondence.
34. David Bryn-Jones, *Frank B. Kellogg: A Biography* (New York, 1937), pp. 107–08; *Minneapolis Journal,* 25 May, 14 June, 16 June 1916; *Breckenridge Telegram,* 3 May 1916; William E. Lee to Frank B. Kellogg, 28 April 1916, and Kellogg to Edmund Pennington, 25 May 1916, Frank B. Kellogg Papers, MinnHS.
35. Lindbergh to Kellogg, 29 May 1916, Kellogg Papers.
36. Kellogg to Lindbergh, 5 June 1916, Kellogg Papers.
37. Charles A. Lindbergh, Sr., "The Force of Human Action," *College Breezes* (Gustavus Adolphus College) 21 (May 1916): 298–304; *St. Peter Herald,* 9 June 1916.
38. "Auto Trip: Spring, 1916," Charles, Jr. Diary, 22 April–8 June

1916, LP. For further comment on Charles, Jr.'s experiences on campaigns, see Lindbergh, *Boyhood*, pp. 28–30.

39. *Ibid.*

40. Charles, Jr. commentary, 1967.

41. *Legislative Manual, 1917*, pp. 190–91, 518–20; *St. Paul Dispatch*, 19 June 1916; *Minneapolis Journal*, 20 June 1916; *Alexandria Post-News*, 22 June 1916; Chrislock, *Progressive Era*, pp. 125–26.

42. *Legislative Manual, 1917*, pp. 192–93, 199, 510–13, 519; Chrislock, *Progressive Era*, p. 126; *Fergus Falls Daily Journal*, 31 October 1916; *Brainerd Tribune*, 27 October 1916; Lindbergh to Eva, 13 October 1916, LP.

43. *Legislative Manual, 1917*, pp. 508–09. See also Minnesota press comment in "Why Wilson Won," *Literary Digest*, 18 November 1916, pp. 1312–15.

44. *Congressional Record*, 64th Cong., 1st sess., Appendix, pp. 2094–95; Land interview; Emory Scott Land, *Winning the War with Ships* (New York, 1958), pp. 100–101. Land is best known for serving as head of both the Maritime Commission and the War Shipping Administration under Franklin D. Roosevelt during World War II.

45. H. Con. Res. 63 and H. Con. Res. 64, House Originals, RG 233, National Archives; *Congressional Record*, 64th Cong., 2nd sess., pp. 7, 78; *New York Times*, 5 December 1916; *Red Lake Falls Gazette*, 7 December 1916; Haines and Haines, *The Lindberghs*, pp. 251–52, 254.

46. Arthur S. Link, *Wilson: Campaigns for Progressivism and Peace, 1916–1917* (Princeton, 1965), pp. 285–303.

47. Haines and Haines, *The Lindberghs*, pp. 256–57.

48. H.R. 20998, 64th Cong., 2nd sess., House Originals, RG 233, National Archives. Benson publicized his advisory war referendum plan in *The Appeal to Reason* in 1915; he also claimed credit for giving the idea to Senators La Follette and Owen, who, in turn, proposed referendum plans in the Congress before Lindbergh. See Harold Currie, "Alan Benson, Salesman of Socialism, 1902–1916," *Labor History* 11 (Summer 1970): 300–303.

49. Holbrook and Appel, *Minnesota in the War*, 1:32–51; Chrislock, *Progressive Era*, pp. 145–63; *Two Harbors Journal-News*, 17 February 1917.

50. *Congressional Record*, 65th Cong., 2nd sess., pp. 2957–58; *Brainerd Dispatch*, 9 February 1917.

51. Dr. Arthur Zimmermann, the German foreign secretary, had sent a note to the German representative in Mexico instructing him to

work out an alliance with Mexico in the event of U.S. entry into the war. In return Mexico was to receive the "lost territory" of Texas, New Mexico, and Arizona.

52. Link, *Wilson: Campaigns for Progressivism*, pp. 350–54; *Congressional Record*, 64th Cong., 2nd sess., p. 4692; Cooper, *Vanity of Power*, p. 179.

53. *Congressional Record*, 64th Cong., 2nd sess., Appendix, p. 701.

54. Lindbergh to Eva, March (undated), 21 March 1917, LP; Holbrook and Appel, *Minnesota in the War*, 1:35, 40–41.

55. *Congressional Record*, 65th Cong., 1st sess., pp. 261, 412–13; Holbrook and Appel, *Minnesota in the War*, 1:52–55; Link, *Wilson: Campaigns for Progressivism*, pp. 390–431.

56. Lindbergh to Eva, March (undated), 14 April, 18 April 1917, LP.

57. *Congressional Record*, 63rd Cong., 2nd sess., pp. 1843–44; 64th Cong., 1st sess., pp. 7–9, 5839, Appendix, pp. 555–59, 1837–45; H. J. Res. 399, 63rd Cong., 3rd sess., H. Res. 36, H. Res. 65, and H. Res. 70, 64th Cong., 1st sess., H. J. Res. 116, 64th Cong., 1st sess., H.R. 12280 and H.R. 13835, 64th Cong., 1st sess., H.R. 18720, 64th Cong., 2nd sess., all items in House Originals, RG 233, National Archives; document files 7677 and 104744, RG 77, Records of the Office of the Chief of Engineers, National Archives.

58. *Congressional Record*, 63rd Cong., 3rd sess., pp. 567–69.

59. *Ibid.*, p. 1417; Lindbergh, Sr., *Why Is Your Country at War*, pp. 195–99.

60. *Congressional Record*, p. 1992, Appendix, p. 354.

61. Investigation by the author at the Kansas State Historical Society, Topeka, uncovered no information about the Free Press Defense League.

62. *Congressional Record*, 64th Cong., 1st sess., Appendix, p. 1839; H. J. Res. 264, 64th Cong., 1st sess., House Originals, RG 233, National Archives; Haines and Haines, *The Lindberghs*, p. 222.

63. *Congressional Record*, 64th Cong., 1st sess., p. 13608, Appendix, pp. 1838, 2092–95; Kerr, *American Railroad Politics*, pp. 33–34; *Real Needs*, no. 1, pp. 135–37; *Real Needs*, no. 2, p. 93.

64. *Congressional Record*, 64th Cong., 2nd sess., p. 3126.

65. *Ibid.*, pp. 3126–30; *Washington Times*, 12 February 1917; Lindbergh to Eva, 17 February 1917, LP.

66. *LF Daily Transcript*, 29 June 1915; "The Mississippi River Trip, from Little Falls, from Itasca," Charles, Jr. Diary; Lindbergh to Eva, March (undated), 30 March, 21 April, 26 December 1915, 30 November 1916, LP.

67. "Some Recollections of My Daughter Lillian, 1916," Charles A.

Lindbergh, Sr., Diary, LP; *LF Daily Transcript,* 6 November 1916.

68. Lindbergh to Eva, July (undated) 1916, 1917 (undated), 15 March, 23 March, 9 April, 11 April 1917, Lindbergh to Carl Bolander, 1917 (undated), LP; Haines and Haines, *The Lindberghs,* pp. 262–63; *Red Lake Falls Gazette,* 7 December 1916.

69. W. H. Dorrance to William Lemke, 23 October 1937, William Lemke Papers, Orrin G. Libby Historical Manuscripts Collection, University of North Dakota, Grand Forks; Lindbergh, Sr., *Why Is Your Country at War,* pp. 5–6, 120, 201–03; Haines and Haines, *The Lindberghs,* pp. 269–70. See Charles A. Lindbergh, *Of Flight and Life* (New York, 1948).

70. Lindbergh, Sr., *Why Is Your Country at War,* pp. 6–7.

71. *Ibid.,* pp. 73, 205–10.

72. *Ibid.,* pp. 214–15.

73. Among the writers who have delineated the relationship between nonintervention and progressive reform are Eric Goldman, *Rendezvous with Destiny* (New York, 1956), pp. 180–81; and Samuel Lubell, *The Future of American Politics,* 3rd rev. ed. (New York, 1965), pp. 136–37; while William E. Leuchtenburg, "Progressivism and Imperialism: The Progressive Moment and American Foreign Policy, 1898–1916," *Mississippi Valley Historical Review* 39 (December 1952): 483–504, has suggested that most progressives embraced an imperialistic attitude on foreign policy. Two later studies, Walter I. Trattner, "Progressivism and World War I: A Re-appraisal," *Mid-America* 44 (July 1962): 131–45; and Howard W. Allen, "Republican Reformers and Foreign Policy, 1913–1917," *Mid-America* 44 (October 1962): 222–29, have concluded from voting behavior that there was no consistent pattern among the progressives. For a synthesis of published data, see Barton J. Bernstein and Franklin A. Leib, "Progressive Republican Senators and American Imperialism, 1898–1916: A Reappraisal," *Mid-America* 50 (July 1968): 163–205.

74. Nye interview. See also Charles A. Beard, *President Roosevelt and the Coming of War, 1941* (New Haven, 1948); Wayne S. Cole, *Senator Gerald P. Nye and American Foreign Relations* (Minneapolis, 1962); Cooper, *Vanity of Power,* p. 238; and Ray Allen Billington, "The Origins of Middle Western Isolationism," *Political Science Quarterly* 60 (March 1945): 44–64. Lubell, in *Future of American Politics,* pp. 131–55, stresses ethnicity, especially German-American, as a factor in American isolationism. He discounts the "myth" of Midwest geographical location, but he

does recognize the relationship of "leftist economics" to antiwar feeling. Lindbergh is mentioned on pp. 131 and 140. Robert P. Wilkins, in his study of Nye's home state, North Dakota, supports the thesis that economic considerations, particularly a "deeply rooted ideological distrust" of the Eastern financial establishment, was the principal reason for strong opposition to World War I in the area. See Wilkins, "North Dakota and the European War, 1914–1917" (Ph.D. dissertation, West Virginia University, 1954), p. 334.

75. Charles, Jr. Commentary, 1967 and 1971. For extensive discussion on Charles, Jr. and the World War II neutrality period, see his recent *Wartime Journals of Charles A. Lindbergh* (New York, 1970); and Wayne S. Cole, *America First: The Battle Against Intervention, 1940–1941* (Madison, 1953).

76. Lindbergh to Eva, 11 March 1917, LP.

Chapter IX: Nonpartisan League Candidate for Governor, pp. 215–249

1. *Congressional Record*, 64th Cong., 1st sess., Appendix, p. 1837.
2. Lindbergh, Sr., *Banking and Currency*, p. 278.
3. The best published work on the Nonpartisan League is Robert L. Morlan, *Political Prairie Fire: The Nonpartisan League, 1915–1922* (Minneapolis, 1955), a portion of which has also been published as "The Nonpartisan League and the Minnesota Campaign of 1918," *Minnesota History* 34 (Summer 1955): 221–32. Briefer accounts may be found in Robinson, *History of North Dakota*, pp. 327–70; and Theodore Saloutos and John D. Hicks, *Agricultural Discontent in the Middle West, 1900–1939* (Madison, 1951), pp. 149–218. Useful early sources include Herbert E. Gaston, *The Non-Partisan League* (New York, 1920); Charles Edward Russell, *The Story of the Non-Partisan League* (New York, 1920); and Andrew A. Bruce, *The Nonpartisan League* (New York, 1921). Data on certain of the key figures in the League movement, including Lindbergh, may be found in H. C. Peterson and Gilbert C. Fite, *Opponents of War, 1917–1918* (Madison, 1957); Edward C. Blackorby, *Prairie Rebel: The Public Life of William Lemke* (Lincoln, 1963); and James M. Youngdale, ed., *Third Party Footprints: An Anthology from Writings and Speeches of Midwest Radicals* (Minneapolis, 1966).
4. H. G. Teigan, "The National Nonpartisan League," *American Labor Yearbook, 1919–1920* (New York, 1920), pp. 280–89.
5. Bruce, *The Nonpartisan League*, p. 4; Russell, *Story of the League*,

p. 11; *Congressional Record,* 67th Cong., special session of the Senate, p. 922; Morlan, *Prairie Fire,* pp. 26, 79, 100; Peterson and Fite, *Opponents of War,* p. 65.

6. *Nonpartisan Leader,* 28 October, 18 November 1915; Lindbergh to Nonpartisan League, 17 January 1917, National Nonpartisan League Papers, MinnHS; H. G. Teigan to Lindbergh, 2 July 1917, Arthur Le Sueur Papers, MinnHS; Teigan to Lindbergh, 25 July 1917, and Lindbergh to Eva, 8 August 1917, LP.

7. Chrislock, *Progressive Era,* pp. 112–13, 145–47, 168; Lindbergh to Eva, 1918 (undated), LP.

8. Morlan, *Prairie Fire,* pp. 142–43; Peterson and Fite, *Opponents of War,* pp. 67–68; statement of Lindbergh speech, 20 September 1917, Le Sueur Papers, copy in LP.

9. Statement of La Follette speech, 20 September 1917, Minnesota Commission of Public Safety Papers, MinnSA; La Follette and La Follette, *Robert M. La Follette,* 2:762–69.

10. La Follette and La Follette, *Robert M. La Follette,* 2:768–865; minutes, Safety Commission meeting, 25 September 1917, John Lind Papers, MinnHS. For discussion on the nature and operation of the Minnesota Safety Commission, see O. A. Hilton, "The Minnesota Commission of Public Safety in World War I, 1917–1919," *Bulletin of the Oklahoma Agricultural and Mechanical College,* 15 May 1951, pp. 1–44.

11. *Resolutions Adopted by the Nonpartisan League Conference,* St. Paul, 18–20 September 1917; testimony of A. C. Townley before the Minnesota Commission of Public Safety, 25 September 1917, Safety Commission Papers; Morlan, *Prairie Fire,* pp. 145–49; Peterson and Fite, *Opponents of War,* p. 72; George Creel to Woodrow Wilson, 7 January, 19 February 1918, Wilson to Creel, 18 February 1918, George Creel Papers, Library of Congress.

12. Lindbergh to Eva, 8 August, 18 October 1917, 1918 (undated), 1 February 1918, LP.

13. *Nonpartisan Leader,* 1 April 1918; Morlan, *Prairie Fire,* pp. 49, 188; Lindbergh to William Kent, 15 May 1918, William Kent Papers, Sterling Library, Yale University, New Haven, Conn.

14. Morlan, *Prairie Fire,* pp. 188–89; J. A. A. Burnquist to Arthur Le Sueur, 11 March 1918, Joseph A. A. Burnquist Papers, MinnHS. For a good analysis of the general Minnesota labor situation during the early twentieth century, see Chrislock, *Progressive Era;* and Donald G. Sofchalk, "Organized Labor and the Iron Ore Miners of Northern Minnesota, 1907–1936," *Labor History* 12 (Spring 1971): 214–42.

15. "The Minnesota Issue," campaign sheet containing extracts from Lindbergh acceptance speech, copy in LP (Yale); *Nonpartisan Leader*, 8 April 1918.

16. Morlan, *Prairie Fire*, p. 190; Haines and Haines, *The Lindberghs*, pp. 280–81; *LF Daily Transcript*, 4 April 1918.

17. Gaston, *Non-Partisan League*, pp. 218–19; Guy Stanton Ford, "Reminiscences," Oral History Collection of Columbia University, 1956, p. 419, copy at University Archives, University of Minnesota, Minneapolis. Ford was a historian and dean of the graduate school.

18. Morlan, *Prairie Fire*, p. 199; *Minnesota Leader*, 8 June 1918.

19. *Minneapolis Journal*, 13 June 1918; *Duluth Herald*, 13 June, 14 June 1918; *Hibbing Daily Tribune*, 14 June 1918.

20. *Svenska Amerikanska Posten*, 12 June 1918; Finis Herbert Capps, *From Isolationism to Involvement: The Swedish Immigrant Press in America, 1914–1945* (Chicago, 1966), pp. 37, 40, 61–62. The *Posten* had a circulation of 56,427 in 1915; Emil Meurling became its editor in March 1918. See Capps, pp. 234–35.

21. *Catholic Bulletin*, 26 August 1916, 8 June, 15 June 1918; Haines and Haines, *The Lindberghs*, pp. 221–23, 292–93; Lindbergh, Sr., *Why Is Your Country at War*, pp. 173–78.

22. Morlan, *Prairie Fire*, pp. 192–93.

23. See *St. Paul Pioneer Press*, 7 June, 11 June, 13 June, 17 June 1918; *Minneapolis Journal*, 27 May, 4 June, 8 June 1918.

24. *Minnesota Leader*, 25 May, 8 June, 15 June 1918; Lindbergh, Sr., *Why Is Your Country at War*, p. 25.

25. *Minnesota Leader*, 8 June 1918; *LF Daily Transcript*, 3 June 1918.

26. U.S. Congress, Senate, Committee on Military Affairs, *Extending Jurisdiction of Military Tribunals: Hearings on S. Doc. 4364*, 65th Cong., 2nd sess., 1918, pt. 2, pp. 82–87.

27. *New York Times*, 29 May, 20 June 1918.

28. *Labor World*, 8 June 1918; Charles W. Ames to Burnquist, 19 February 1918, Safety Commission Papers.

29. Charles A. Lindbergh, Sr., *Your Country at War and What Happens to You After a War* (reprint ed., Philadelphia, 1934), p. 7. The title was slightly changed with republication in 1934, when the book also appeared serially in the *Washington Daily News*, 13 April–12 May 1934. See also *Washington Daily News*, 13 April 1934; *LF Daily Transcript*, 1 March 1934; "Honorable Lindbergh, M.C.," *American Monthly* 20 (October 1927): 3.

30. Burrill A. Peterson to the author, 22 March 1966; J. Edgar Hoover to the author, 9 May 1966.

31. Frank Parrish to C. K. Howe, 18 February 1933, and Joseph B. Keenan to William Snead, 9 May 1934, RG 60, General Records of the Department of Justice, National Archives.

32. Two of six copies of the original edition of *Why Is Your Country at War* examined by the author have been missing pp. 173–78.

33. Peterson and Fite, *Opponents of War*, pp. 189–91; McGee statement in Haines and Haines, *The Lindberghs*, pp. 281–82; John F. McGee to Knute Nelson, 23 May 1918, Knute Nelson Papers; Morlan, *Prairie Fire*, p. 198. For comment on civil liberties and the Safety Commission during the 1918 campaign see Carol Jenson, "Loyalty as a Political Weapon: The 1918 Campaign in Minnesota," *Minnesota History* 43 (Summer 1972): 42–57.

34. Morlan, *Prairie Fire*, pp. 198–99; Haines and Haines, *The Lindberghs*, p. 292; *LF Daily Transcript*, 11 June 1918; *Duluth Herald*, 28 May, 30 May, 7 June 1918; *The Poison Book of Lindbergh*, 13-page pamphlet prepared and published by Tom Parker Junkin, St. Paul; *New York Times*, 28 May, 29 May, 9 June 1918; *Labor World*, 1 June 1918.

35. *Minnesota Leader*, 8 June, 15 June 1918.

36. Interview with Henry R. Martinson, 7 September 1966. On Martinson's activities, see also his article "Comes the Revolution . . . A Personal Memoir," *North Dakota History* 36 (Winter 1969): 40–109.

37. Lindbergh to Charles, Jr., 12 June 1918, LP; John Baer interview.

38. *Fairmont Daily Sentinel*, 10 June 1918; Eric Olson to John Lind, 5 December 1918, Lind Papers, MinnHS.

39. No record of the Lindbergh arrest could be found in the Martin County courthouse, but the author located a justice docket documenting the arrest in the office of Fairmont lawyer C. F. Gaarenstroom. See justice docket, 1917–18, County Attorney's Register of Criminal Actions, Martin County, Minn., p. 257; interview with C. F. Gaarenstroom, 1 February 1966.

40. Lindbergh to Eva, 12 April, 18 May 1918, LP.

41. Lindbergh to Eva, 31 May 1918, LP.

42. *Minnesota Leader*, 25 May, 8 June 1918; *Fairmont Daily Sentinel*, 14 June 1918.

43. Olson to Lind, 5 December 1918, Lind Papers, MinnHS; interview with Claude N. Swanson, 6 September 1967. Swanson, an agent with the Federal Bureau of Investigation in late 1917 and on the *Sentinel* staff in 1918, labeled Allen a "self-appointed patriot" and accused him of being one of the many local officials who had a "perverted idea of patriotism."

44. Albert R. Allen to W. S. Carver, 13 February 1918, and Allen to Nonpartisan League, 13 February 1918, NPL Papers; Lindbergh to Charles, Jr., 12 June 1918, LP.

45. Lindbergh to Eva, 28 April 1918, 1918 (undated), LP; *Red Lake Falls Gazette*, 6 June 1918; Eva Lindbergh Christie Spaeth interviews, 12 July 1965, 12 October 1972.

46. Morlan, *Prairie Fire*, pp. 197–98; Lindbergh to Eva, 1918 (undated), LP; *Fargo Forum*, 15 June 1918.

47. Interview with John M. Baer, 27 August 1965; interview with Arthur C. Townley by Russell Fridley and Lucile Kane, 11 December 1956, MinnHS.

48. *Minnesota Leader*, 15 June 1918; Charles A. Lindbergh for Governor campaign leaflet, 1918, copy in Burnquist Papers.

49. *Legislative Manual*, 1917, pp. 190–93, 510–13; *Legislative Manual*, 1919, pp. 250–53. See also Morlan, *Prairie Fire*, pp. 200–201; Saloutos and Hicks, *Agricultural Discontent*, p. 187.

50. Townley interview; Peterson and Fite, *Opponents of War*, p. 193; Lindbergh telegram to Eva, 2 August 1918, LP; Baer interview, 24 August 1965.

51. Justice docket, 1917–18, Martin County, p. 257; Lindbergh to Eva, 1918 (undated), LP; *Fairmont Daily Sentinel*, 16 July 1918.

52. *Minnesota Leader*, 22 June 1918; *Minneapolis Tribune*, 18 June, 24 June 1918; *New York Times*, 20 June 1918.

53. *Minnesota Leader*, 22 June 1918; Morlan, *Prairie Fire*, p. 207; Chrislock, *Progressive Era*, pp. 171–72.

54. *Legislative Manual*, 1919, insert opp. p. 670; Chrislock, *Progressive Era*, pp. 172–77.

55. *Legislative Manual*, 1919, pp. 250–53, opp. 670, 671; Chrislock, *Progressive Era*, pp. 177–81; Lubell, *Future of American Politics*, p. 131.

56. *Legislative Manual*, 1919, pp. 250–53, opp. 670, 671; Chrislock, *Progressive Era*, pp. 177–81; *Minnesota Leader*, 9 November 1918.

57. *Legislative Manual*, 1919, pp. 250–53, opp. 670.

58. Chrislock, *Progressive Era*, p. 181.

59. *Ibid.*, p. 182.

Chapter X: Farmer-Labor Politics, pp. 250–281

1. Knud Wefald to H. G. Teigan, 7 September 1923, Knud Wefald Papers, MinnHS.

2. Useful sources dealing with the Farmer-Labor movement from

1918 through 1924, the period of Lindbergh's involvement, include Folwell, *A History of Minnesota,* 3:319–22, 547–56; Congressman Ernest Lundeen's detailed statement, "Farmer-Labor Party—History, Platforms, and Programs," *Congressional Record,* 74th Cong., 2nd sess., pp. 9694–9725; Arthur Naftalin, "A History of the Farmer-Labor Party of Minnesota" (Ph.D. dissertation, University of Minnesota, 1948), pp. 1–131 (Naftalin was an active participant in the Democratic–Farmer-Labor merger of 1944 and later became mayor of Minneapolis; his study is the best to date on the Farmer-Labor movement); Saloutos and Hicks, *Agricultural Discontent,* pp. 342–71; the appropriate references to Farmer-Labor development in Morlan, *Prairie Fire;* and James Weinstein, "Radicalism in the Midst of Normalcy," *Journal of American History* 52 (March 1966): 773–90. Also informative are the following studies on leading figures in the movement during the early period: Martin Ross, *Shipstead of Minnesota* (Chicago, 1940); George H. Mayer, *The Political Career of Floyd B. Olson* (Minneapolis, 1951); Jon Wefald, "Congressman Knud Wefald: A Minnesota Voice for Farm Parity," *Minnesota History* 38 (December 1962): 177–85; Sister Mary Rene Lorentz, "Henrik Shipstead: Minnesota Independent, 1923–1946" (Ph.D. dissertation, Catholic University, 1963); Walfrid Engdahl, "Magnus Johnson—Colorful Farmer-Labor Senator from Minnesota," *Swedish Pioneer Historical Quarterly* 16 (July 1965): 122–36; and Youngdale, *Third Party Footprints.*

3. Naftalin, "Farmer-Labor Party," p. 89.
4. Examination by the author of the Bernard M. Baruch Papers, including files on the War Industries Board, Princeton University, Princeton, N.J., revealed no correspondence or items concerning the Lindbergh appointment to the WIB in 1918.
5. Telegram from Bernard M. Baruch to Lindbergh, 23 August 1918, and telegram from Lindbergh to Baruch, 26 August 1918, cited in Lindbergh to Eva, 13 September 1918, LP.
6. Telegram from Lindbergh to Bernard M. Baruch, 28 August 1918, and Lindbergh to Eva, 26 August, September (undated), 9 September 1918, LP.
7. Statement by George Creel (undated), Creel Papers; George Creel, "Beware the Superpatriots," *American Mercury,* September 1940, p. 38; Lindbergh to Eva, 13 September 1918, LP.
8. Creel statement (undated), and Woodrow Wilson to George Creel, 1 April 1918, Creel Papers; Creel to Wilson, 2 April 1918, and William Kent to Wilson, 22 April 1918, Woodrow Wilson

Papers; William Kent to Woodrow Wilson, 5 October 1918, and Woodrow Wilson to Thomas Gregory, 7 October 1918, Thomas Gregory Papers, Library of Congress. See also Seward W. Livermore, *Politics Is Adjourned: Woodrow Wilson and the War Congress, 1916–1918* (Middletown, Conn., 1966), pp. 154–58.

9. *Minneapolis Tribune,* 8 September 1918; *Minneapolis Journal,* 13 September 1918; Knute Nelson to Elmer E. Adams, 28 June 1918, telegram from P. A. Gough to Knute Nelson, 12 September 1918, and Nelson to Gough, 12 September 1918, Knute Nelson Papers.

10. Lindbergh to Bernard M. Baruch, 10 September 1918, copy in Lind Papers, MinnHS; see also Stephenson, *John Lind,* pp. 338–39.

11. Lindbergh to Eva, 13 September 1918, LP.

12. *Ibid.;* the entire letter is quoted in Haines and Haines, *The Lindberghs,* pp. 286–88.

13. Creel to Wilson, 18 September 1918, Creel Papers; Lindbergh to Eva (later note by Eva on the letter), Summer 1918, LP.

14. Manahan and Lindbergh statements in Haines and Haines, *The Lindberghs,* p. 296.

15. Lindbergh to Eva, 9 January, 13 January, 15 January, 21 January, 2 March 1919, LP.

16. *Lindbergh's National Farmer,* no. 1 (March 1919): 1–16, copy in MinnHS. Lindbergh originally announced that he would call his journal the *Progressive Farmer,* but he discovered that another journal by that title already existed.

17. See March 1919 through December 1919 issues of *Lindbergh's National Farmer;* Lindbergh telegram to Eva, 22 March 1920, LP.

18. See January and March 1920 issues of *Lindbergh's National Farmer.* For a general discussion of the farm problem during the period, see James H. Shideler, *Farm Crisis, 1919–1923* (Berkeley, 1957).

19. Publisher Johnson supported the views of Lindbergh and the NPL, but not Townley personally. He agreed to promote Lindbergh's journal in the state, but he experienced some difficulties with Lindbergh in agreeing on publishing costs. According to Johnson, Lindbergh occasionally appeared at the printers and requested changes in type that had already been set, in pagination, and in the number of copies to be run; he then wondered why the original cost estimate was not met. For discussion of the publishing aspects of *Lindbergh's National Farmer,* see A. C. Johnson to Lindbergh, 28 April, 21 June, 28 November, 12 December 1919,

and Lindbergh to Johnson, November (undated), 27 November, 10 December 1919, LP.

20. Naftalin, "Farmer-Labor Party," pp. 58–59; William Mahoney, "Notes on the History of the Farmer Labor Movement," William Mahoney Papers, MinnHS; Morlan, *Prairie Fire*, pp. 262–63.

21. Naftalin, "Farmer-Labor Party," pp. 59–60; Ernest Lundeen, "A Farmer-Labor Party for the Nation," Farmer-Labor Association of Minnesota Papers, MinnHS; radio speech by Elmer A. Benson, 1936, Elmer A. Benson Papers, MinnHS; Lindbergh to William Lemke, 18 March 1920, LP.

22. Naftalin, "Farmer-Labor Party," pp. 60–61; Morlan, *Prairie Fire*, pp. 281–84; *Legislative Manual, 1921*, pp. 100–101, 106–09.

23. Lindbergh to Eva, 1920 (undated), LP; *LF Daily Transcript*, 23 August 1920; *Minnesota Leader*, 28 August 1920.

24. *LF Daily Transcript*, 29 October, 5 November 1920; *Brainerd Dispatch*, 22 October 1920; *St. Cloud Daily Times*, 2 October, 28 October 1920; *Minnesota Leader*, 9 October, 16 October, 6 November 1920; Charles A. Lindbergh, Sr., "The Voter and the Economic Pinch," copy in LP.

25. *Legislative Manual, 1921*, pp. 524–27; Naftalin, "Farmer-Labor Party," pp. 62–63; Morlan, *Prairie Fire*, p. 301; David A. Shannon, *The Socialist Party of America: A History* (Chicago, 1967), pp. 122–23. For a more thorough comment on the fear of radicalism in America after World War I, see Robert K. Murray, *Red Scare: A Study in National Hysteria, 1919–1920* (Minneapolis, 1951).

26. Lindbergh to Eva, 27 November 1919, Lindbergh to Frank Lindbergh, 1919 (undated), Lindbergh to William Agard, 11 August 1921, and Lindbergh to A. M. Opsahl, 22 August 1922, LP; Lindbergh to Andrew Volstead, 9 November 1920, Andrew J. Volstead Papers, MinnHS.

27. Lindbergh to Eva, 29 February 1920, 1921 (undated), 21 November 1921, Lindbergh to Charles, Jr., 8 December 1921, and Lindbergh to Agard, 26 November 1920, 6 February, 17 March, 8 August, 16 September 1922, LP; Charles, Jr. commentary, 1971.

28. Lindbergh to Eva, 23 April 1921, 1 May 1922, LP; Lindbergh to Evangeline (undated), LP (Yale); Lindbergh, *Spirit of St. Louis*, pp. 383–84.

29. Lindbergh to Evangeline, 1921 (undated), 17 July 1921, and Lindbergh to Charles, Jr., 13 April 1921, LP (Yale); Charles, Jr. commentary, 1967 and 1971; Lindbergh, *Spirit of St. Louis*, pp. 384–85.

30. Lindbergh to Evangeline, 18 March 1924, LP (Yale).

31. Naftalin, "Farmer-Labor Party," pp. 70–77; *Minnesota Leader,* 8 April 1922.

32. Naftalin, "Farmer-Labor Party," pp. 68, 75–76; Morlan, *Prairie Fire,* pp. 339, 341.

33. Knud Wefald to Henrik Shipstead, 3 May 1922, Lindbergh to Wefald, 22 August 1922, and F. A. Pike to Wefald, 10 November 1922, Wefald Papers; *Minnesota Leader,* 20 May 1922.

34. Lindbergh to committeeman, 7 September 1922, LP; Morlan, *Prairie Fire,* pp. 341–42.

35. Comment on Lindbergh's campaign activities in 1922 is either limited or nonexistent in LP, the *Minnesota Leader,* and Farmer-Labor records.

36. Naftalin, "Farmer-Labor Party," pp. 76–82; Lorentz, "Henrik Shipstead," pp. 22–23; Christianson, *Minnesota,* 3:152–53.

37. Naftalin, "Farmer-Labor Party," pp. 76–77; Engdahl, "Magnus Johnson," pp. 122–27; Folwell, *A History of Minnesota,* 3:551; Christianson, *Minnesota,* 2:427.

38. *Legislative Manual,* 1923, pp. 452–53, insert opp. 452; Morlan, *Prairie Fire,* p. 345; interview with Magnus Wefald, 21 July 1965.

39. Naftalin, "Farmer-Labor Party," pp. 82–90; Shideler, *Farm Crisis,* p. 223.

40. Lindbergh to Dorrance and Company, 25 September, 14 November, 9 December, 18 December, 22 December, 26 December 1922, 17 January 1923, and Dorrance and Company to Lindbergh, 30 September, 17 November, 22 November 1922, LP.

41. Lindbergh to Dorrance and Company, [1923] (undated), 28 March, April (undated), 10 April, 14 April, 17 April, 20 April, 26 April 1923, and Dorrance and Company to Lindbergh, 22 November 1922, 10 April, 30 April 1923, LP.

42. Lindbergh to Dorrance and Company, 25 November 1922, LP; Charles A. Lindbergh, Sr., *The Economic Pinch* (Philadelphia, 1923), pp. 17–24, 77–93, 99–107, 120–42.

43. Lindbergh, Sr., *The Economic Pinch,* pp. 222, 243–45.

44. *Ibid.,* pp. 145, 175–78, 186–87, 191, 202–03, 208.

45. Christianson, *Minnesota,* 2:439–40; Naftalin, "Farmer-Labor Party," pp. 90–91; *Legislative Manual,* 1925, pp. 298–99, 672.

46. Lindbergh to Eva, 19 May 1923, LP; interview with Francis Johnson, 16 June 1972; interview with T. R. Fritsche, 12 October 1972; Benjamin Drake to Lynn Haines, 25 May 1923, Haines Papers.

47. *New Ulm Review,* 6 June, 13 June 1923; *Brown County Journal,* 8 June 1923; *Minnesota Union Advocate,* 31 May 1923; *Minne-*

apolis Journal, 7 June 1923; *St. Paul Dispatch,* 12 June 1923;
Fritsche interview; Ole Langhaug to Knud Wefald, 31 May 1923,
and Wefald to Langhaug, 15 June 1923, Wefald Papers.

48. Lindbergh to Charles, Jr., 17 May 1923, LP.

49. Lindbergh, *Spirit of St. Louis,* p. 448; Minnesota interview;
Charles, Jr. commentary, 1967. It is often thought that this campaign flight was the only time Lindbergh went up with Charles,
Jr. in his plane. But that is not the case. On at least one other
occasion, probably more, C. A. flew with his son. In July 1923
they both flew over the Little Falls area. Lindbergh wrote Eva:
"I wanted to see the town and the farm from the sky, and it was
wonderful." See Lindbergh to Eva, 19 July 1923; *LF Daily
Transcript,* 16 July 1923; Minnesota interview.

50. Minnesota interview; Charles, Jr. commentary, 1967; P. P. Orn-
berg to Dora Haines, 8 August 1930, Haines Papers; *Litchfield
Saturday Review,* 16 June 1923; *McLeod County Republic,*
15 June 1923; Lindbergh to Eva, 3 July 1923, LP.

51. *Legislative Manual, 1925,* pp. 298–99; Haines and Haines, *The
Lindberghs,* pp. 301–02; Benjamin Drake to Lynn Haines, 25 May
1923, Haines Papers.

52. Naftalin, "Farmer-Labor Party," pp. 91–92; *New York Times,*
17 June 1923; *Labor,* 30 June 1923; Engdahl, "Magnus Johnson,"
pp. 128–29; *Minnesota Union Advocate,* 28 June 1923; interview
with J. A. O. Preus by Lucile M. Kane and June D. Holmquist,
1960, MinnHS.

53. *Legislative Manual, 1925,* pp. 300–301; Naftalin, "Farmer-Labor
Party," pp. 92–93.

54. Blackorby, *Prairie Rebel,* p. 190; William Lemke, *You and Your
Money* (Philadelphia, 1938); Lemke's well-marked personal copy
of Lindbergh, Sr., *Banking and Currency,* Lemke Papers; Lundeen, "Farmer-Labor Party"; Cheney, *Minnesota Politics,* pp. 69–
70; Nye interview; Benson interview; James M. Shields, *Mr. Progressive: A Biography of Elmer Austin Benson* (Minneapolis,
1971), pp. 14, 205.

55. Gaarenstroom interview; Johnson interview; Wefald interview.
Knud Wefald's poem, originally written in Norwegian, was entered in the *Congressional Record,* 6 January 1928, by Congressman Kvale. See Wefald Papers; and *Congressional Record,* 70th
Cong., 1st sess., pp. 1–2.

56. Lindbergh to William Agard, 24 November 1922, 16 April, 29
July 1923, 12 February 1924, and Lindbergh to Carl Bolander,
18 July 1923, LP; Spaeth commentary, 1971; statement on Peo-

ple's National Bank, Shakopee, Minn., and Lindbergh to Evangeline, 22 March 1924, LP (Yale).

57. Spaeth commentary, 1971; statement on Charles A. Lindbergh, Sr., estate, 1927, LP (Yale); statements and official documents on Charles A. Lindbergh, Sr., estate, 1924, 1925, 1926, 1931, 1960, Charles A. Lindbergh estate file, Probate Court office, Morrison County, Little Falls; Case 24994, State of Minnesota, *In Supreme Court.*

58. In 1931 the Lindbergh home and farm, comprising 110 acres, was given to the state of Minnesota by Evangeline Lodge Land Lindbergh, Eva Lindbergh Christie, Colonel Charles A. Lindbergh, and the heirs of Lillian Lindbergh Roberts as a memorial to the elder Lindbergh. The area was named Charles A. Lindbergh State Park in honor of the former congressman, and it remains in 1973 as both a historic site and a state park. See June D. Holmquist and Jean A. Brookins, *Minnesota's Major Historic Sites: A Guide* (St. Paul, 1963), pp. 74–79.

59. Haines and Haines, *The Lindberghs*, pp. 303–04; Charles A. Lindbergh, Sr., *This Pamphlet Tells Who and What Caused the Panic and Who Can Stop the Panic*, copyrighted by Co-Operators Industrial Securities Company, Minneapolis (n.d., but likely 1924, at some point after the late November 1923 farmers' meeting).

60. Lindbergh to Charles L. Coy, 16 January 1924, LP; Lindbergh to William Lemke, 26 February 1924, Lemke Papers; Mayer, *Floyd B. Olson*, pp. 27–28; Naftalin, "Farmer-Labor Party," pp. 126–27; William Mahoney statement, Mahoney Papers; *LF Daily Transcript*, 13 March, 14 March 1924; "Vote for Chas. A. Lindbergh for Governor" pamphlet, prepared by Lindbergh for Governor Committee, W. C. Bredenhagen, secretary, copy in LP.

61. Interviews with Eva Lindbergh Christie Spaeth, 1 April 1967, 22 June 1972; Spaeth commentary, 1971; *LF Daily Transcript*, 21 April, 26 April, 29 April, 30 April 1924; Mayer, *Floyd B. Olson*, p. 28; Gaarenstroom interview.

62. *LF Daily Transcript*, 24 May, 26 May, 27 May 1924; Charles, Jr., commentary, 1967. In the 22 June 1972 interview, Eva remembered that Lindbergh had once told her that he wanted "no marble monuments" to himself. "Money is for the living," he had said.

Chapter XI: The Measure of the Man, pp. 282–288

1. Charles, Jr. interview, 22 March 1971.
2. Lindbergh to Dorrance and Company, 21 November 1922, LP.

3. See Hicks, *The Populist Revolt;* and Nye, *Midwestern Progressive Politics.*
4. See Kolko, *Triumph of Conservatism;* and Wiebe, *Search for Order.*
5. See David P. Thelen, *The New Citizenship: Origins of Progressivism in Wisconsin, 1885–1900* (Columbia, Mo., 1972).
6. Lindbergh to Eva, 31 January 1924, LP.
7. See Leuchtenburg, "Progressivism and Imperialism, 1898–1916."
8. Lindbergh, Sr., *Why Is Your Country at War,* p. 186.
9. Knud Wefald to editor, *Minneapolis Daily Star,* 24 May 1927, Wefald Papers.
10. Lindbergh, Sr., *The Economic Pinch,* p. 245.

Bibliography

Publications of Charles A. Lindbergh, Sr.

Banking and Currency and the Money Trust. Washington, D.C., 1913.
The Economic Pinch. Philadelphia, 1923.
The Law of Rights: Realized and Unrealized, Individual and Public.
    A quarterly magazine. Little Falls, Minn., 1905.
Lindbergh's National Farmer. A monthly journal. Minneapolis, March
    1919–March 1920.
Real Needs: A Magazine of Co-ordination. A quarterly magazine.
    Washington, D.C., March and June 1916.
*This Pamphlet Tells Who and What Caused the Panic and Who Can
    Stop the Panic.* Minneapolis, n.d., but likely early 1924.
*Why Is Your Country at War and What Happens to You After the War
    and Related Subjects.* Washington, D.C., 1917.

Manuscript Collections

Nelson Aldrich Papers, Library of Congress, Washington, D.C.
Elmer A. Benson Papers, Minnesota Historical Society, St. Paul.
Joseph A. A. Burnquist Papers, Minnesota Historical Society, St. Paul.
Moses Clapp Papers, Minnesota Historical Society, St. Paul.
Edwin Clark Papers, Minnesota Historical Society, St. Paul.
George Creel Papers, Library of Congress, Washington, D.C.
Farmer-Labor Association of Minnesota Papers, Minnesota Historical
    Society, St. Paul.
Carter Glass Papers, Alderman Library, University of Virginia, Char-
    lottesville.
Thomas Gregory Papers, Library of Congress, Washington, D.C.
Lynn Haines and Family Papers, Minnesota Historical Society, St.
    Paul.

Bibliography

Frank B. Kellogg Papers, Minnesota Historical Society, St. Paul.
William Kent Papers, Sterling Library, Yale University, New Haven, Conn.
Mathias N. Koll Papers, Minnesota Historical Society, St. Paul.
Robert M. La Follette, Sr., Papers, Library of Congress, Washington, D.C.
W. Jett Lauck Papers, Alderman Library, University of Virginia, Charlottesville.
William Lemke Papers, Orrin G. Libby Historical Manuscripts Collection, University of North Dakota, Grand Forks.
Arthur Le Sueur Papers, Minnesota Historical Society, St. Paul.
John Lind Papers, Minnesota Historical Society, St. Paul.
Charles A. Lindbergh, Jr., Papers, Sterling Library, Yale University, New Haven, Conn.
Charles A. Lindbergh, Sr., and Family Papers, Minnesota Historical Society, St. Paul. Principal collection on Lindbergh, Sr. Twelve boxes, including two volumes, and two additional volumes.
William Mahoney Papers, Minnesota Historical Society, St. Paul.
James Manahan Papers, Minnesota Historical Society, St. Paul.
James Manahan correspondence, private collection in possession of James H. Manahan, Mankato, Minn.
Austin Mires Diary, Michigan Historical Collections, University of Michigan, Ann Arbor.
National Nonpartisan League Papers, Minnesota Historical Society, St. Paul.
John M. Nelson Papers, Wisconsin State Historical Society, Madison.
Knute Nelson Papers, Minnesota Historical Society, St. Paul.
George W. Norris Papers, Library of Congress, Washington, D.C.
Gifford Pinchot Papers, Library of Congress, Washington, D.C.
Theodore Roosevelt Papers, Library of Congress, Washington, D.C.
William Howard Taft Papers, Library of Congress, Washington, D.C.
Andrew J. Volstead and Family Papers, Minnesota Historical Society, St. Paul.
Knud Wefald Papers, Minnesota Historical Society, St. Paul.
Woodrow Wilson Papers, Library of Congress, Washington, D.C.

Interviews

Personal interviews
John M. Baer. Washington, D.C., 24 August, 27 August 1965.
Elmer A. Benson. St. Paul, Minn., 21 February 1970.
Elizabeth Gaspar Brown. Ann Arbor, Mich., 7 July 1969.

Gladys M. Brown. Little Falls, Minn., 21 June 1967.

Mrs. G. V. Butler. Luverne, Minn., 19 June 1965.

Eva Lindbergh Christie (now Spaeth). Minneapolis, Minn., 12 July 1965; Red Lake Falls, Minn., 1 April 1967; St. Paul, Minn., 21 October 1971, 22 June, 12 October 1972.

Eva Lindbergh Christie and Charles A. Lindbergh, Jr. Red Lake Falls, Little Falls, and St. Paul, Minn., and en route, 16–20 April 1966.

Frank Dewey. Little Falls, Minn., 23 June 1967.

Ben Du Bois. Sauk Centre, Minn., 24 October 1972.

Martin Engstrom. Little Falls, Minn., 22 June 1967.

T. R. Fritsche. New Ulm, Minn., 12 October 1972.

C. F. Gaarenstroom. Fairmont, Minn., 1 February 1966.

Mrs. P. W. Huntemer. Chicago, Ill., 27 April 1967.

Francis Johnson. Darwin, Minn., 16 June 1972.

Fola La Follette. Washington, D.C., 5 May 1966.

Emory Scott Land. Washington, D.C., 11 May 1970.

Fred Larson. Little Falls, Minn., June and July 1966, 10 September 1967.

Charles A. Lindbergh, Jr. Darien, Conn., 9 May 1966; Little Falls, Minn., 22 March 1971.

Frank A. Lindbergh. Crosby, Minn., 26 June 1964.

Mrs. Frank A. Lindbergh. Crosby, Minn., 7 April 1971.

Henry R. Martinson. Fargo, N.Dak., 7 September 1966.

Grace L. Nelson. Madison, Wis., 31 October 1970.

Gerald P. Nye. Washington, D.C., 16 July 1969.

John C. Patience. Little Falls, Minn., 22 June 1967.

Roy F. Proffitt. Ann Arbor, Mich., 7 July 1969.

Nina Hollister Sullivan. Lake Alexander, Minn., 2 August 1970.

Claude N. Swanson. Fairmont, Minn., 6 September 1967.

Magnus Wefald. Hawley, Minn., 21 July 1965.

Other interviews

Carl Bolander. Interviewed by Sarah Thorp Heald, Little Falls, Minn., June 1937. WPA Project 3870. In possession of Morrison County Historical Society, Little Falls, Minn.

John M. Nelson. Interviewed by Kenneth Hechler, 5–7 February 1939. In John M. Nelson Papers, Wisconsin State Historical Society, Madison.

J. A. O. Preus. Interviewed by Lucile M. Kane and June D. Holmquist, 1960, Minnesota Historical Society, St. Paul.

A. C. Townley. Interviewed by Russell W. Fridley and Lucile M. Kane, 11 December 1956, Minnesota Historical Society, St. Paul.

Bibliography

Correspondence

John M. Baer, Magnus Bolander, Eva Lindbergh Christie Spaeth, J. Edgar Hoover, Mrs. P. W. Huntemer, Fola La Follette, Charles A. Lindbergh, Jr. (including extended commentary on the 1966 interview), Mrs. Frank A. Lindbergh, Grace L. Nelson, Bengt Olof Nilsson, and Burrill A. Peterson to the author.

N. K. Strande to Edward Karrigan, and Gust Levorson to Pope County Historical Society, in possession of the Pope County Historical Society, Glenwood, Minn.

Archives

Attorney Generals' Papers, Minnesota State Archives, St. Paul.

John A. Johnson Papers, Governors' Archives, Minnesota State Archives, St. Paul.

John Lind Papers, Governors' Archives, Minnesota State Archives, St. Paul.

Minnesota Commission of Public Safety Papers, Minnesota State Archives, St. Paul.

U.S. Congress. Record Group 233, Records of the House of Representatives, National Archives, Washington, D.C.

U.S. Department of Justice. Record Group 60, General Records, National Archives, Washington, D.C.

U.S. War Department. Record Group 94, Records of the Adjutant General's Office, 1780's–1917, National Archives, Washington, D.C.

U.S. War Department. Record Group 77, Records of the Office of the Chief of Engineers, National Archives, Washington, D.C.

Public Documents

United States

U.S. Congress. *Congressional Directory.* 60th–64th Congs. Washington, D.C., 1907–17.

U.S. Congress. *Congressional Record.* 60th–64th Congs.; 65th Cong., 1st sess.; 67 Cong., special session of the Senate; 70th Cong., 1st sess.

U.S. Congress. House. Committee on Banking and Currency. *Changes in the Banking and Currency System of the United States.* 63rd Cong., 1st sess., 1913, Rept. 69.

U.S. Congress. House. Committee on Rules. *Hearings on House Resolution No. 314.* 62nd Cong., 2nd sess., 1911.

U.S. Congress. House. *Journal of the House of Representatives of the United States.* 60th–64th Congs., 1908–17.

U.S. Congress. National Monetary Commission. *History of Crises Under the National Banking System,* by O. M. W. Sprague. 61st Cong., 2nd sess., 1910, S. Doc. 538, *Reports,* vol. 5. Washington, D.C., 1910.

U.S. Congress. Senate. Commission on Industrial Relations. *Final Report and Testimony Submitted to Congress by the Commission on Industrial Relations Created by the Act of August 23, 1912.* 64th Cong., 1st sess., 1916, Doc. 415.

U.S. Congress. Senate. Committee on Military Affairs. *Hearings on S. Doc. 4364.* 65th Cong., 2nd sess., 1918, pt. 2.

Michigan

Department of Law Records; and *Proceedings of the Board of Regents,* January 1881–January 1886. University of Michigan, Ann Arbor.

Minnesota

Abstract of Votes Polled: Minnesota Election Returns, 1890, and Minnesota Primary Election Returns, 1906. Secretary of States' Collection, Minnesota State Archives, St. Paul.

In Supreme Court. Case 24994. Respondent's Brief and Appellant's Brief regarding the estate of C. A. Lindbergh.

Legislative Manual of the State of Minnesota, 1891–1925. St. Paul.

Martin County (Fairmont, Minn.)

Justice docket, 1917–18. County Attorney's Register of Criminal Actions. Office of C. F. Gaarenstroom.

Morrison County (Little Falls, Minn.)

Affidavits in Case 3228 (1891) of Seventh Judicial District Court of Minnesota.

Deeds, Book 12, 1895–99; Incorporations, Book H-9; Miscellaneous, Book D-4. Office of the Register of Deeds.

Judgment Records, Book A, 1881–87; Register of Actions, Books B–G, 1857–1907. Office of the Clerk of Court.

Charles A. Lindbergh, Sr., estate file. Office of Probate Court.

Stearns County (St. Cloud, Minn.)

Record Book A. Office of the Clerk of Court.

Village of Melrose, Minn.

Book of Financial Records, 1887–96; minutes of Village Council Proceedings, 1881–97. In possession of City of Melrose.

Bibliography

Newspapers

Ada Norman County Herald
Alexandria Citizen
Alexandria Post-News
Brainerd Arena
Brainerd Daily Dispatch
Brainerd Dispatch
Brainerd Tribune
Breckenridge Telegram
Brown County Journal
   (New Ulm)
Buffalo Journal
Cass Lake Voice
The Catholic Bulletin (St. Paul)
Dassel Anchor
Der Nordstern (St. Cloud)
Duluth Herald
Duluth News-Tribune
Fairmont Daily Sentinel
Fargo Forum
Fergus Falls Daily Journal
Hubbard County Enterprise
   (Park Rapids)
Labor (Washington, D.C.)
Labor World (Duluth)
Litchfield News Ledger
Litchfield Saturday-Review
Little Falls Daily Transcript
Little Falls Herald
Little Falls Transcript
Little Falls Weekly Transcript
Long Prairie Leader
McLeod County Republic
   (Glencoe)

Melrose Beacon
Minneapolis Journal
Minneapolis Tribune
Minnesota Leader (St. Paul)
Minnesota Union Advocate
   (St. Paul)
New Ulm Review
New York Times
New York Tribune
Nonpartisan Leader (Fargo and
   St. Paul)
Osakis Review
Pine Tree Blaze (Pine River)
Red Lake Falls Gazette
St. Cloud Daily Journal-Press
St. Cloud Daily Times
St. Cloud Democrat
St. Cloud Journal-Press
St. Paul Dispatch
St. Paul Pioneer Press
Svenska Amerikanska Posten
   (Minneapolis)
St. Peter Herald
Todd County Argus (Long
   Prairie)
Two Harbors Journal-News
Wadena Pioneer-Journal
Washington Daily News
Washington Herald
Washington Times
Winona Republican-Herald

Selected Books, Articles, and Unpublished Material

Anderson, George L. "Banks, Mails, and Rails, 1880–1915." In *The Frontier Challenge: Responses to the Trans-Mississippi West*, edited by John G. Clark. Lawrence, Kans., 1971, pp. 275–307.
———. *Essays on the History of Banking*. Lawrence, Kans., 1972.

————. "The National Banking System, 1865–1875: A Sectional Institution." Ph.D. dissertation, University of Illinois, 1933.

Andersson, Ingvar. *A History of Sweden*. London, 1956.

Blegen, Theodore C. *Minnesota: A History of the State*. Minneapolis, 1963.

Brown, Elizabeth Gaspar. *Legal Education at Michigan, 1859–1959*. Ann Arbor, 1959.

Cheney, Charles B. *The Story of Minnesota Politics*. Minneapolis, 1947.

Chrislock, Carl H. *The Progressive Era in Minnesota, 1899–1918*. St. Paul, 1971.

Christensen, Harald P. "The Political Ideas of Charles A. Lindbergh, Sr." Master's thesis, State University of Iowa, 1940.

Cooper, John Milton, Jr. *The Vanity of Power: American Isolationism and World War I, 1914–1917*. Westport, Conn., 1969.

Creese, James. "Charles Augustus Lindbergh." *American-Scandinavian Review* 15 (August 1927): 488–92.

Folwell, William Watts. *A History of Minnesota*. 4 vols. St. Paul, 1921–32.

Friedman, Milton, and Schwartz, Anna Jacobson. *A Monetary History of the United States, 1867–1960*. Princeton, 1963.

Fuller, Clara. *History of Morrison and Todd Counties, Minnesota*. 2 vols. Indianapolis, 1915.

Gaston, Herbert E. *The Non-Partisan League*. New York, 1920.

Gieske, Millard L. "The Politics of Knute Nelson, 1912–1920." Ph.D. dissertation, University of Minnesota, 1965.

Haines, Lynn. *Law Making in America: The Story of the 1911–1912 Session of the Sixty-second Congress*. Bethesda, Md., 1912.

Haines, Lynn, and Haines, Dora. *The Lindberghs*. New York, 1931.

Hechler, Kenneth W. *Insurgency: Personalities and Politics of the Taft Era*. 1940. Reprint. New York, 1970.

Helmes, Winifred G. *John A. Johnson, the People's Governor: A Political Biography*. Minneapolis, 1949.

Hicks, John D. *The Populist Revolt*. Minneapolis, 1931.

Holbrook, Franklin F., and Appel, Livia. *Minnesota in the War with Germany*. 2 vols. St. Paul, 1928–32.

Holt, James. *Congressional Insurgents and the Party System, 1909–1916*. Cambridge, Mass., 1967.

"Honorable Lindbergh, M.C." *American Monthly* 20 (October 1927): 3–6.

Jenson, Carol. "Loyalty as a Political Weapon: The 1918 Campaign in Minnesota." *Minnesota History* 43 (Summer 1972): 42–57.

Jones, Alan. "Thomas M. Cooley and 'Laissez-Faire Constitutionalism':

A Reconsideration." *Journal of American History* 53 (March 1967): 751–71.

Kolko, Gabriel. *The Triumph of Conservatism: A Reinterpretation of American History, 1900–1916.* New York, 1963.

Krooss, Herman E., ed. *Documentary History of Banking and Currency in the United States.* 4 vols. New York, 1969.

La Follette, Belle Case, and La Follette, Fola. *Robert M. La Follette: June 14, 1855–June 18, 1925.* 2 vols. New York, 1953.

Leuchtenburg, William E. "Progressivism and Imperialism: The Progressive Movement and American Foreign Policy, 1898–1916." *Mississippi Valley Historical Review* 39 (December 1952): 483–504.

Lindbergh, Charles A. *Boyhood on the Upper Mississippi: A Reminiscent Letter.* St. Paul, 1972.

————. *Of Flight and Life.* New York, 1948.

————. *The Spirit of St. Louis.* New York, 1953.

————. *The Wartime Journals of Charles A. Lindbergh.* New York, 1970.

Lindmark, Sture. *Swedish America, 1914–1932: Studies in Ethnicity with Emphasis on Illinois and Minnesota.* Chicago, 1971.

Link, Arthur S. *Wilson.* 5 vols. Princeton, 1947–64.

————. *Woodrow Wilson and the Progressive Era, 1910–1917.* New York, 1963.

Ljungmark, Lars. *For Sale—Minnesota: Organized Promotion of Scandinavian Immigration, 1866–1873.* Chicago, 1971.

Lowitt, Richard. *George W. Norris: The Making of a Progressive, 1861–1912.* Syracuse, 1963.

Lubell, Samuel. *The Future of American Politics.* 3rd rev. ed. New York, 1965.

Mayer, George. *The Political Career of Floyd B. Olson.* Minneapolis, 1951.

Merrill, Horace Samuel, and Merrill, Marion Galbraith. *The Republican Command, 1897–1913.* Lexington, Ky., 1971.

Mitau, G. Theodore. *Politics in Minnesota.* Minneapolis, 1960.

Morlan, Robert L. *Political Prairie Fire: The Nonpartisan League, 1915–1922.* Minneapolis, 1955.

Mowry, George E. *The Era of Theodore Roosevelt and the Birth of Modern America, 1900–1912.* New York, 1958.

————. *Theodore Roosevelt and the Progressive Movement.* Madison, 1946.

Naftalin, Arthur. "A History of the Farmer-Labor Party of Minnesota." Ph.D. dissertation, University of Minnesota, 1948.

Nute, Grace Lee, ed. "The Lindbergh Colony." *Minnesota History* 20 (September 1939): 243–58.

Nye, Russel B. *Midwestern Progressive Politics: A Historical Study of Its Origins and Development, 1870–1958.* New York, 1965.

Penick, James, Jr. *Progressive Politics and Conservation: The Ballinger-Pinchot Affair.* Chicago, 1968.

Peterson, H. C., and Fite, Gilbert C. *Opponents of War, 1917–1918.* Madison, 1957.

Pollack, Norman. *The Populist Response to Industrial America.* Cambridge, Mass., 1962.

Pringle, Henry F. *The Life and Times of William Howard Taft: A Biography.* 2 vols. 1938. Reprint. Hamden, Conn., 1964.

Saloutos, Theodore, and Hicks, John D. *Agricultural Discontent in the Middle West, 1900–1939.* Madison, 1951.

Scheiner, Seth M. "President Theodore Roosevelt and the Negro." *Journal of Negro History,* 47 (July 1962): 169–82.

Shideler, James H. *Farm Crisis: 1919–1923.* Berkeley, 1957.

Stephenson, George M. *John Lind of Minnesota.* Minneapolis, 1935.

Stevens, Hiram F. *History of the Bench and Bar of Minnesota.* 2 vols. Minneapolis and St. Paul, 1904.

Tarbell, Ida M. "The Hunt for a Money Trust." *American Magazine,* May 1913, pp. 3–17.

Thelen, David P. *The New Citizenship: Origins of Progressivism in Wisconsin, 1885–1900.* Columbia, Mo., 1972.

Trattner, Walter I. "Progressivism and World War I: A Re-appraisal." *Mid-America* 44 (July 1962): 131–145.

Tweton, D. Jerome. "The Border Farmer and the Canadian Reciprocity Issue, 1911–1912." *Agricultural History* 37 (October 1963): 235–41.

Upham, Warren, and Dunlap, Rose Barteau, comps. *Minnesota Biographies, 1655–1912. Collections of the Minnesota Historical Society,* vol. 14. St. Paul, 1912.

Wefald, Jon. *A Voice of Protest: Norwegians in American Politics, 1890–1917.* Northfield, Minn., 1971.

Youngdale, James M., ed. *Third Party Footprints: An Anthology from Writings and Speeches of Midwest Radicals.* Minneapolis, 1966.

Index

Index

357

Index

Index

Poindexter, Miles, 69, 134, 146
Populists, 3, 46, 64, 67, 70, 88, 159, 270, 284
Power, Victor, 221
Powers, Caleb, 214
Prescott, William: *History of the Conquest of Mexico*, 33; *History of the Conquest of Peru*, 33
Press: and Nonpartisan League, 224, 226, 229, 232, 244–45; questioned Lindbergh's loyalty, 229–30, 232, 234, 236, 245, 253; and World War I, 181, 182, 183, 184, 187, 190, 198, 219, 229, 230. *See also* individual newspapers
Preus, Jacob A. O., 259, 260, 266–267, 270–71, 272, 275
Progressive Federation of Publicists and Editors, 135
Progressive party, 144–49 *passim*, 162, 177, 283
Progressives, 38, 87, 150, 153, 158, 168, 215, 221, 246, 249, 270, 284–286. *See also* Republican party, progressives
Prohibition: supported by Lindbergh, 205
Prohibitionist party, 198, 246
Prudential Insurance Co., 117
Pujo, Arsène, 126, 151, 152

Quick, Herbert, 144
Quigley, Walter E., 40, 233

Ragsdale, J. Willard, 159
Railroads, xiii, 8, 50, 109, 118, 124; farmers and, 12; labor and, 207–208; rates and regulations for, 70, 88–94, 97, 109
Raymond, Gust, 196
Real Needs: A Magazine of Coordination, 182–83, 188, 208, 285
Record, George, 134, 138
Red Cross, 223, 229, 230, 231
Red Lake Falls, Minn., 210
Red Lake Falls Gazette, 210
Red Wing, Minn., 235
Reed, James A., 231
Republican party, 36, 57, 88, 94, 176–77, 215–16, 261; conservatives, 150, 159, 186; convention and election of 1912, 133–49; in Minnesota, 3, 12, 44–46, 48–49, 145, 223, 243–44, 249, 252, 254, 260–61, 264; progressives (insurgents), 69–74, 78–79, 81–89

passim, 96, 97–98, 100, 105, 115, 133–46 *passim*, 150, 185, 192–94, 282, 283, 327n.; split in, 63, 84
Roberts, Clifton, 172
Roberts, Dr. Loren B., 132, 172, 210
Roberts, Mrs. Loren B., 132, 206, 210. *See also* Lindbergh, Lillian
Roberts, Louise (granddaughter), 210
Rockefeller, John D., 81, 109, 111, 123
Rockefeller, William, 123
Rockefeller Institute, 187
Roman Catholic church, 224, 264; role of, questioned by Lindbergh, 206, 207, 226–29, 234, 247
Roosevelt, Theodore, 46, 48, 55, 67, 70, 85, 192, 215, 230, 284; and economy, 59, 60; and election of 1912, 133, 135–36, 137, 138, 139–149 *passim*, 194; and Panama Canal, 75–76; and racial issue, 37; and Republican progressives, 71–72
Rosenberger Brothers, 19
Royalton Banner, 52
Ruble, Rollor, 239
Russia, 50, 224

St. Cloud, Minn., 6, 8, 18, 44, 55, 90, 259
St. Cloud Daily Journal-Press, 181, 191
St. Cloud Daily Times, 49, 55, 148, 178
St. Cloud Democrat, 6
St. Louis, Mo., 123
St. Paul, Minn., 247
St. Paul Pioneer Press, 229–30
Sauk Centre, Minn., 11, 44, 49
Schiff, Jacob H., 123
Schmidt, Oscar, 33
Schwartz, Anna Jacobson, 59
Seal, Joseph, 28
Seal, Mrs. Joseph, 28. *See also* Lindbergh, Linda
Searle, D. B., 24
Sharkey, Thomas J., 178
Sherman Antitrust Act, 89, 155, 165
Shields, James, 276
Shipstead, Henrik, 250, 259, 260, 264, 266–67, 275
Singer Manufacturing Co., 19
Sioux Indians, 8
Smith, Edward E., 148
Smith, Gerald L. K., 214

Index

E
748
L74
L33

Larson. Bruce L
    Lindbergh of Minnesota; a political biography [by]
Bruce L. Larson. Foreword by Charles A. Lindbergh, Jr.
[1st ed.] New York, Harcourt Brace Jovanovich [1973]

    xix. 363 p. illus. 22 cm. $14.50

    Based on the author's thesis, University of Kansas.
    Bibliography: p. 343–351.

    1. Lindbergh. Charles August, 1859–1924. 2. United States—Poli-
tics and government—1901–1953. 3. Minnesota—Politics and government.   I. Title.

    E748.L74L37   328.73′092′4 [B]   73–6596
2'74947'' ISBN 0-15-152400-9   MARC
    Library of Congress   73 [4]